SORCERERS & SECRETARIES

SECRETARIES

Volume 1

By Amy Kim Ganter

HAMBURG // LONDON // LOS ANGELES // TOKYO

Sorcerers & Secretaries Vol. 1
Created by Amy Kim Ganter

Production Artists - James Dashiell and Jason Milligan
Cover Design - Anne Marie Horne

Editor - Lillian Diaz-Przybyl
Digital Imaging Manager - Chris Buford
Production Managers - Jennifer Miller and Mutsumi Miyazaki
Managing Editor - Lindsey Johnston
VP of Production - Ron Klamert
Publisher and E.I.C. - Mike Kiley
President and C.O.O. - John Parker
C.E.O. - Stuart Levy

A  Manga

TOKYOPOP Inc.
5900 Wilshire Blvd. Suite 2000
Los Angeles, CA 90036

E-mail: info@TOKYOPOP.com
Come visit us online at www.TOKYOPOP.com

ISBN: 1-59816-409-0

First TOKYOPOP printing: February 2006
10 9 8 7 6 5 4 3 2 1
Printed in the USA

contents

CHAPTER ONE——————5

CHAPTER TWO——————33

CHAPTER THREE——————59

CHAPTER FOUR——————89

CHAPTER FIVE——————119

CHAPTER SIX——————145

Chapter One

Starts With A Dream

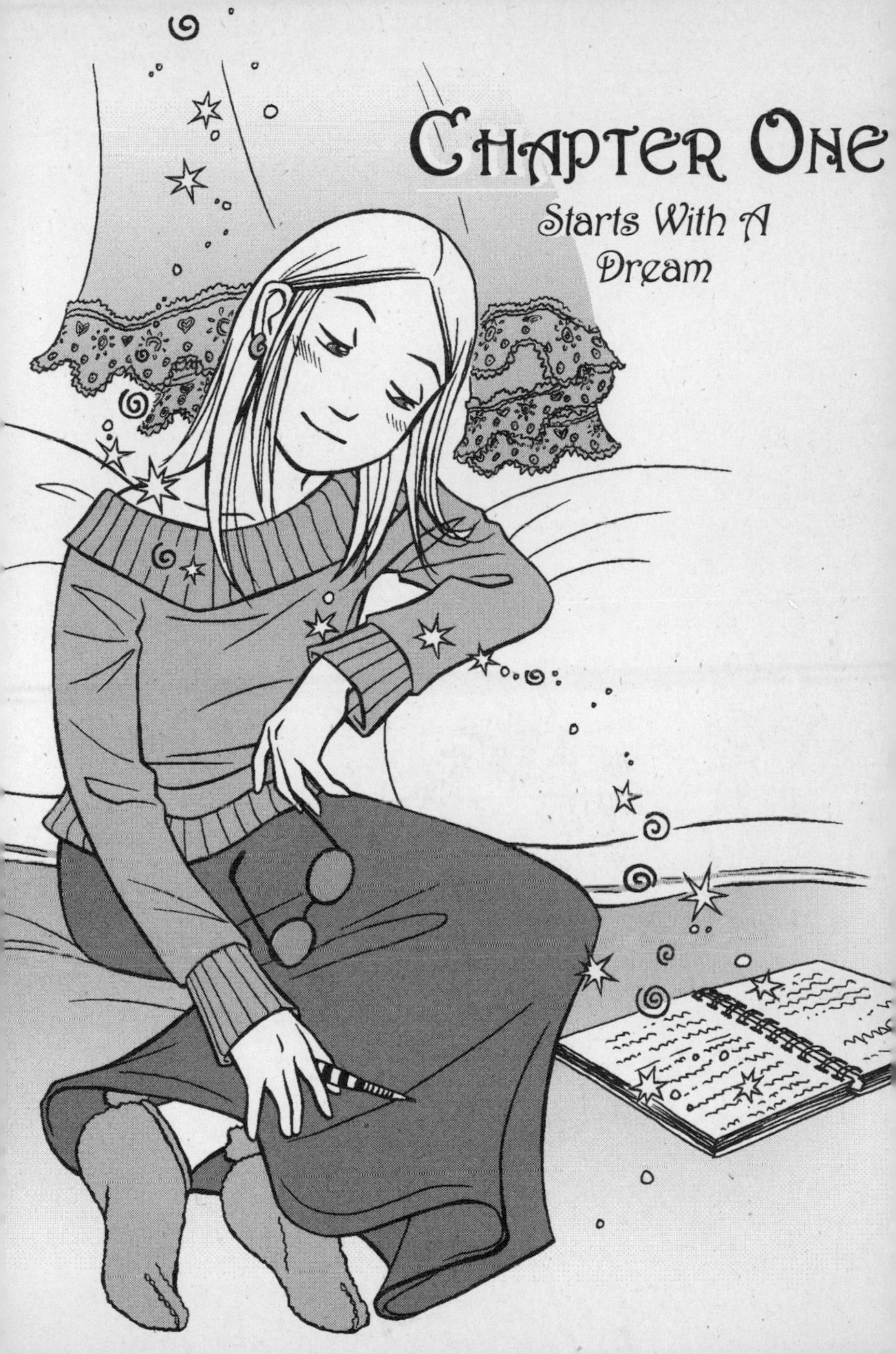

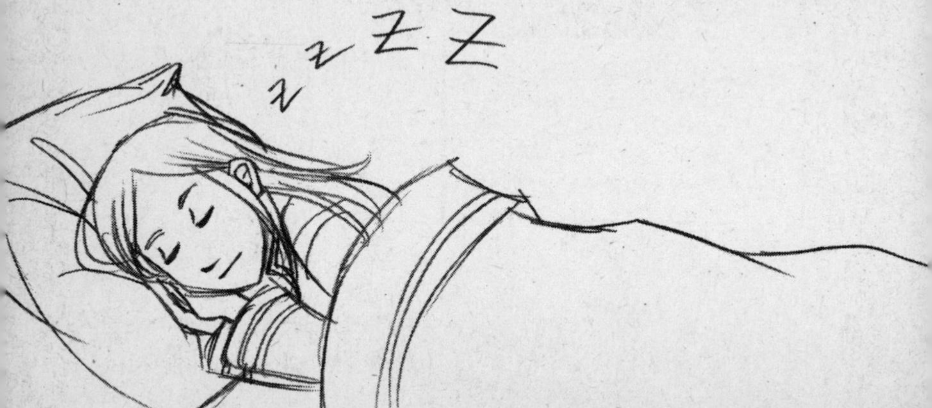
zzZZ

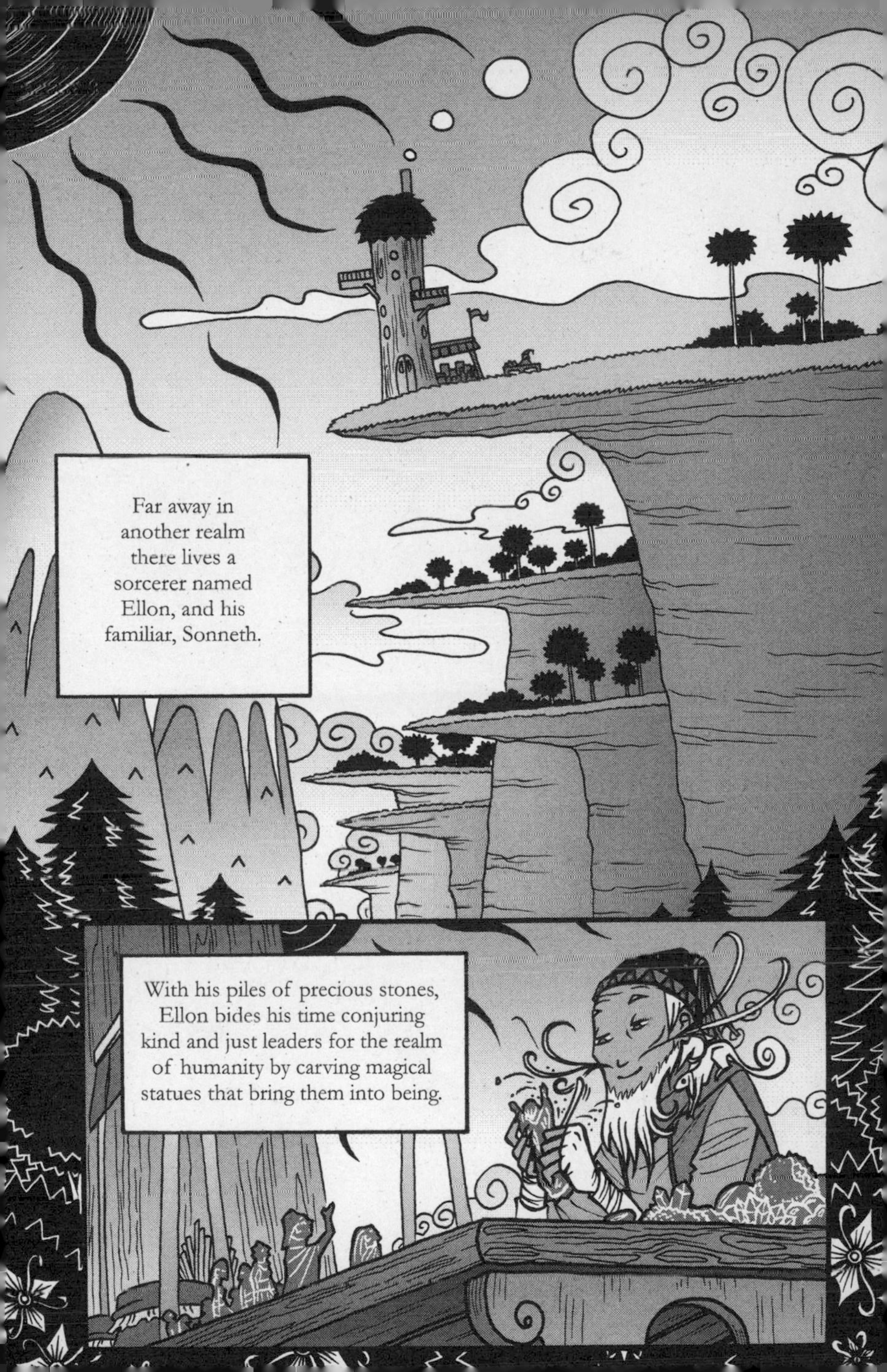
Far away in another realm there lives a sorcerer named Ellon, and his familiar, Sonneth.
With his piles of precious stones, Ellon bides his time conjuring kind and just leaders for the realm of humanity by carving magical statues that bring them into being.

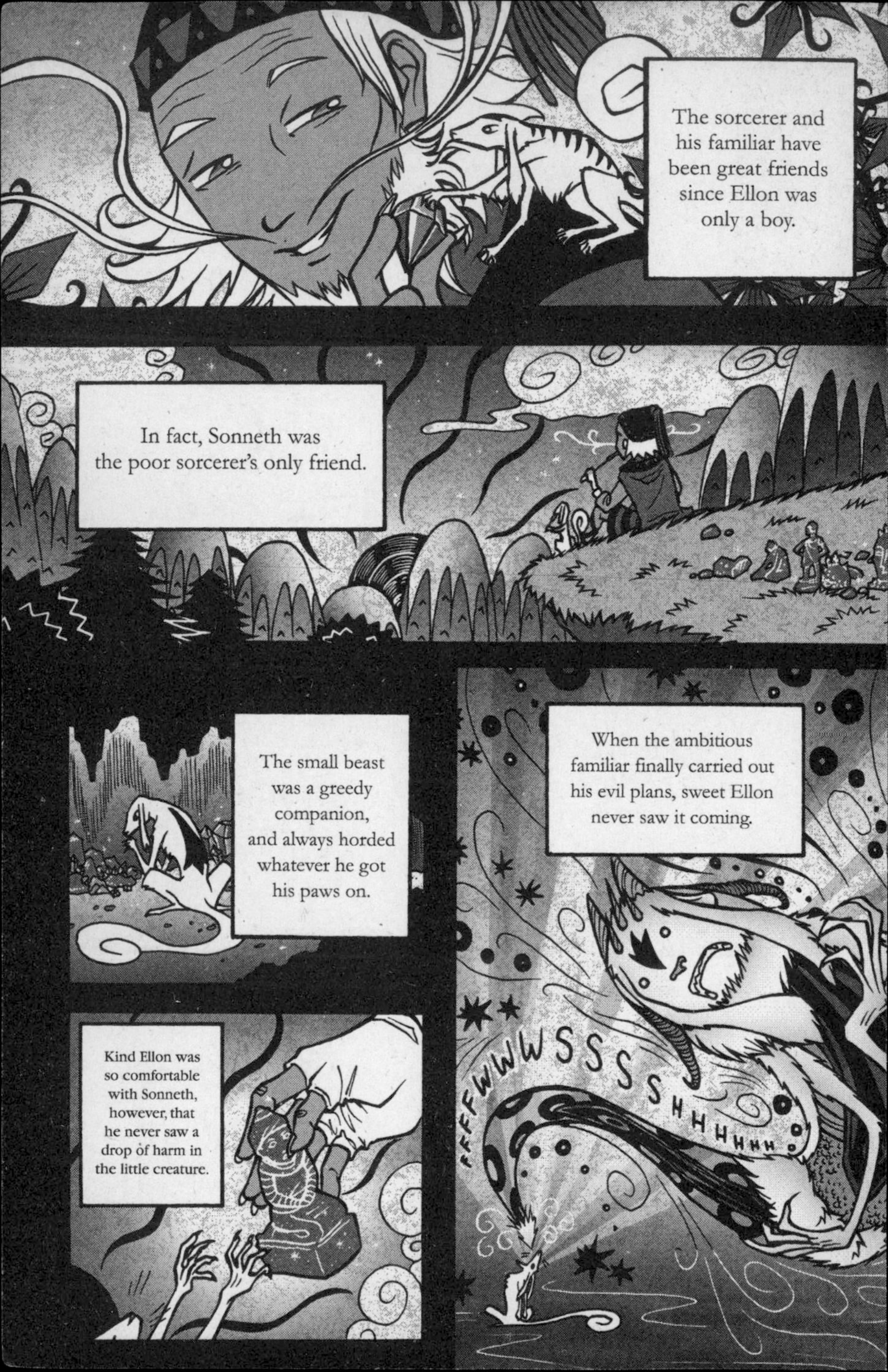
The sorcerer and his familiar have been great friends since Ellon was only a boy.
In fact, Sonneth was the poor sorcerer's only friend.
The small beast was a greedy companion, and always horded whatever he got his paws on.
Kind Ellon was so comfortable with Sonneth, however, that he never saw a drop of harm in the little creature.
When the ambitious familiar finally carried out his evil plans, sweet Ellon never saw it coming.
FFFFWWWWSSSSSHHHHHHHH

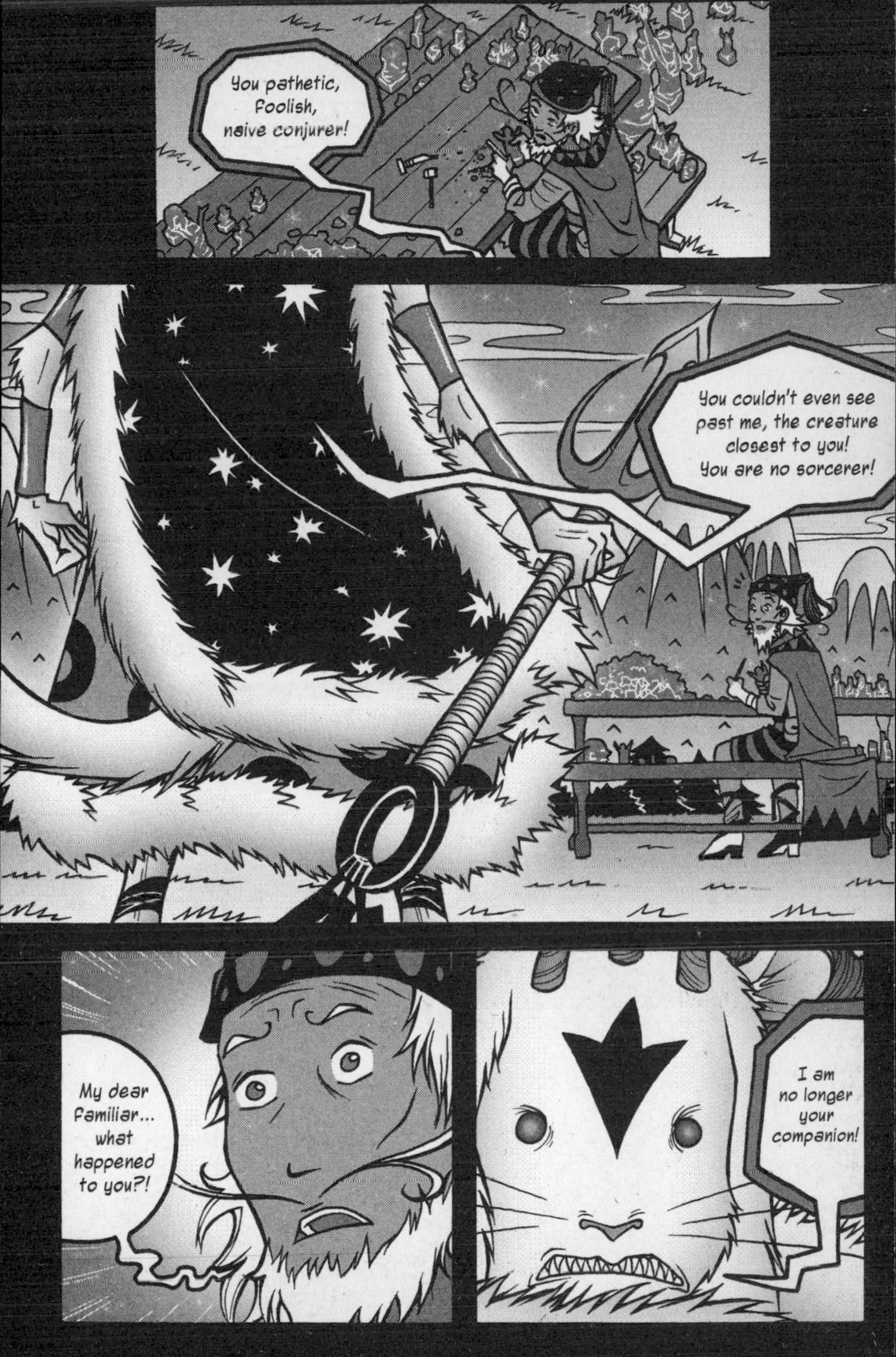
You pathetic, foolish, naive conjurer!
You couldn't even see past me, the creature closest to you! You are no sorcerer!
My dear familiar... what happened to you?!
I am no longer your companion!

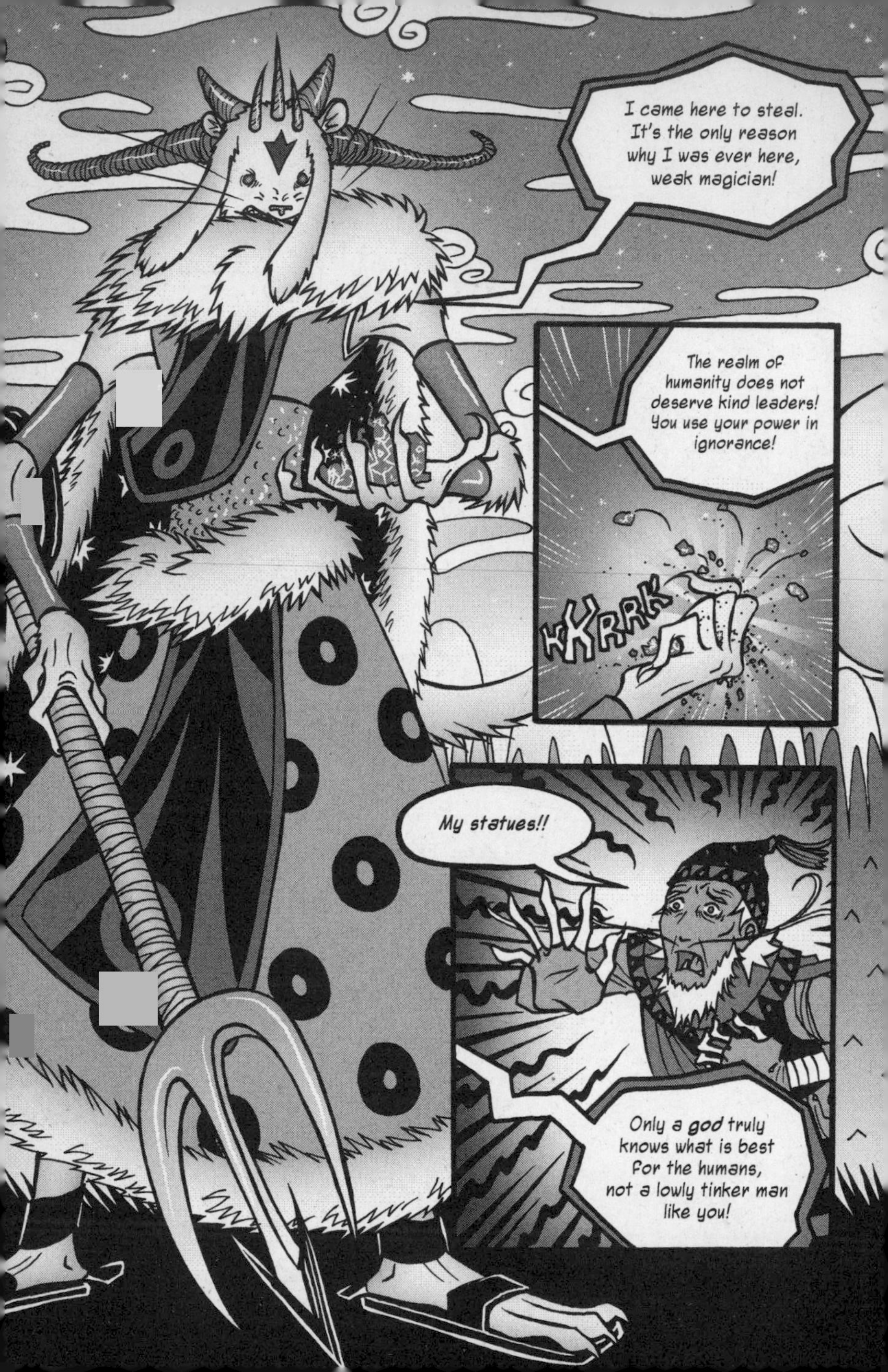
I came here to steal. It's the only reason why I was ever here, weak magician!
The realm of humanity does not deserve kind leaders! You use your power in ignorance!
KKRRK
My statues!!
Only a god truly knows what is best for the humans, not a lowly tinker man like you!

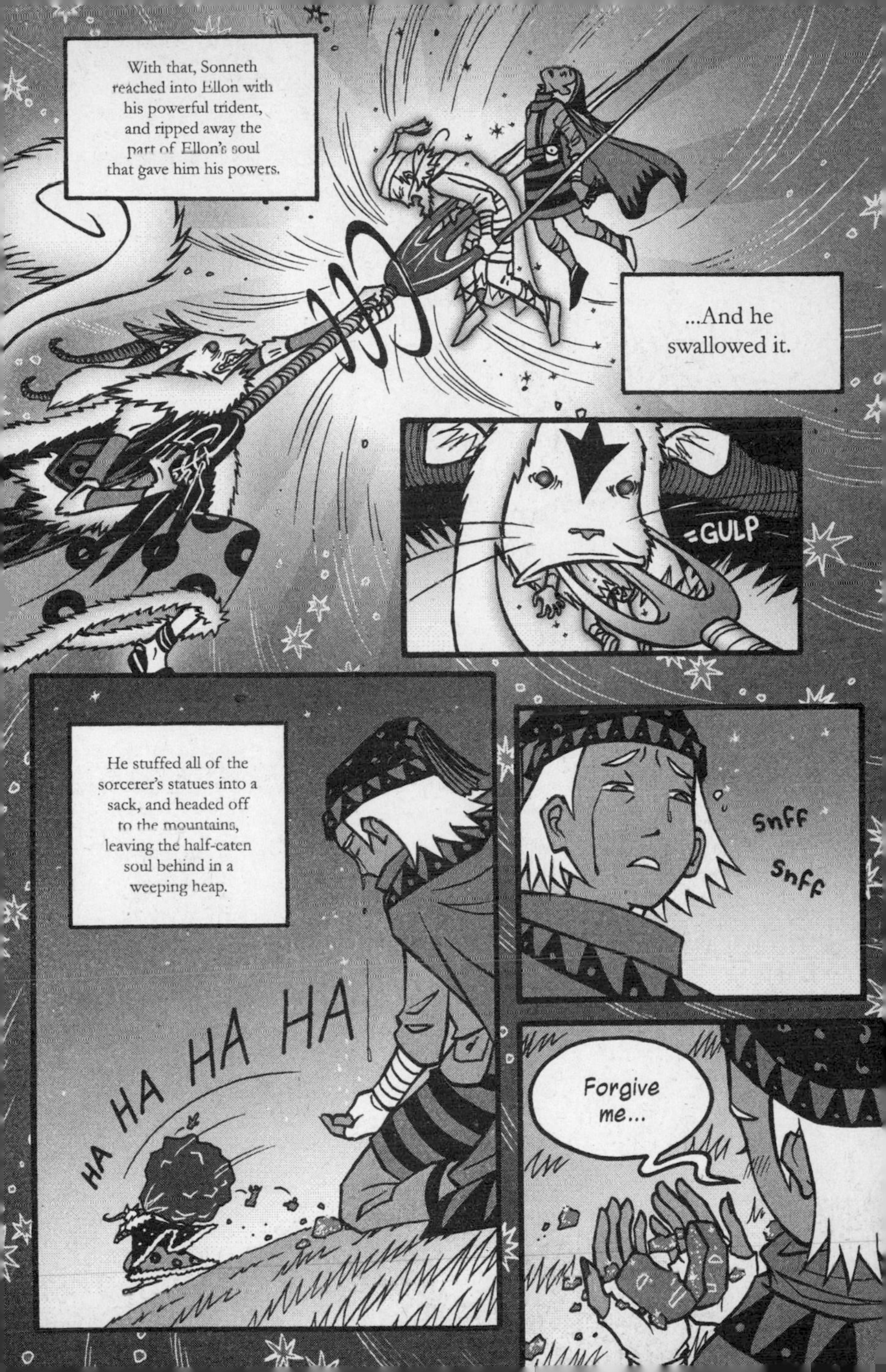
With that, Sonneth reached into Ellon with his powerful trident, and ripped away the part of Ellon's soul that gave him his powers.
...And he swallowed it.
GULP
He stuffed all of the sorcerer's statues into a sack, and headed off to the mountains, leaving the half-eaten soul behind in a weeping heap.
HA HA HA HA HA
Snff
Snff
Forgive me...

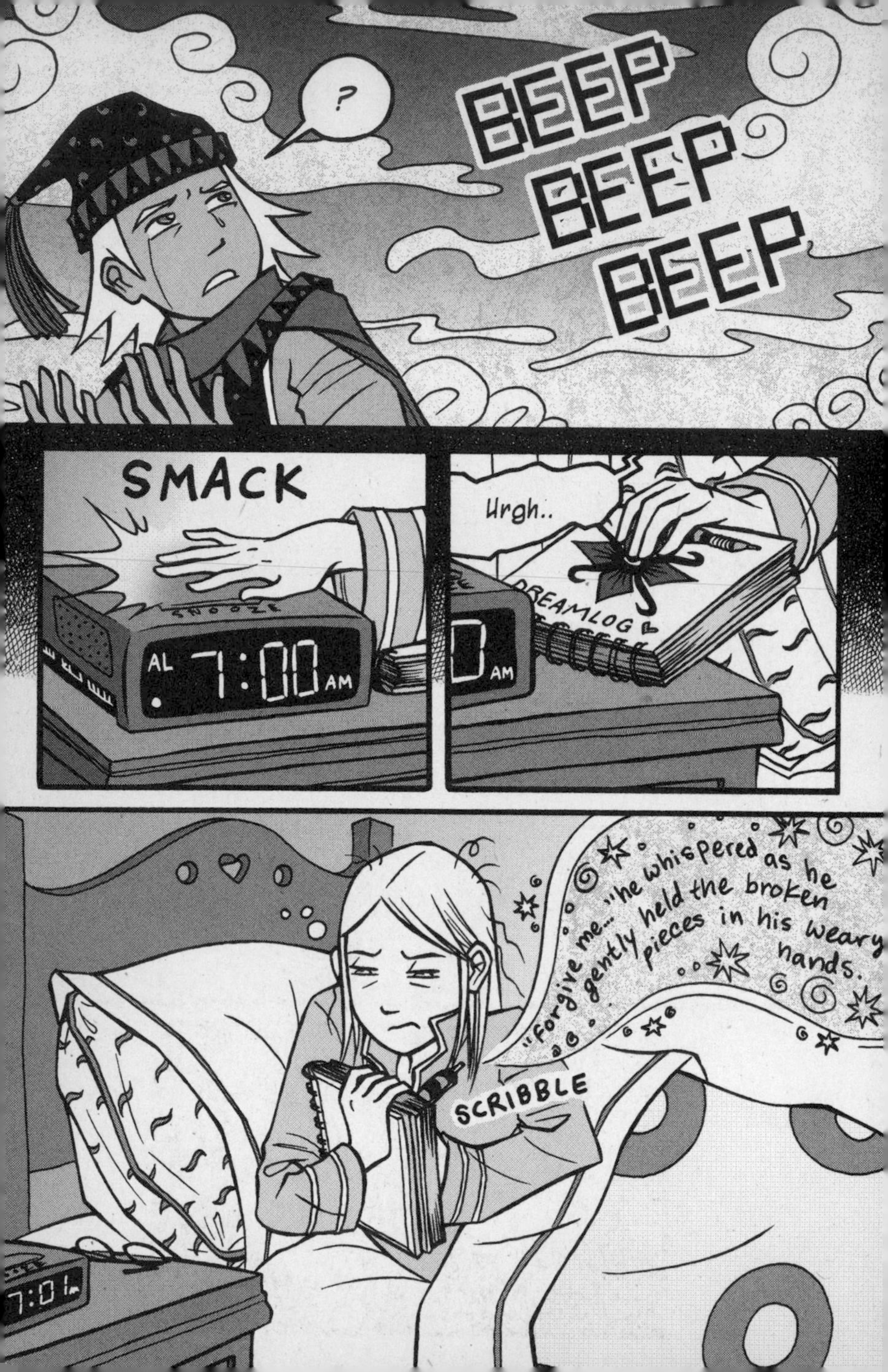
?
BEEP BEEP BEEP
SMACK
Urgh..
DREAMLOG
AL 7:00 AM
"Forgive me..." he whispered as he gently held the broken pieces in his weary hands.
SCRIBBLE
7:01

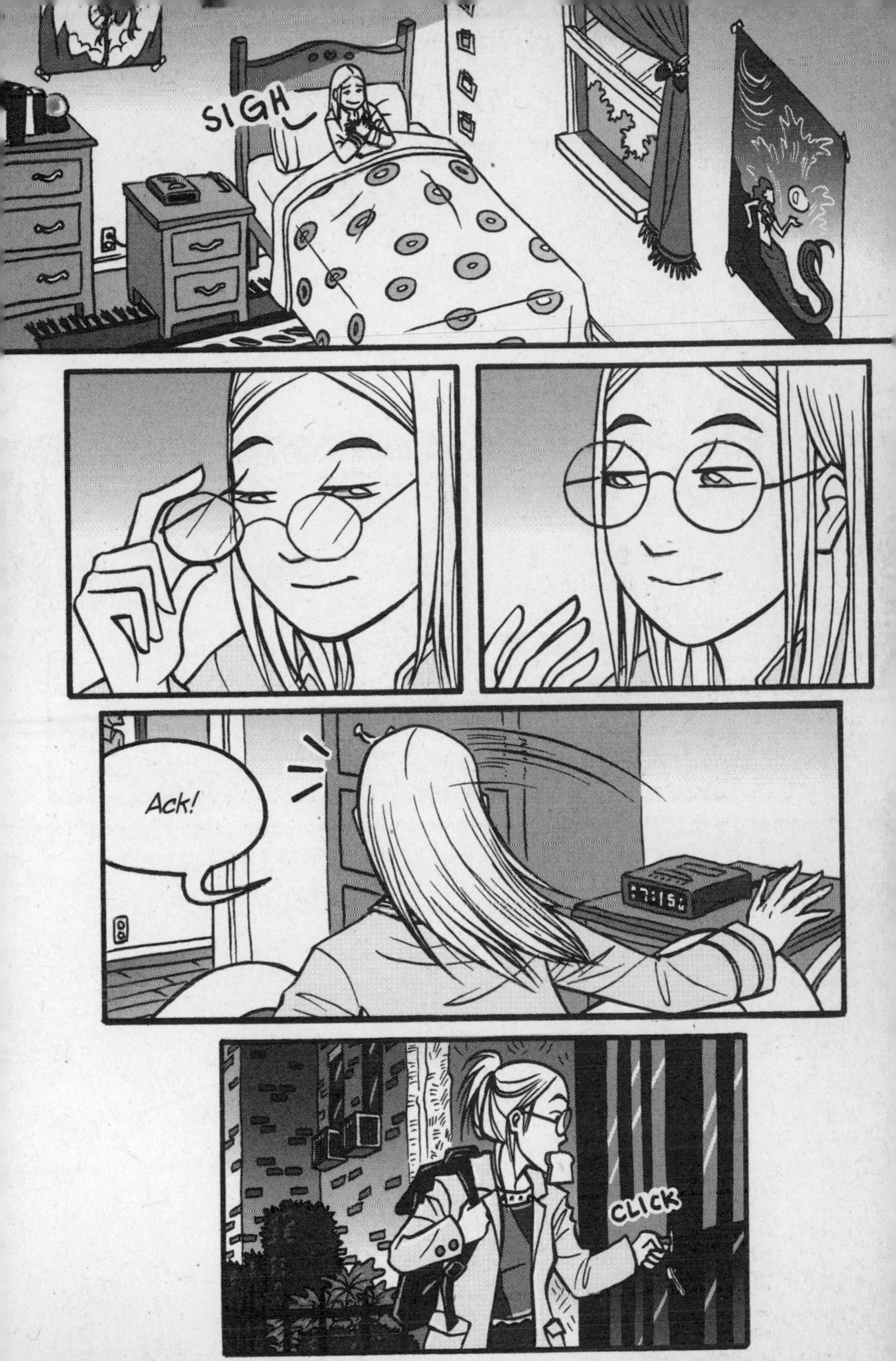
SIGH
Ack!
7:15
CLICK

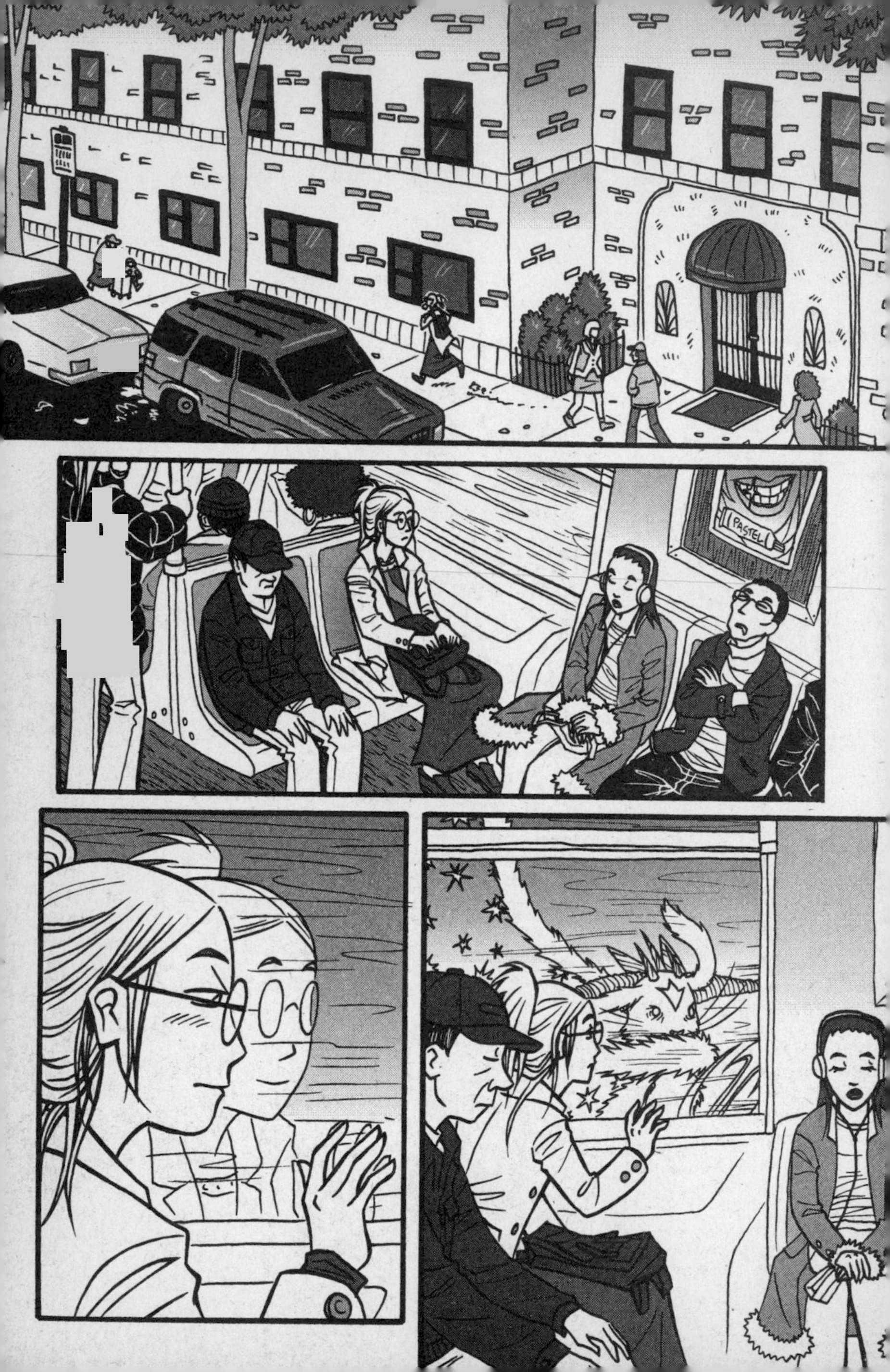
PASTEL

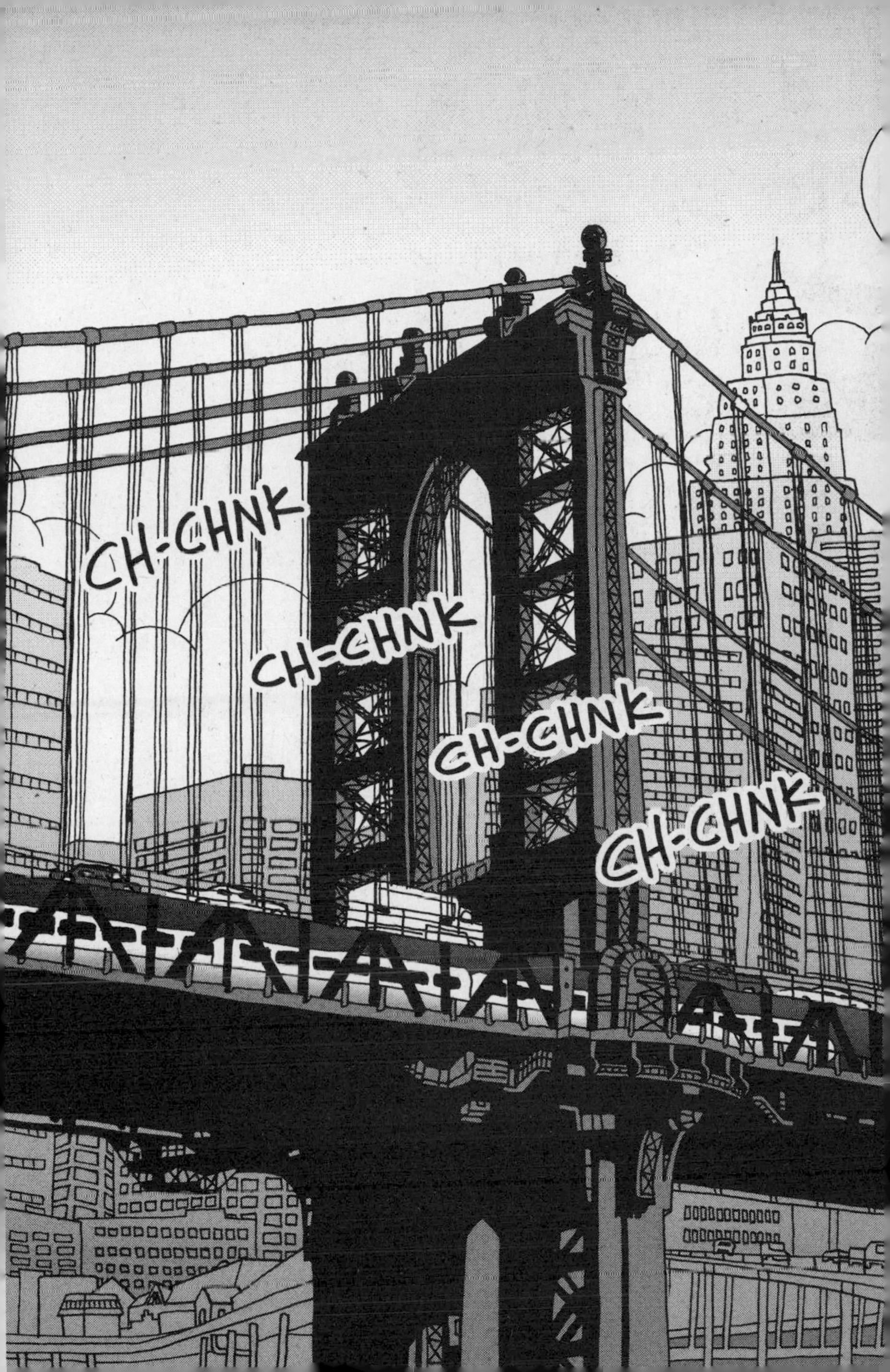
CH-CHNK
CH-CHNK
CH-CHNK
CH-CHNK

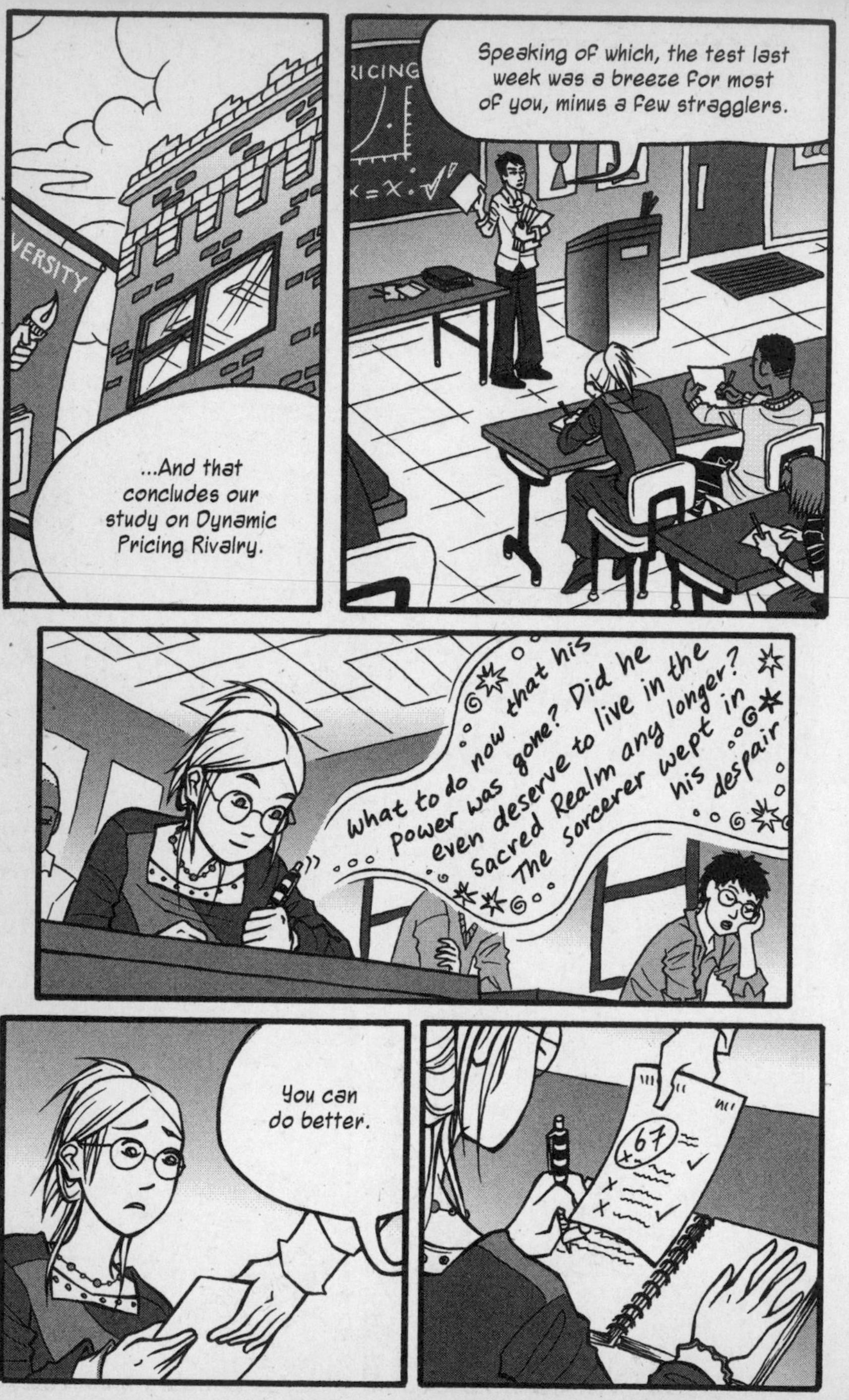

...And that concludes our study on Dynamic Pricing Rivalry.
Speaking of which, the test last week was a breeze for most of you, minus a few stragglers.
What to do now that his power was gone? Did he even deserve to live in the Sacred Realm any longer? The sorcerer wept in his despair
You can do better.
67

The Sorcerer prayed and the gods and for several days. And so, he co... For the half of his soul that w... stripped from him...

=SIGH=

I just bought this shirt, and I saw Allison Stiles wearing it on the way here. Now I have to return it!

I mean, what if we show up in the same class one day and we're both wearing the same thing? That would be sooo embarassing!

But I guess this is what happens when I buy things I saw in *Girlfriend!* *Magazine*, huh?

=POOMF=

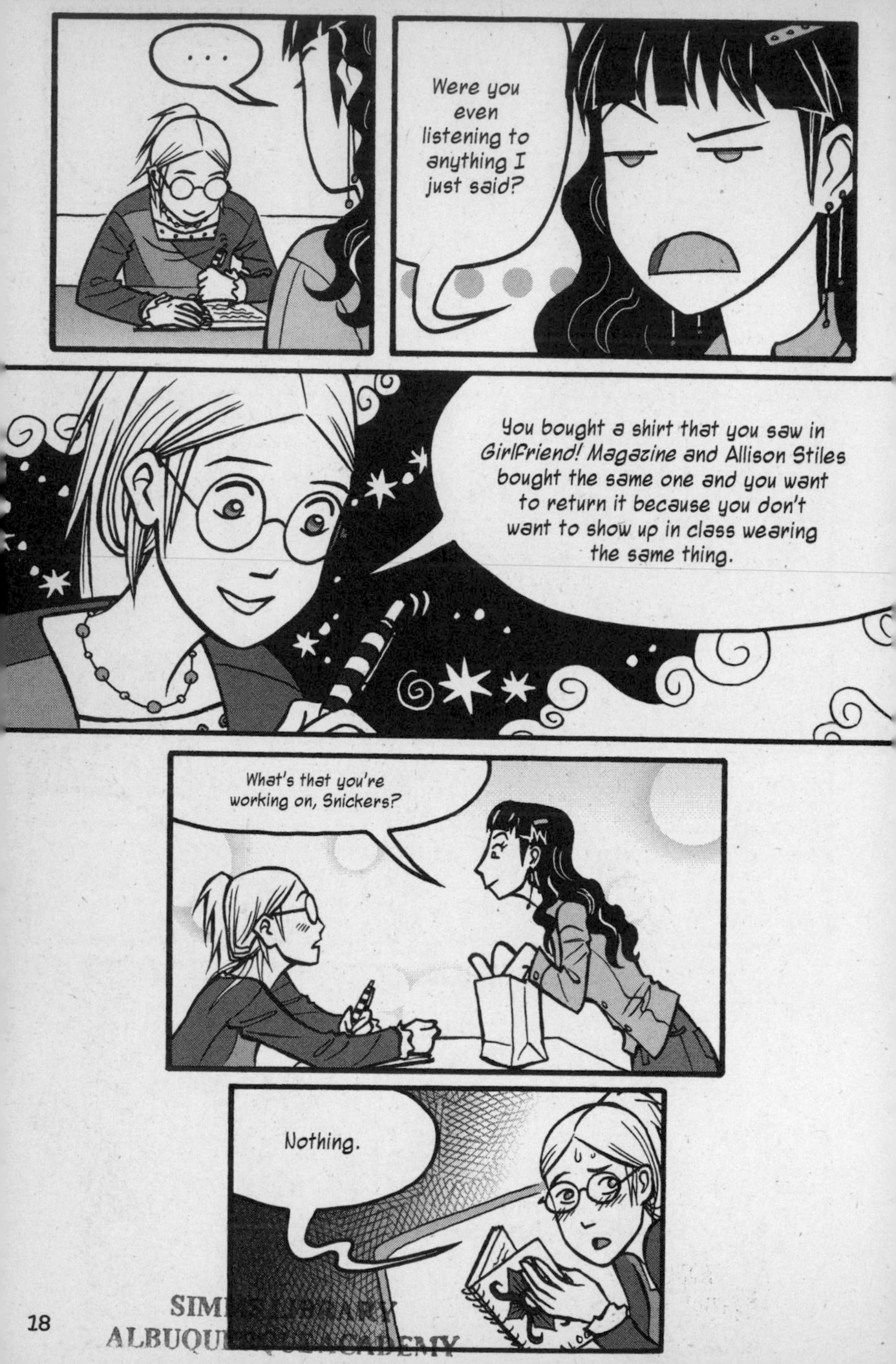
. . .
Were you even listening to anything I just said?
You bought a shirt that you saw in Girlfriend! Magazine and Allison Stiles bought the same one and you want to return it because you don't want to show up in class wearing the same thing.
What's that you're working on, Snickers?
Nothing.

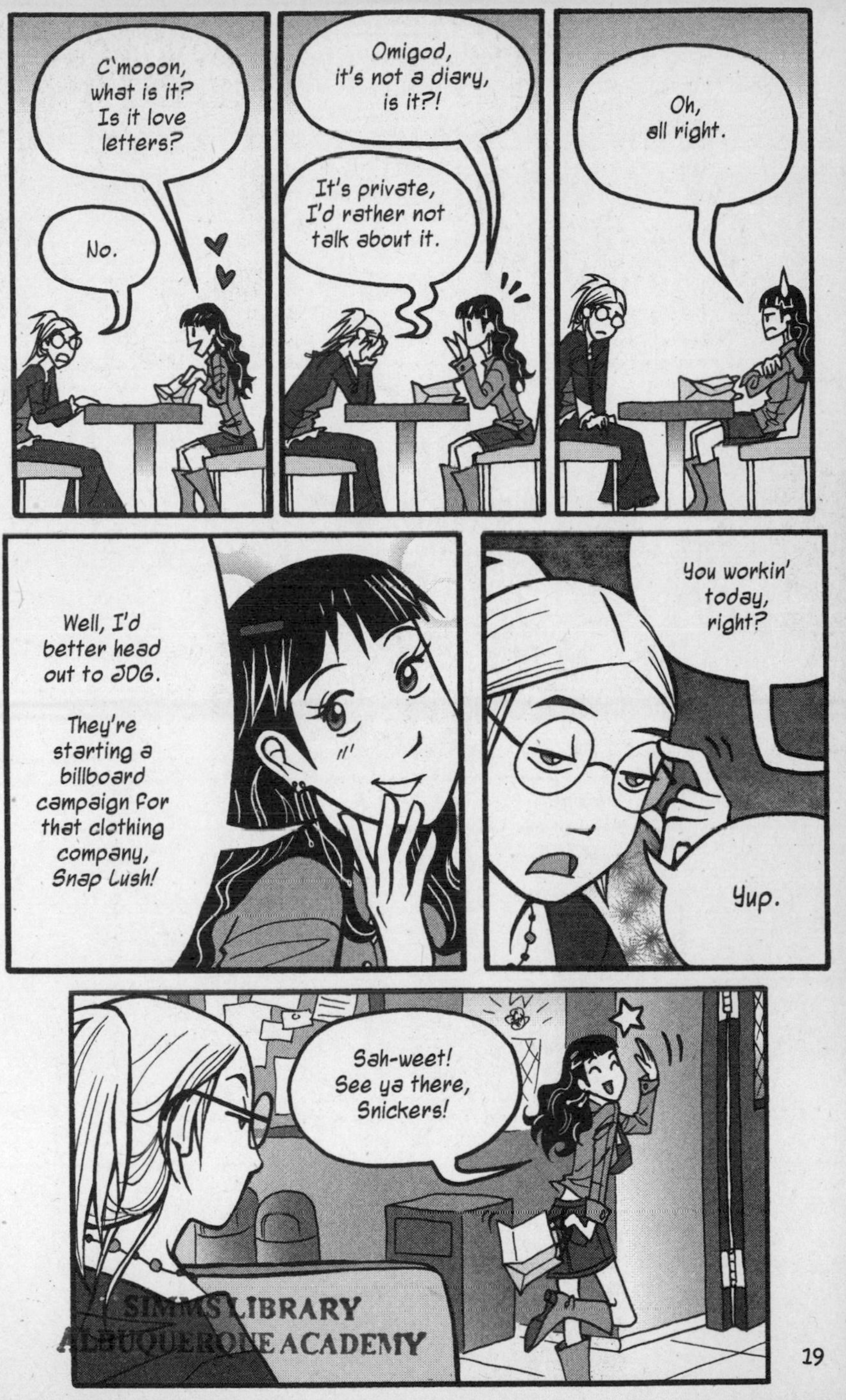
C'mooon, what is it? Is it love letters?
No.
Omigod, it's not a diary, is it?!
It's private, I'd rather not talk about it.
Oh, all right.
Well, I'd better head out to JOG.
They're starting a billboard campaign for that clothing company, Snap Lush!
You workin' today, right?
Yup.
Sah-weet! See ya there, Snickers!
SIMMS LIBRARY
ALBUQUERQUE ACADEMY

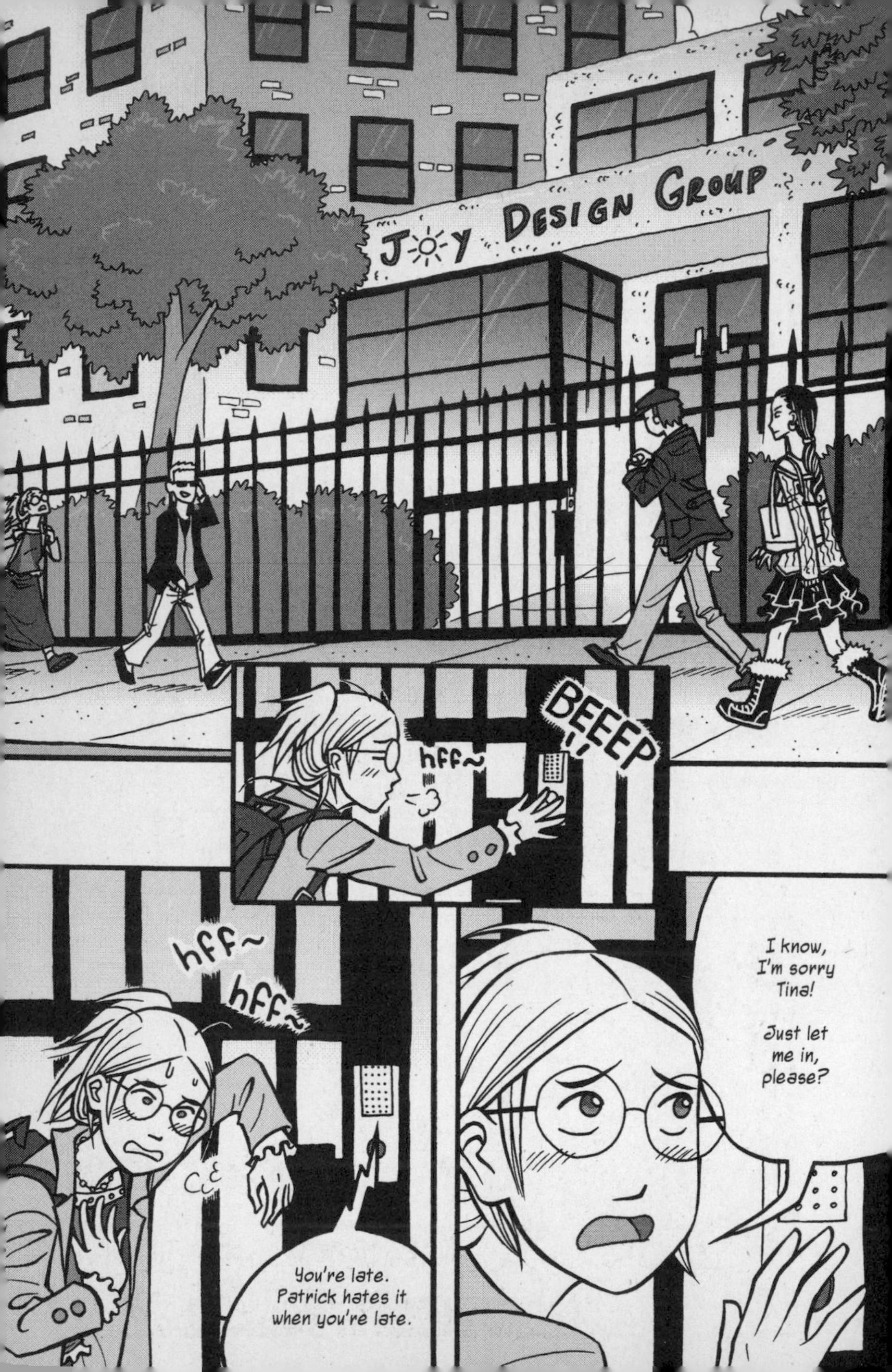
JOY DESIGN GROUP
hff~
BEEEEP
hff~
hff~
You're late. Patrick hates it when you're late.
I know, I'm sorry Tina!
Just let me in, please?

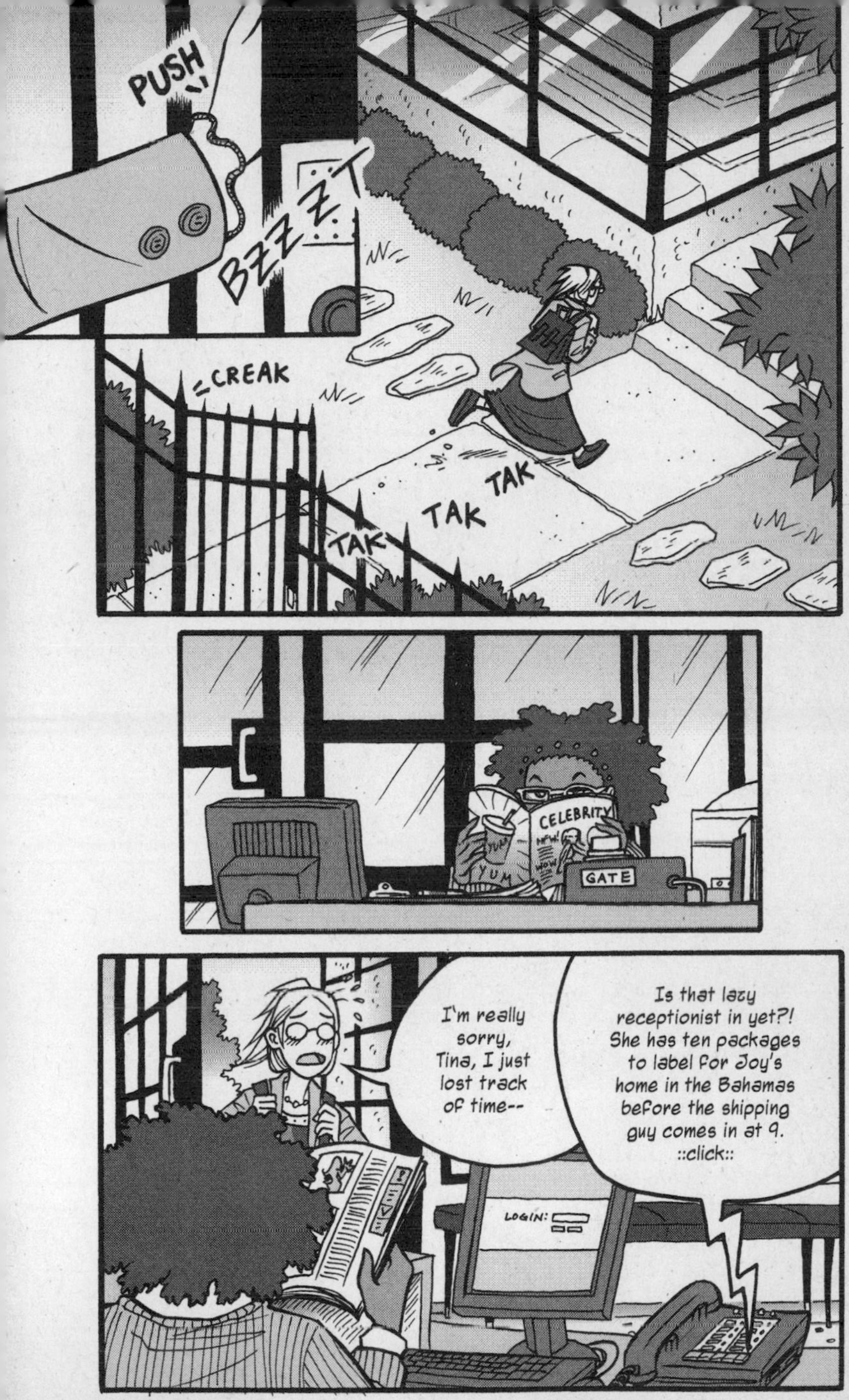
PUSH
BZZZZT
CREAK
TAK
TAK
TAK
CELEBRITY
YUM
YUM
GATE
I'm really sorry, Tina, I just lost track of time--
Is that lazy receptionist in yet?! She has ten packages to label for Joy's home in the Bahamas before the shipping guy comes in at 9. ::click::
LOGIN:

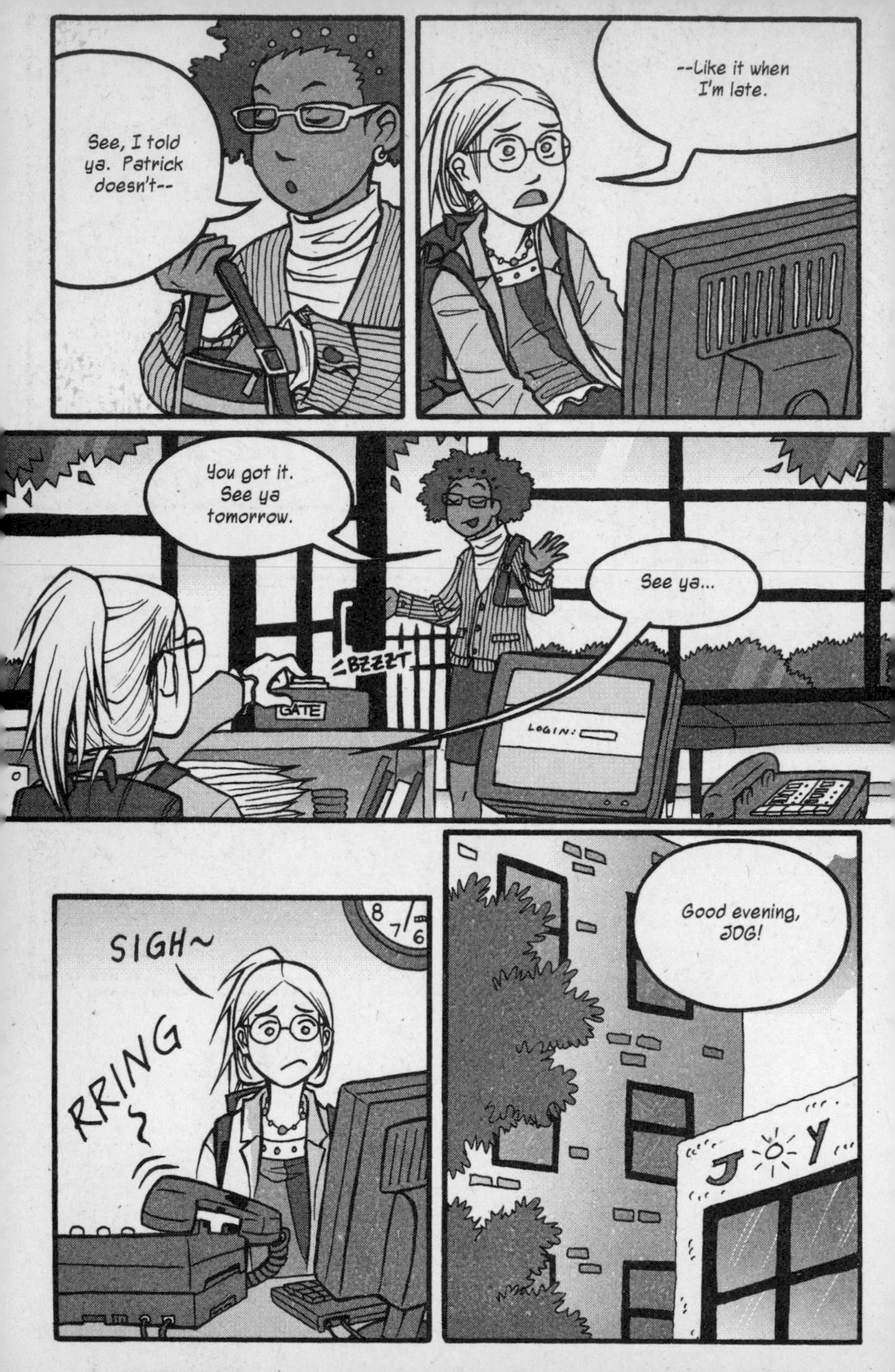

See, I told ya. Patrick doesn't--
--Like it when I'm late.
You got it. See ya tomorrow.
See ya...
BZZZT
GATE
LOGIN:
SIGH~
RRING
Good evening, JOG!
JOY

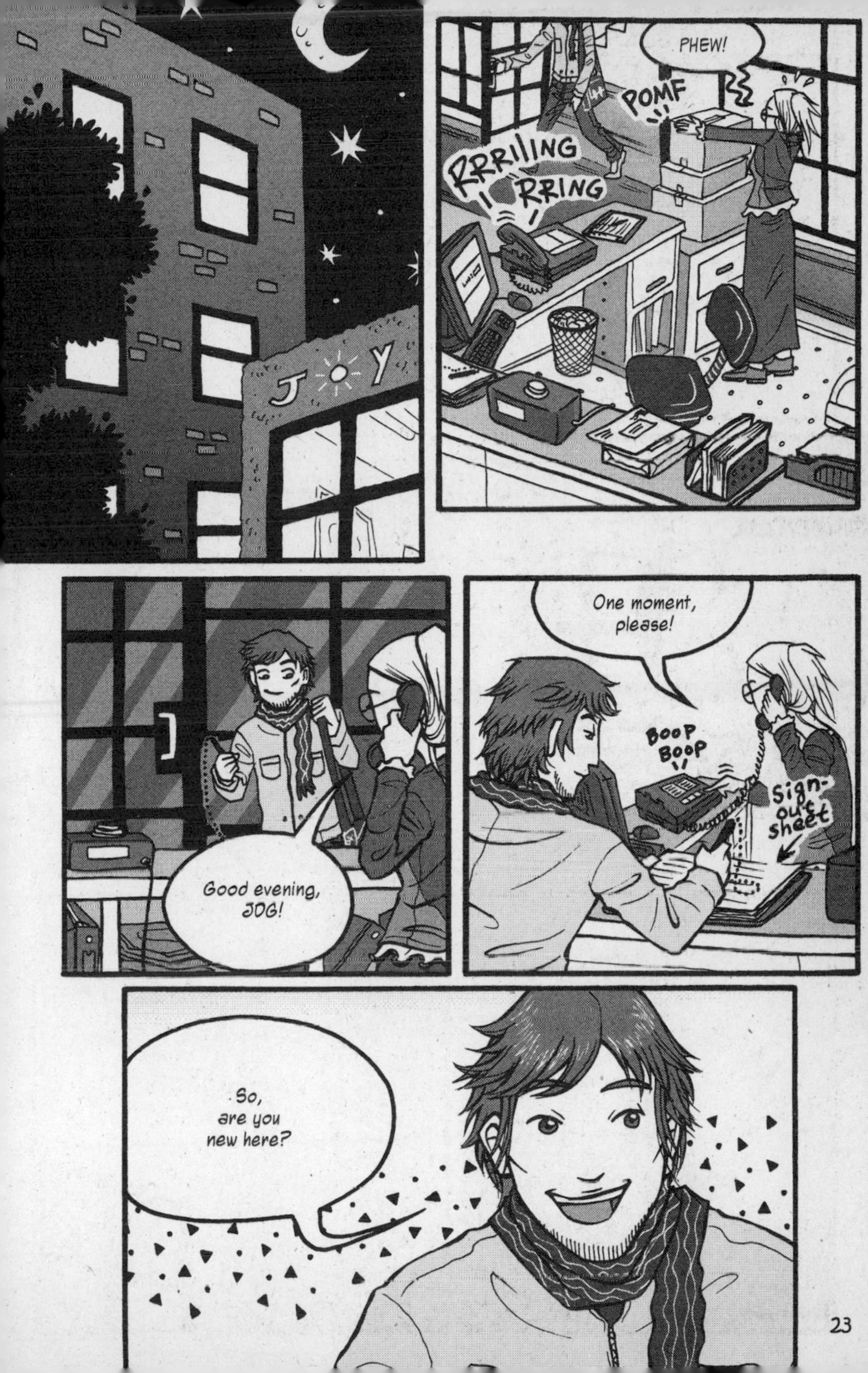
J☼Y
PHEW!
POMF
RRRIIING RRING
Good evening, JOG!
One moment, please!
BOOP BOOP
Sign-out sheet
So, are you new here?

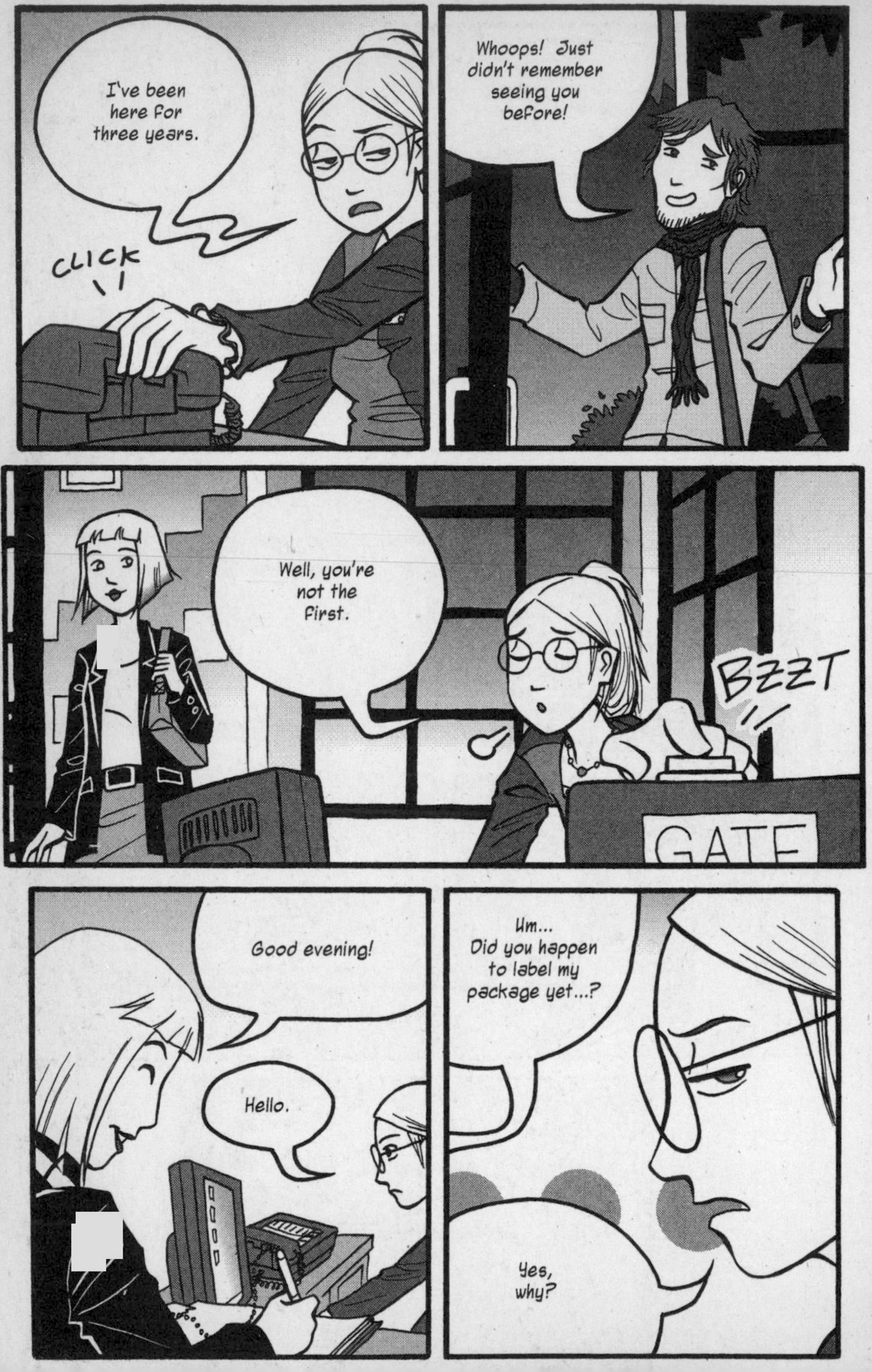
I've been here for three years.
CLICK
Whoops! Just didn't remember seeing you before!
Well, you're not the first.
BZZT
GATE
Good evening!
Hello.
Um... Did you happen to label my package yet...?
Yes, why?

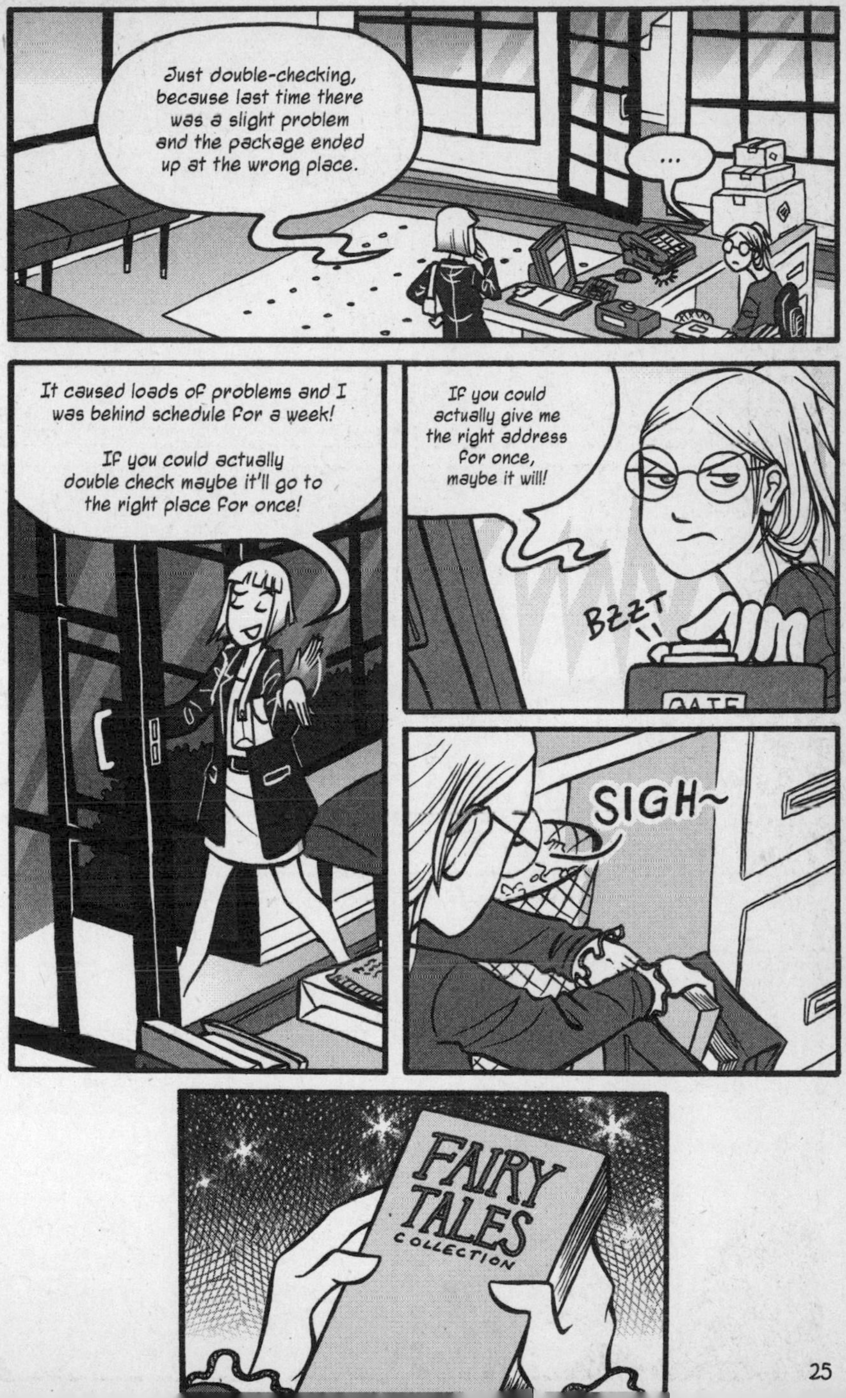
Just double-checking, because last time there was a slight problem and the package ended up at the wrong place.
...
It caused loads of problems and I was behind schedule for a week!
If you could actually double check maybe it'll go to the right place for once!
If you could actually give me the right address for once, maybe it will!
BZZT
SIGH~
FAIRY TALES
COLLECTION

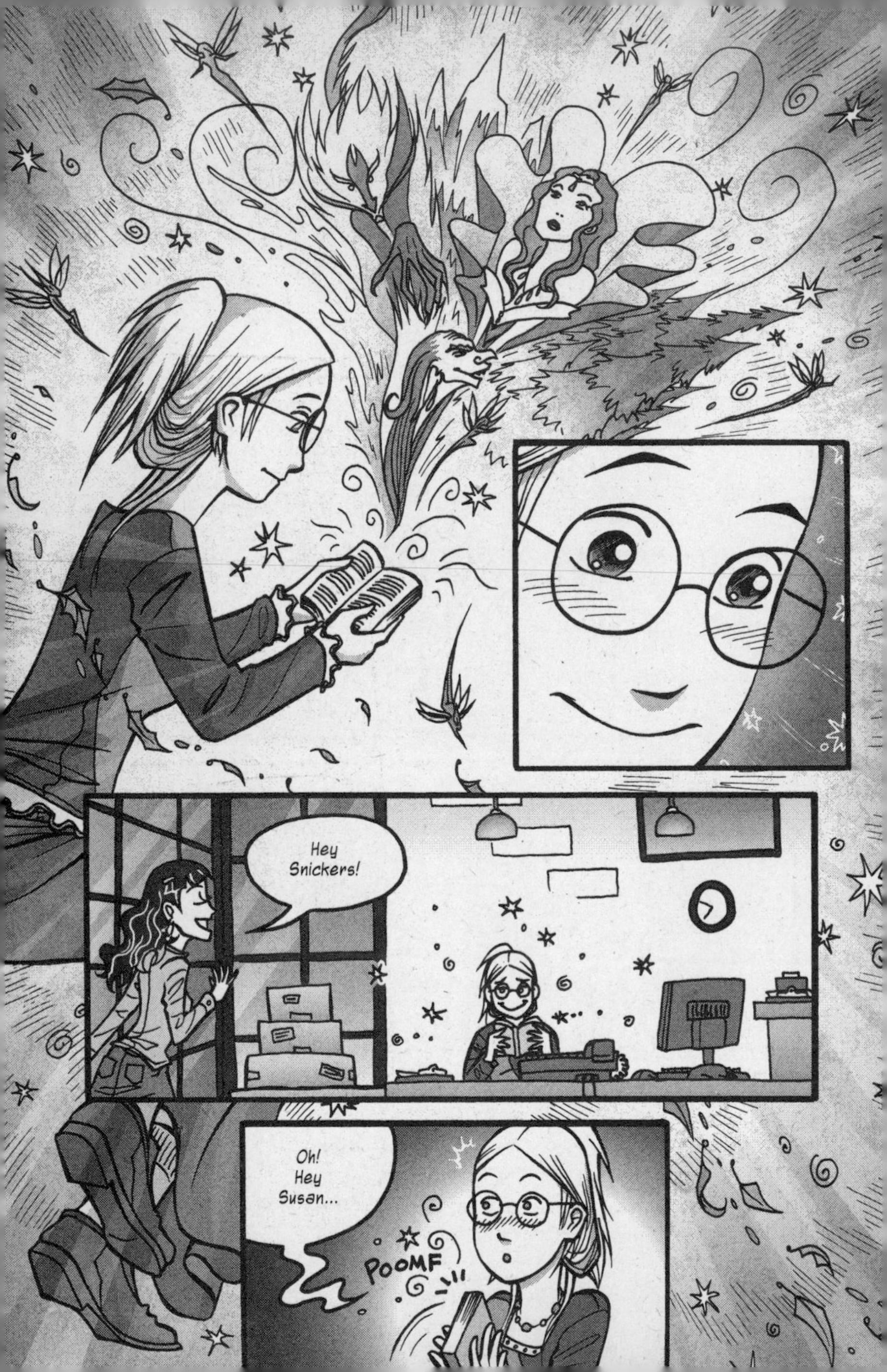
Hey Snickers!
Oh! Hey Susan...
POOMF

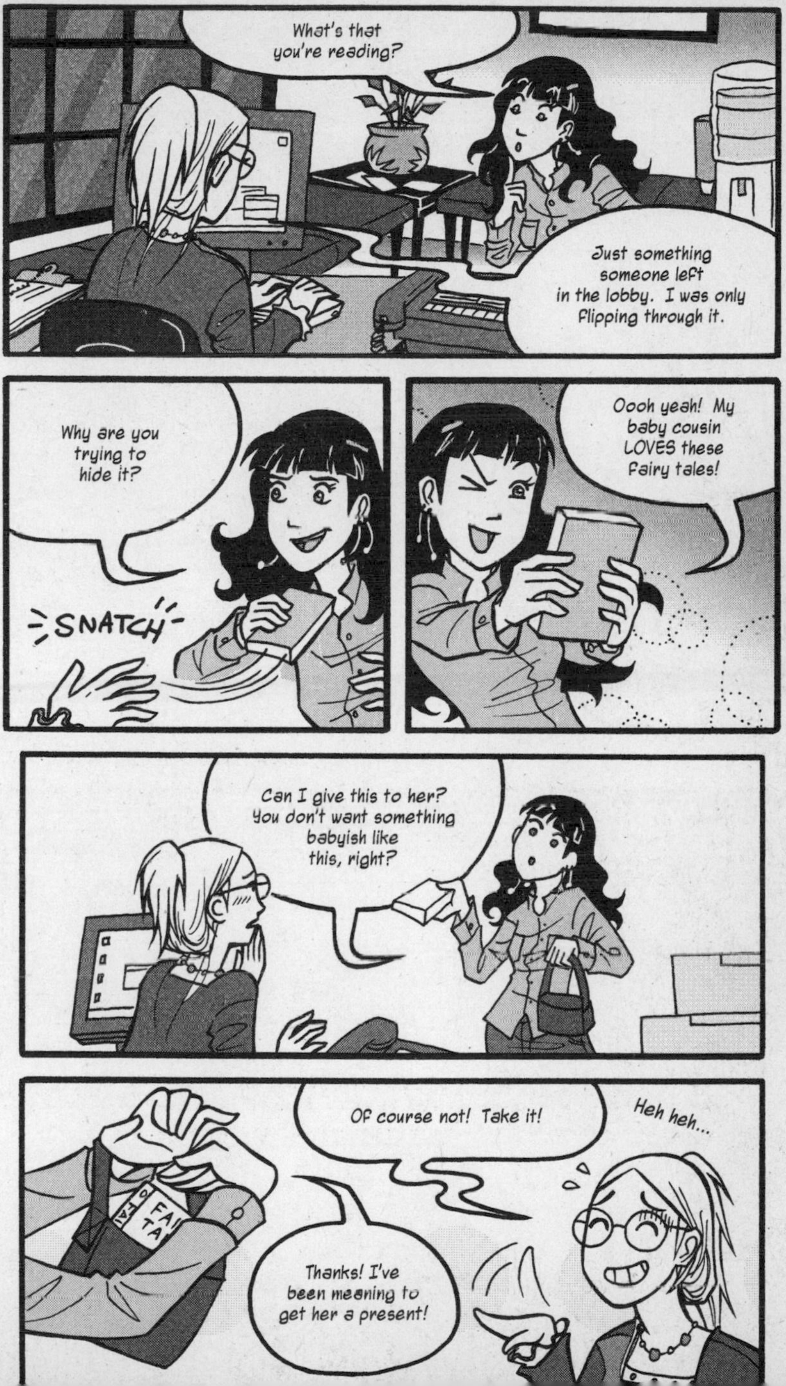
What's that you're reading?
Just something someone left in the lobby. I was only flipping through it.
Why are you trying to hide it?
SNATCH
Oooh yeah! My baby cousin LOVES these fairy tales!
Can I give this to her? You don't want something babyish like this, right?
Of course not! Take it!
Heh heh...
Thanks! I've been meaning to get her a present!

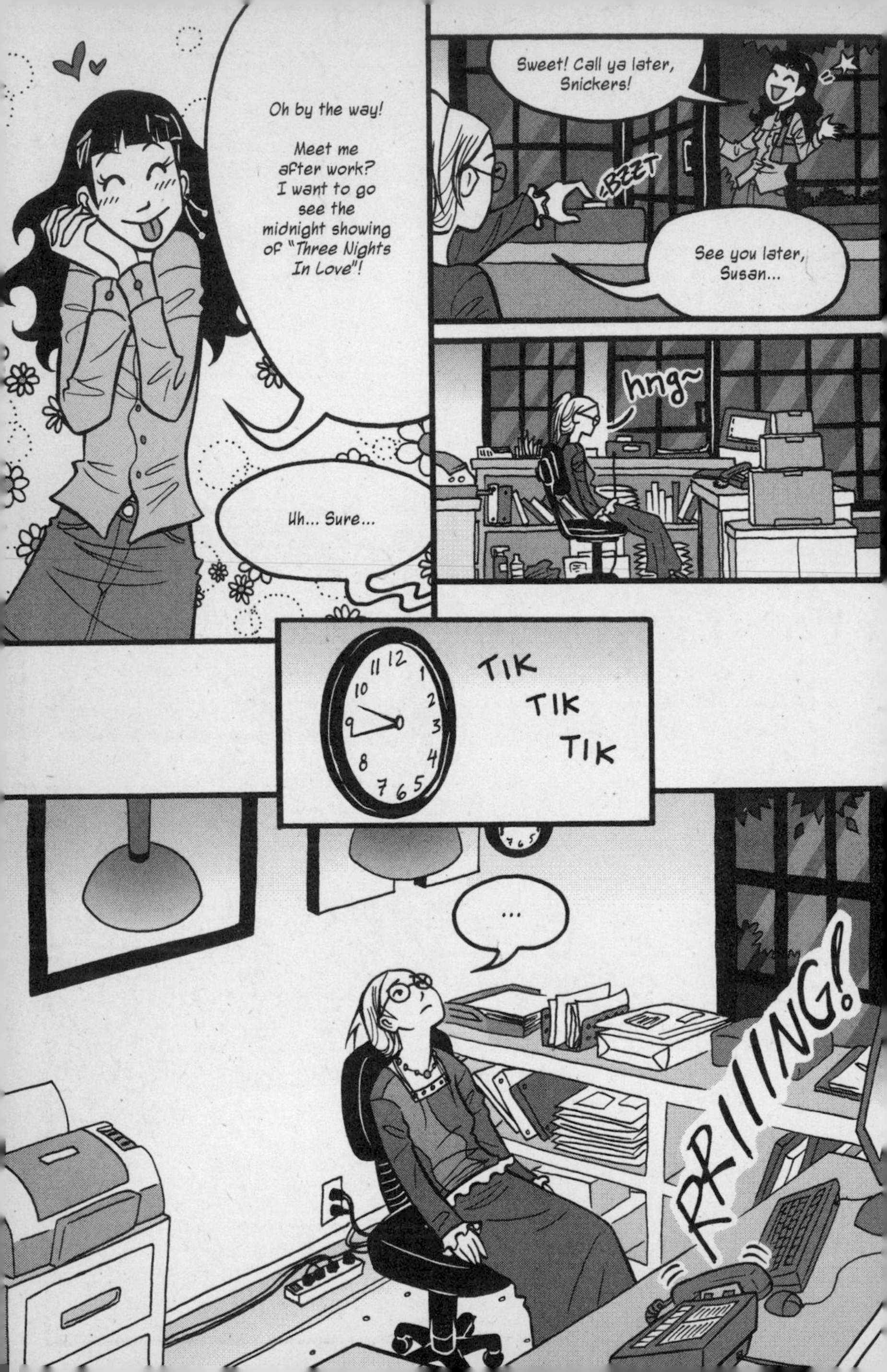
Oh by the way!
Meet me after work? I want to go see the midnight showing of "Three Nights In Love"!
Uh... Sure...
Sweet! Call ya later, Snickers!
BZZT
See you later, Susan...
hng~
TIK
TIK
TIK
...
RRIIING!

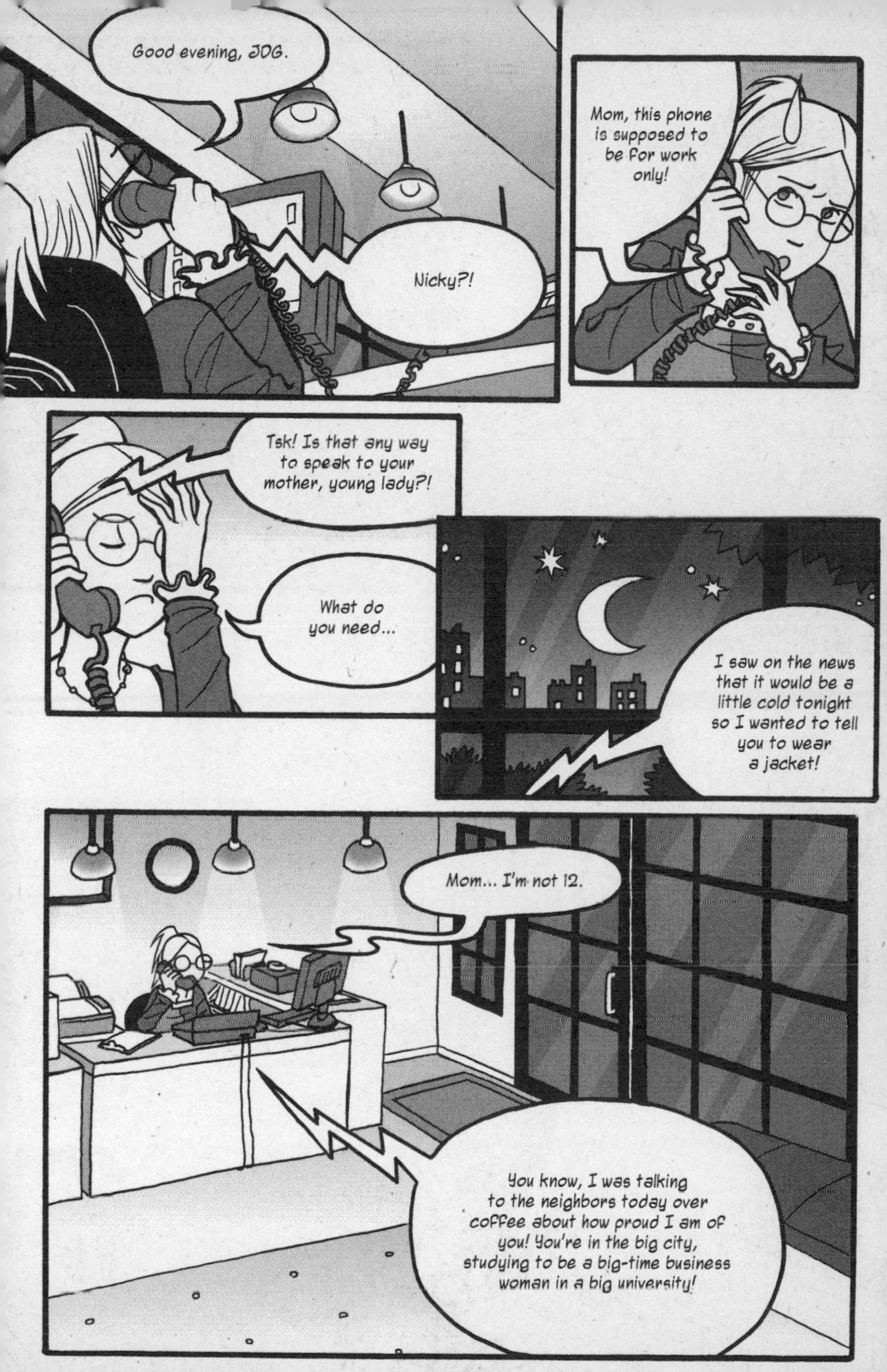
Good evening, JOG.
Nicky?!
Mom, this phone is supposed to be for work only!
Tsk! Is that any way to speak to your mother, young lady?!
What do you need...
I saw on the news that it would be a little cold tonight so I wanted to tell you to wear a jacket!
Mom... I'm not 12.
You know, I was talking to the neighbors today over coffee about how proud I am of you! You're in the big city, studying to be a big-time business woman in a big university!

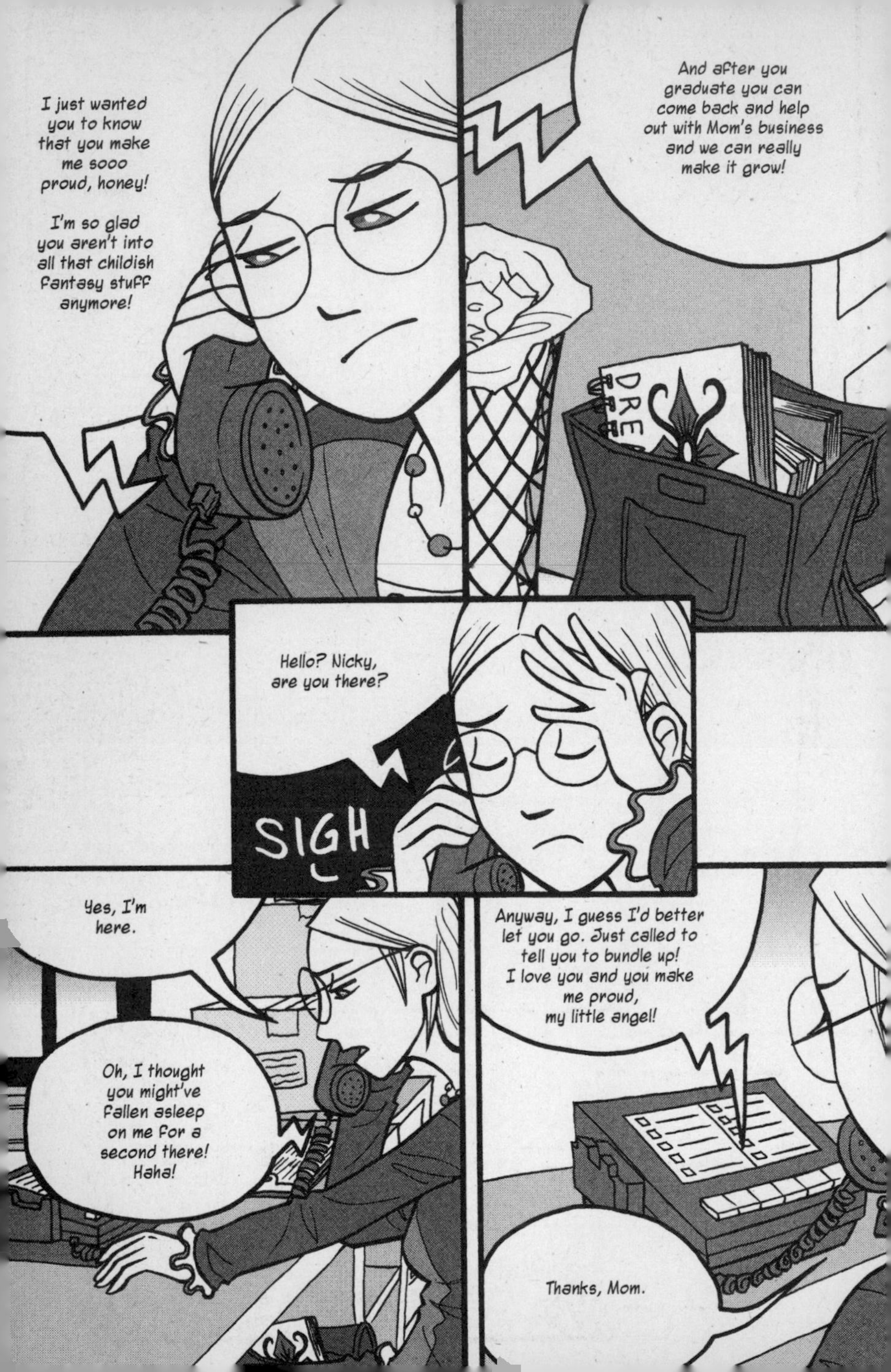
I just wanted you to know that you make me sooo proud, honey!
I'm so glad you aren't into all that childish fantasy stuff anymore!
And after you graduate you can come back and help out with Mom's business and we can really make it grow!
Hello? Nicky, are you there?
SIGH
Yes, I'm here.
Oh, I thought you might've fallen asleep on me for a second there! Haha!
Anyway, I guess I'd better let you go. Just called to tell you to bundle up! I love you and you make me proud, my little angel!
Thanks, Mom.

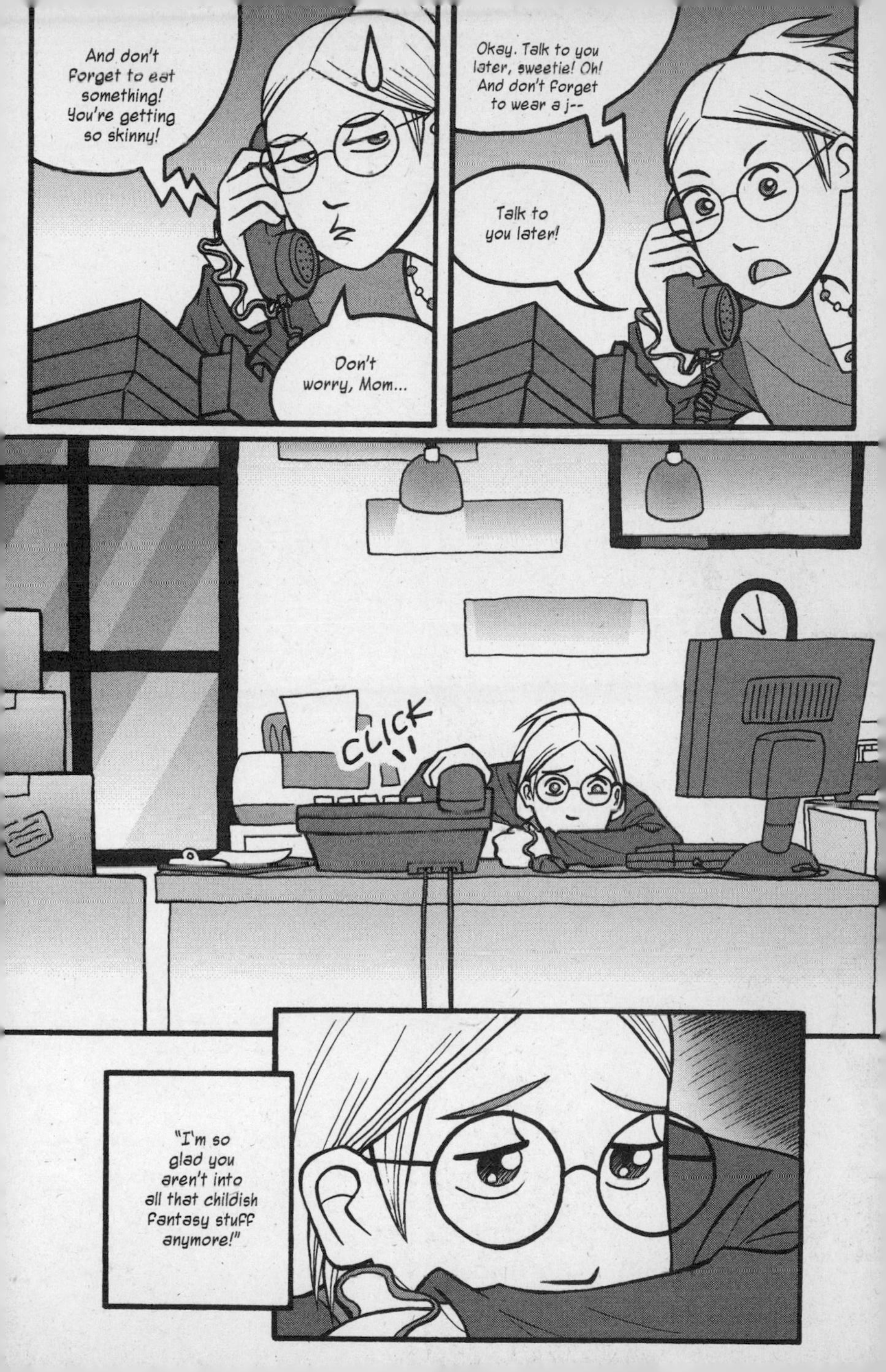
And don't forget to eat something! You're getting so skinny!
Don't worry, Mom...
Okay. Talk to you later, sweetie! Oh! And don't forget to wear a j--
Talk to you later!
CLICK
"I'm so glad you aren't into all that childish fantasy stuff anymore!"

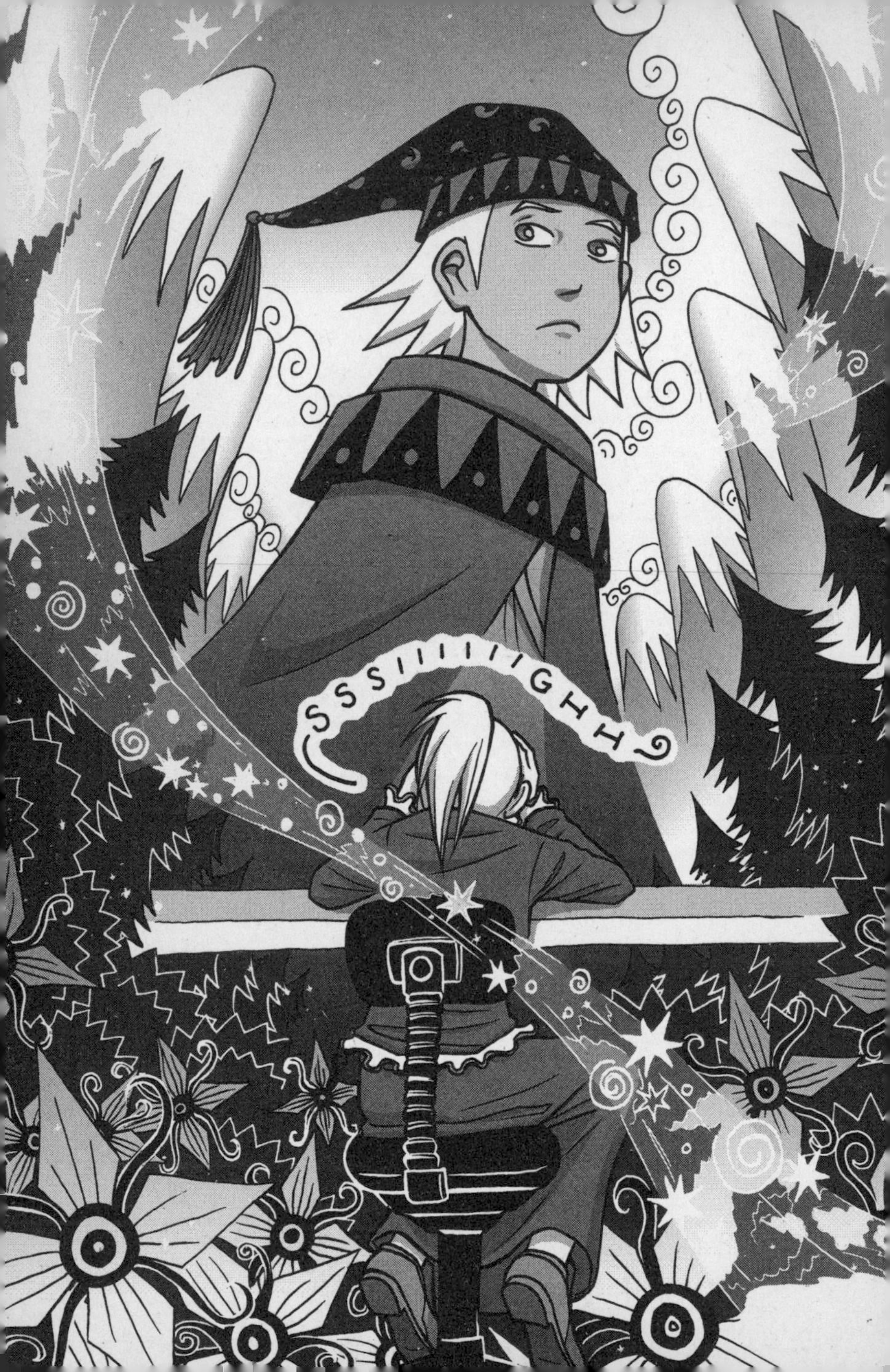
SSSIIIIIIGHH

CHAPTER TWO

Is About A Lost Pen

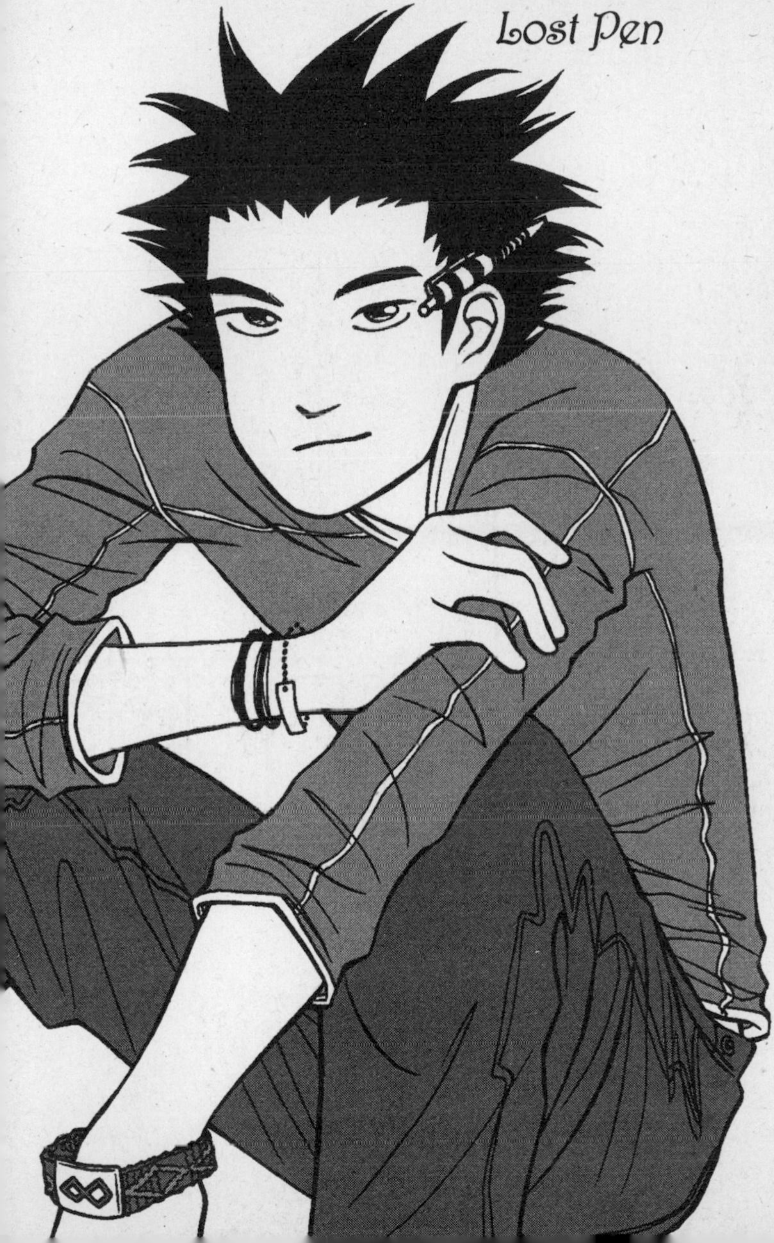

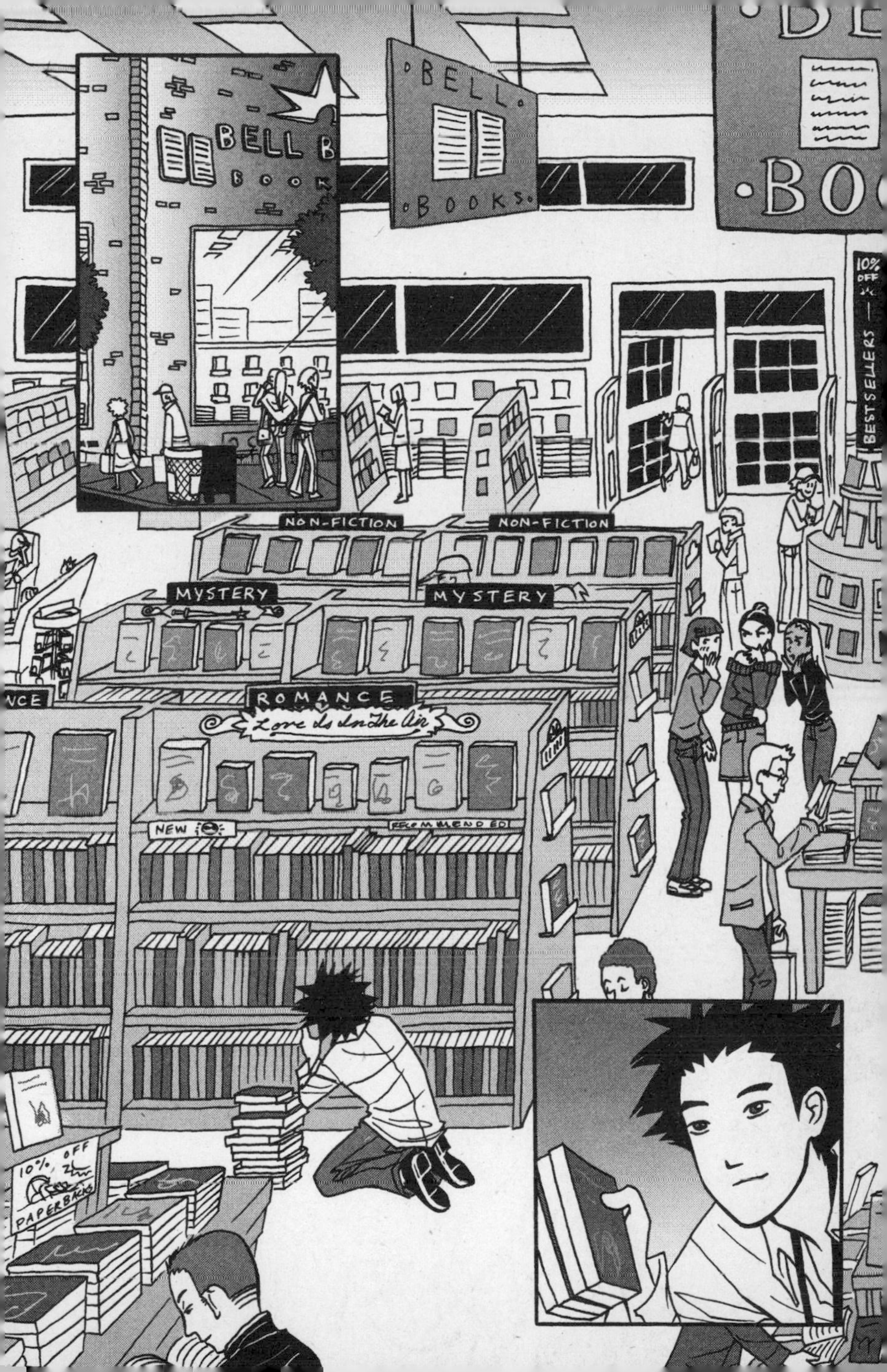

BELL B
BOOK
BELL
BOOKS
BO
10% OFF
BESTSELLERS
NON-FICTION
NON-FICTION
MYSTERY
MYSTERY
ROMANCE
Love Is In The Air
NEW
RECOMMENDED
10% OFF
PAPERBACKS

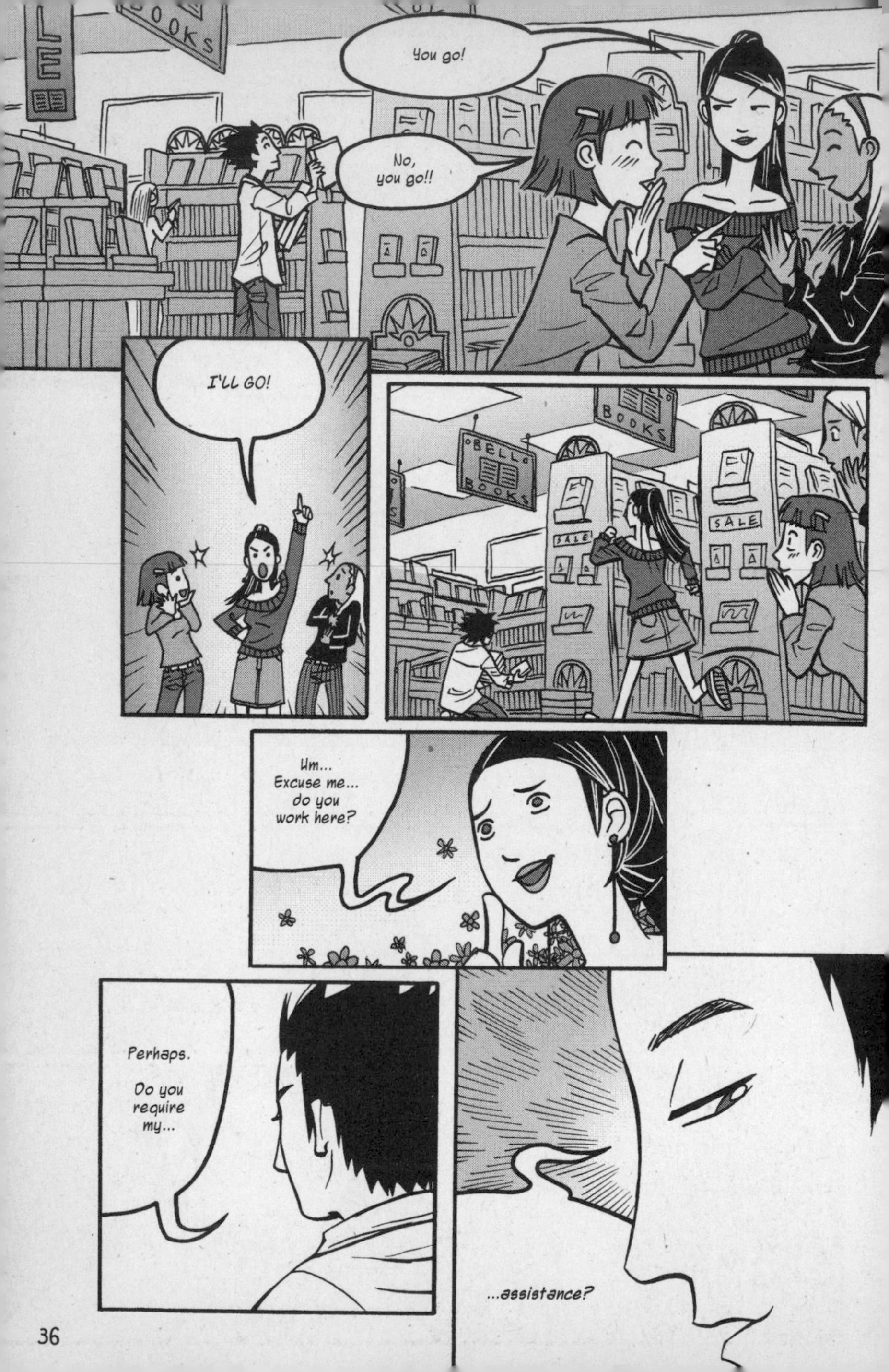
You go!
No, you go!!
I'LL GO!
Um... Excuse me... do you work here?
Perhaps.
Do you require my...
...assistance?

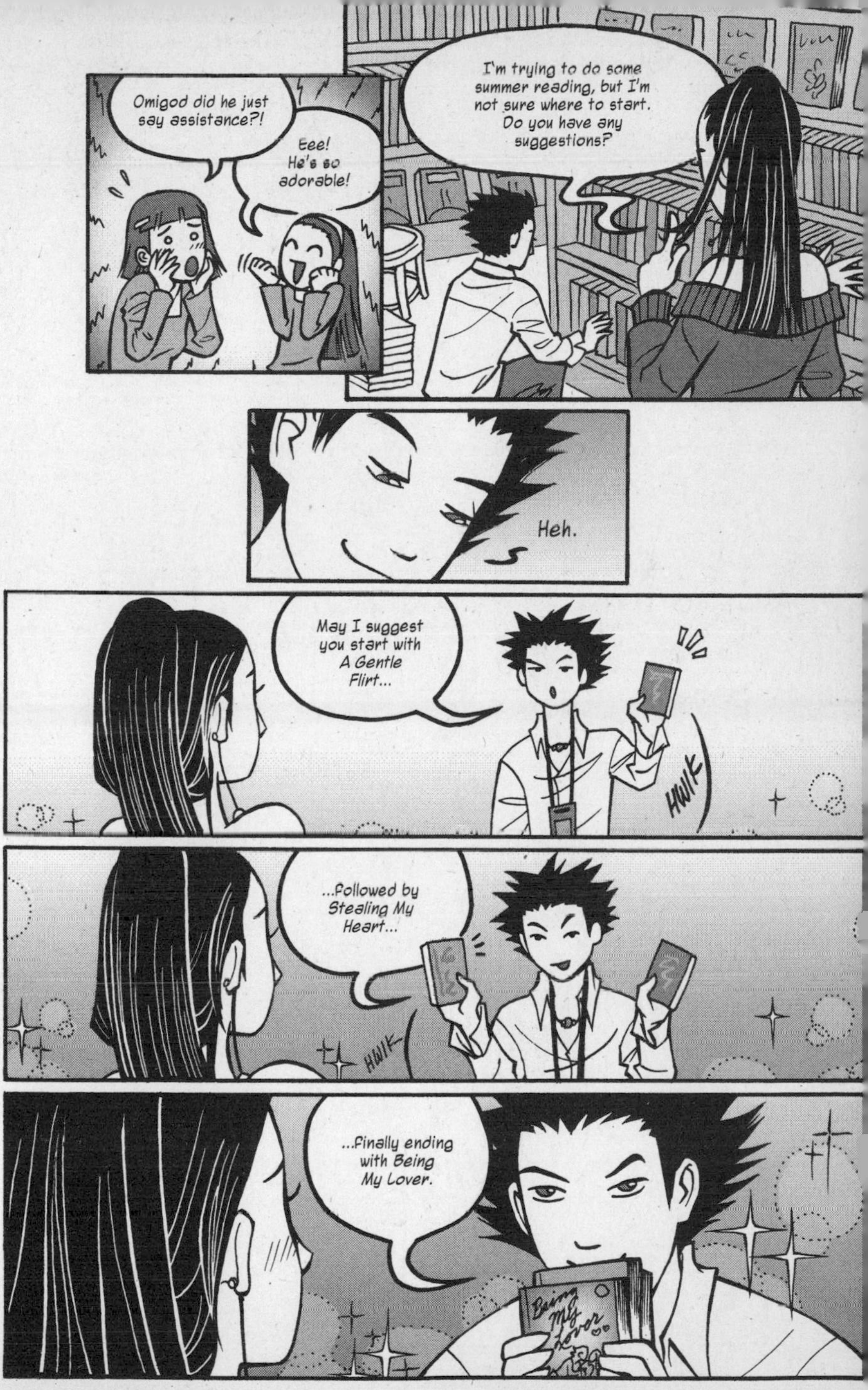
Omigod did he just say assistance?!
Eee! He's so adorable!
I'm trying to do some summer reading, but I'm not sure where to start. Do you have any suggestions?
Heh.
May I suggest you start with A Gentle Flirt...
HWIK
...followed by Stealing My Heart...
HWIK
...finally ending with Being My Lover.
Being My Lover

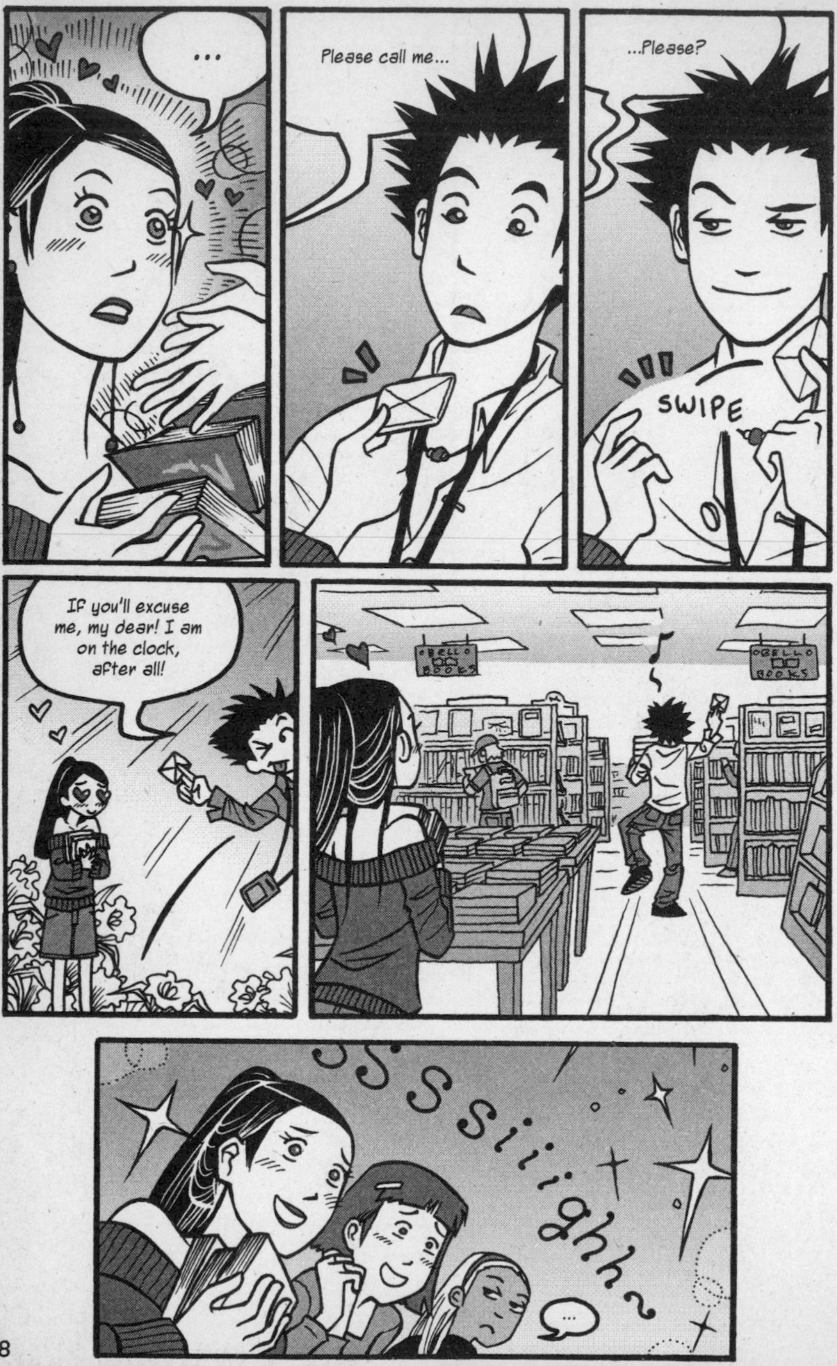
...
Please call me...
...Please?
SWIPE
If you'll excuse me, my dear! I am on the clock, after all!
BELLO BOOKS
BELLO BOOKS
SSSiiiighh~
...

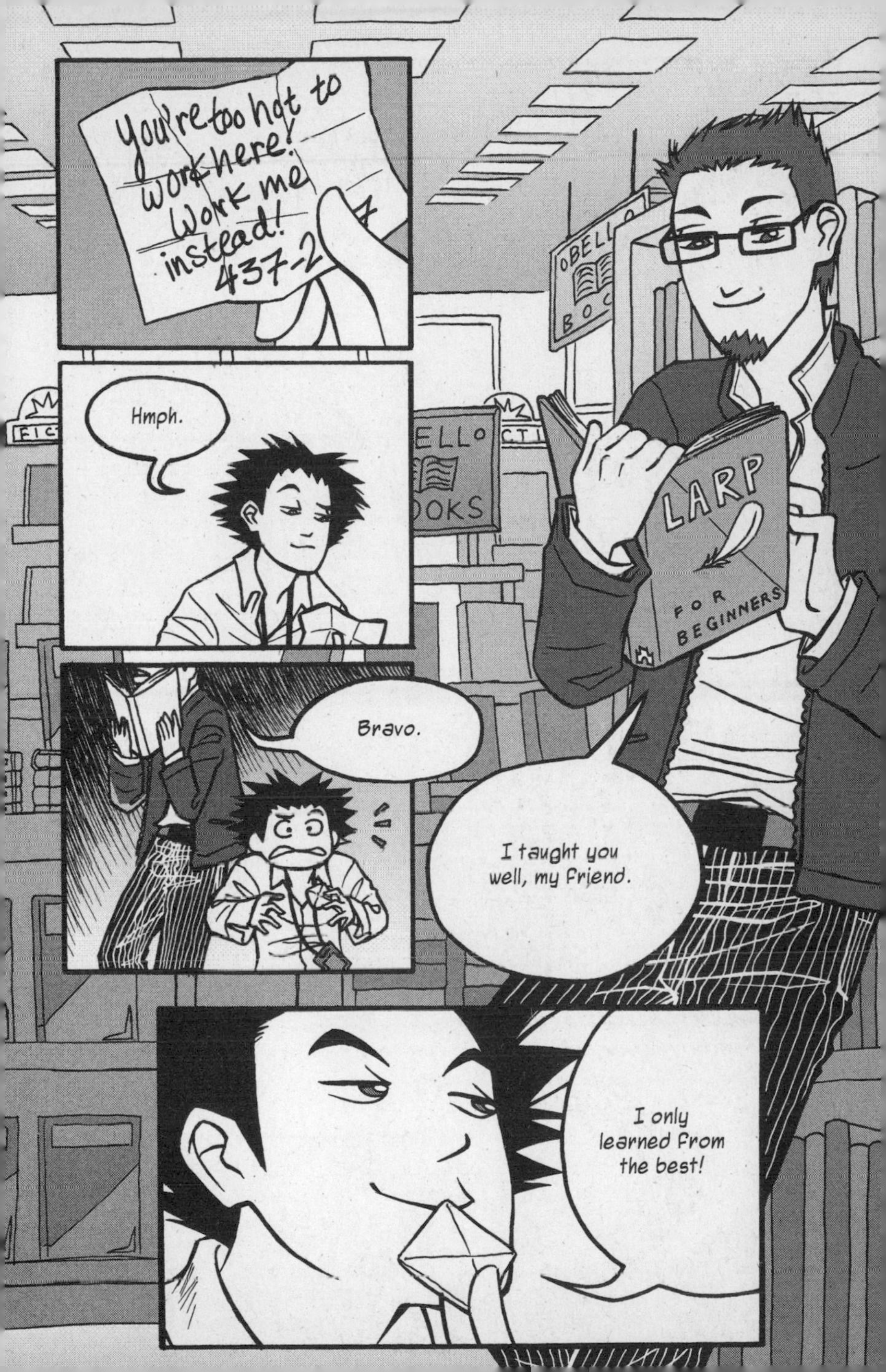
You're too hot to work here! Work me instead! 437-2
Hmph.
Bravo.
LARP
FOR BEGINNERS
I taught you well, my friend.
I only learned from the best!

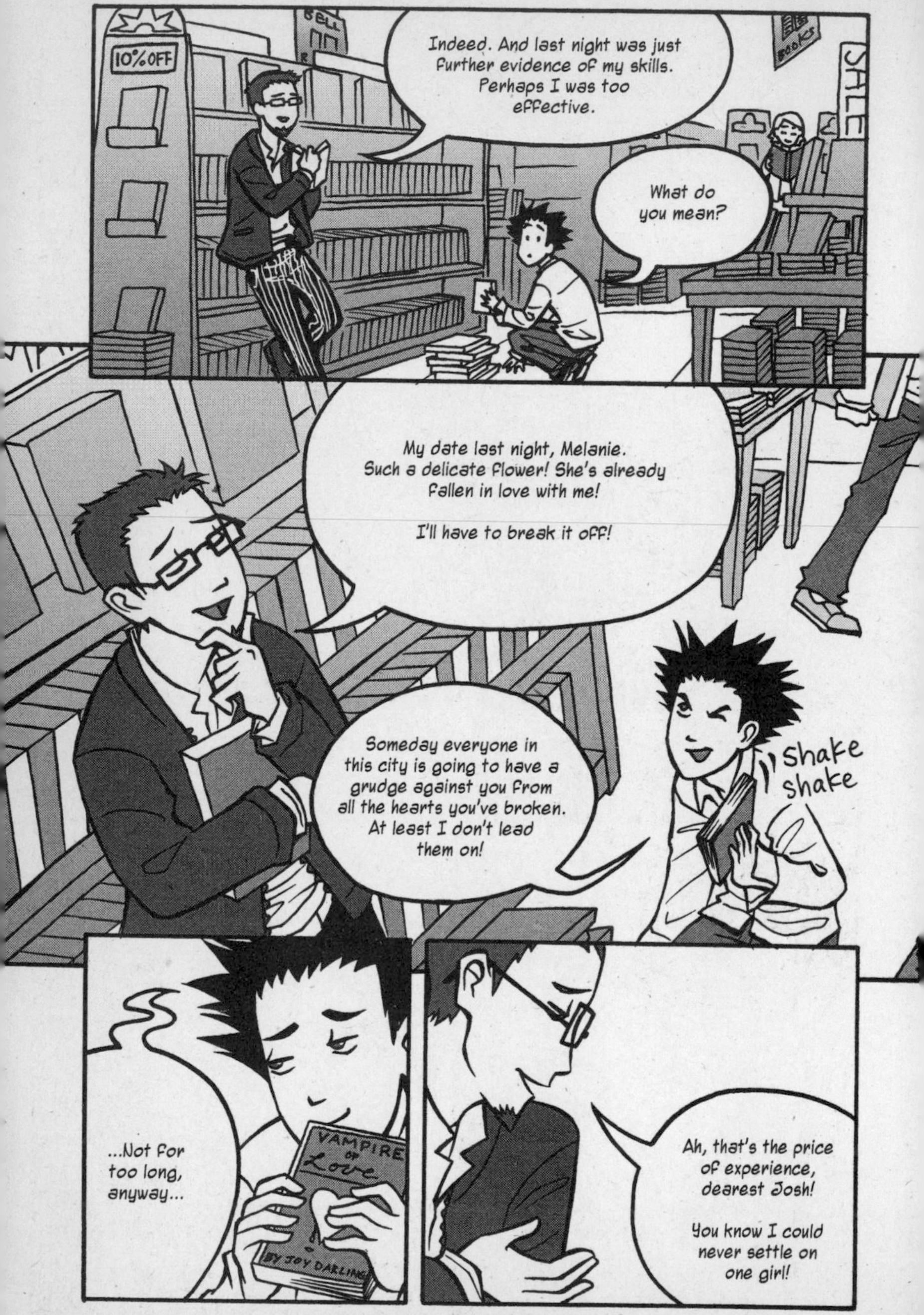
10% OFF
SALE
Indeed. And last night was just further evidence of my skills. Perhaps I was too effective.
What do you mean?
My date last night, Melanie. Such a delicate flower! She's already fallen in love with me!
I'll have to break it off!
Someday everyone in this city is going to have a grudge against you from all the hearts you've broken. At least I don't lead them on!
shake shake
...Not for too long, anyway...
VAMPIRE OF Love
BY JOY DARLING
Ah, that's the price of experience, dearest Josh!
You know I could never settle on one girl!

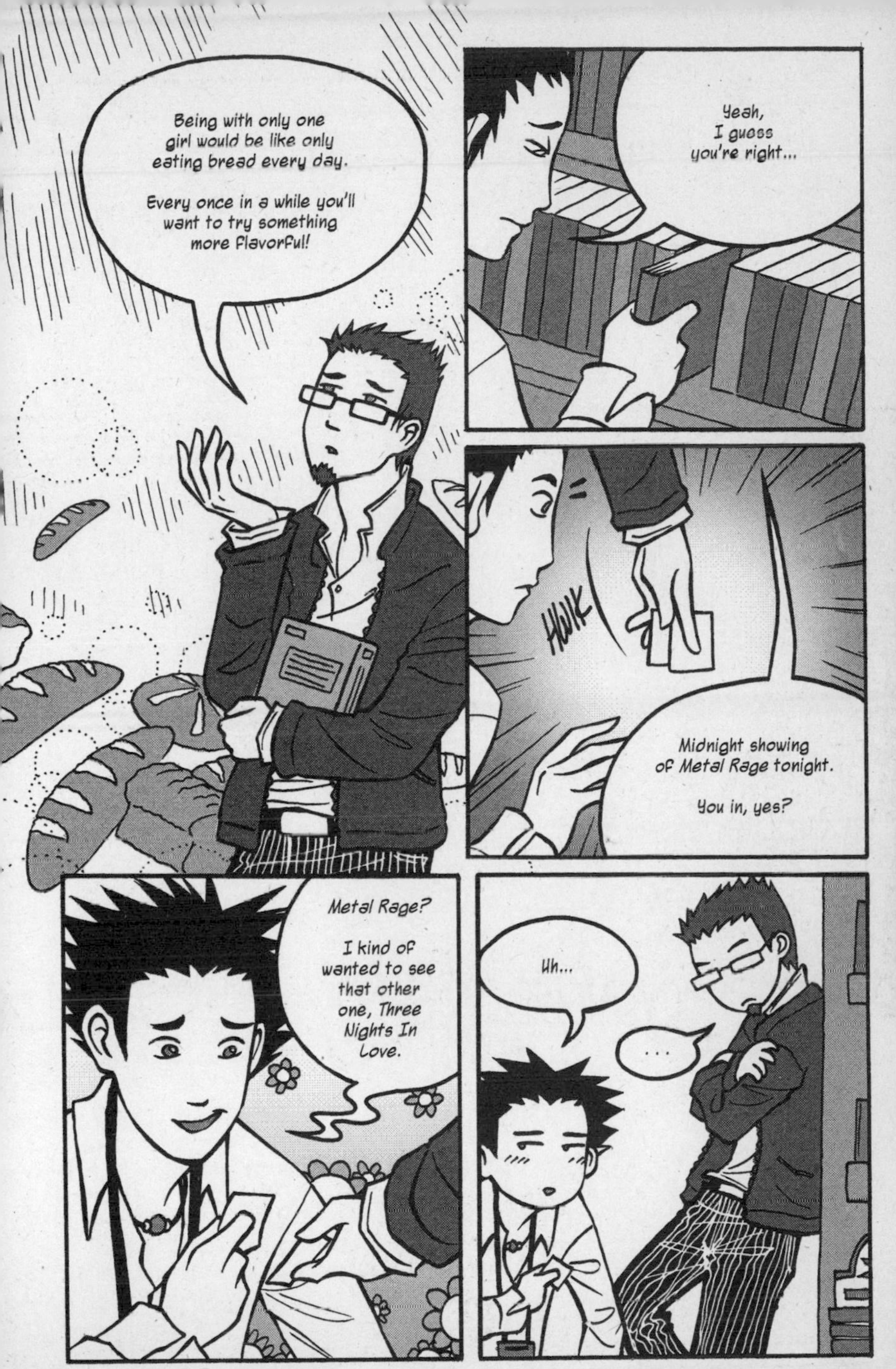
Being with only one girl would be like only eating bread every day.
Every once in a while you'll want to try something more flavorful!
Yeah, I guess you're right...
Midnight showing of Metal Rage tonight.
You in, yes?
Metal Rage?
I kind of wanted to see that other one, Three Nights In Love.
Uh...
. . .

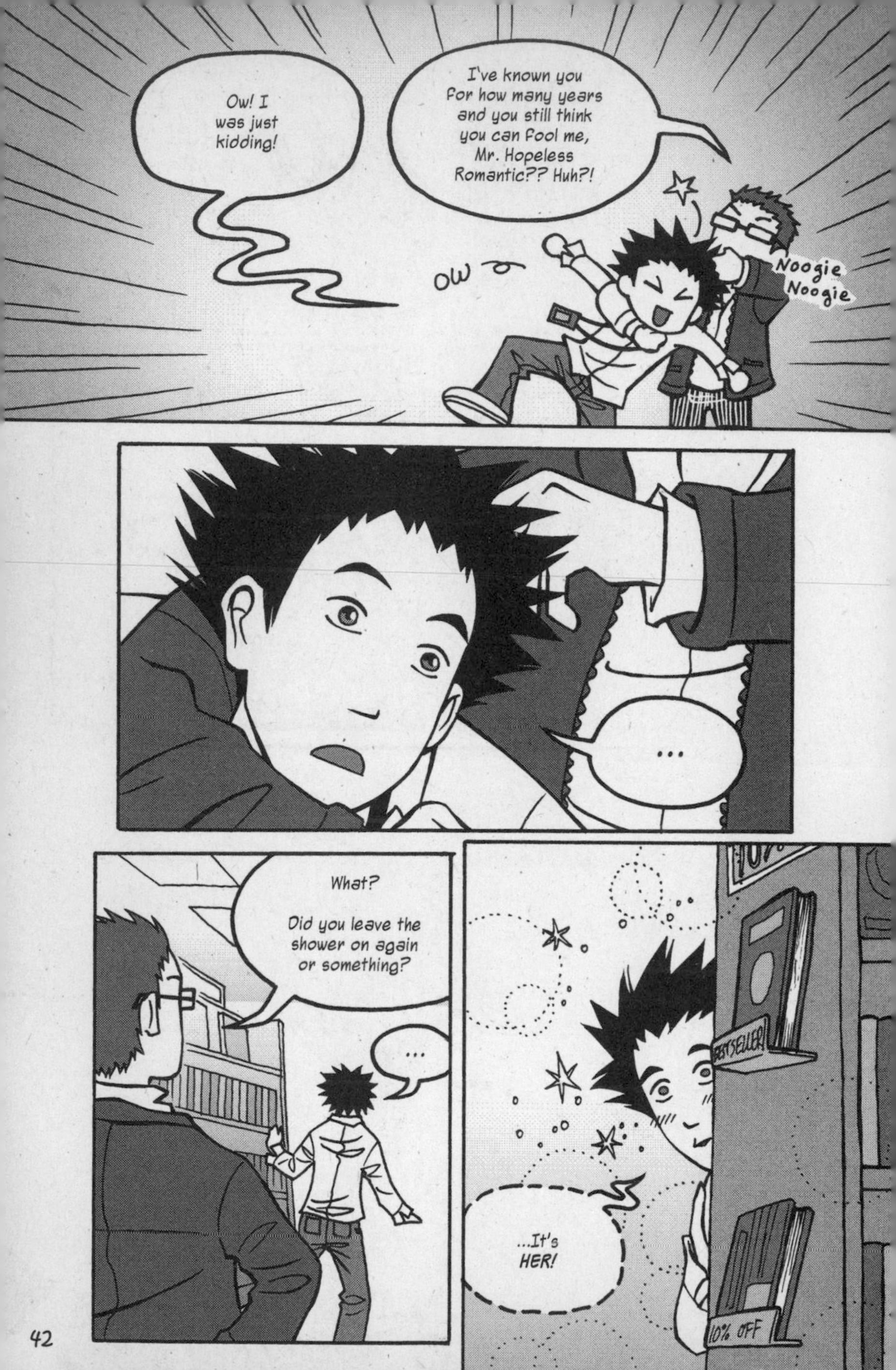

Ow! I was just kidding!
I've known you for how many years and you still think you can fool me, Mr. Hopeless Romantic?? Huh?!
OW
Noogie Noogie
...
What?
Did you leave the shower on again or something?
...
BESTSELLER
10% OFF
...It's HER!

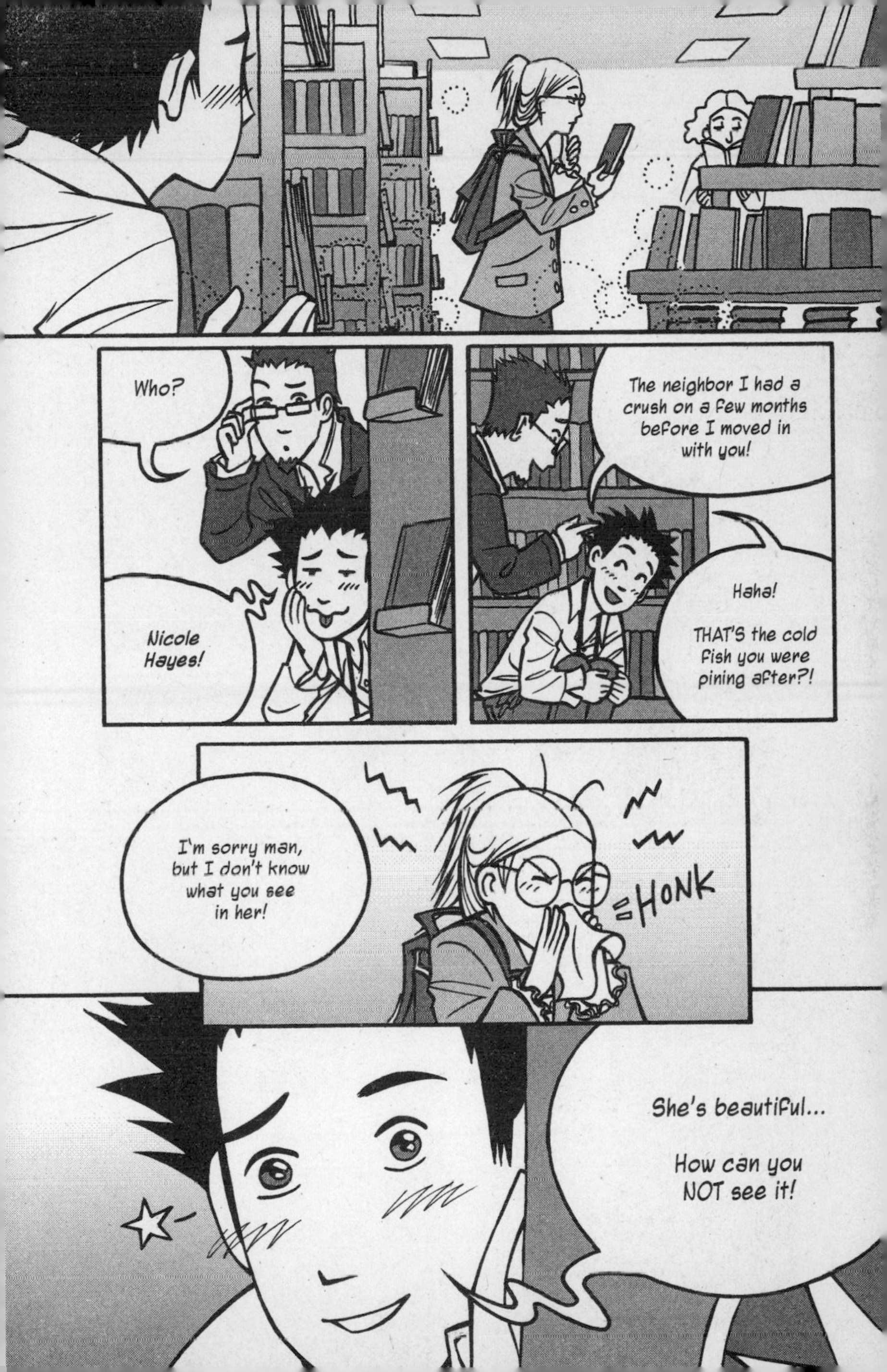
Who?
Nicole Hayes!
The neighbor I had a crush on a few months before I moved in with you!
Haha!
THAT'S the cold fish you were pining after?!
I'm sorry man, but I don't know what you see in her!
HONK
She's beautiful...
How can you NOT see it!

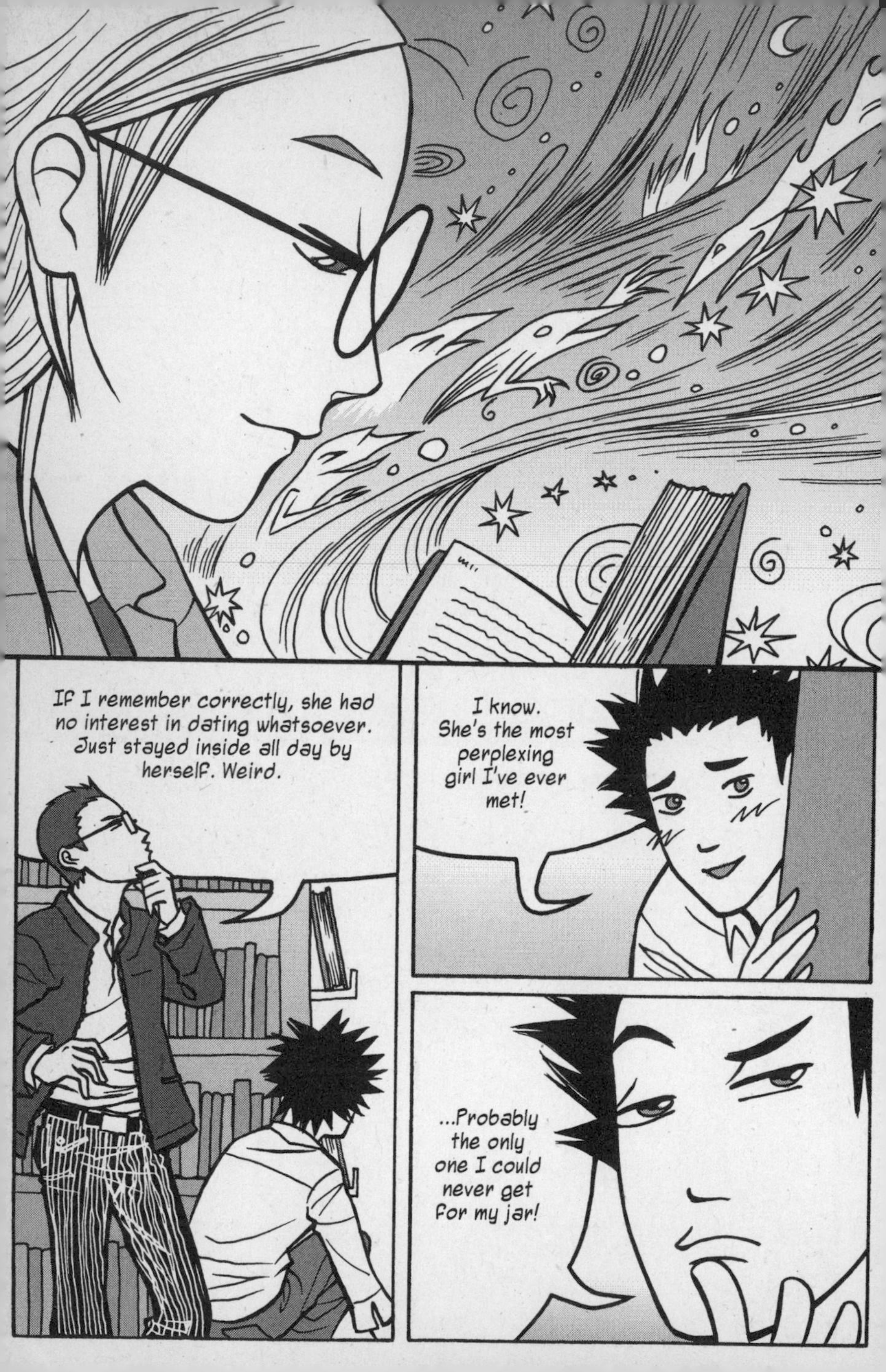
If I remember correctly, she had no interest in dating whatsoever. Just stayed inside all day by herself. Weird.
I know. She's the most perplexing girl I've ever met!
...Probably the only one I could never get for my jar!

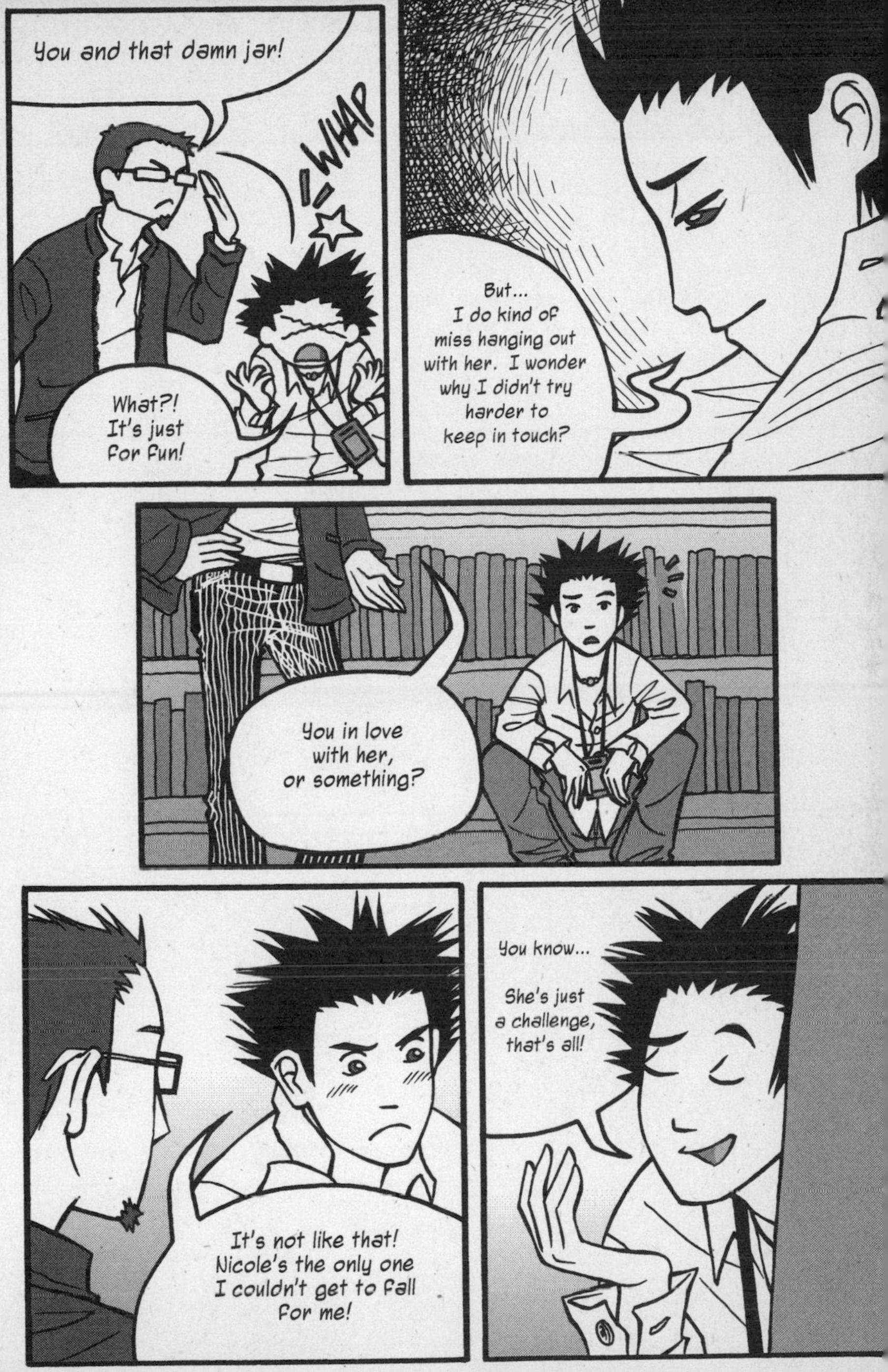
You and that damn jar!
WHAP
What?! It's just for fun!
But... I do kind of miss hanging out with her. I wonder why I didn't try harder to keep in touch?
You in love with her, or something?
It's not like that! Nicole's the only one I couldn't get to fall for me!
You know...
She's just a challenge, that's all!

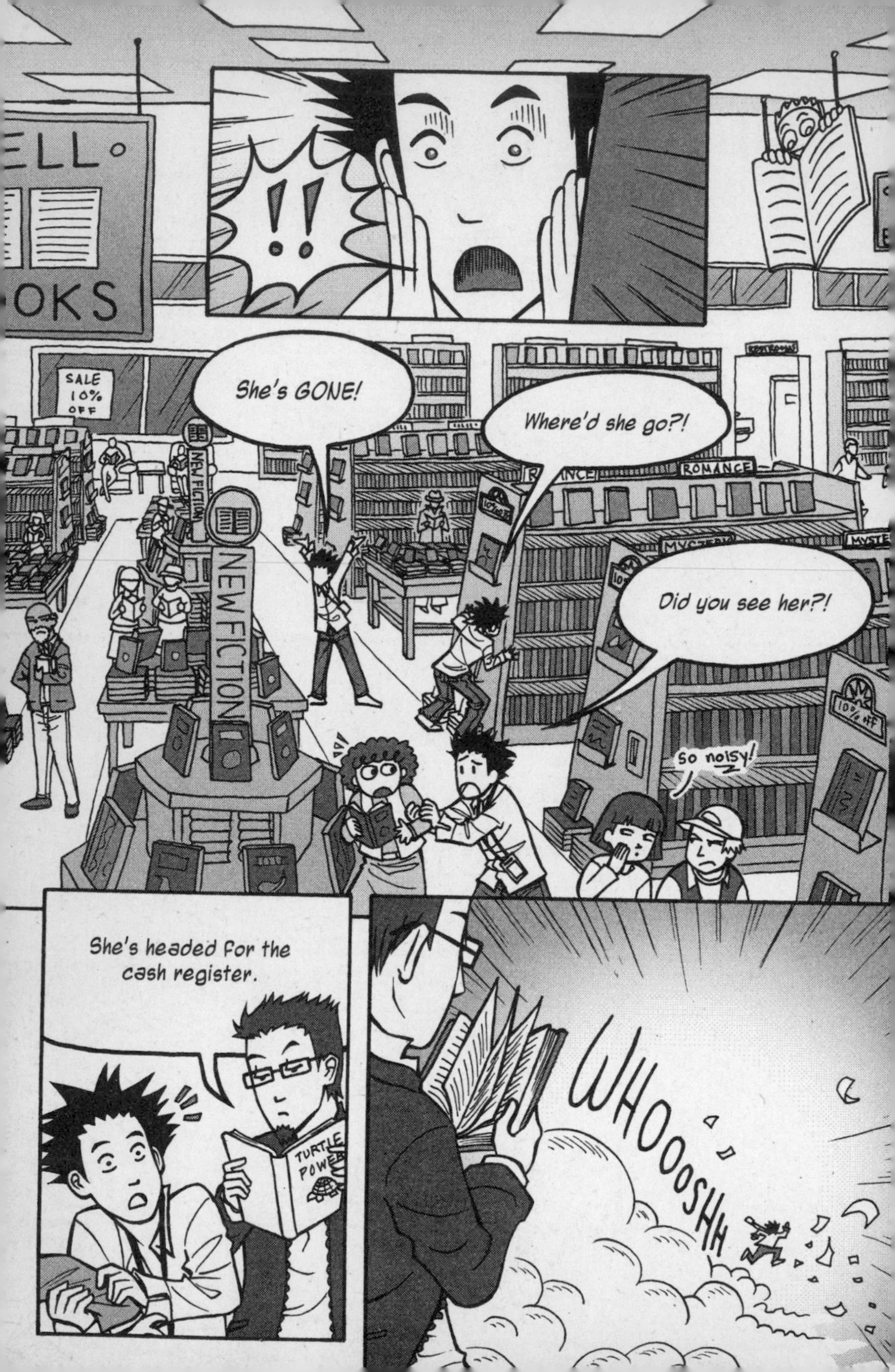

!!
SALE 10% OFF
NEW FICTION
She's GONE!
Where'd she go?!
ROMANCE
Did you see her?!
10% OFF
So noisy!
She's headed for the cash register.
TURTLE POWER
WHOOOOSHH

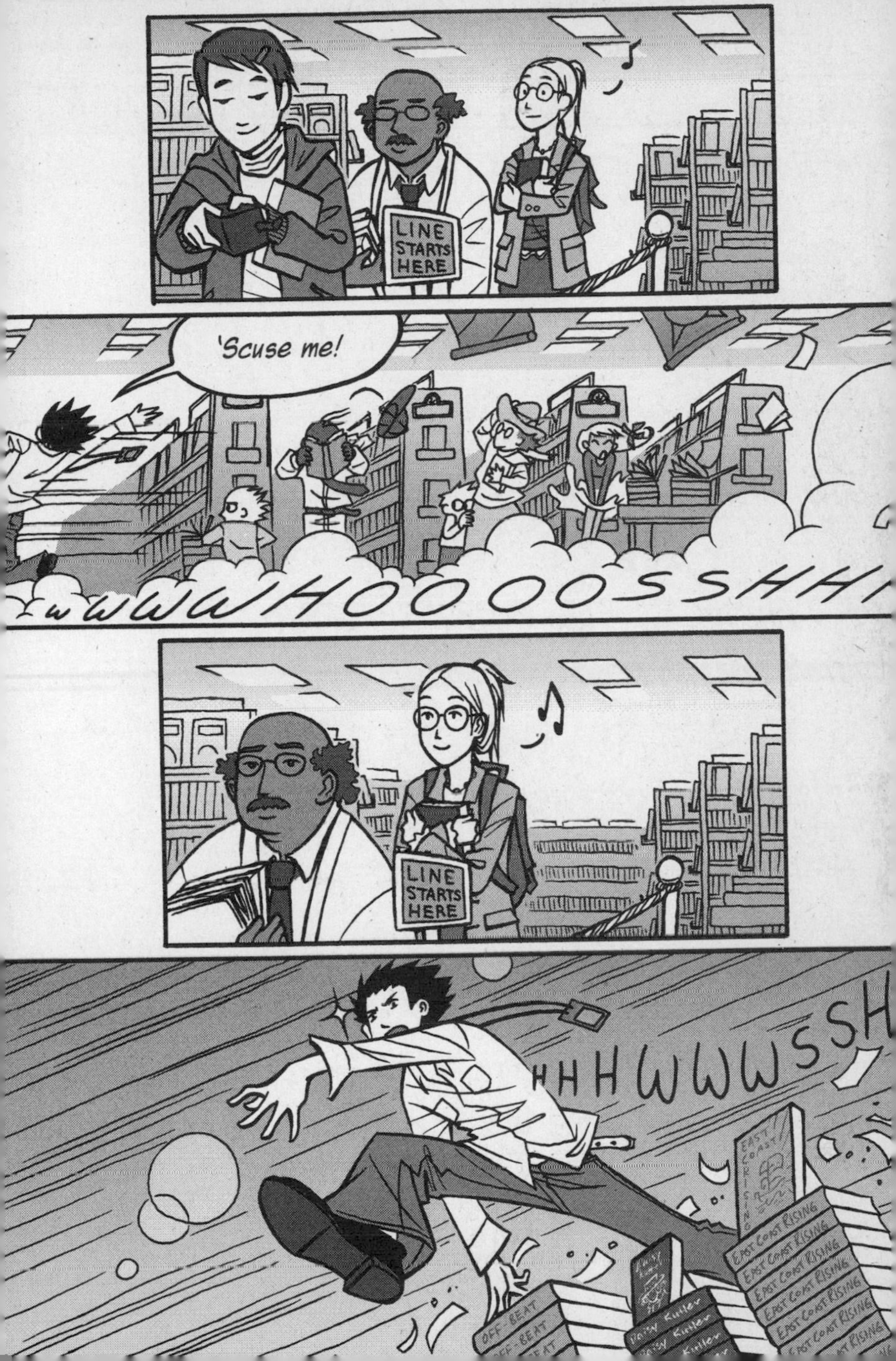
LINE STARTS HERE
'Scuse me!
wWWWHOOOOOSSHH
LINE STARTS HERE
HHHWWWSSH
EAST COAST RISING
EAST COAST RISING
Daisy Kutter
OFF-BEAT

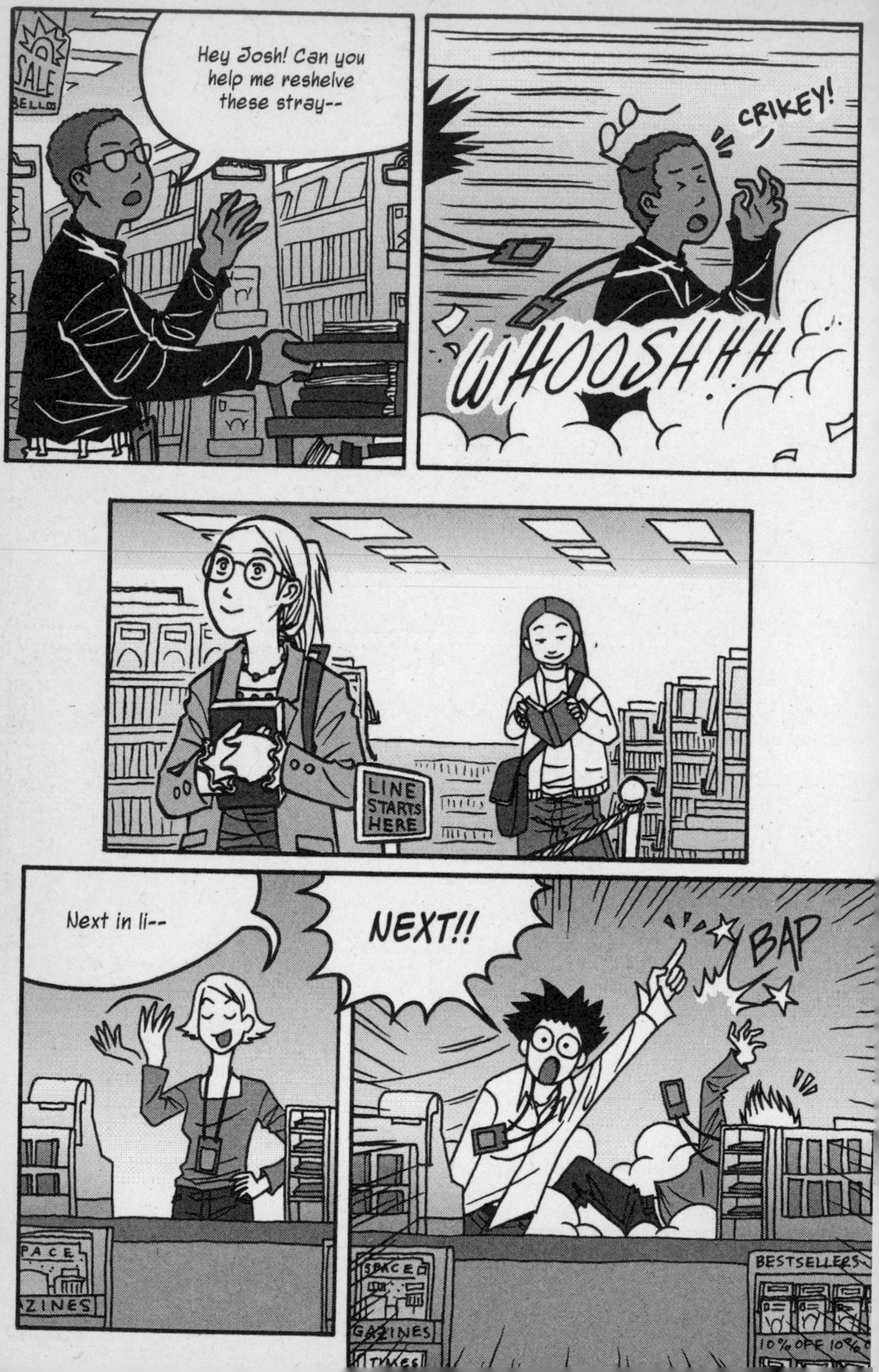
SALE
Hey Josh! Can you help me reshelve these stray--
CRIKEY!
WHOOSHHH!!
LINE STARTS HERE
Next in li--
NEXT!!
BAP
BESTSELLERS

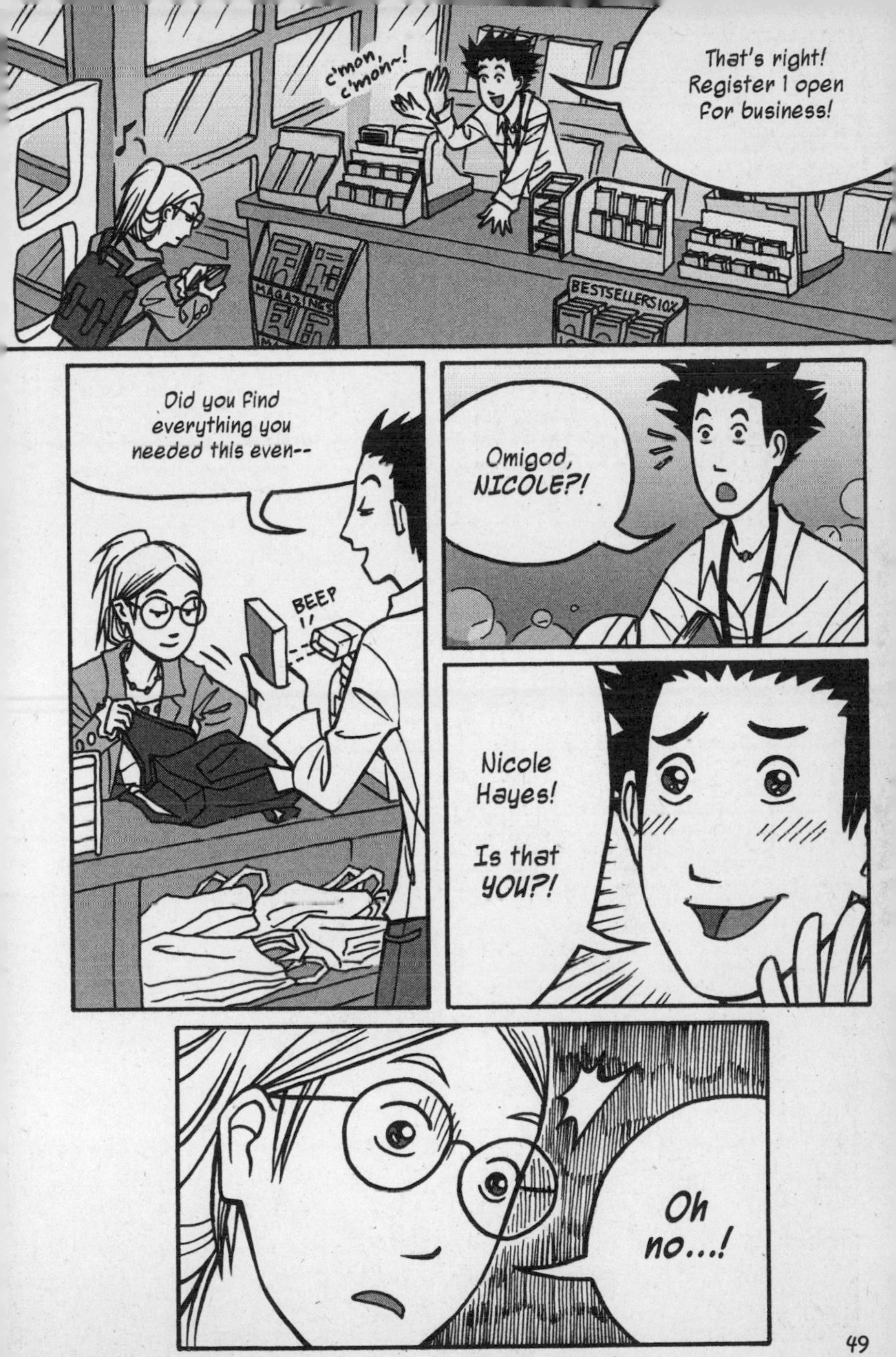
c'mon, c'mon~!
That's right! Register 1 open for business!
MAGAZINES
BESTSELLERS 10%
Did you find everything you needed this even--
BEEP
Omigod, NICOLE?!
Nicole Hayes!
Is that YOU?!
Oh no...!

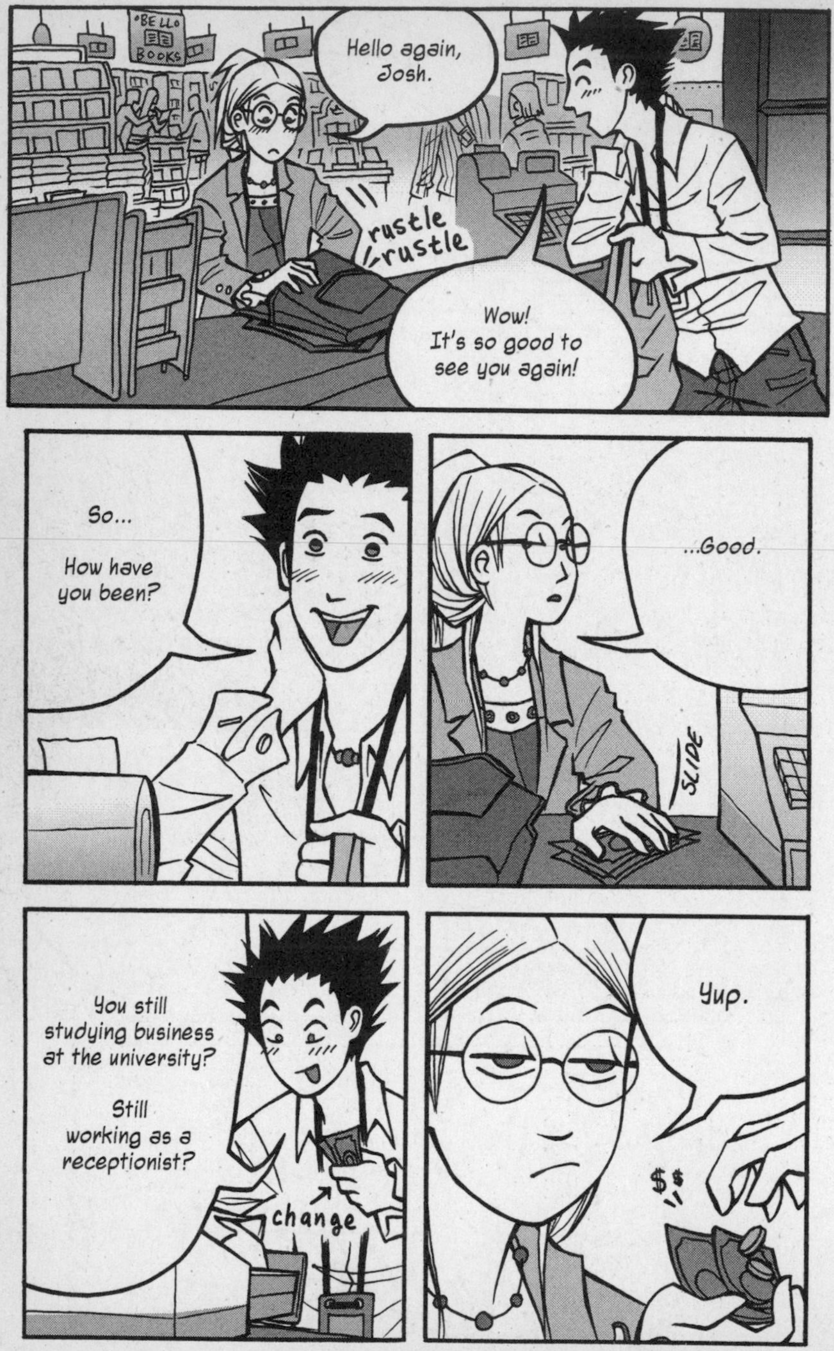
BELLO BOOKS
Hello again, Josh.
rustle rustle
Wow! It's so good to see you again!
So...
How have you been?
...Good.
SLIDE
You still studying business at the university?
Still working as a receptionist?
change
Yup.
$$

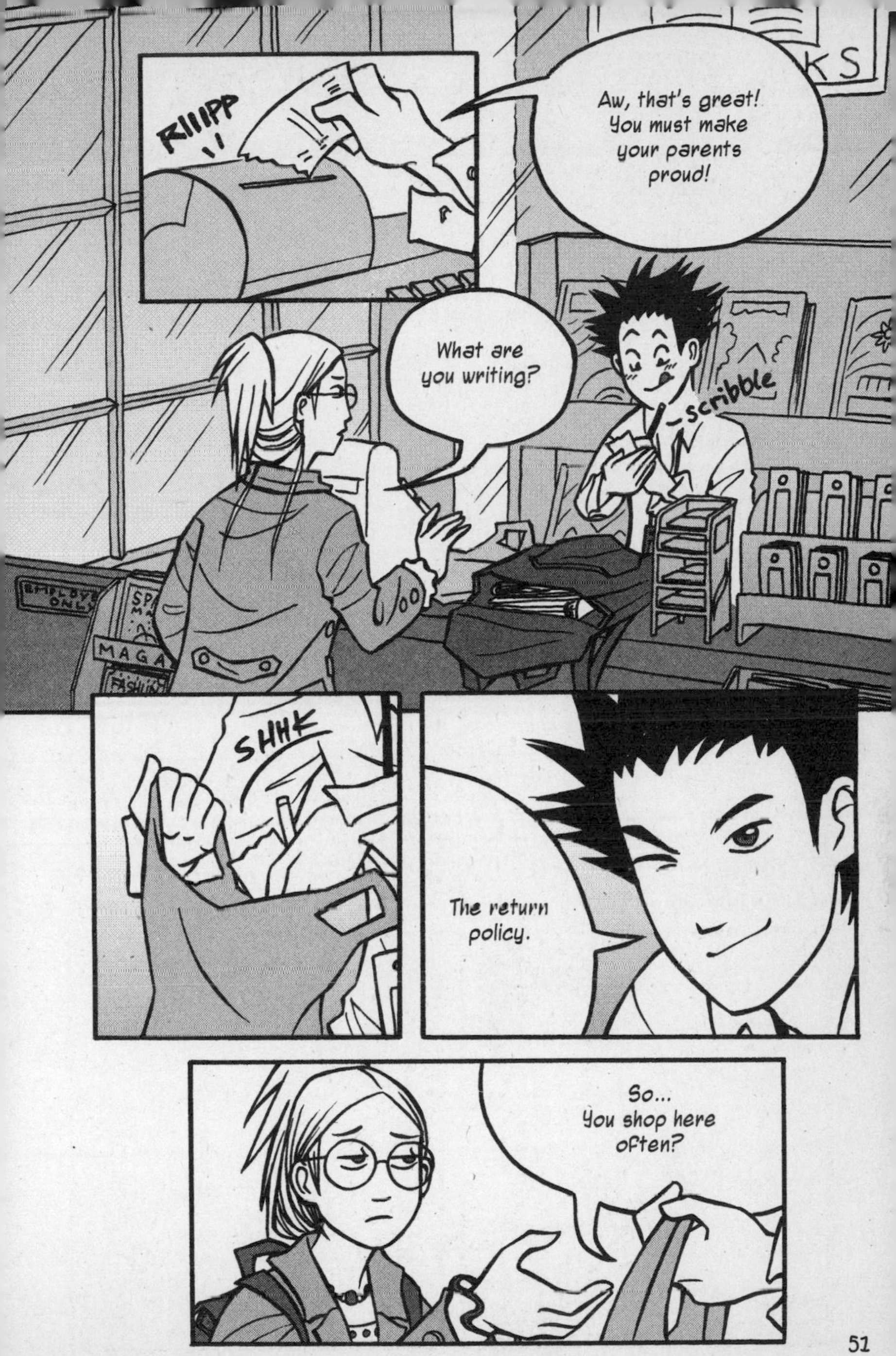
RIIIPP
Aw, that's great! You must make your parents proud!
What are you writing?
scribble
SHHK
The return policy.
So... You shop here often?

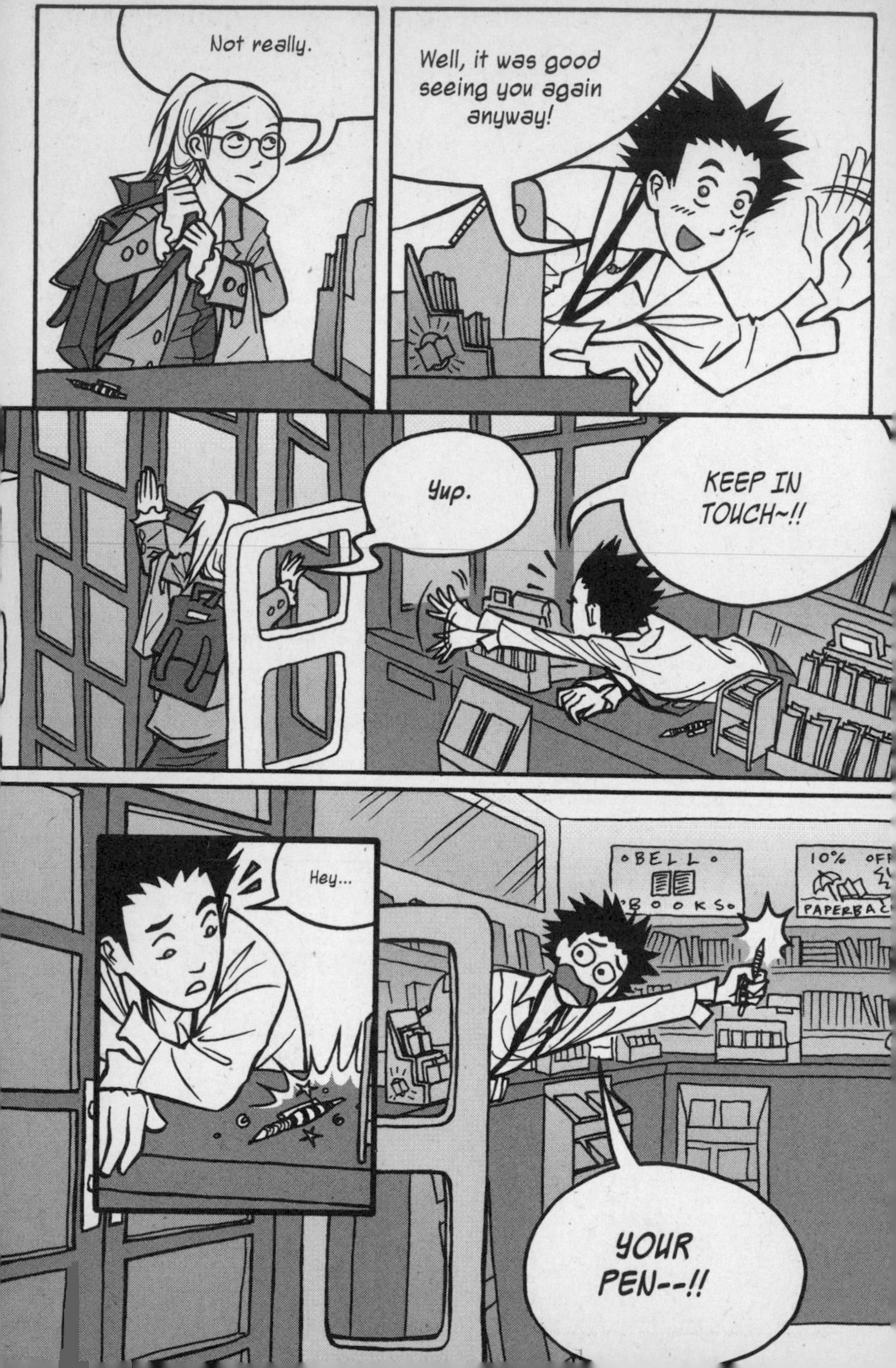
Not really.
Well, it was good seeing you again anyway!
Yup.
KEEP IN TOUCH~!!
Hey...
•BELL• BOOKS•
10% OFF PAPERBA
YOUR PEN--!!

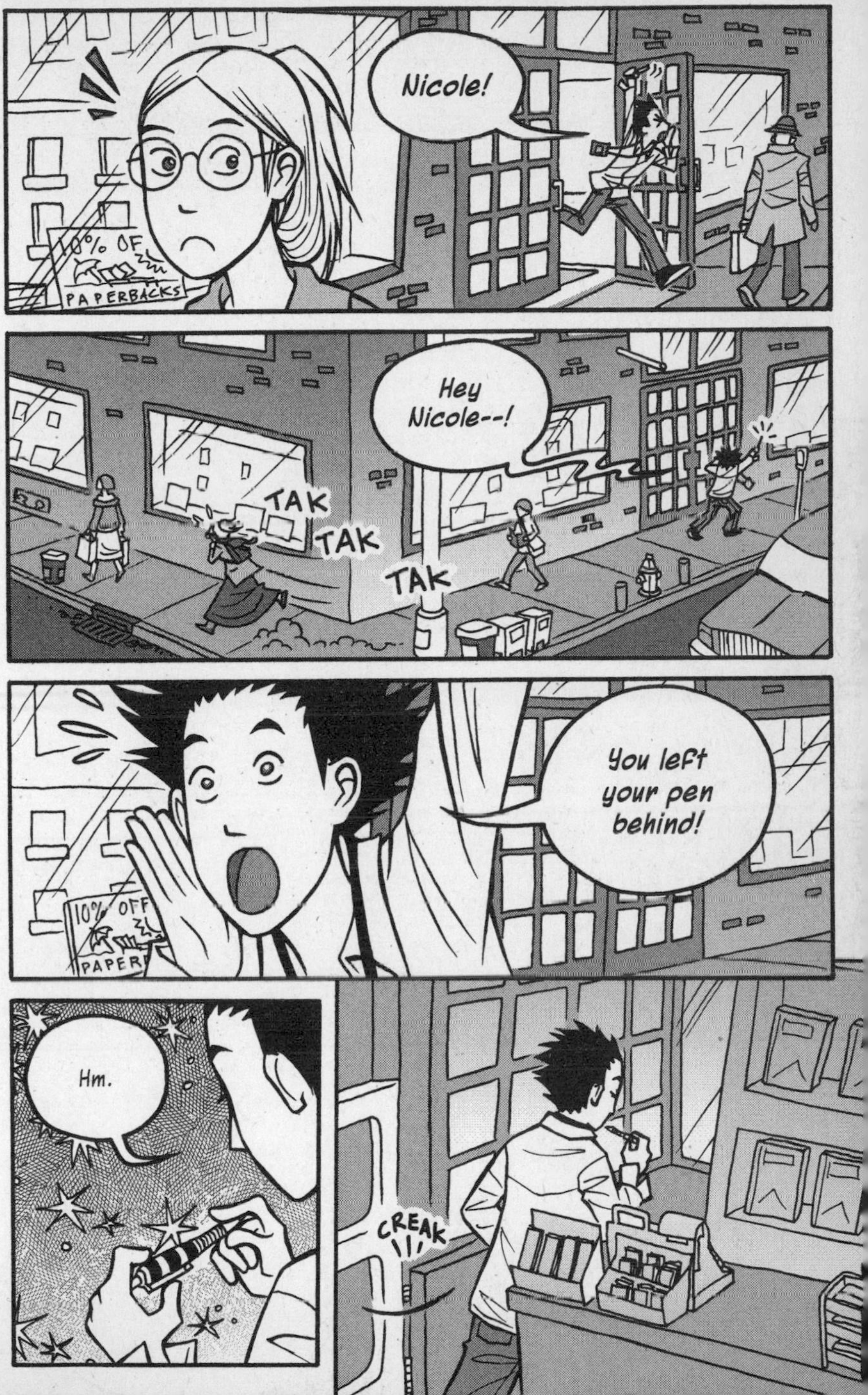
10% OFF
PAPERBACKS
Nicole!
Hey Nicole--!
TAK
TAK
TAK
10% OFF
PAPER
You left your pen behind!
Hm.
CREAK

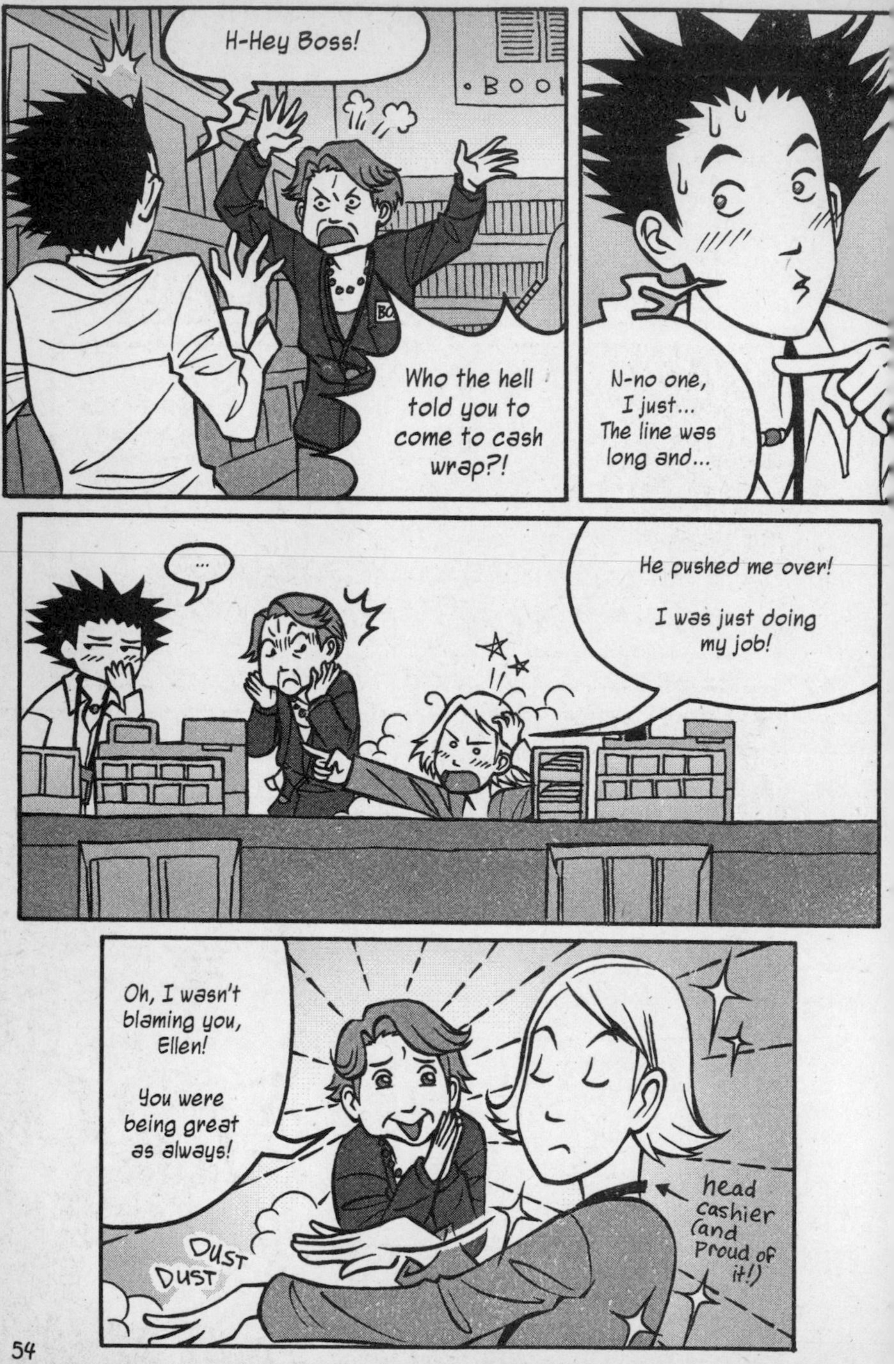
H-Hey Boss!
BOO
Who the hell told you to come to cash wrap?!
N-no one, I just... The line was long and...
...
He pushed me over!
I was just doing my job!
Oh, I wasn't blaming you, Ellen!
You were being great as always!
head cashier (and Proud of it!)
DUST
DUST

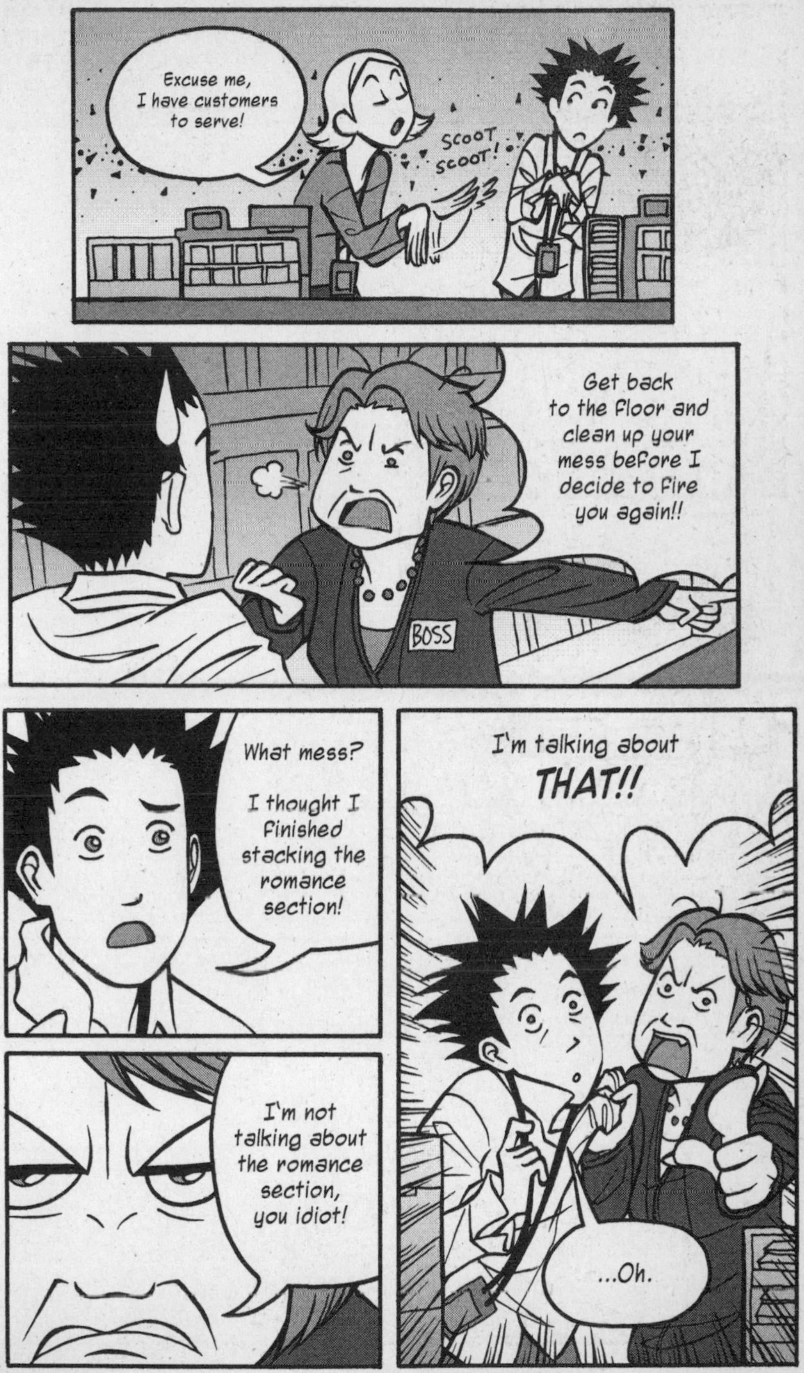
Excuse me, I have customers to serve!
SCOOT SCOOT!
Get back to the floor and clean up your mess before I decide to fire you again!!
BOSS
What mess?
I thought I finished stacking the romance section!
I'm talking about THAT!!
I'm not talking about the romance section, you idiot!
...Oh.

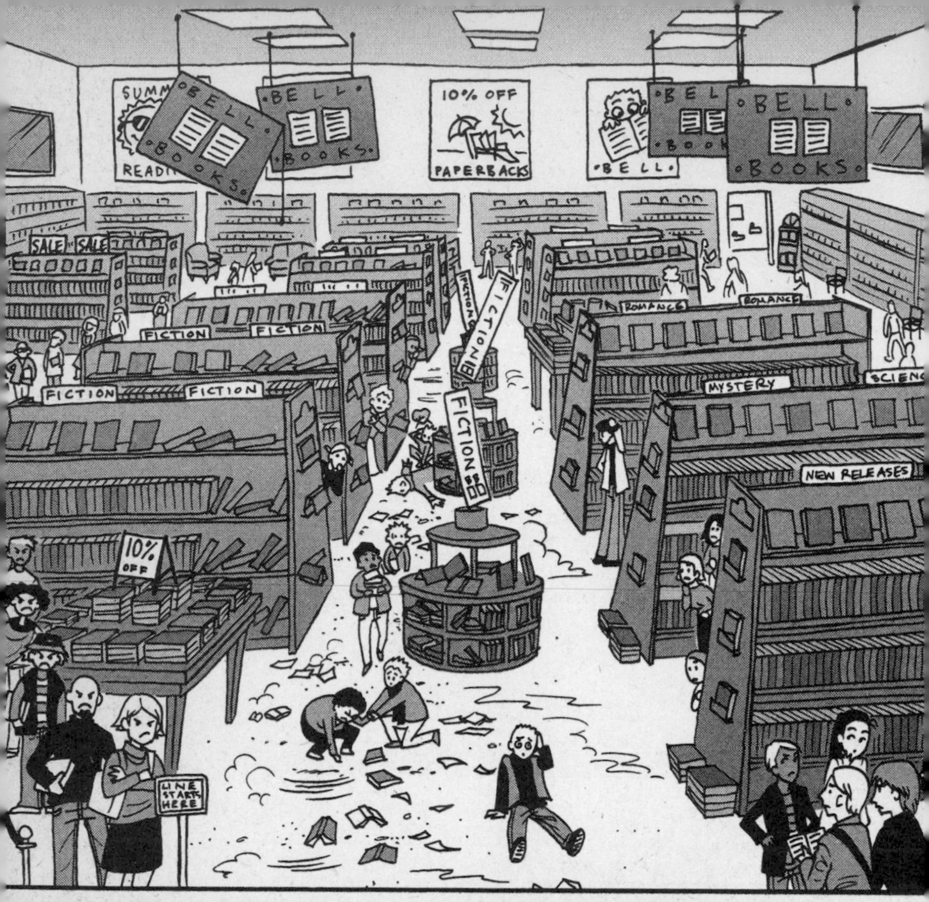
BELL BOOKS
BELL BOOKS
10% OFF
PAPERBACKS
BELL
BELL BOOKS
BELL BOOKS
SALE
SALE
FICTION
FICTION
FICTION
FICTION
FICTION
FICTION $$
ROMANCE
ROMANCE
MYSTERY
NEW RELEASES
10% OFF
LINE STARTS HERE

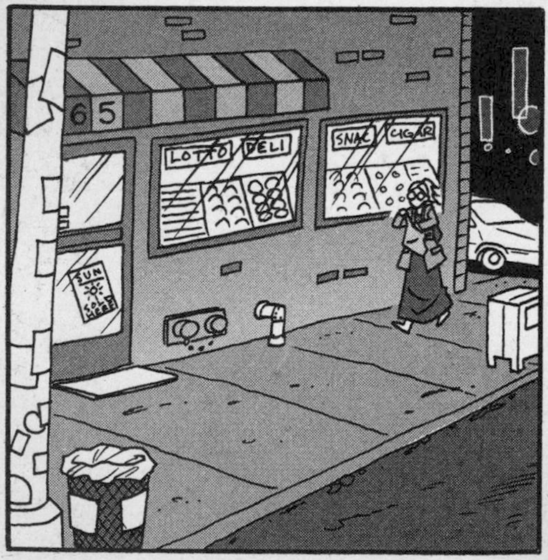
65
LOTTO
DELI
CIGAR

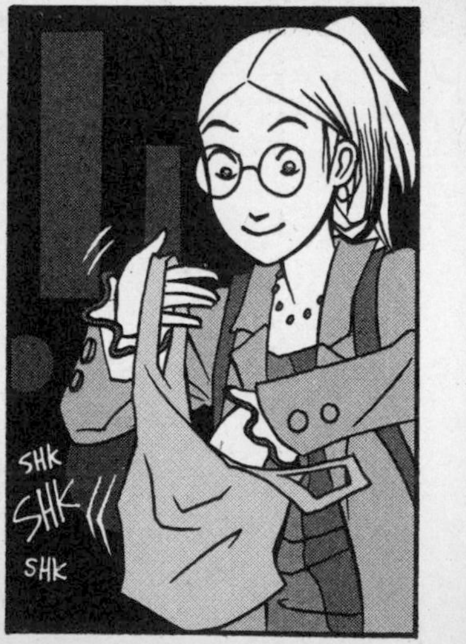
SHK
SHK
SHK

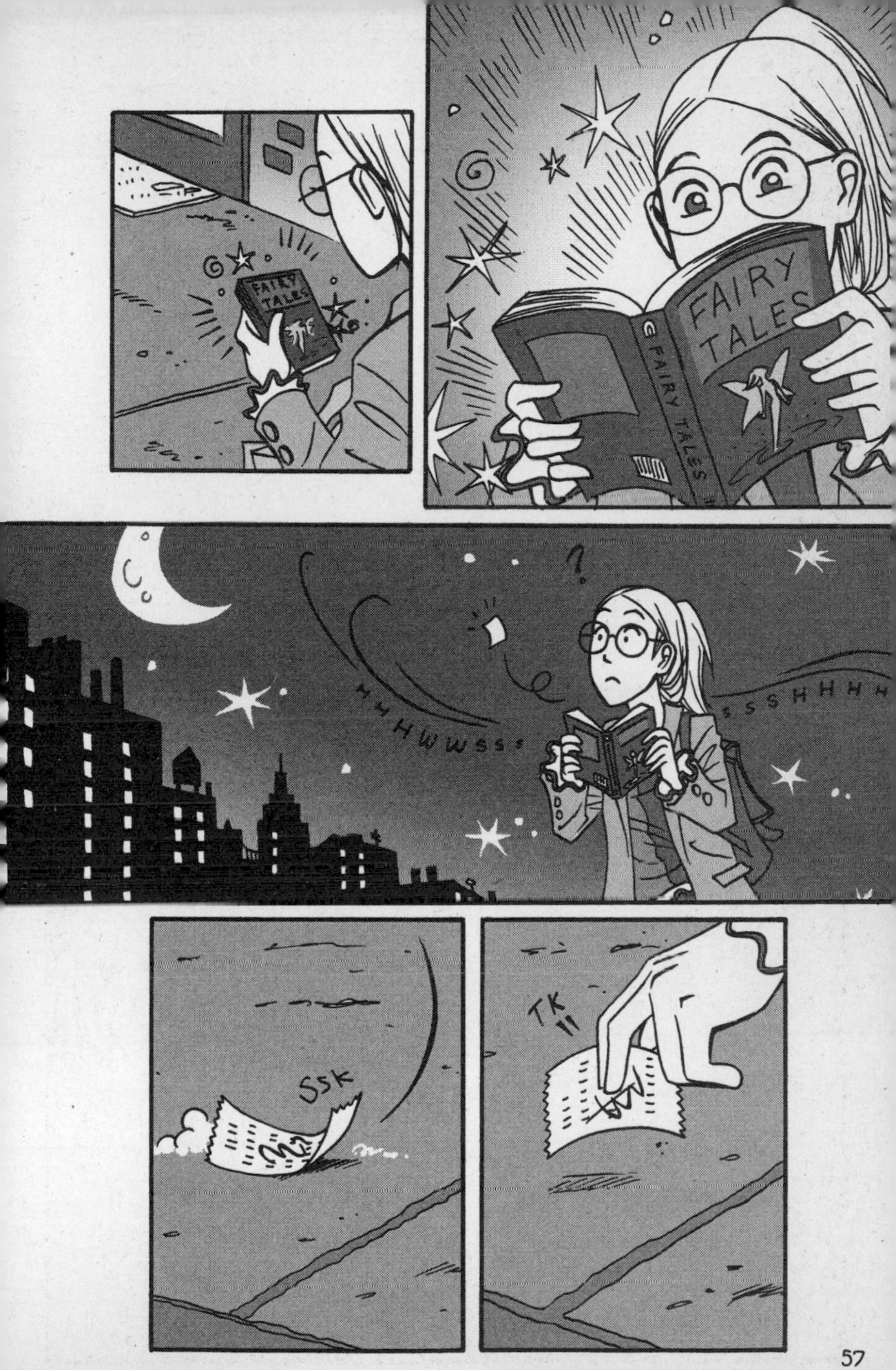
FAIRY TALES
FAIRY TALES
FAIRY TALES
?
HHHWWSSS
SSSHHHH
SSK
TK

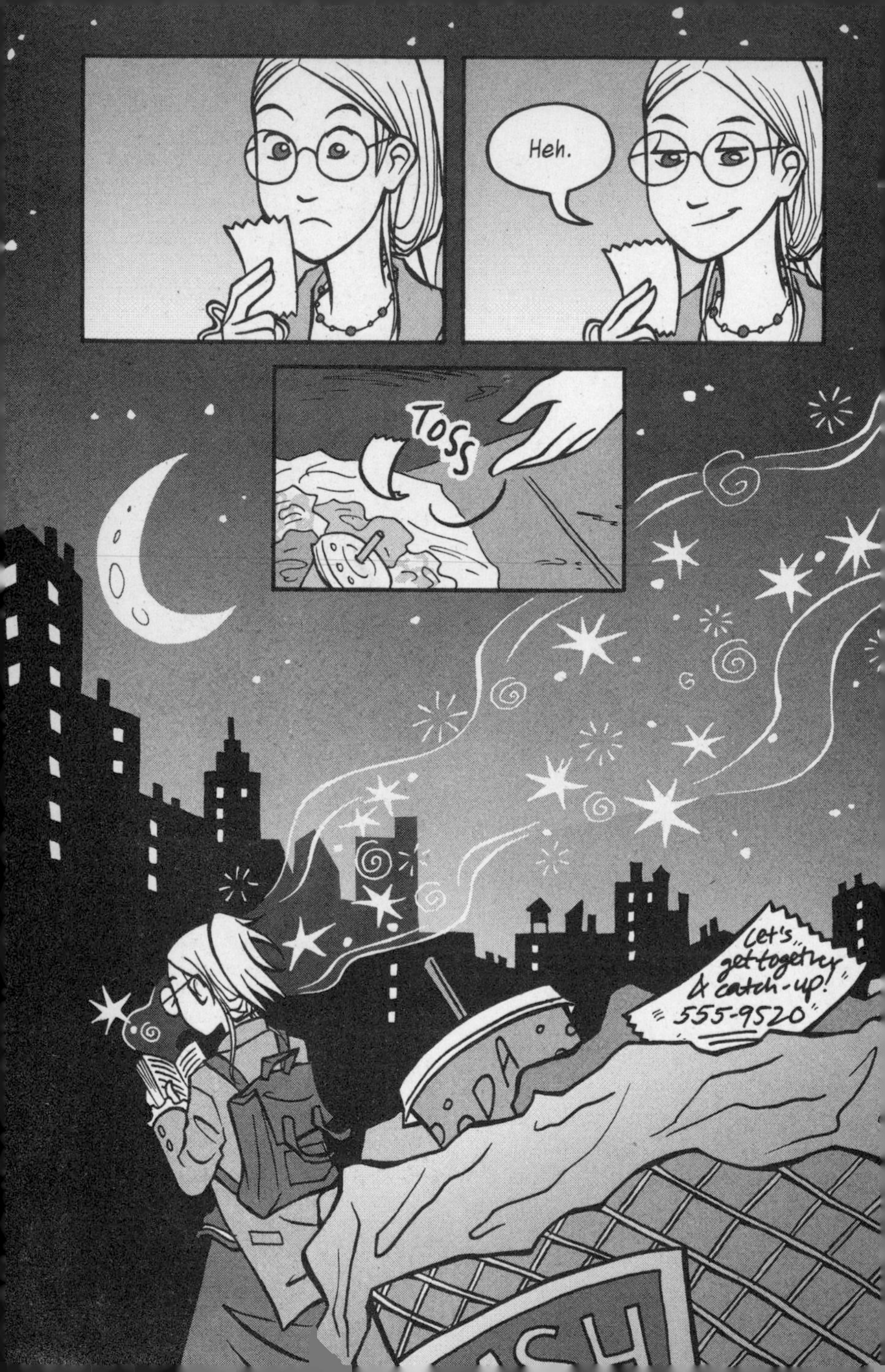
Heh.
TOSS
Let's get together & catch-up!
555-9520

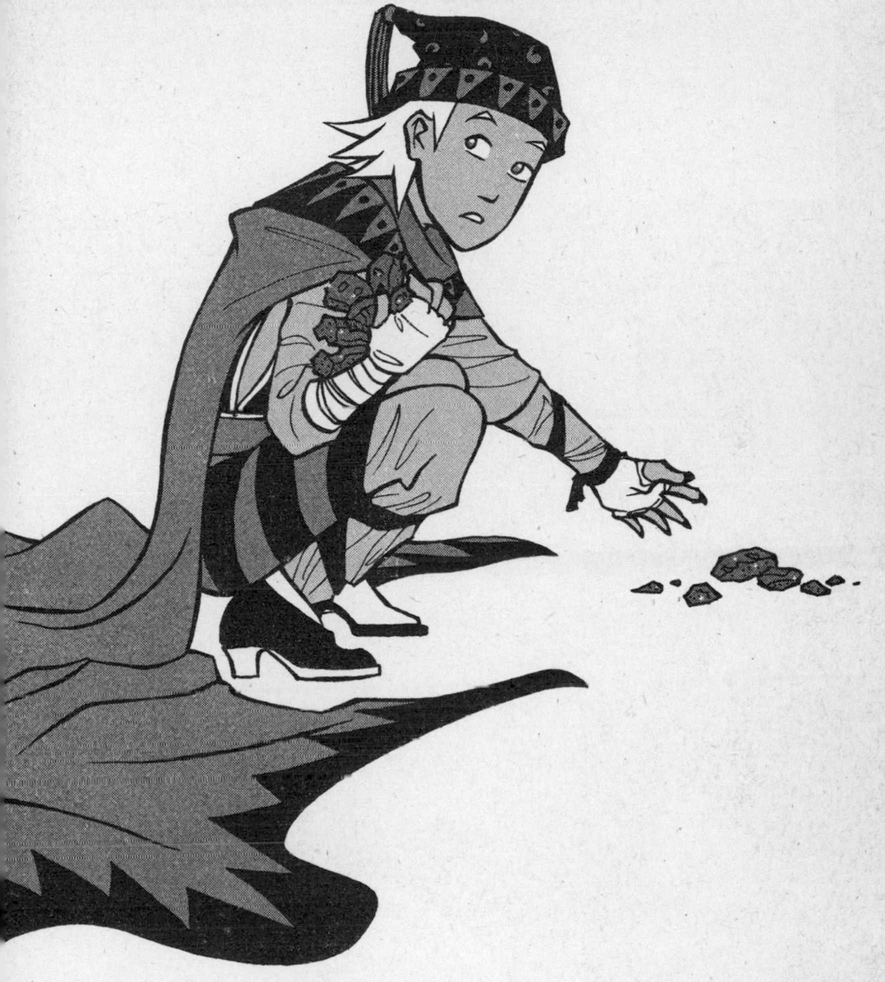

CHAPTER THREE

Feels So Lonely

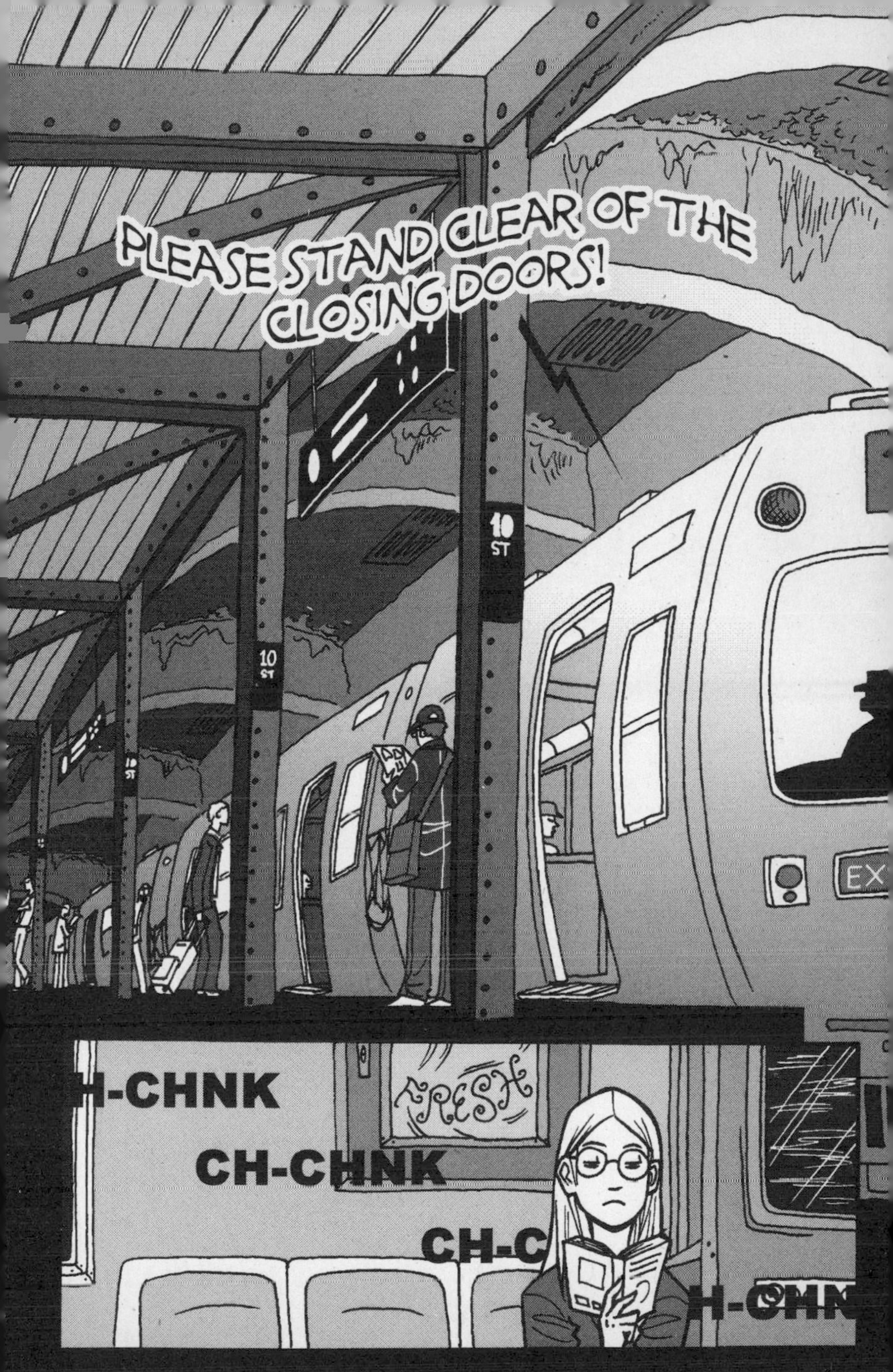
PLEASE STAND CLEAR OF THE CLOSING DOORS!
10 ST
10 ST
FRESH
H-CHNK
CH-CHNK
CH-C
H-CHN

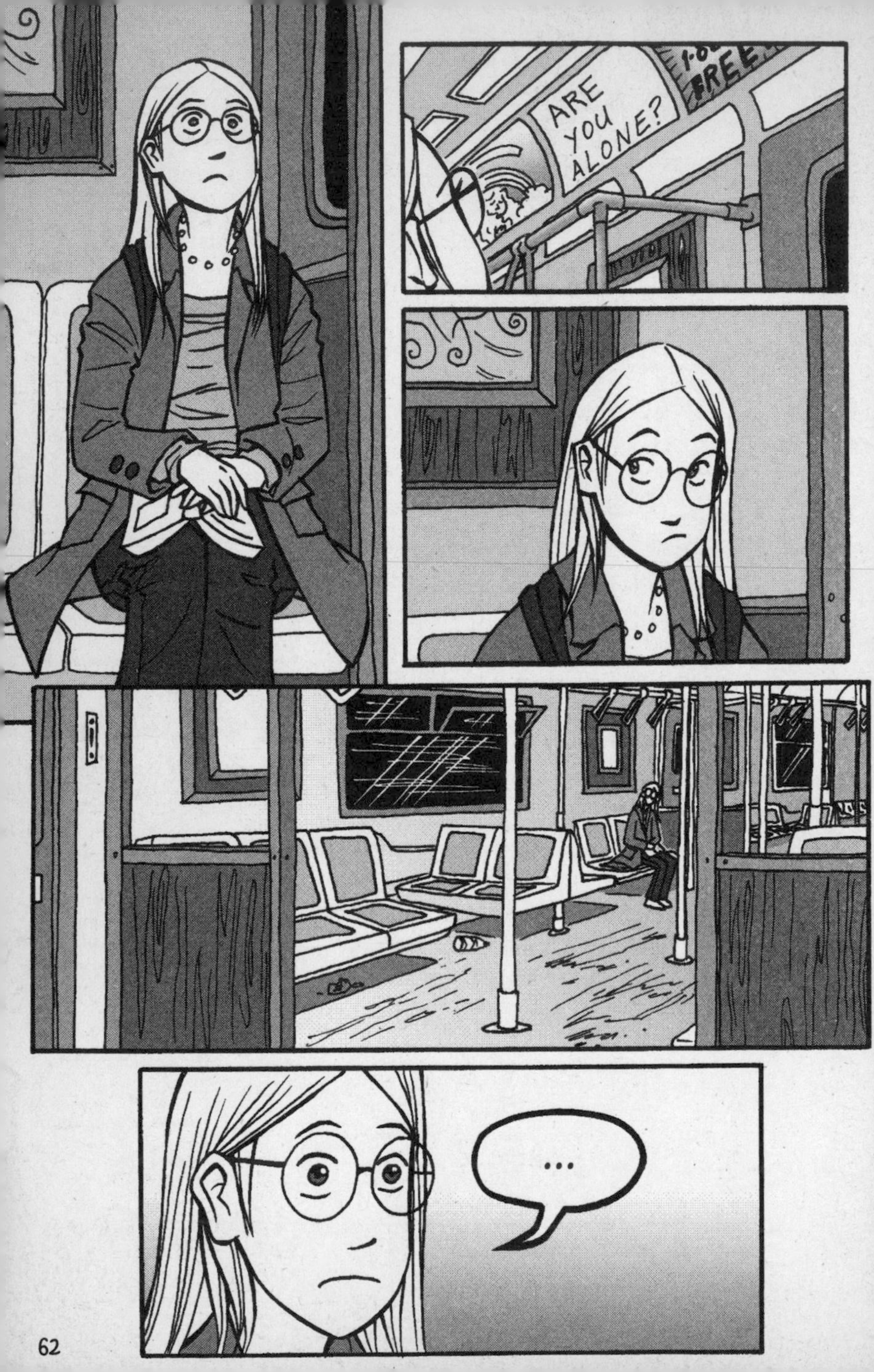
ARE YOU ALONE?
...

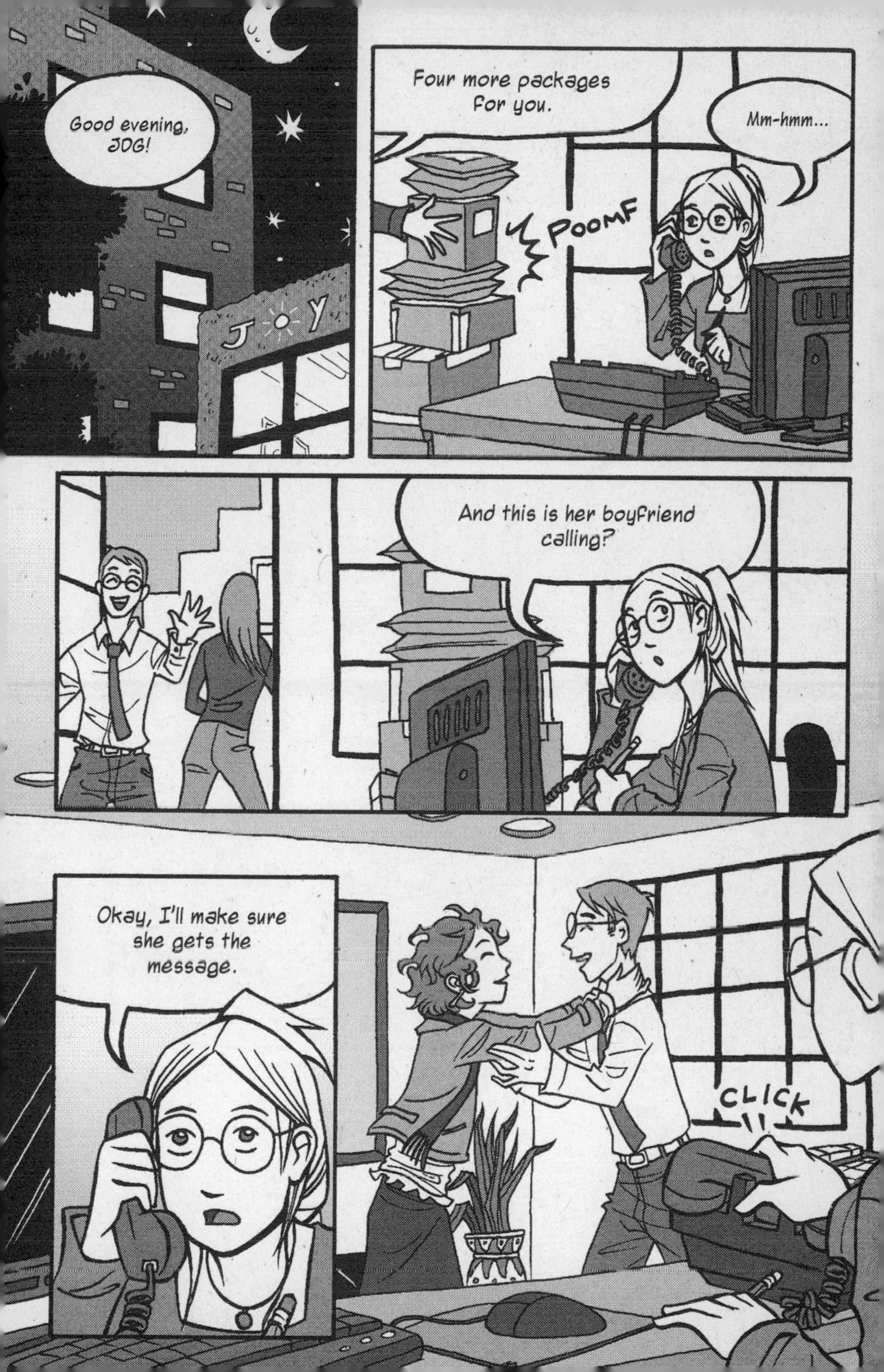
Good evening, JOG!
Four more packages for you.
Mm-hmm...
POOMF
And this is her boyfriend calling?
Okay, I'll make sure she gets the message.
CLICK

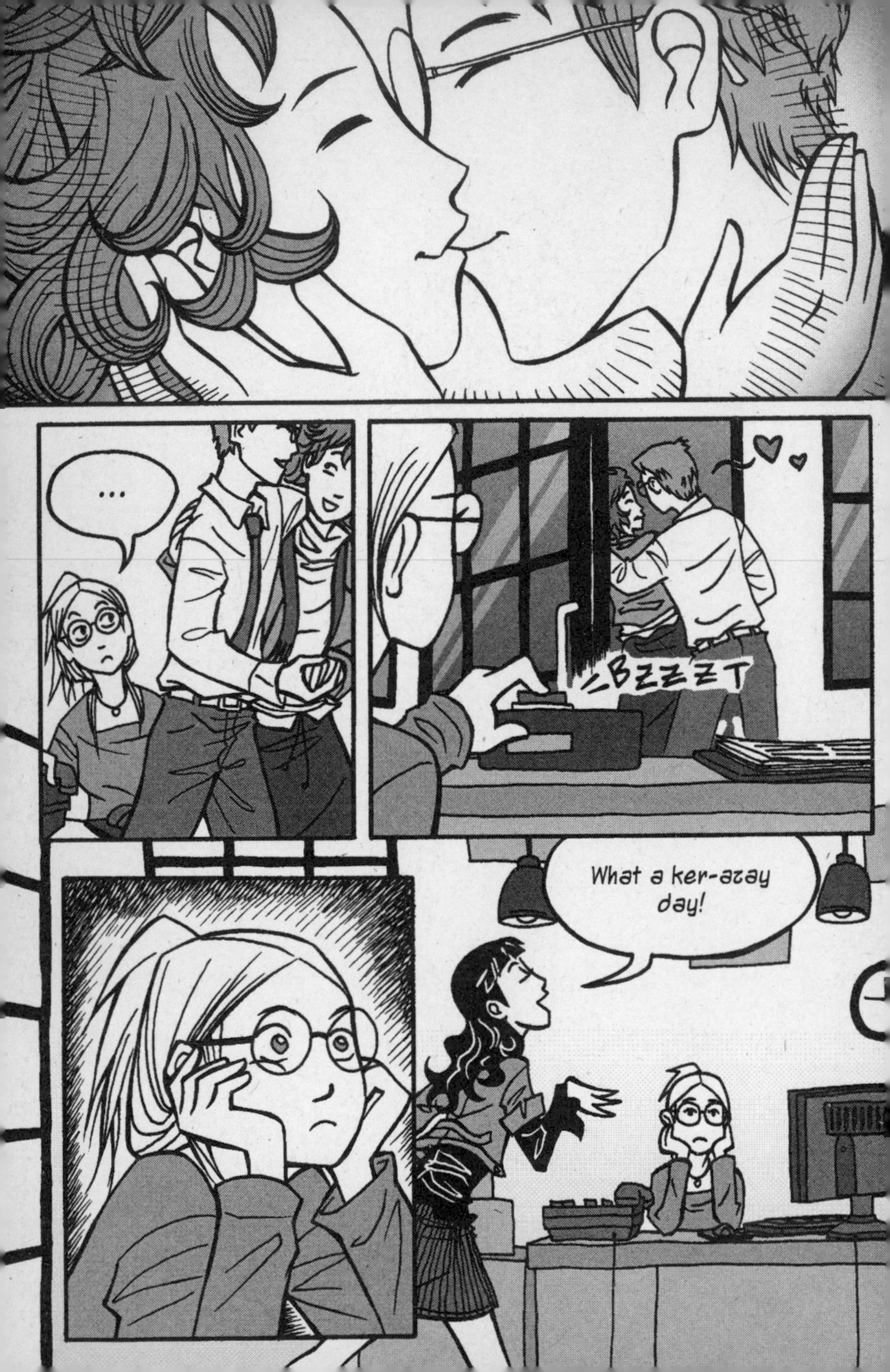
...
BZZZZT
What a ker-azay day!

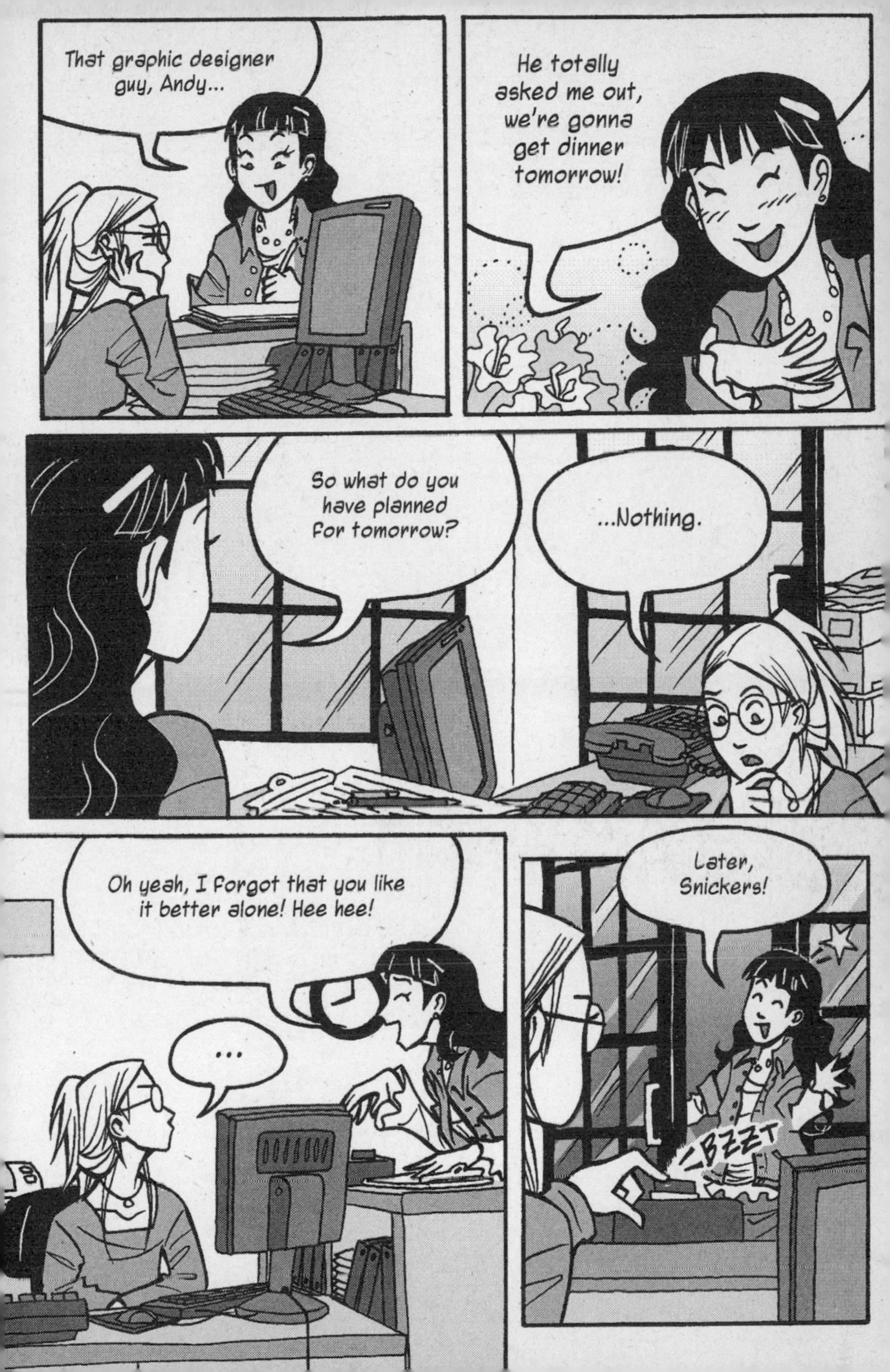
That graphic designer guy, Andy...
He totally asked me out, we're gonna get dinner tomorrow!
So what do you have planned for tomorrow?
...Nothing.
Oh yeah, I forgot that you like it better alone! Hee hee!
...
Later, Snickers!
BZZT

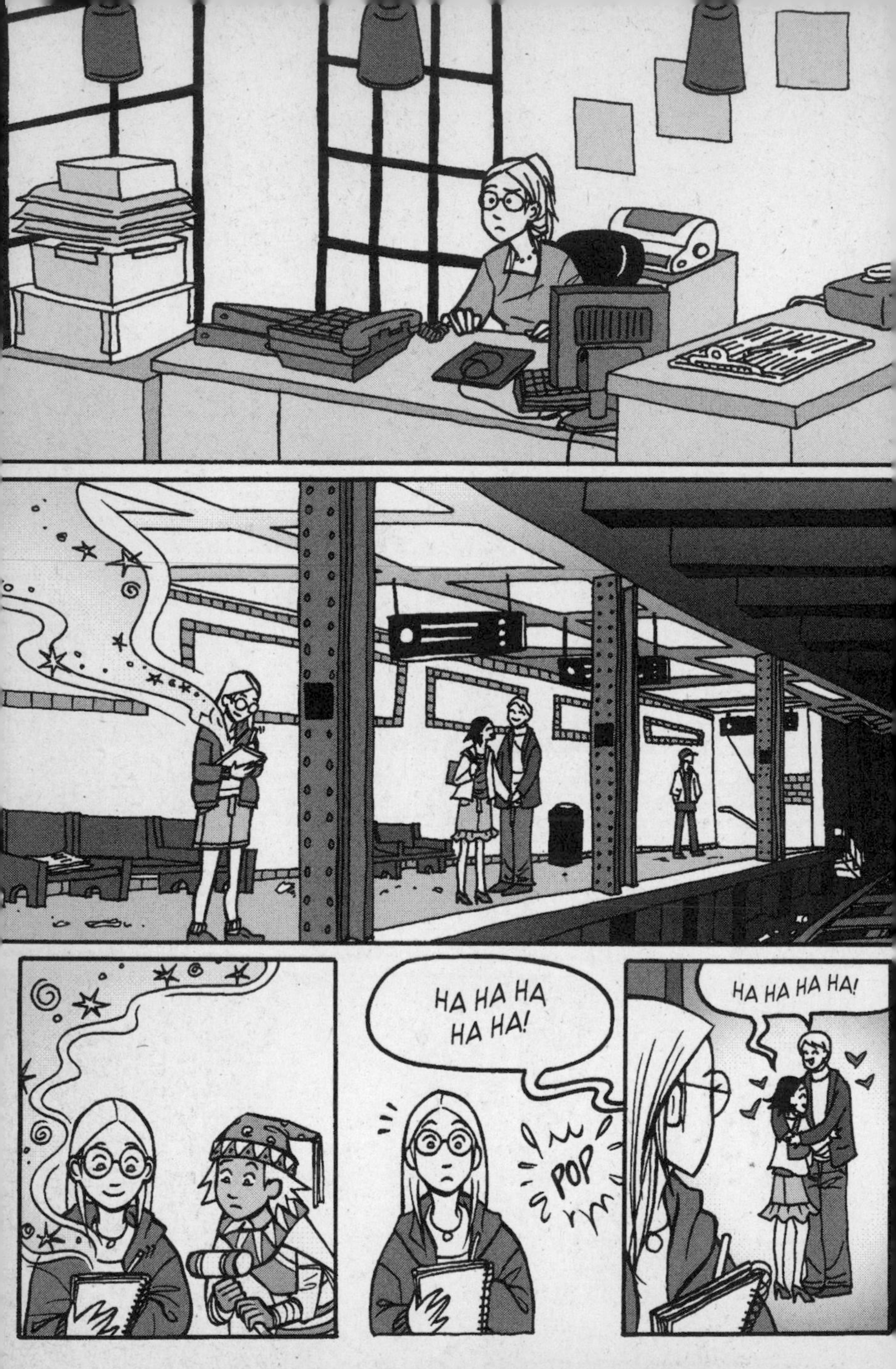
HA HA HA
HA HA!
POP
HA HA HA HA!

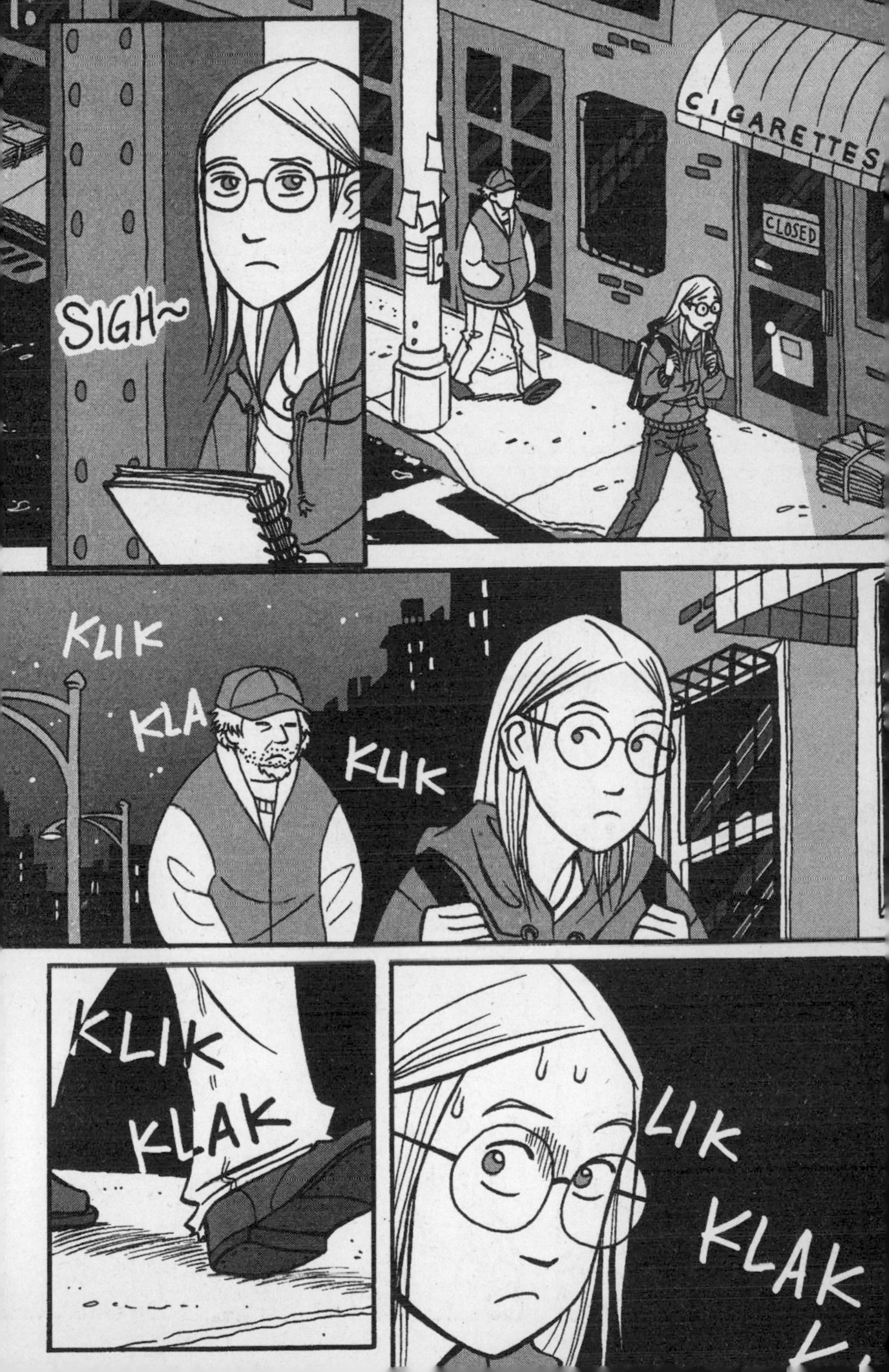
SIGH~
CIGARETTES
CLOSED
KLIK
KLA
KLIK
KLIK
KLAK
LIK
KLAK

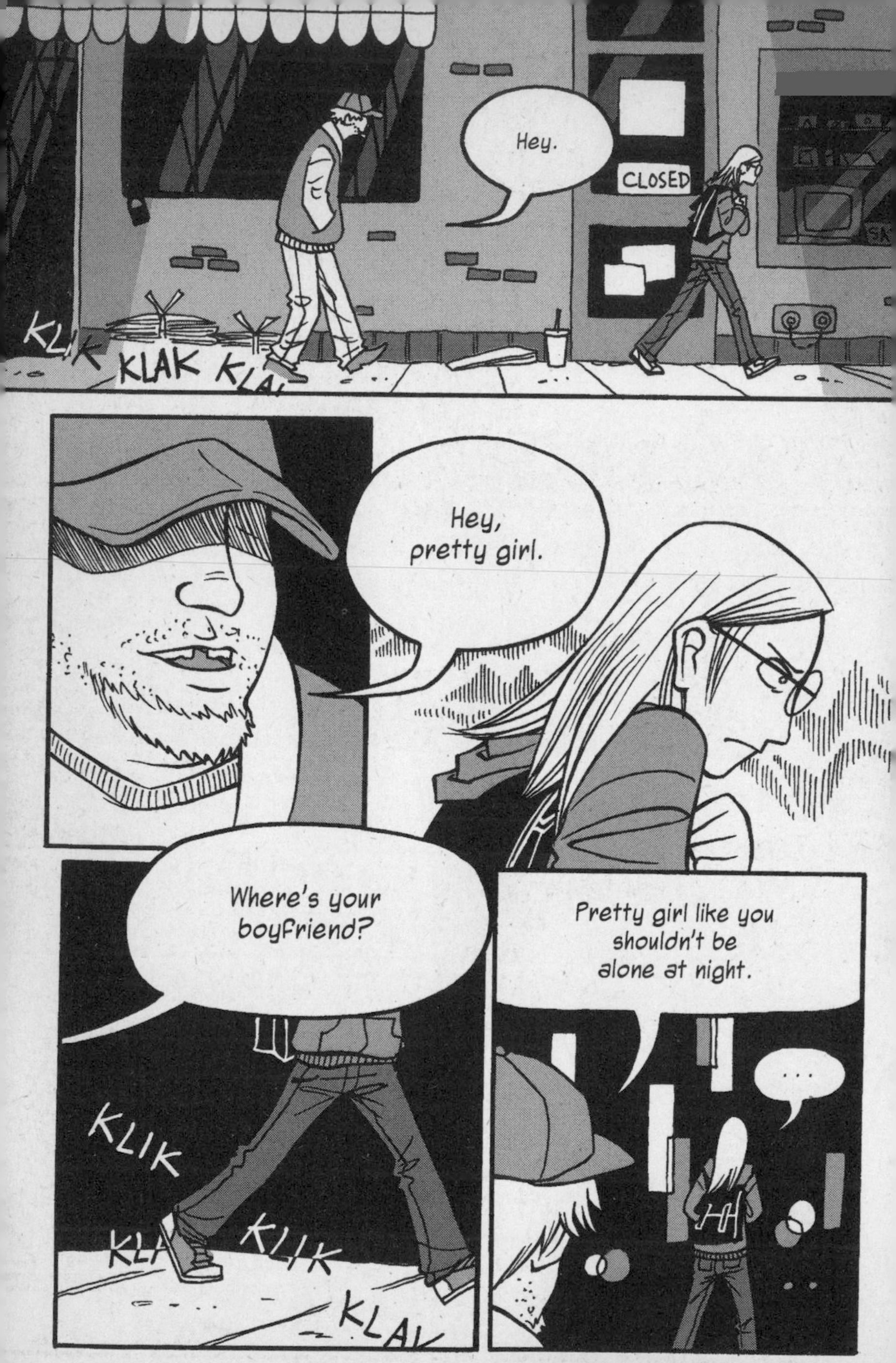
Hey.
CLOSED
KLIK
KLAK
Hey, pretty girl.
Where's your boyfriend?
KLIK
KLIK
Pretty girl like you shouldn't be alone at night.
. . .

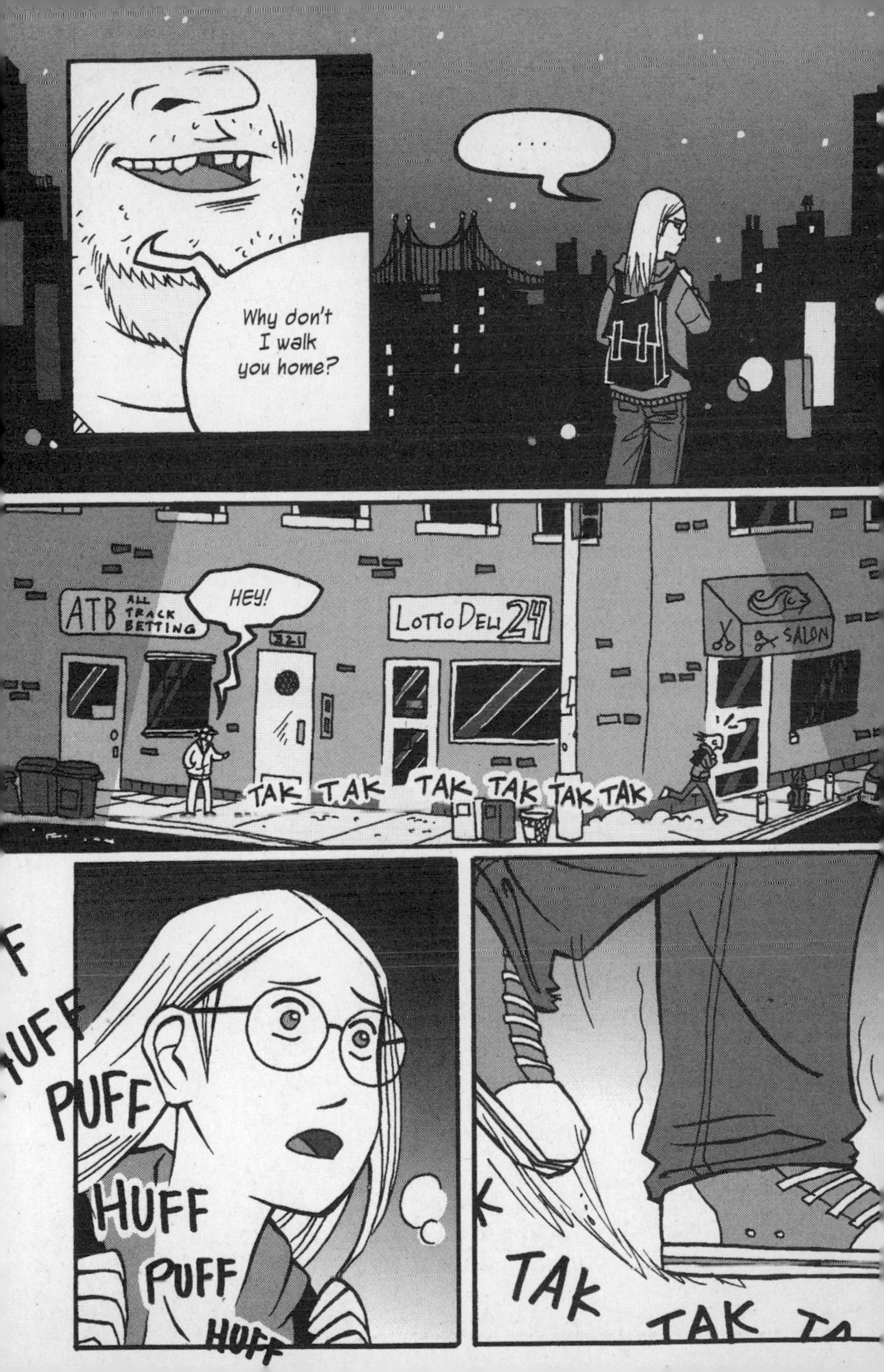
Why don't I walk you home?
...
ATB ALL TRACK BETTING
HEY!
321
LOTTO DELI 24
SALON
TAK TAK TAK TAK TAK TAK
PUFF
HUFF
PUFF
HUFF
TAK
TAK

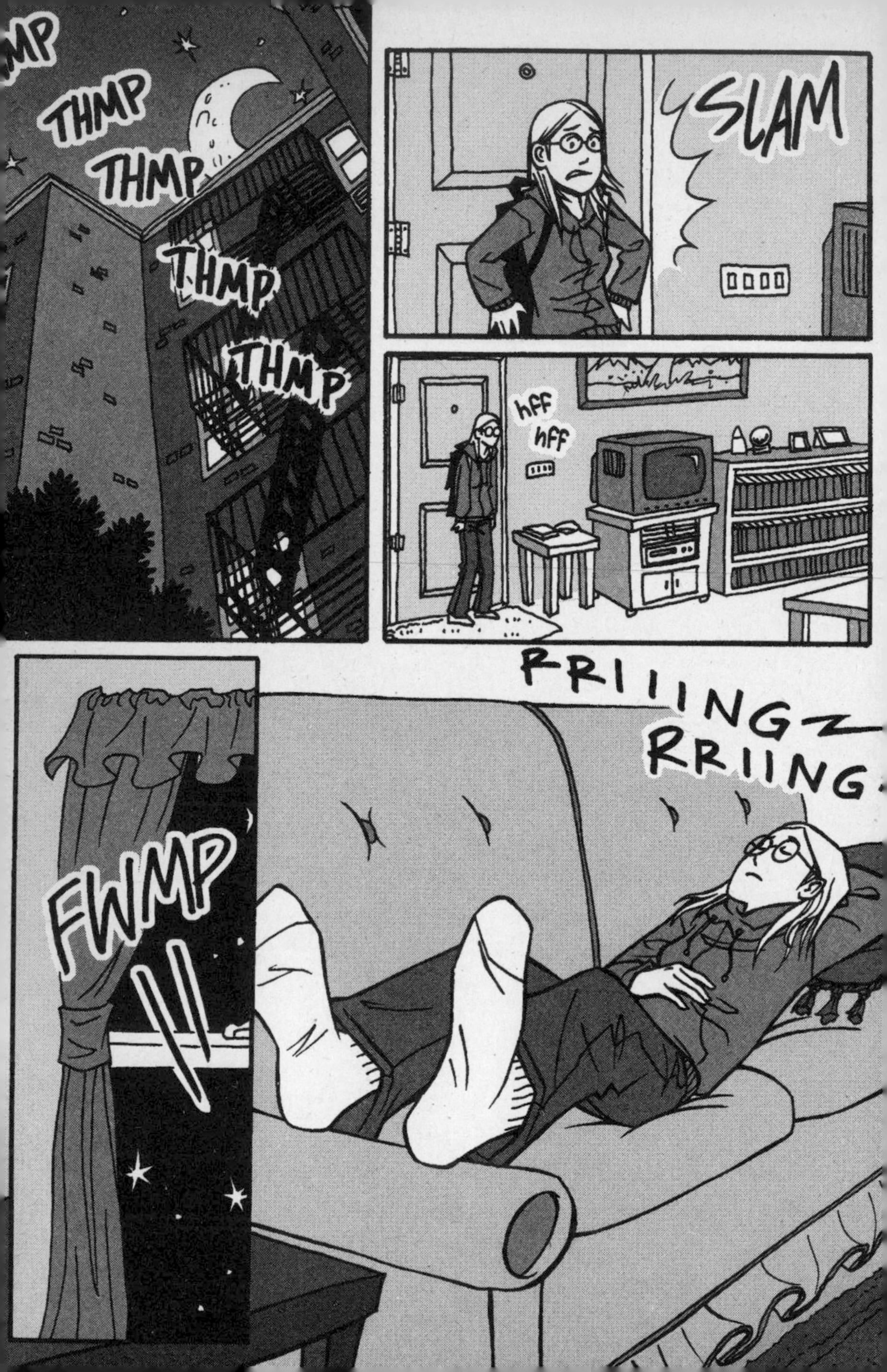
MP
THMP
THMP
THMP
THMP
SLAM
hff
hff
RRIIING
RRIING
FWMP

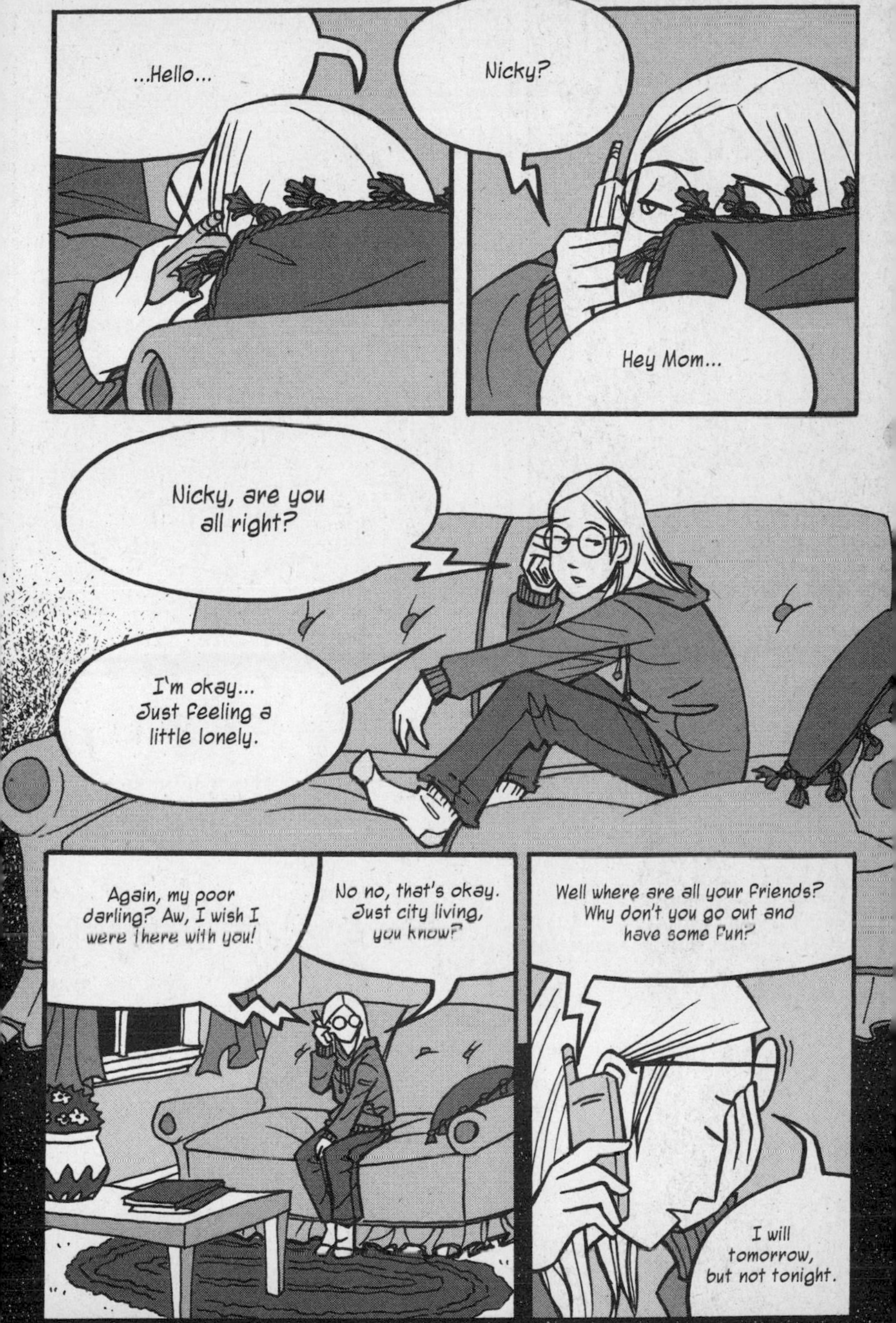
...Hello...
Nicky?
Hey Mom...
Nicky, are you all right?
I'm okay... Just feeling a little lonely.
Again, my poor darling? Aw, I wish I were there with you!
No no, that's okay. Just city living, you know?
Well where are all your friends? Why don't you go out and have some fun?
I will tomorrow, but not tonight.

I just want to be by myself right now.

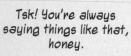

Tsk! You're always saying things like that, honey.

No wonder you're always feeling lonely!

...

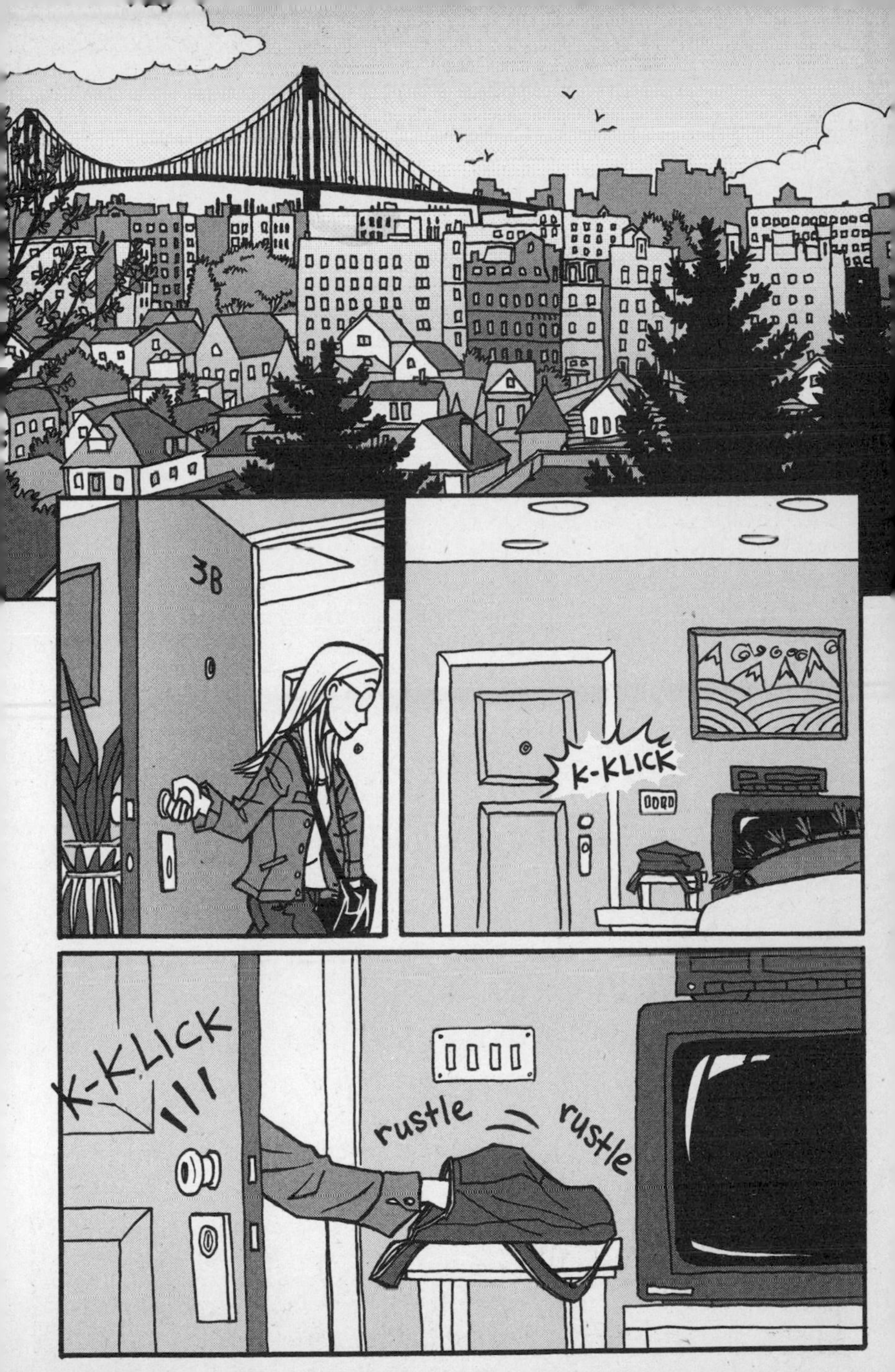
3B
K-KLICK
K-KLICK
rustle
rustle

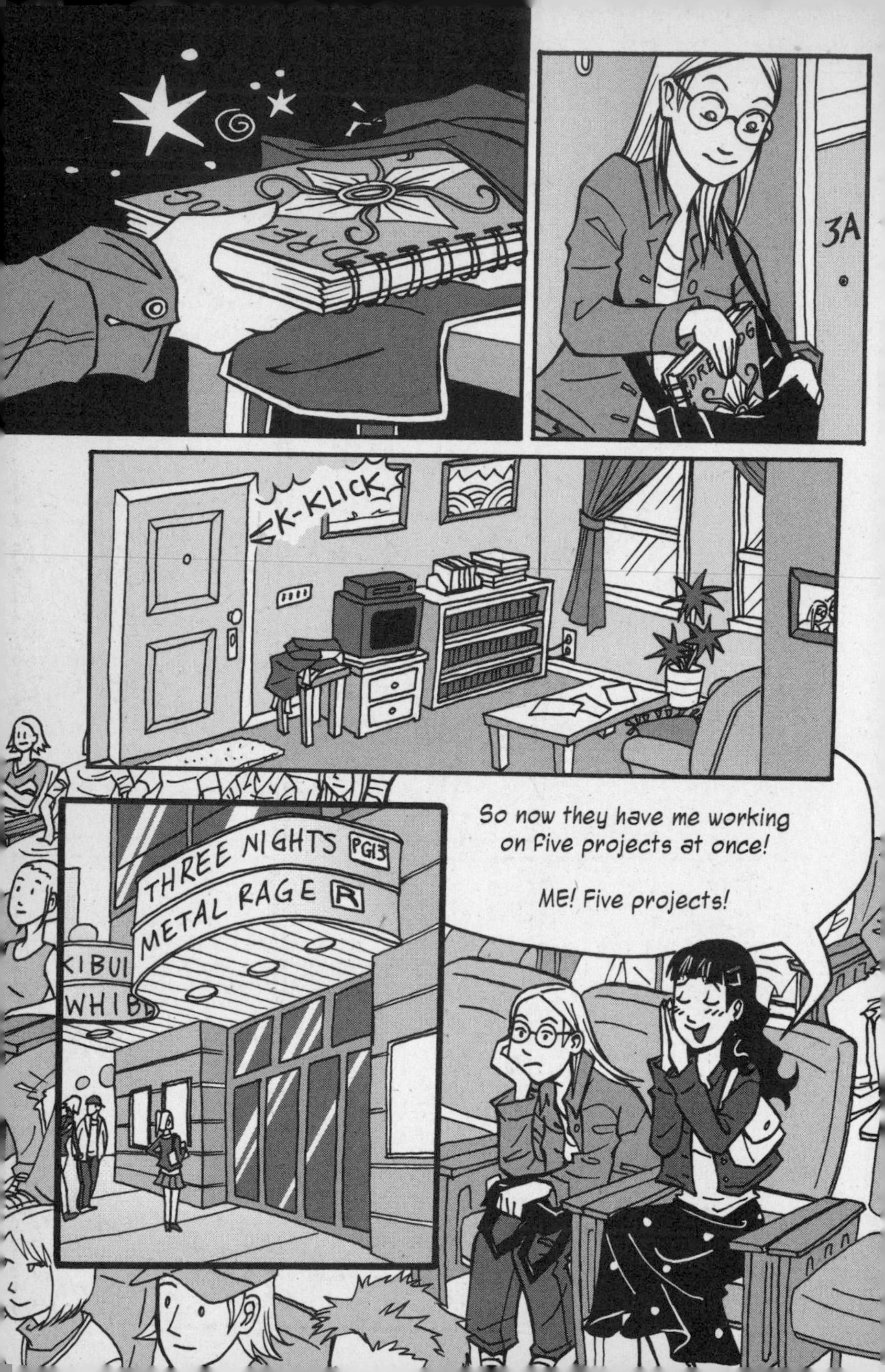

DRE
3A
DREAG
K-KLICK
THREE NIGHTS PG13
METAL RAGE R
KIBUI
WHIB
So now they have me working on five projects at once!
ME! Five projects!

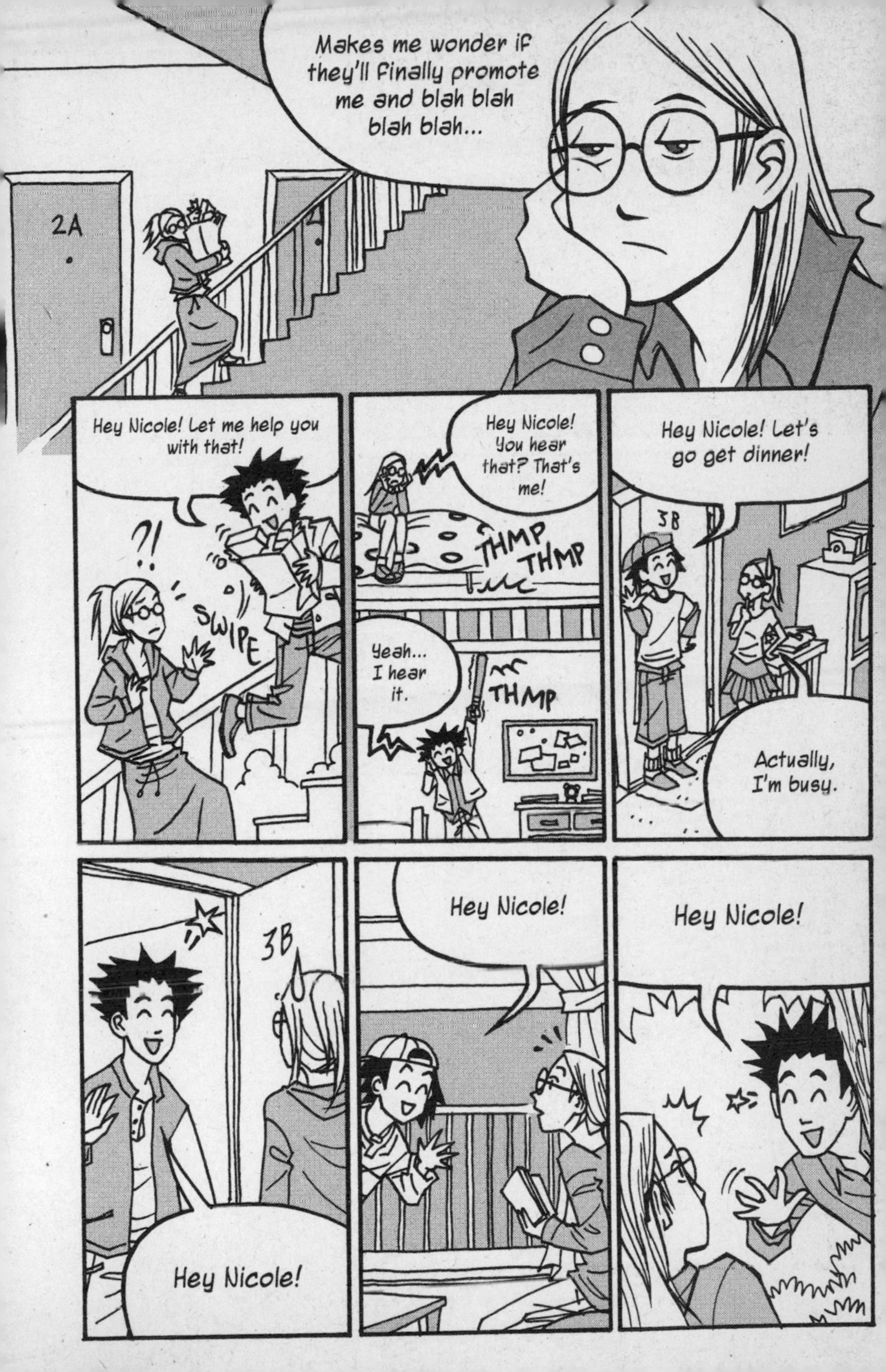
Makes me wonder if they'll finally promote me and blah blah blah blah...
2A
Hey Nicole! Let me help you with that!
?!
SWIPE
Hey Nicole! You hear that? That's me!
THMP THMP
Yeah... I hear it.
THMP
Hey Nicole! Let's go get dinner!
3B
Actually, I'm busy.
3B
Hey Nicole!
Hey Nicole!
Hey Nicole!

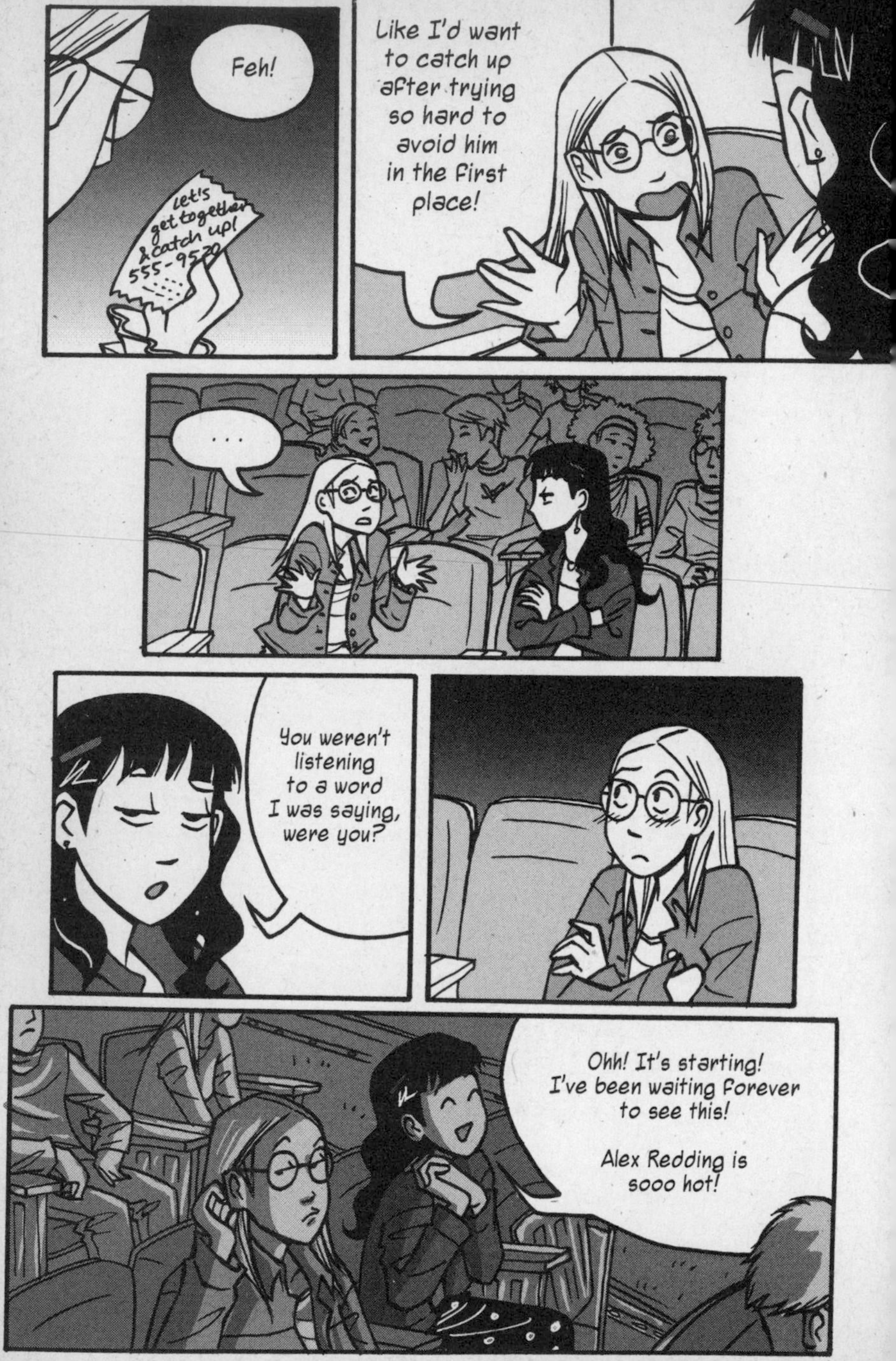
Feh!
Let's get together & catch up! 555-9520
Like I'd want to catch up after trying so hard to avoid him in the first place!
. . .
You weren't listening to a word I was saying, were you?
Ohh! It's starting! I've been waiting forever to see this!
Alex Redding is sooo hot!

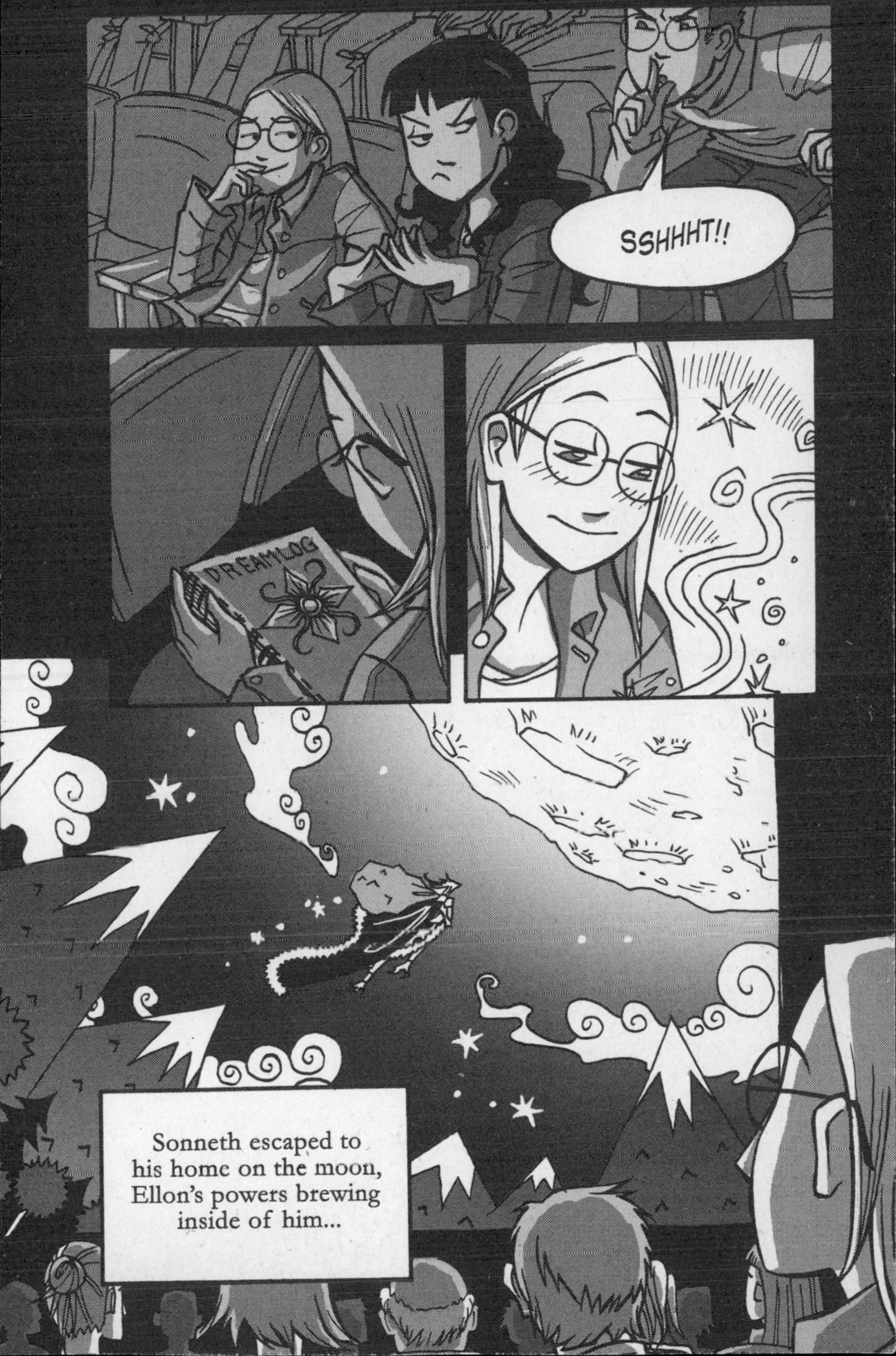
SSHHHT!!
DREAMLOG
Sonneth escaped to his home on the moon, Ellon's powers brewing inside of him...

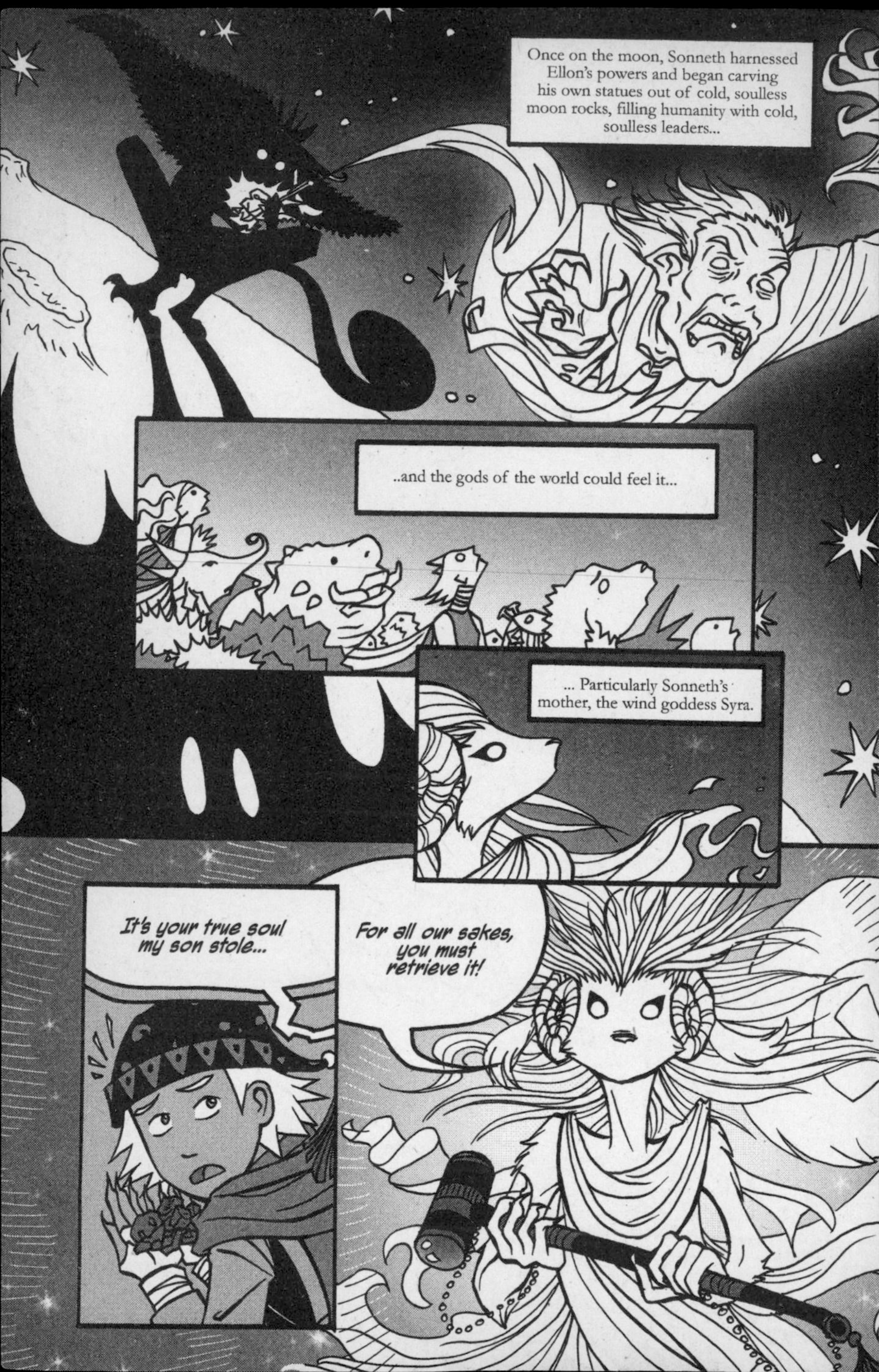
Once on the moon, Sonneth harnessed Ellon's powers and began carving his own statues out of cold, soulless moon rocks, filling humanity with cold, soulless leaders...
..and the gods of the world could feel it...
... Particularly Sonneth's mother, the wind goddess Syra.
It's your true soul my son stole...
For all our sakes, you must retrieve it!

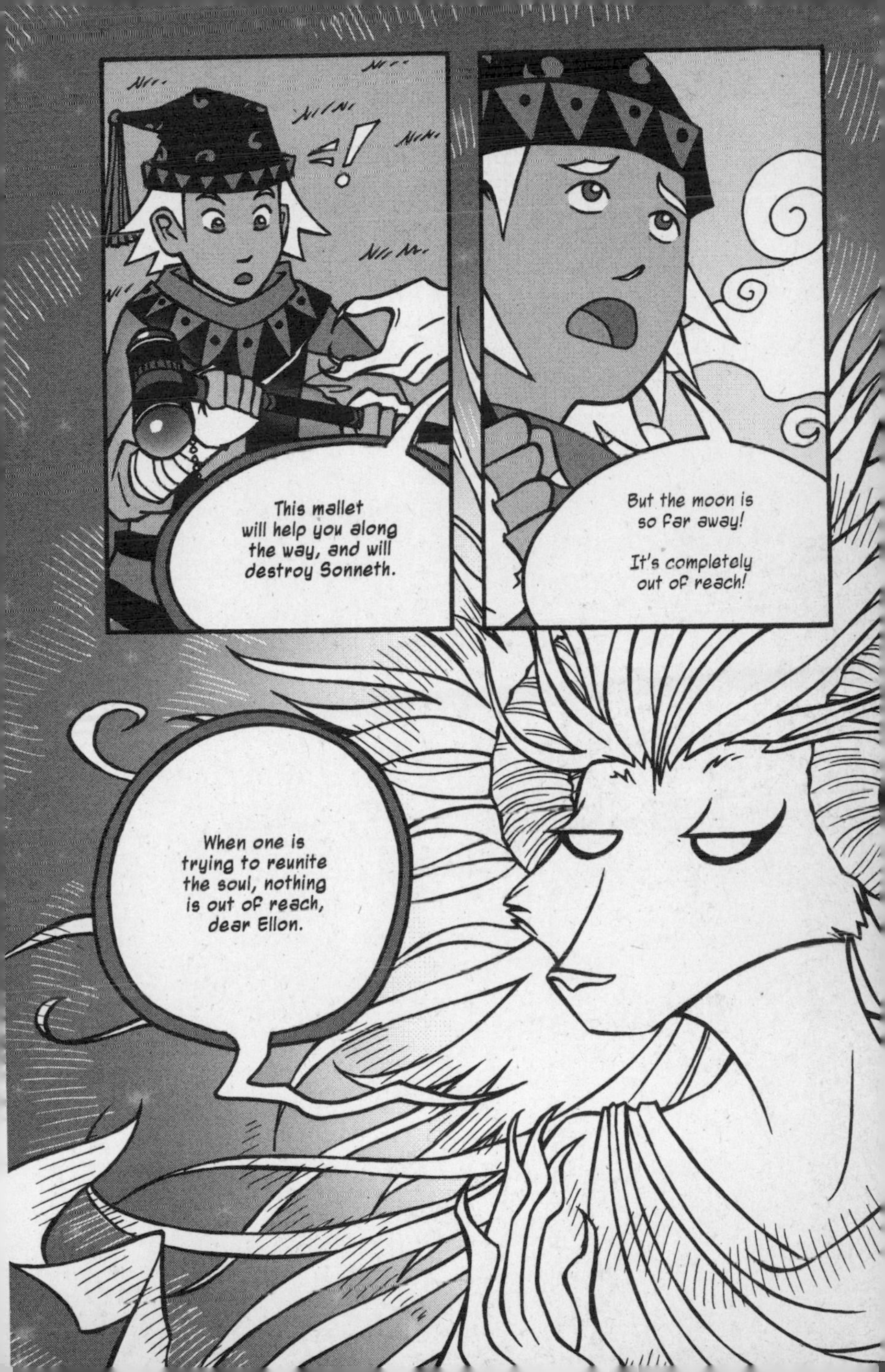
!
This mallet will help you along the way, and will destroy Sonneth.
But the moon is so far away!
It's completely out of reach!
When one is trying to reunite the soul, nothing is out of reach, dear Ellon.

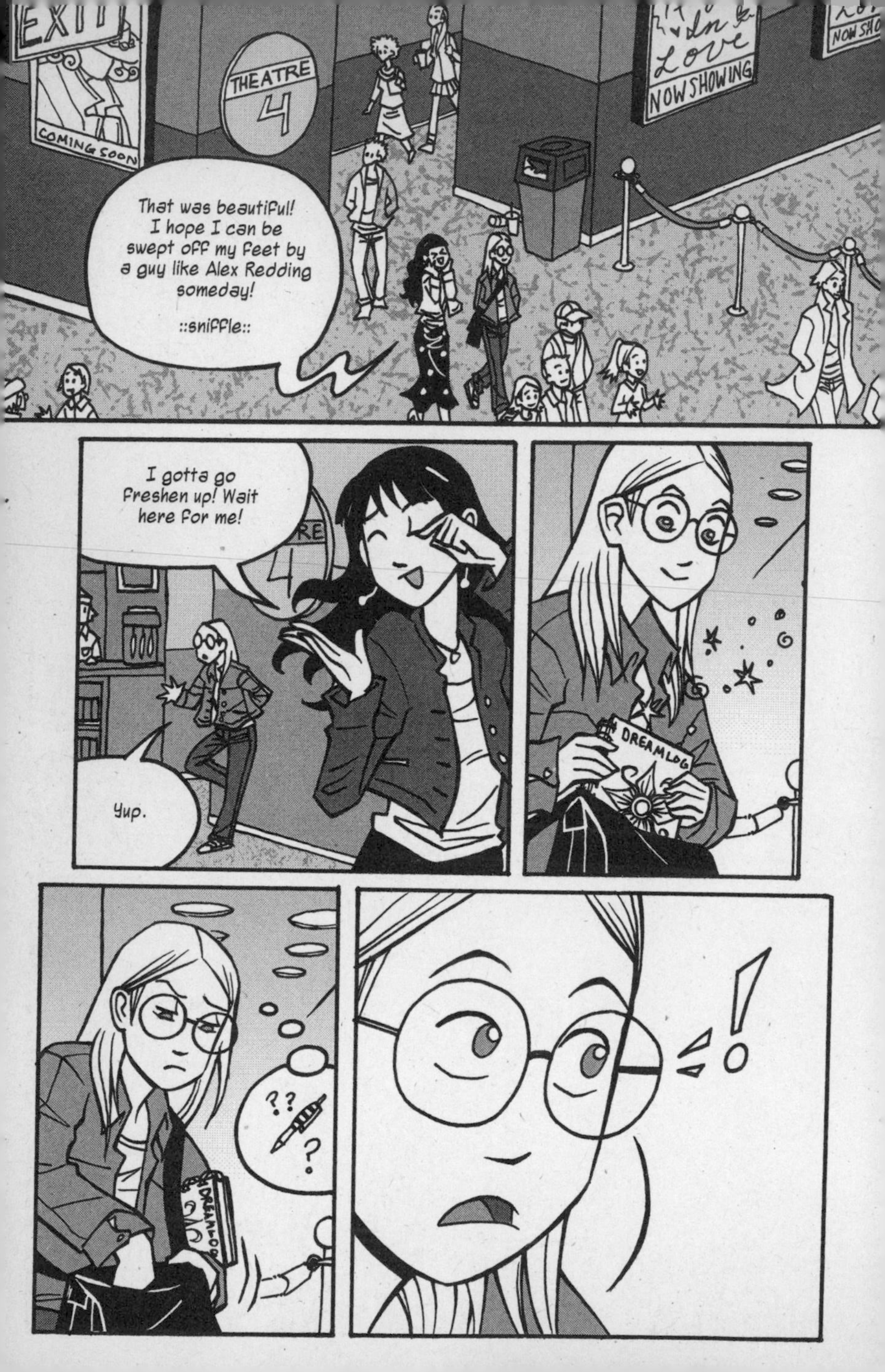
EXIT
COMING SOON
THEATRE 4
In Love
NOW SHOWING
NOW SHOWING
That was beautiful! I hope I can be swept off my feet by a guy like Alex Redding someday!
::sniffle::
I gotta go freshen up! Wait here for me!
Yup.
DREAMLOG
??
?
!

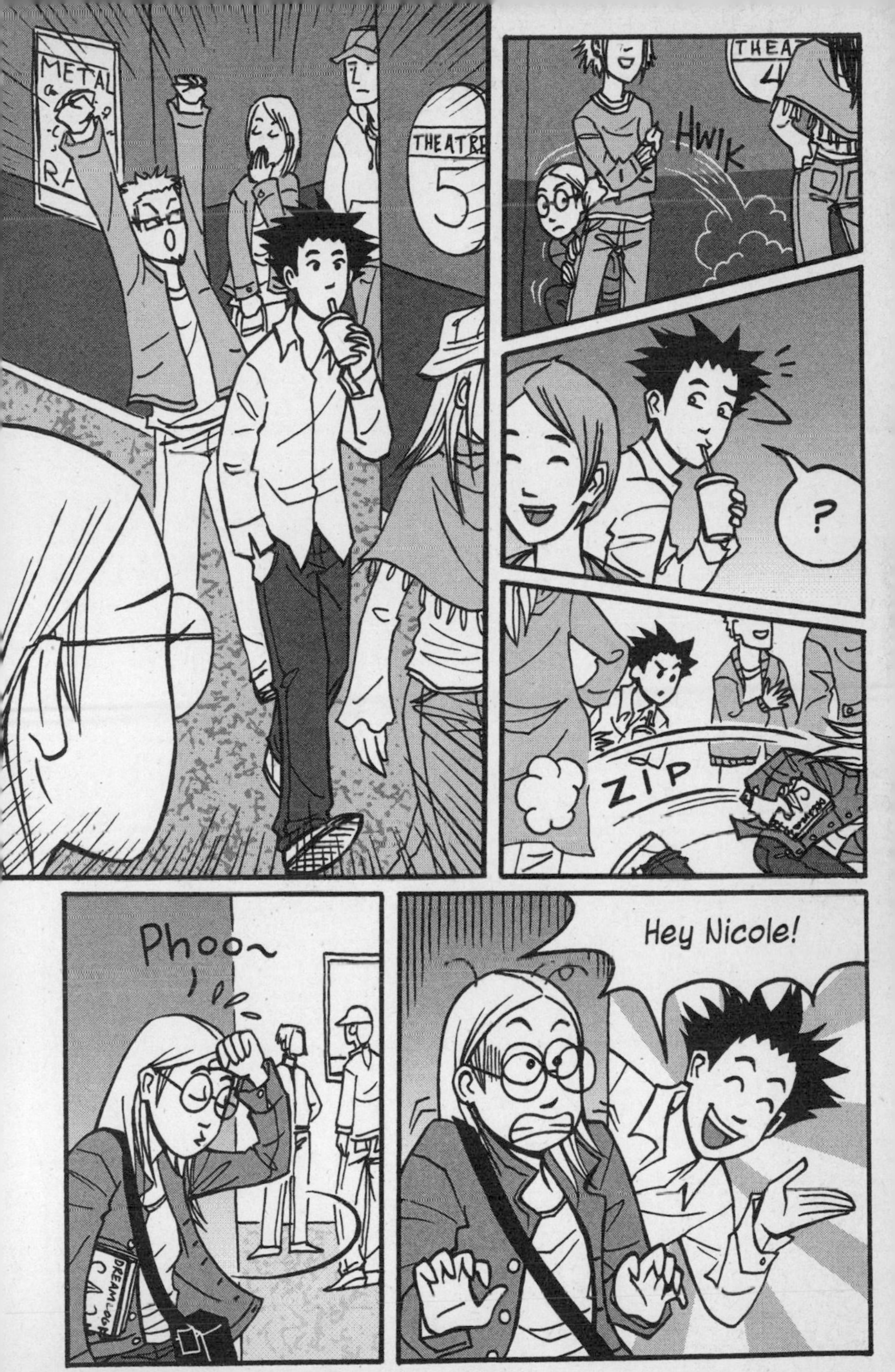
METAL
RA
THEATRE
5
THEA
4
HWIK
?
ZIP
Phoo~
Hey Nicole!

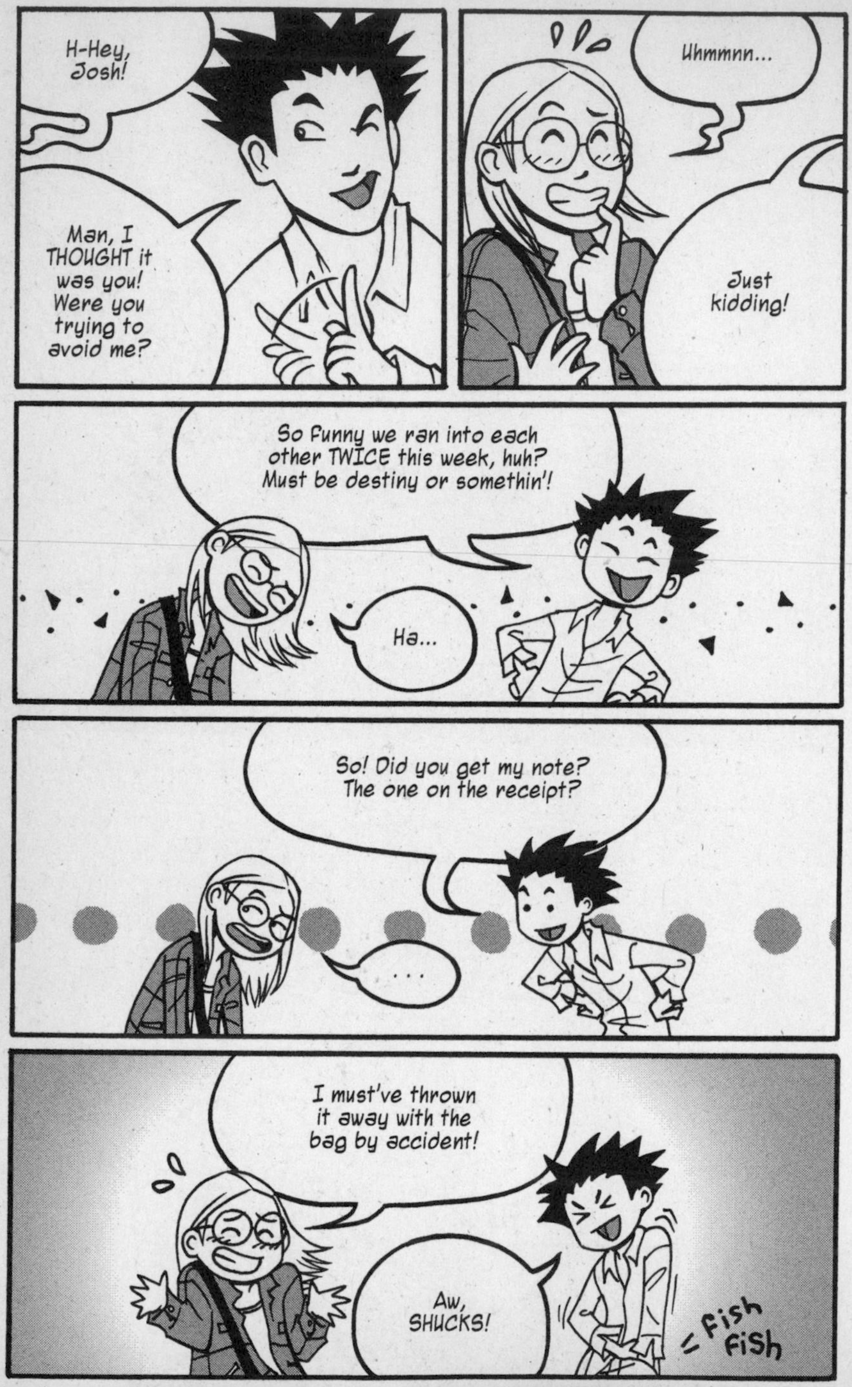
H-Hey, Josh!
Man, I THOUGHT it was you! Were you trying to avoid me?
Uhmmnn...
Just kidding!
So funny we ran into each other TWICE this week, huh? Must be destiny or somethin'!
Ha...
So! Did you get my note? The one on the receipt?
...
I must've thrown it away with the bag by accident!
Aw, SHUCKS!
fish fish

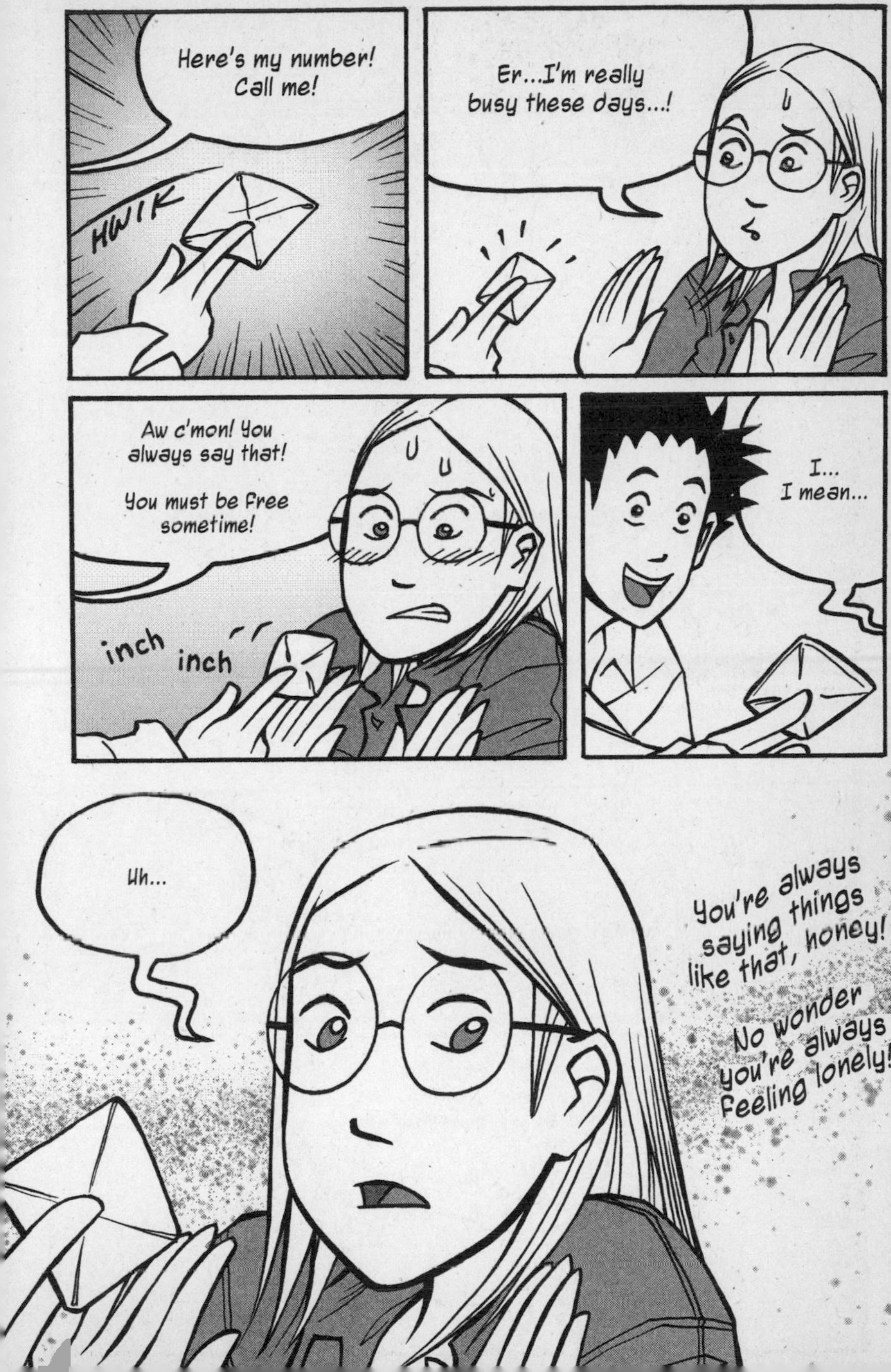
Here's my number! Call me!
HWIK
Er...I'm really busy these days...!
Aw c'mon! You always say that!
You must be free sometime!
inch inch
I... I mean...
Uh...
You're always saying things like that, honey!
No wonder you're always feeling lonely!

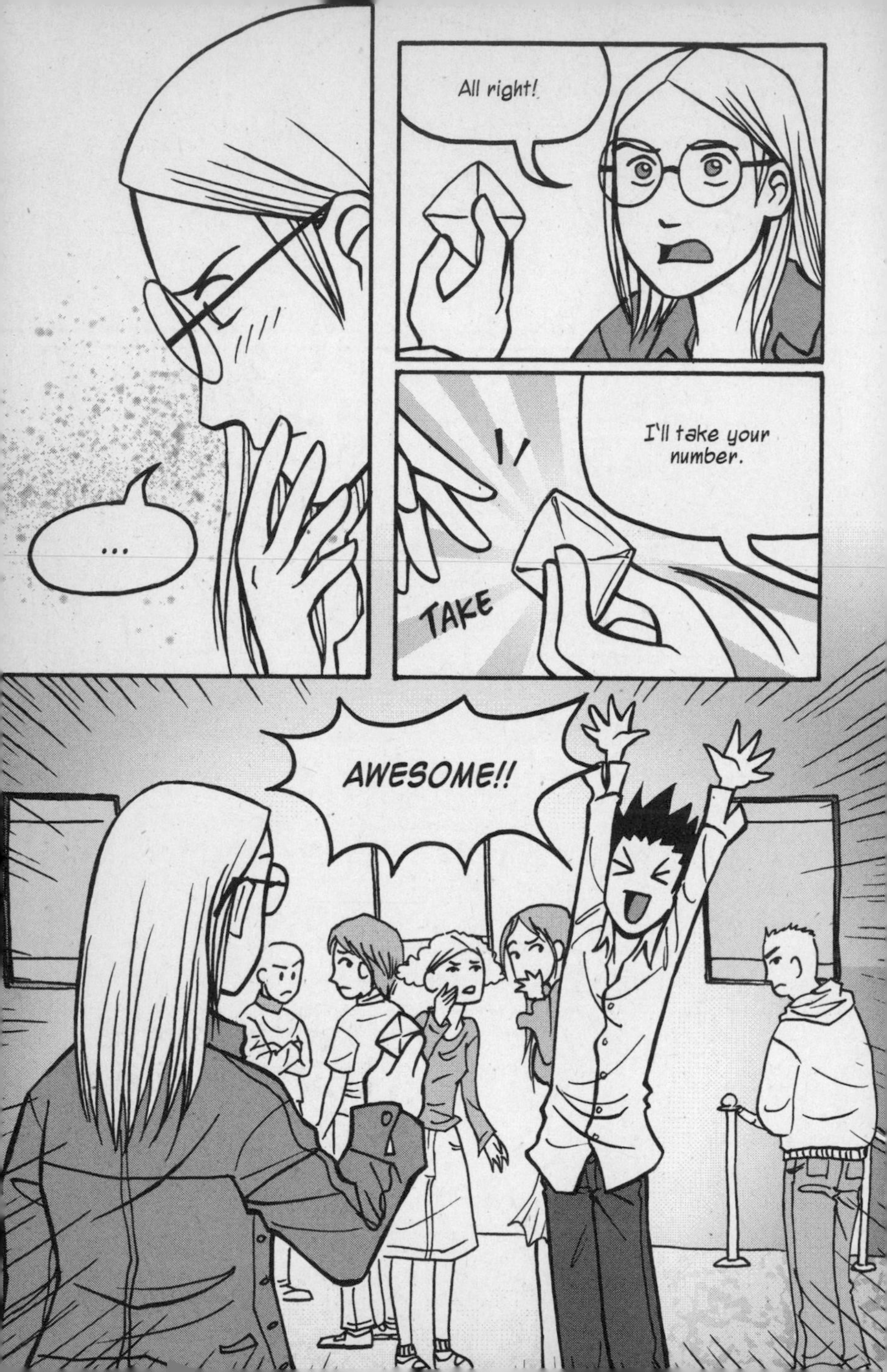
...
All right!
I'll take your number.
!/
TAKE
AWESOME!!

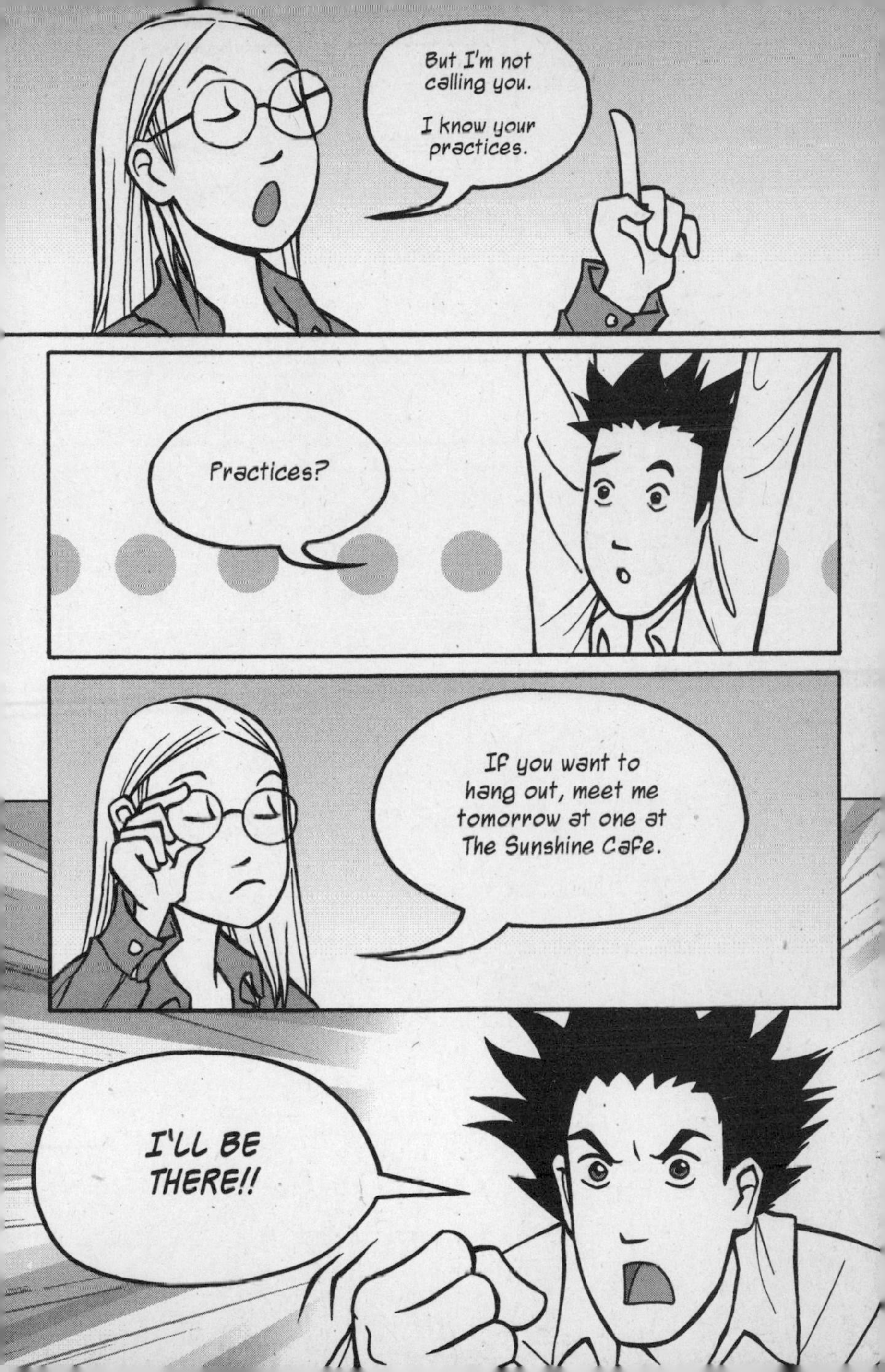
But I'm not calling you.
I know your practices.
Practices?
If you want to hang out, meet me tomorrow at one at The Sunshine Cafe.
I'LL BE THERE!!

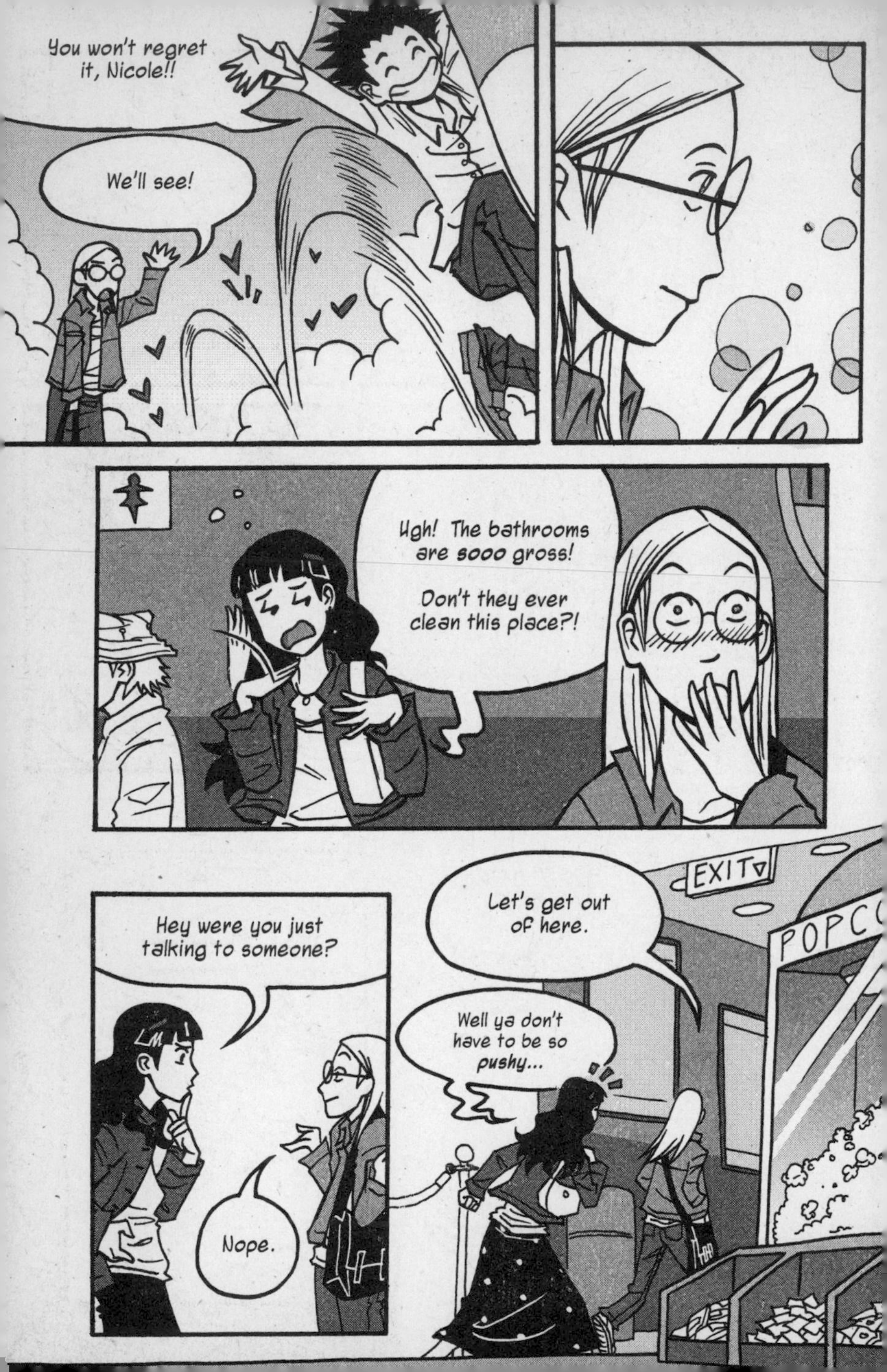
You won't regret it, Nicole!!
We'll see!
Ugh! The bathrooms are sooo gross!
Don't they ever clean this place?!
Hey were you just talking to someone?
Nope.
Let's get out of here.
EXIT
POPC
Well ya don't have to be so *pushy*...

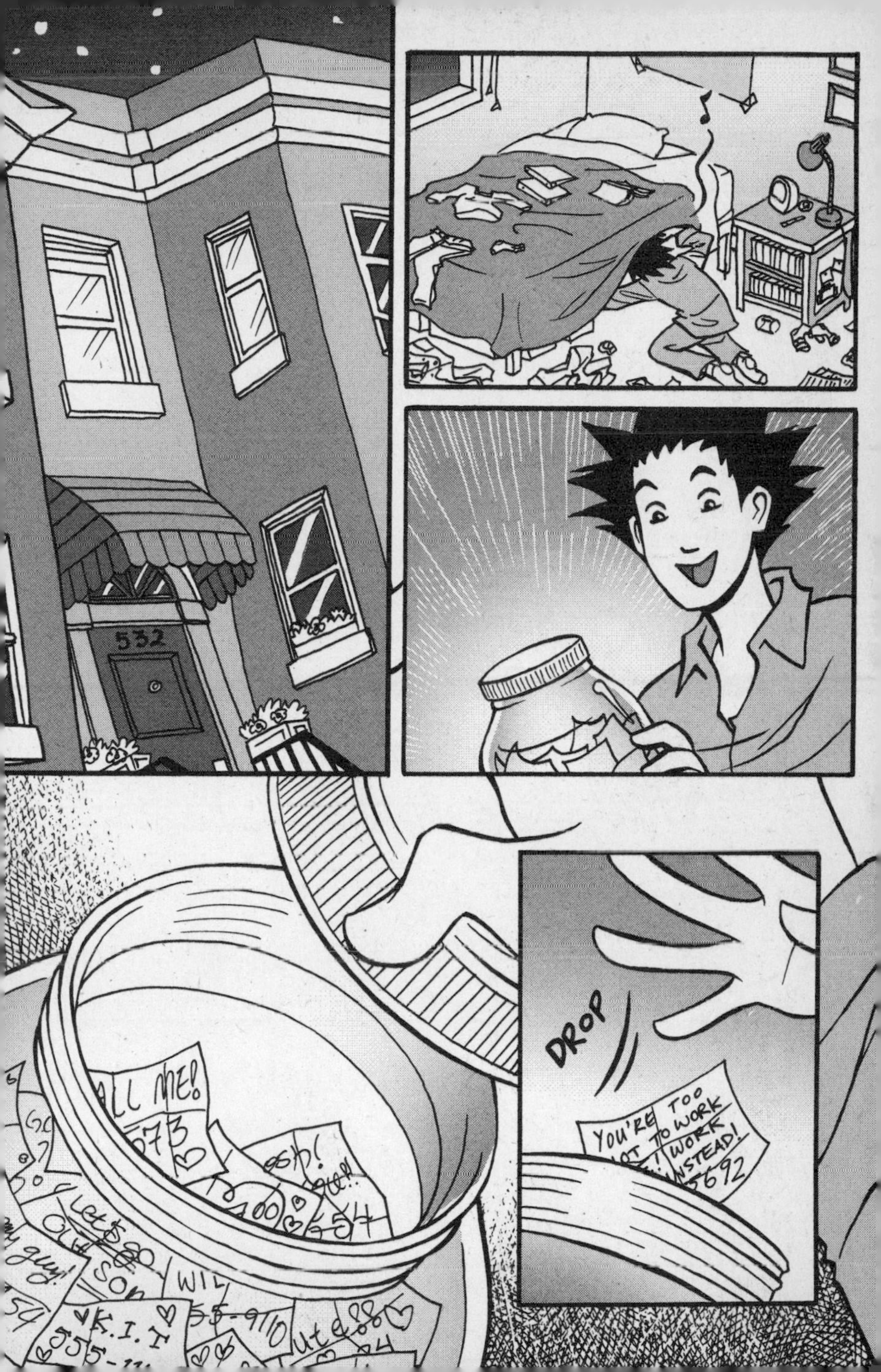
532
DROP

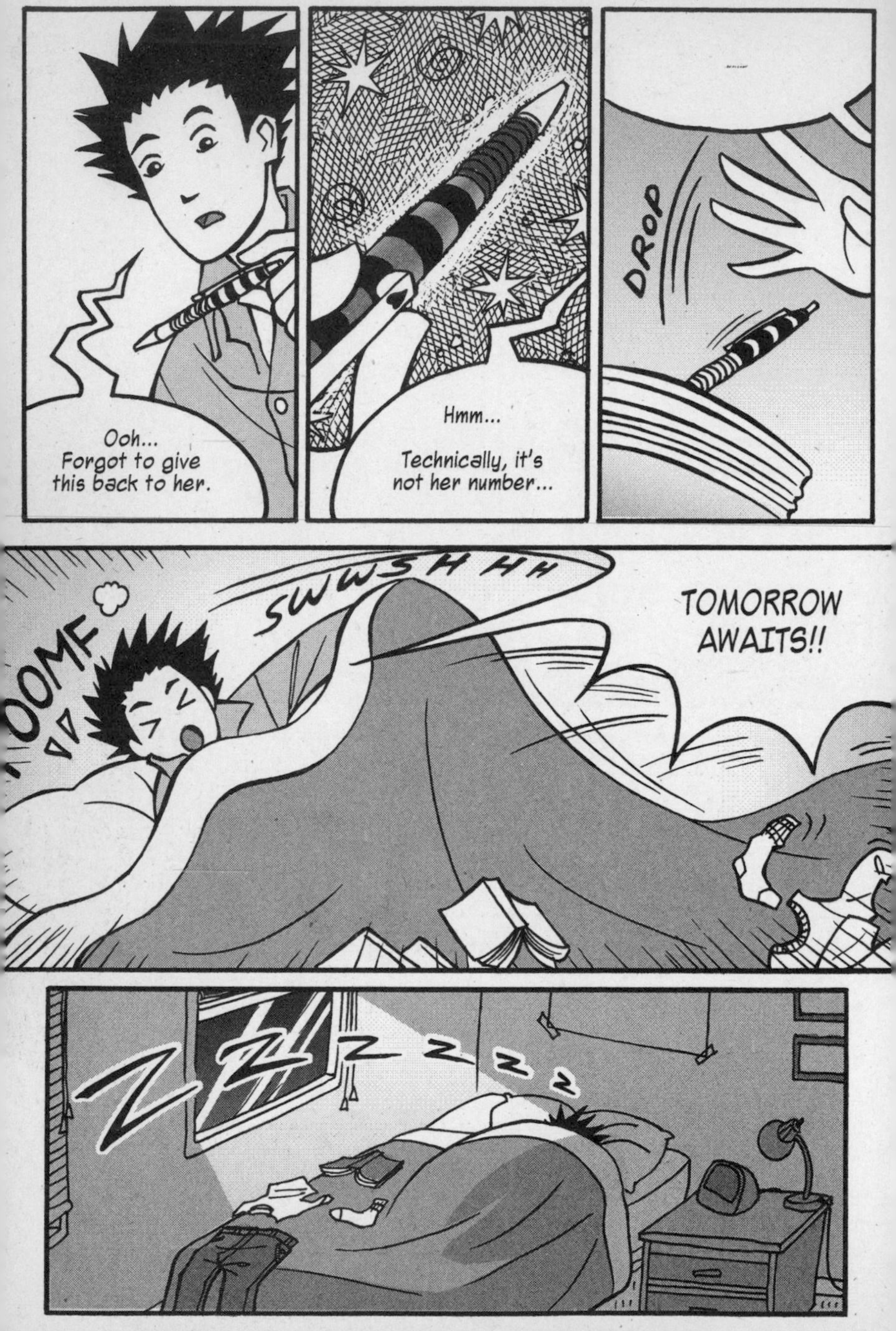
Ooh...
Forgot to give this back to her.
Hmm...
Technically, it's not her number...
DROP
OOMF
SWWSHHH
TOMORROW AWAITS!!
ZZZZZZZ

CHAPTER FOUR

Ignites A Spark

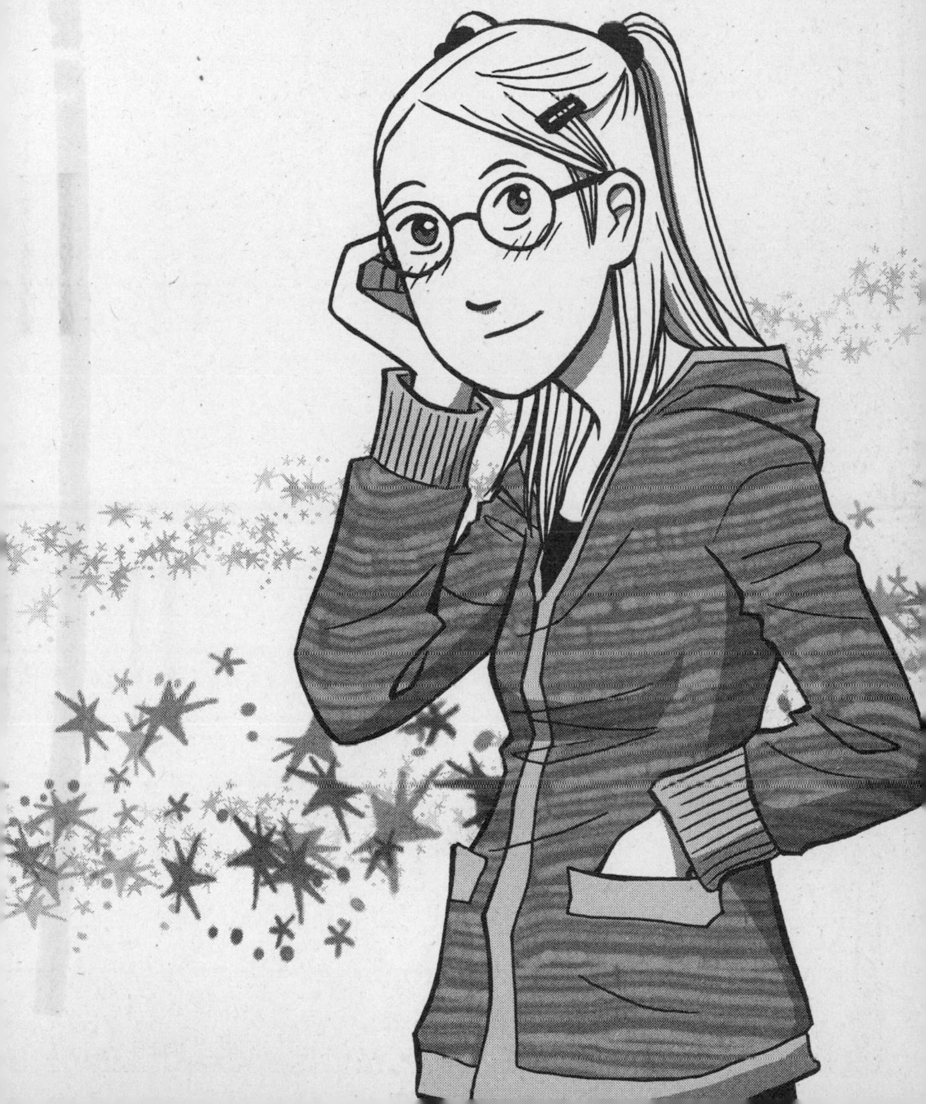

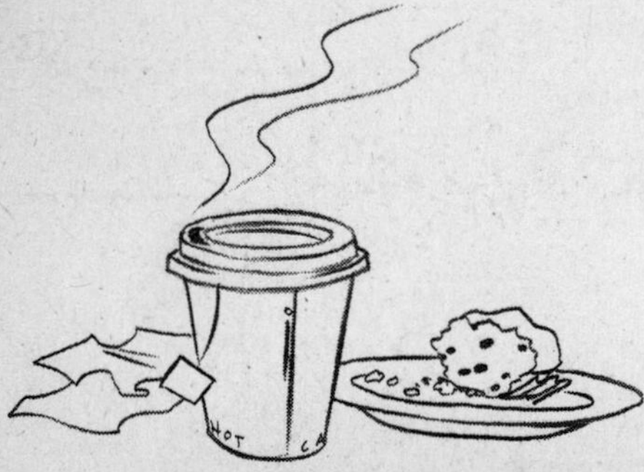
HOT

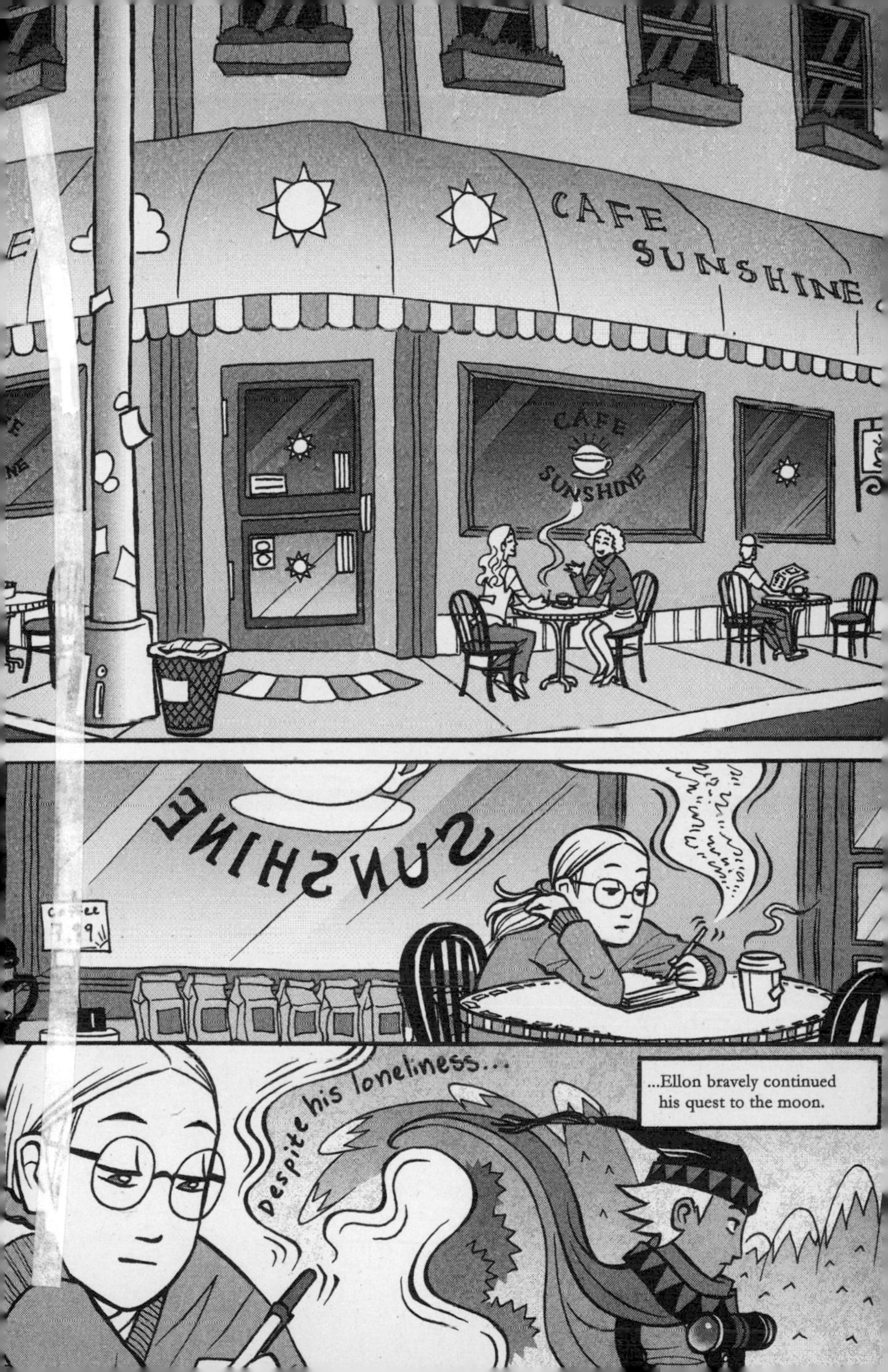
CAFE SUNSHINE
CAFE SUNSHINE
SUNSHINE
Despite his loneliness...
...Ellon bravely continued his quest to the moon.

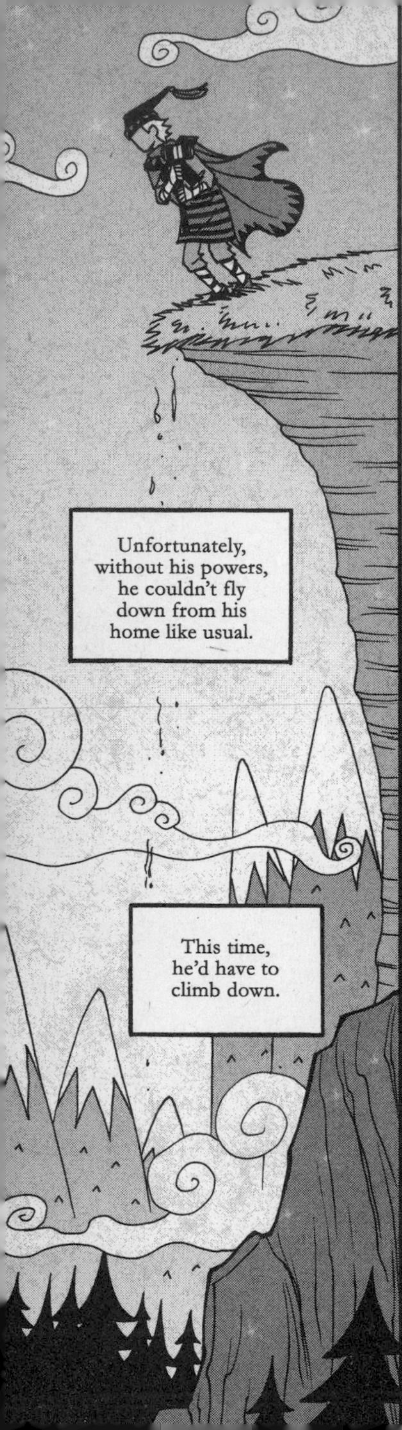
Unfortunately, without his powers, he couldn't fly down from his home like usual.
This time, he'd have to climb down.
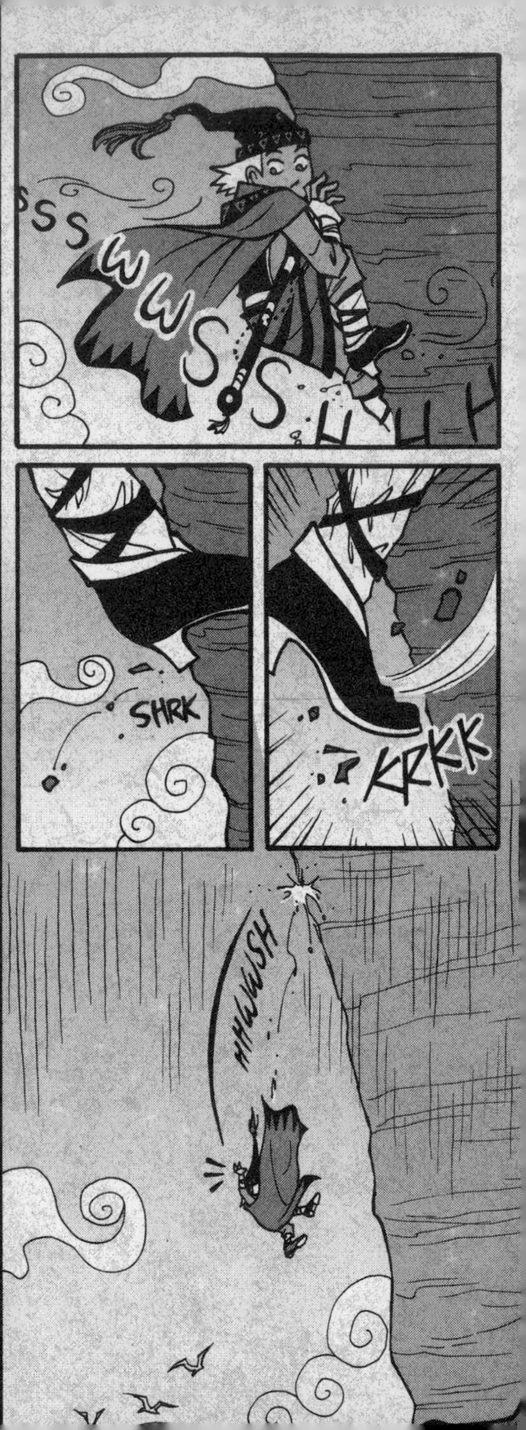
SSSWWSSSHHH
SHRK
KRKK
HHWWSH

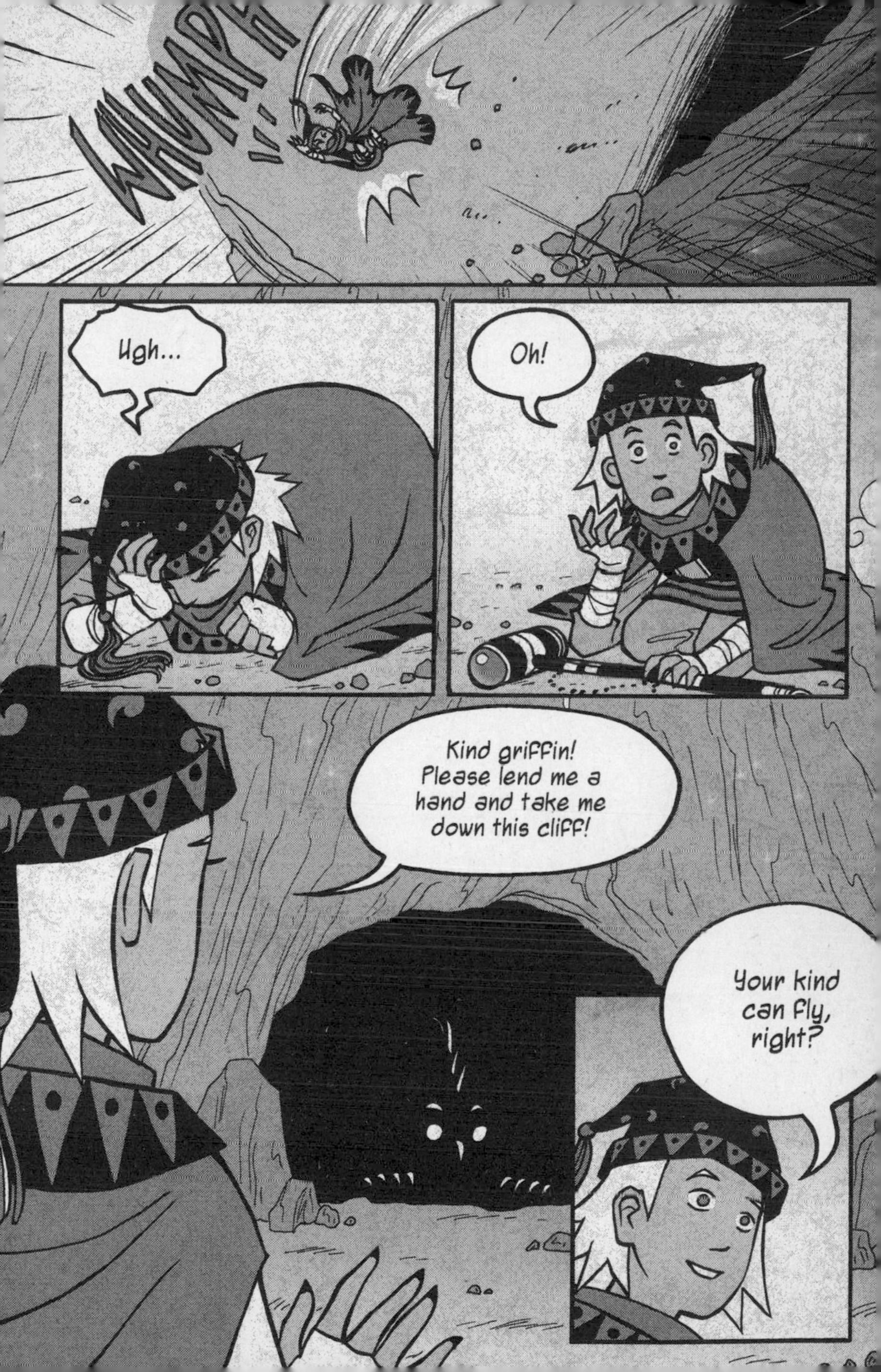
WHUMPH
Ugh...
Oh!
Kind griffin! Please lend me a hand and take me down this cliff!
Your kind can fly, right?

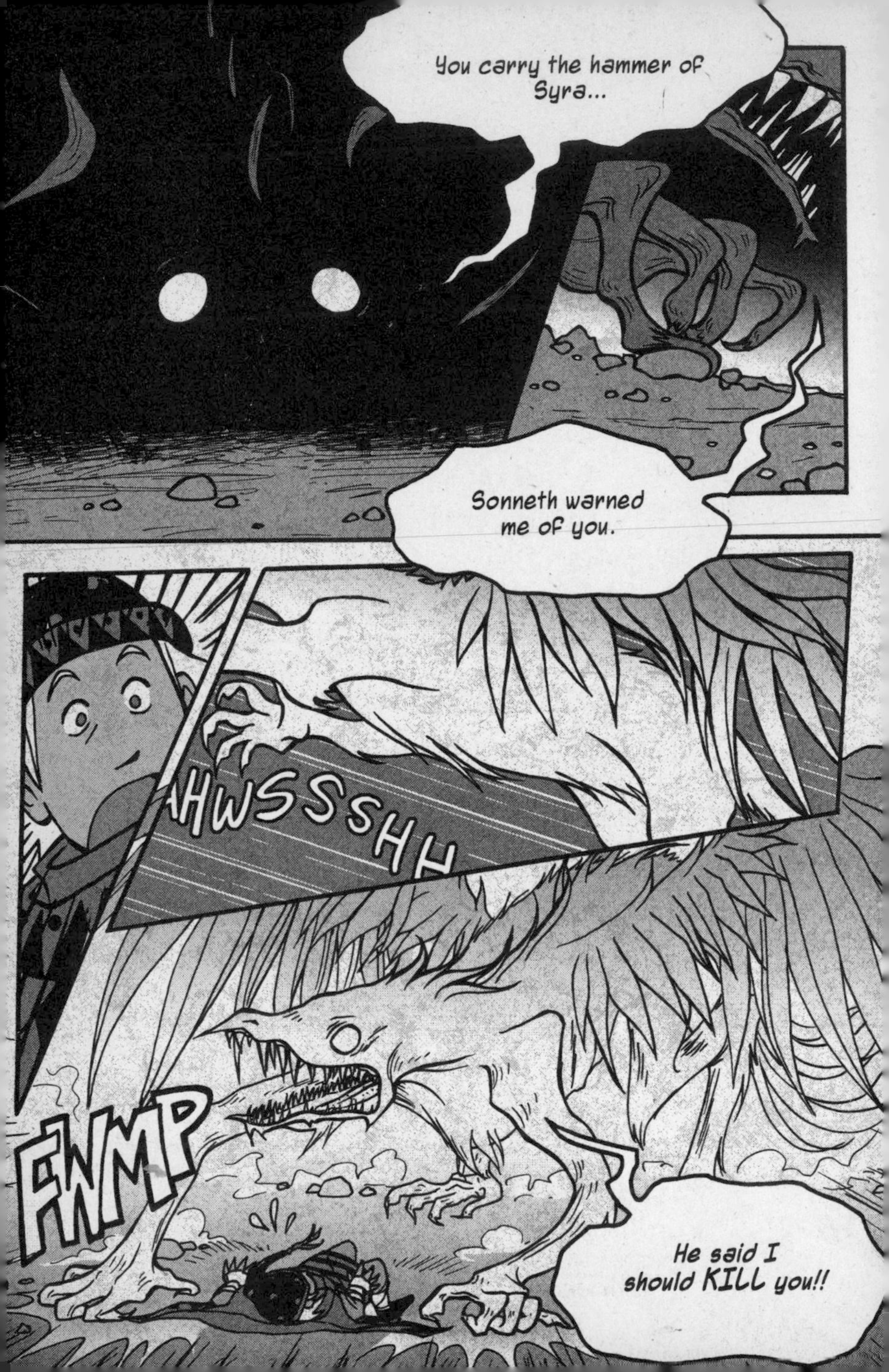
You carry the hammer of Syra...
Sonneth warned me of you.
AHWSSSHH
FWMP
He said I should KILL you!!

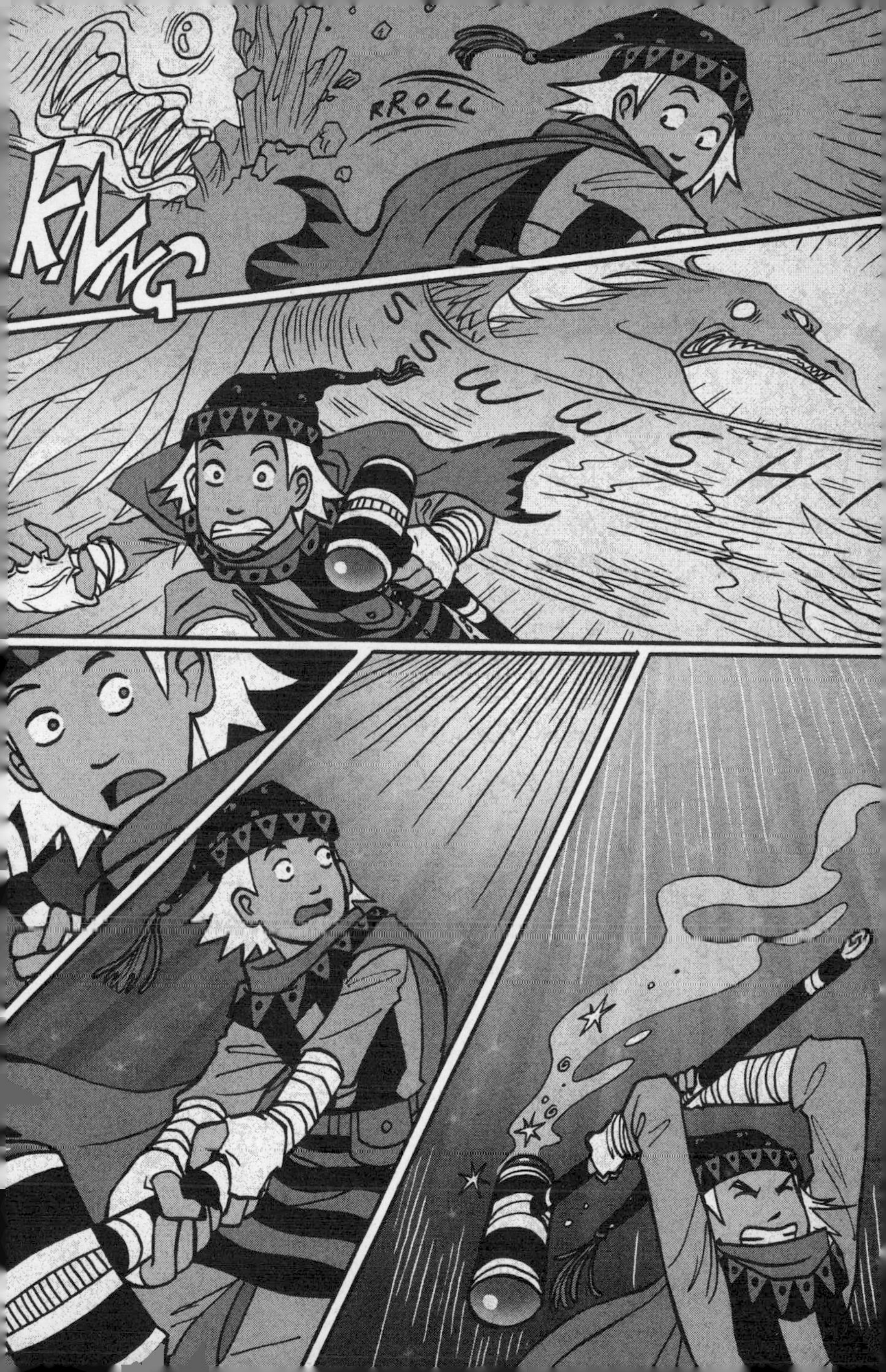
K-NNG
RROLL
SWUSSH

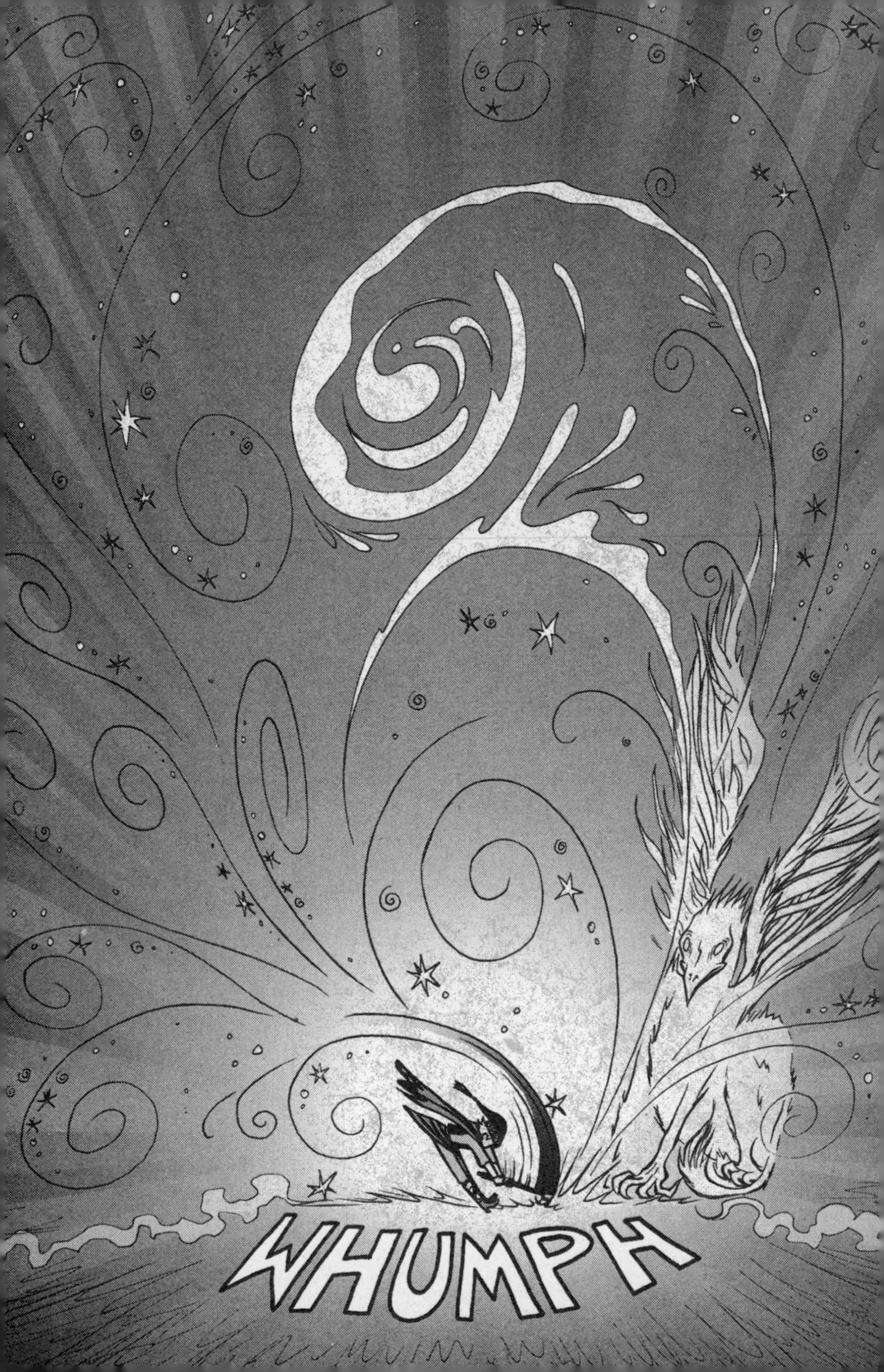
WHUMPH

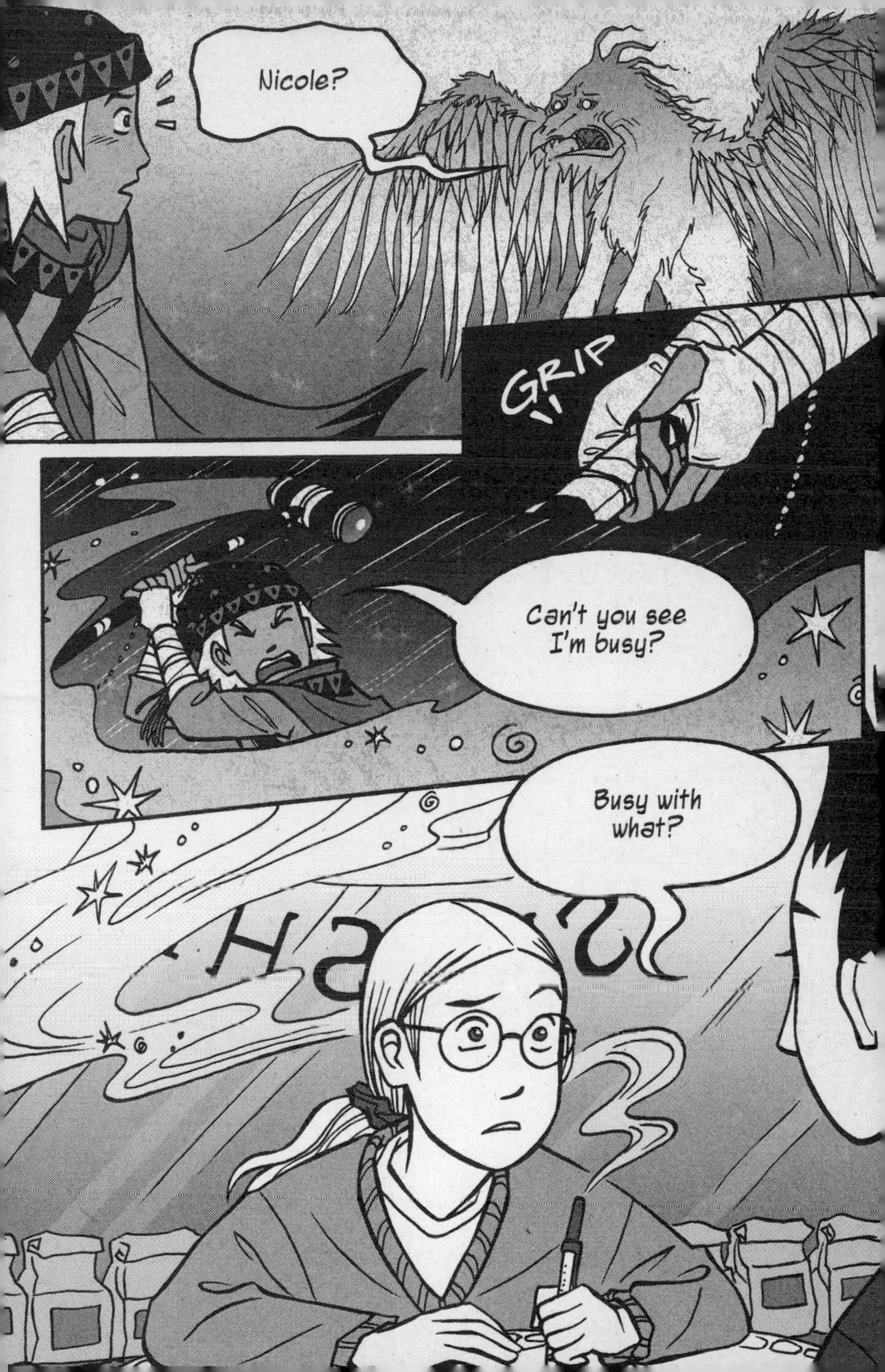
Nicole?
GRIP
Can't you see I'm busy?
Busy with what?

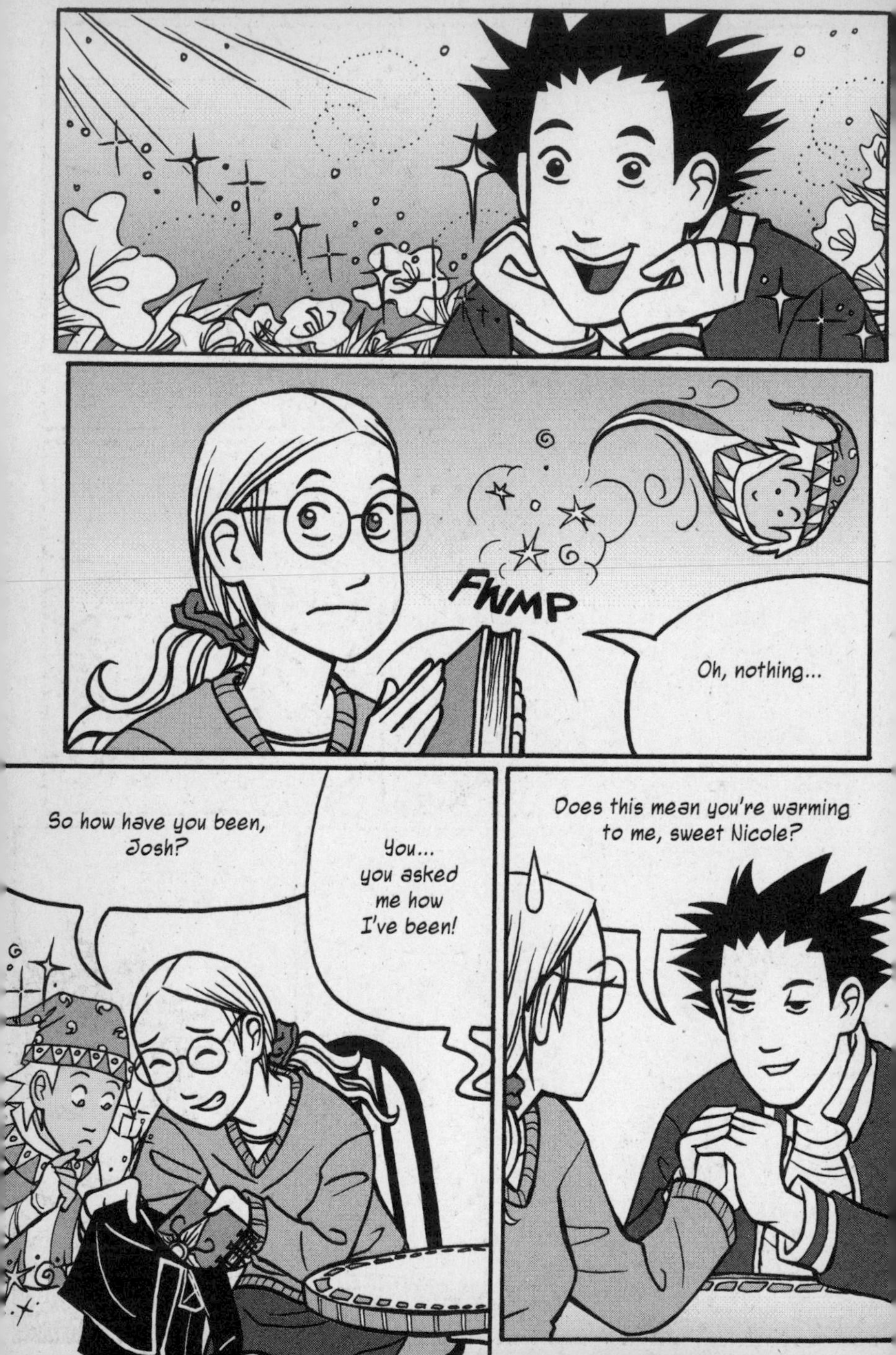
FWMP
Oh, nothing...
So how have you been, Josh?
You... you asked me how I've been!
Does this mean you're warming to me, sweet Nicole?

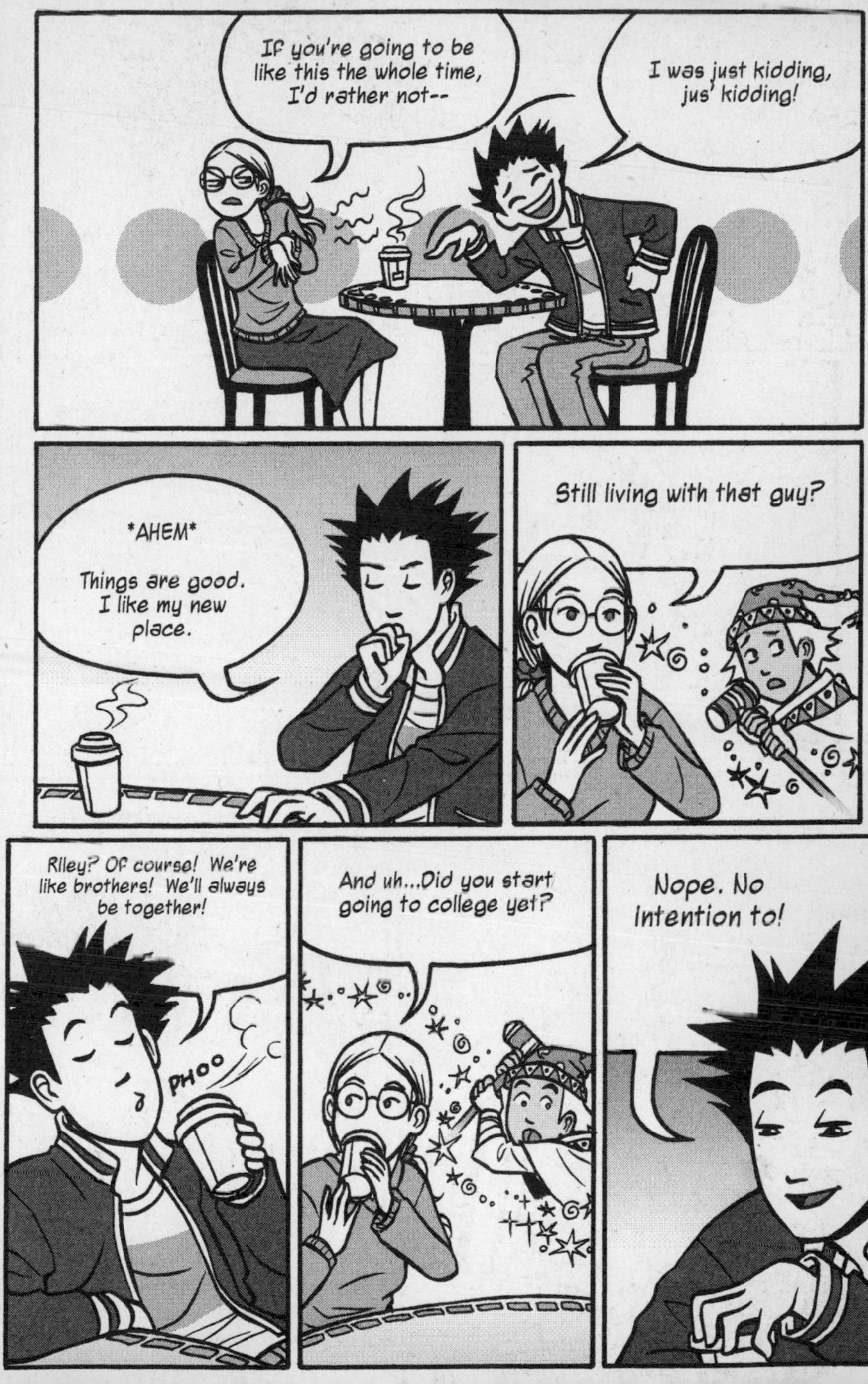
If you're going to be like this the whole time, I'd rather not--
I was just kidding, jus' kidding!
AHEM
Things are good. I like my new place.
Still living with that guy?
Riley? Of course! We're like brothers! We'll always be together!
PHOO
And uh...Did you start going to college yet?
Nope. No intention to!

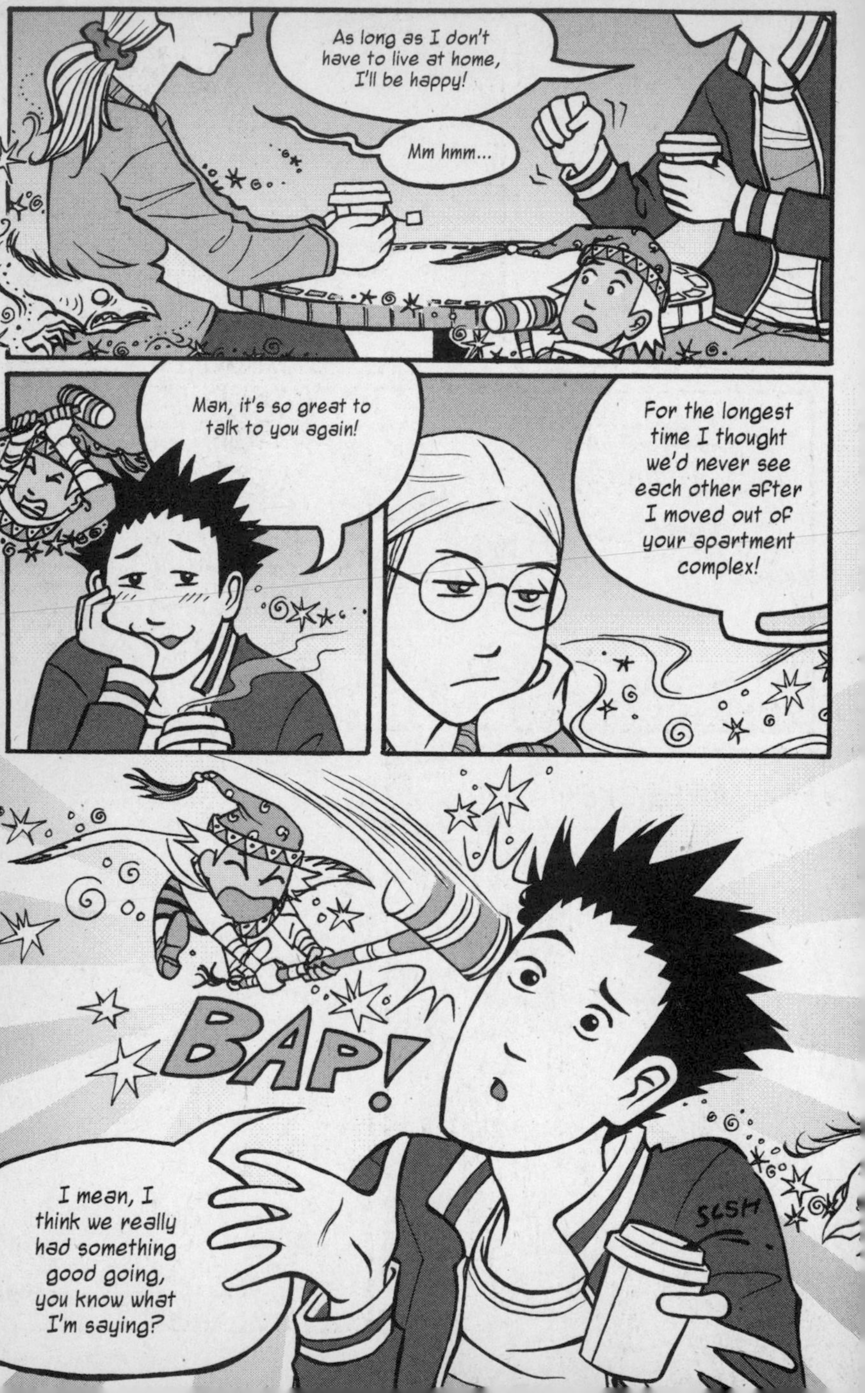
As long as I don't have to live at home, I'll be happy!
Mm hmm...
Man, it's so great to talk to you again!
For the longest time I thought we'd never see each other after I moved out of your apartment complex!
BAP!
I mean, I think we really had something good going, you know what I'm saying?
SLSH

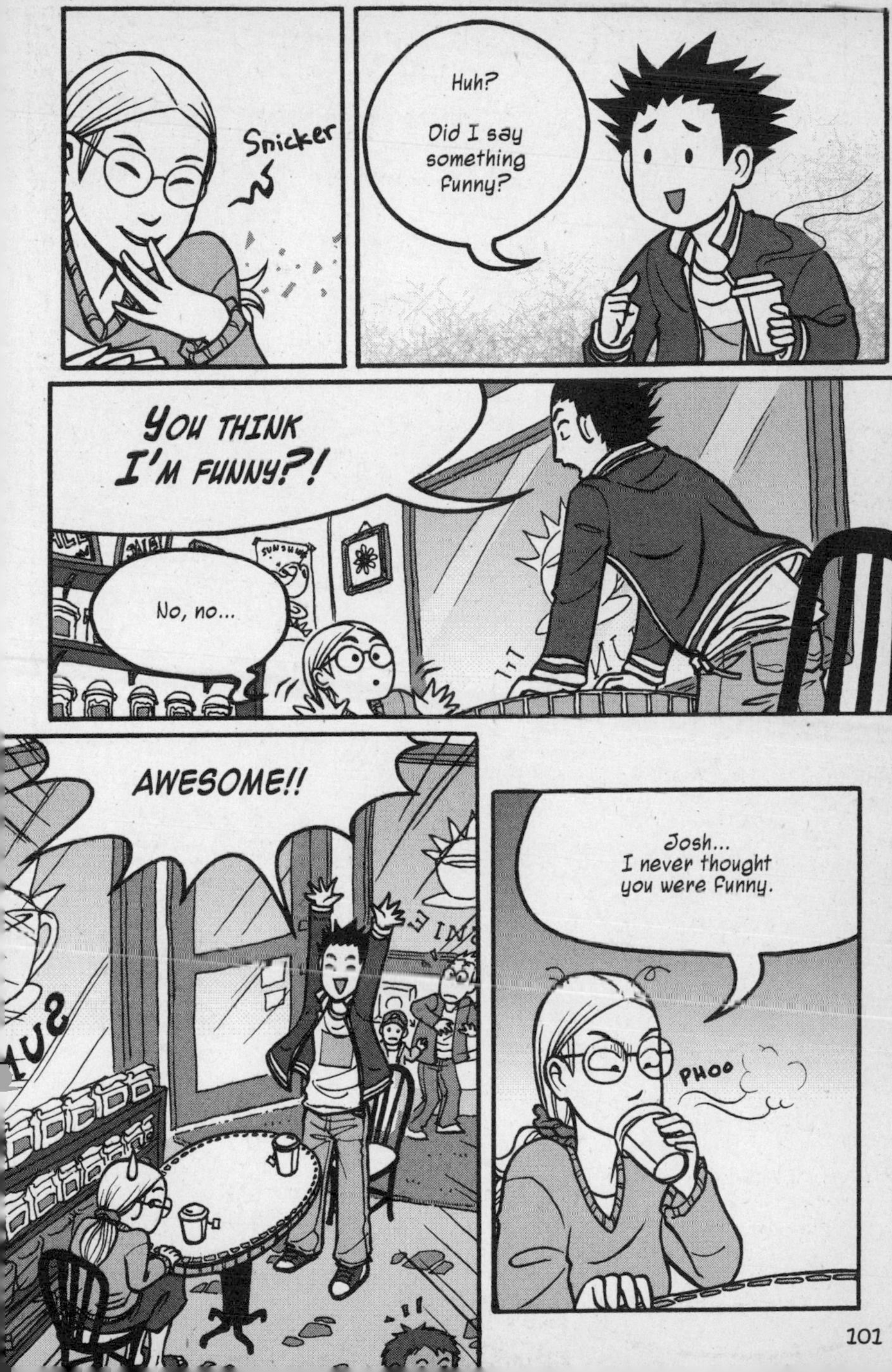
Snicker
Huh?
Did I say something funny?
YOU THINK I'M FUNNY?!
No, no...
AWESOME!!
Josh... I never thought you were funny.
PHOO

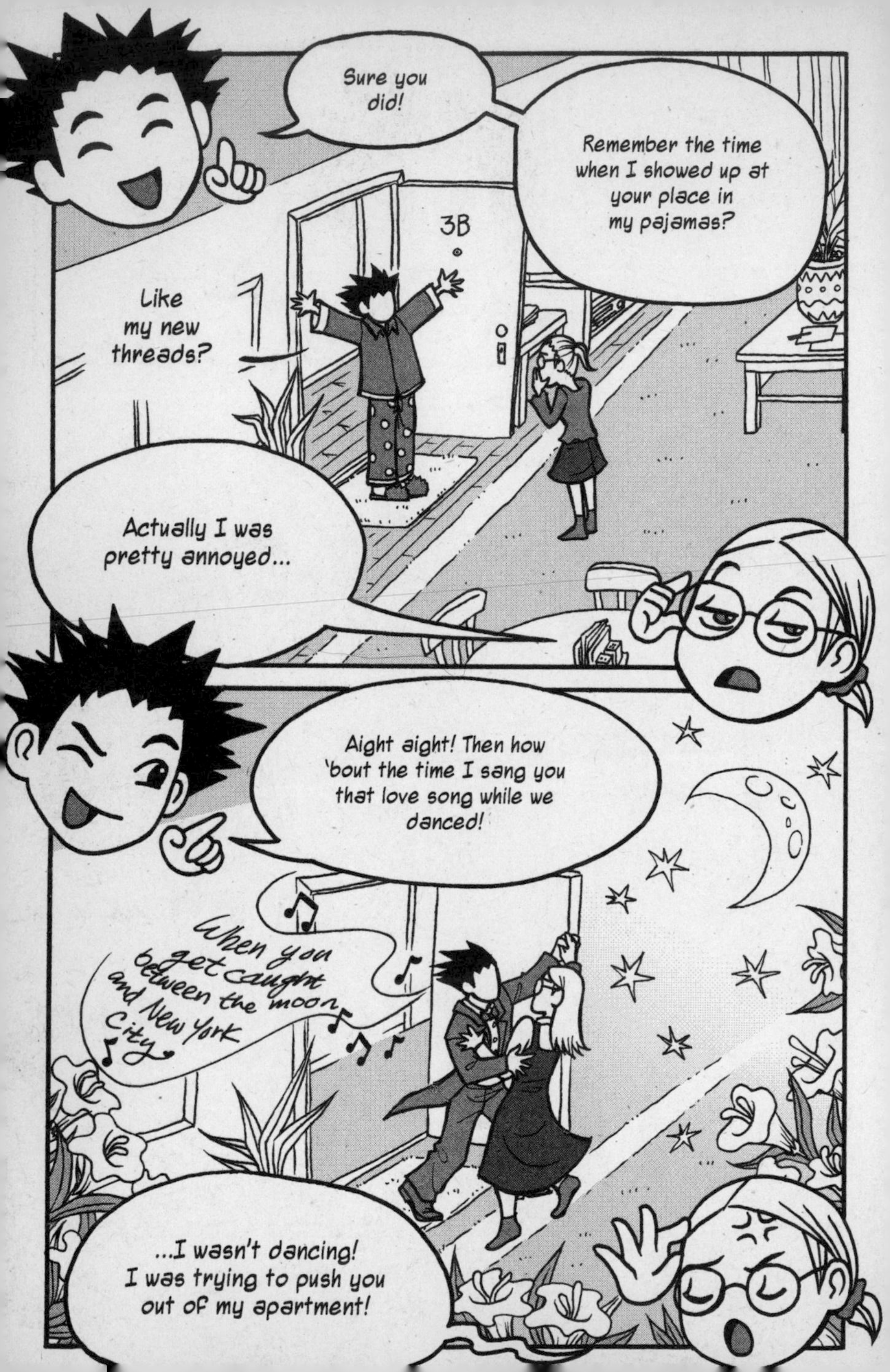
Sure you did!
Remember the time when I showed up at your place in my pajamas?
3B
Like my new threads?
Actually I was pretty annoyed...
Aight aight! Then how 'bout the time I sang you that love song while we danced!
When you get caught between the moon and New York City
...I wasn't dancing! I was trying to push you out of my apartment!

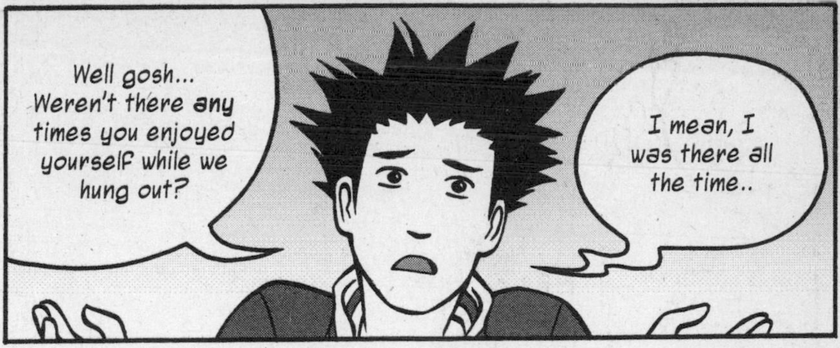
Well gosh... Weren't there any times you enjoyed yourself while we hung out?
I mean, I was there all the time..

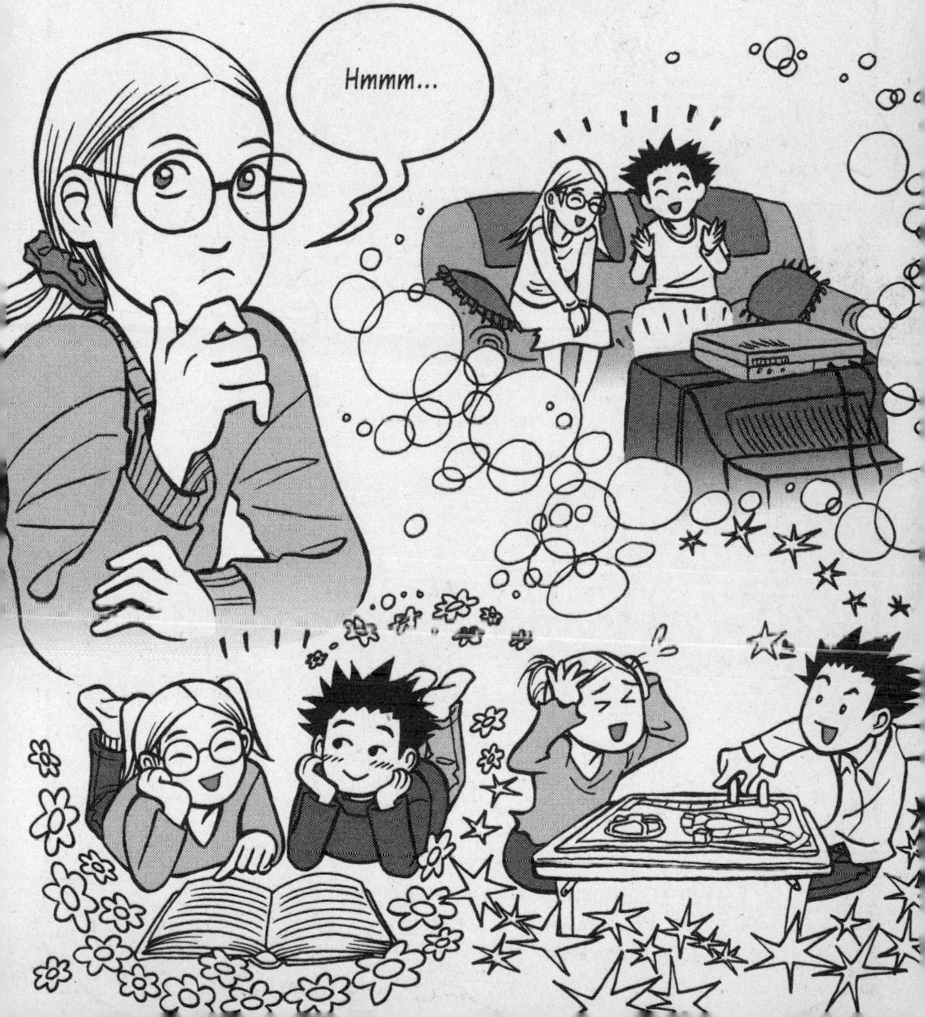
Hmmm...

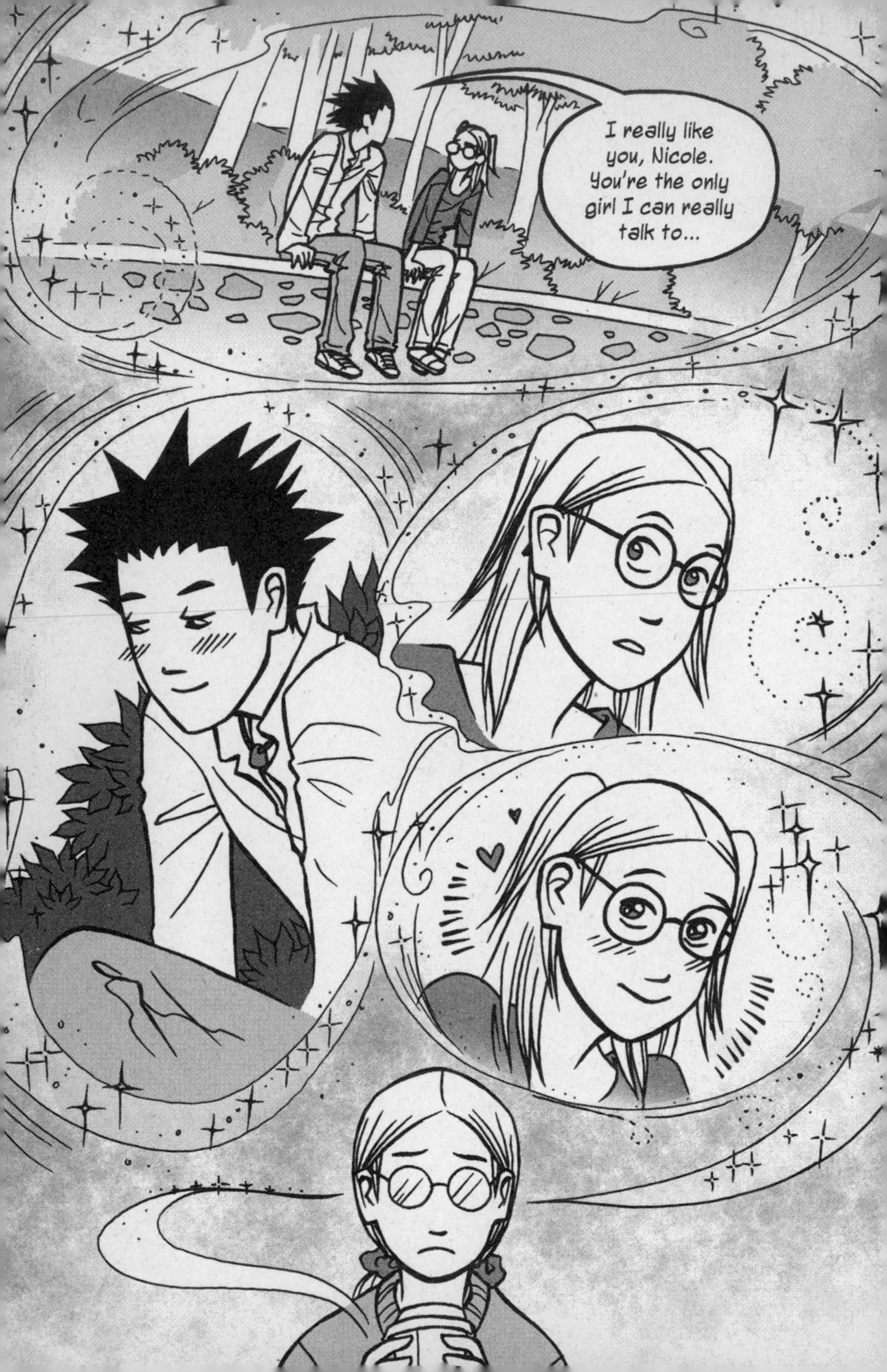
I really like you, Nicole. You're the only girl I can really talk to...

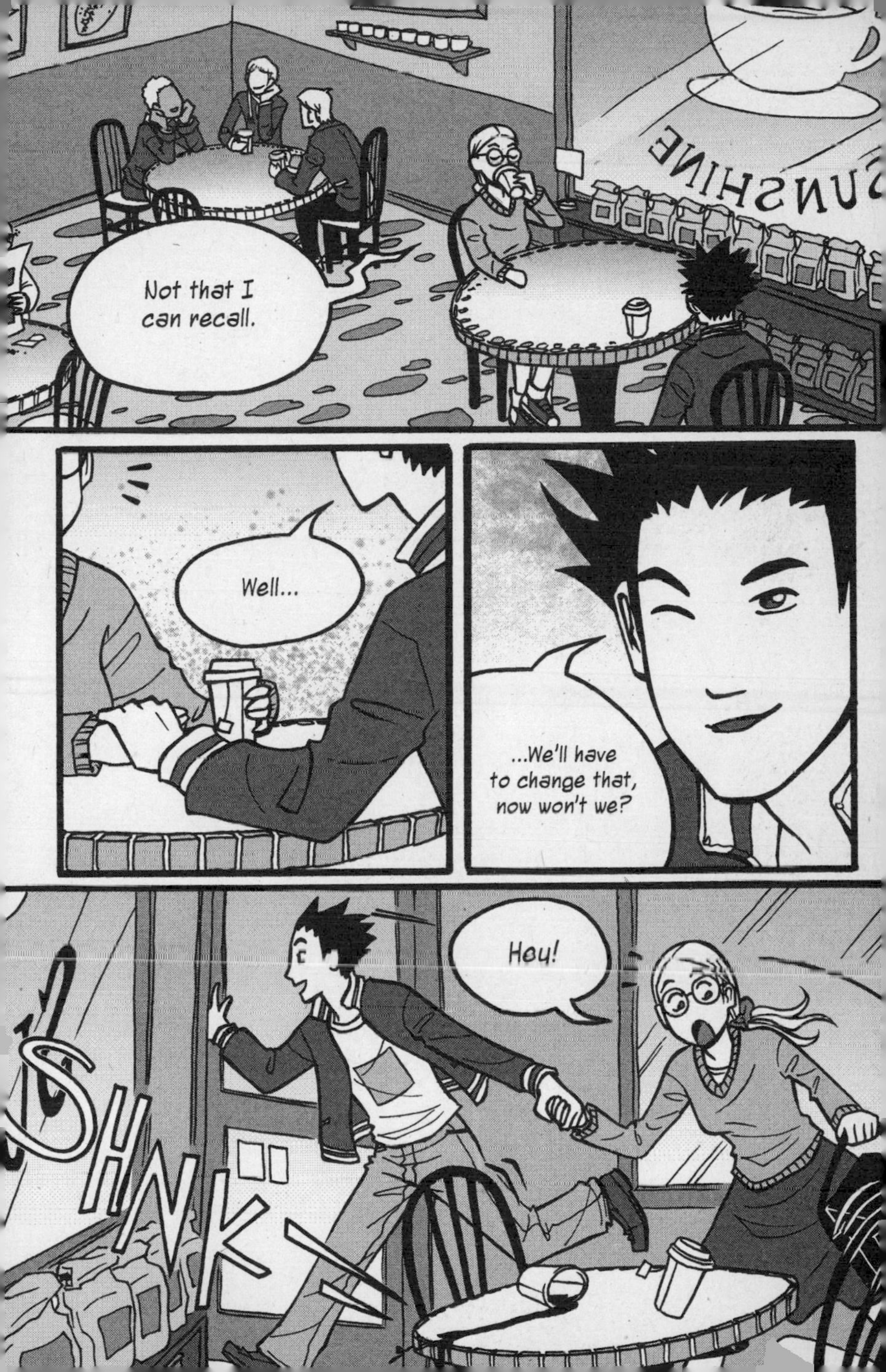
SUNSHINE
Not that I can recall.
Well...
...We'll have to change that, now won't we?
Hey!
SHNK

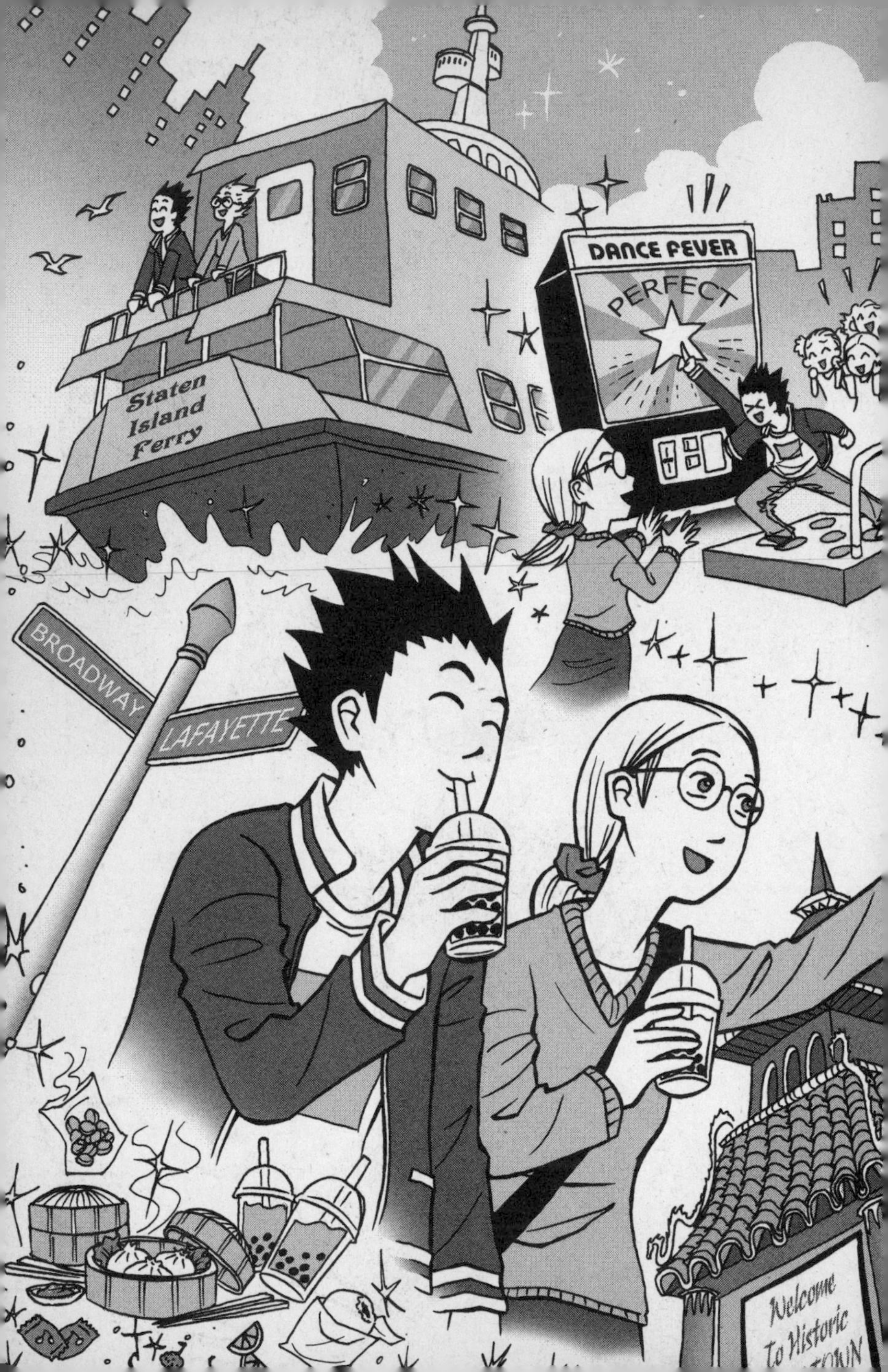

Staten Island Ferry
DANCE FEVER
PERFECT
BROADWAY
LAFAYETTE
Welcome To Historic

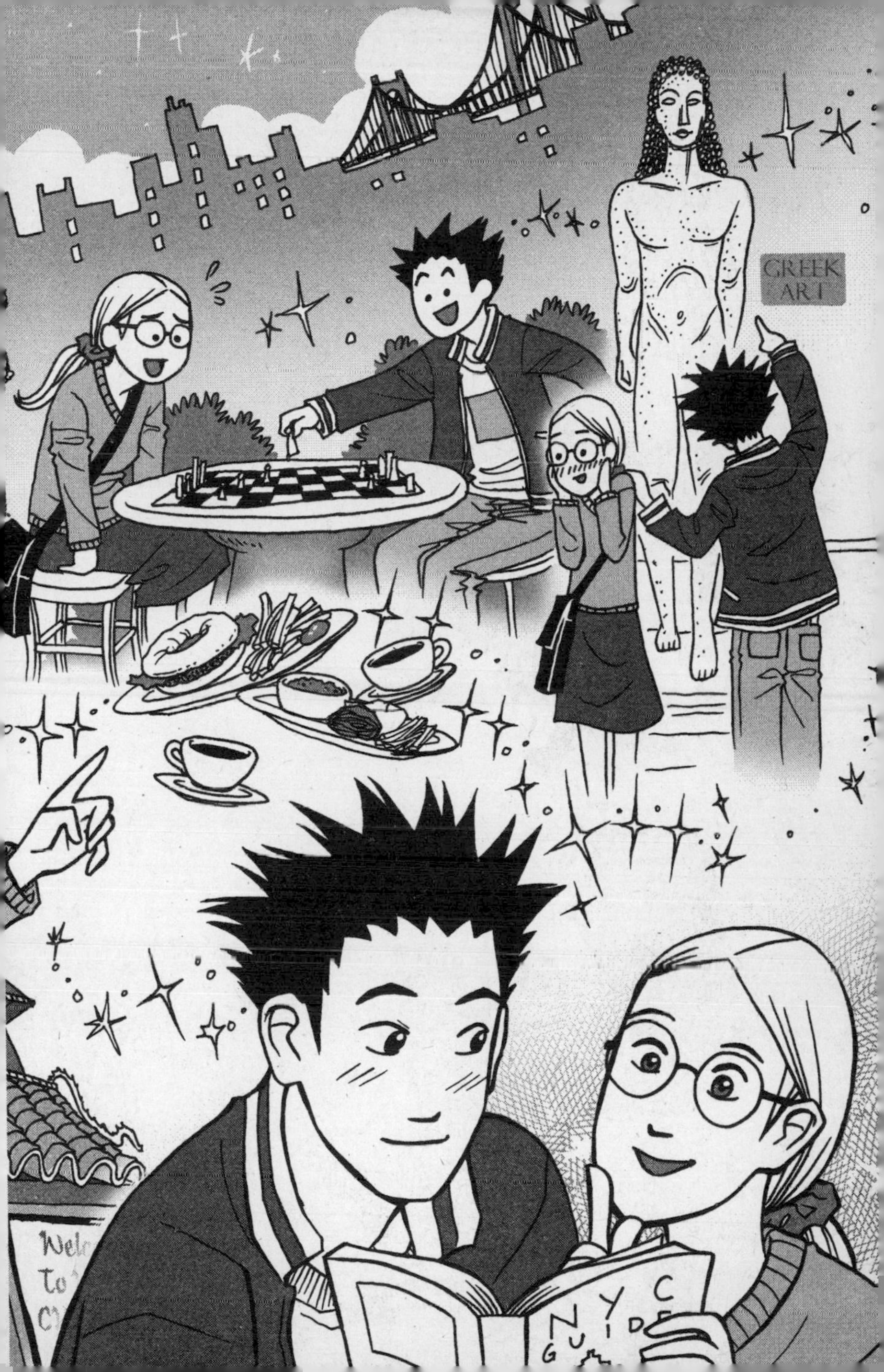
GREEK ART
NYC GUIDE

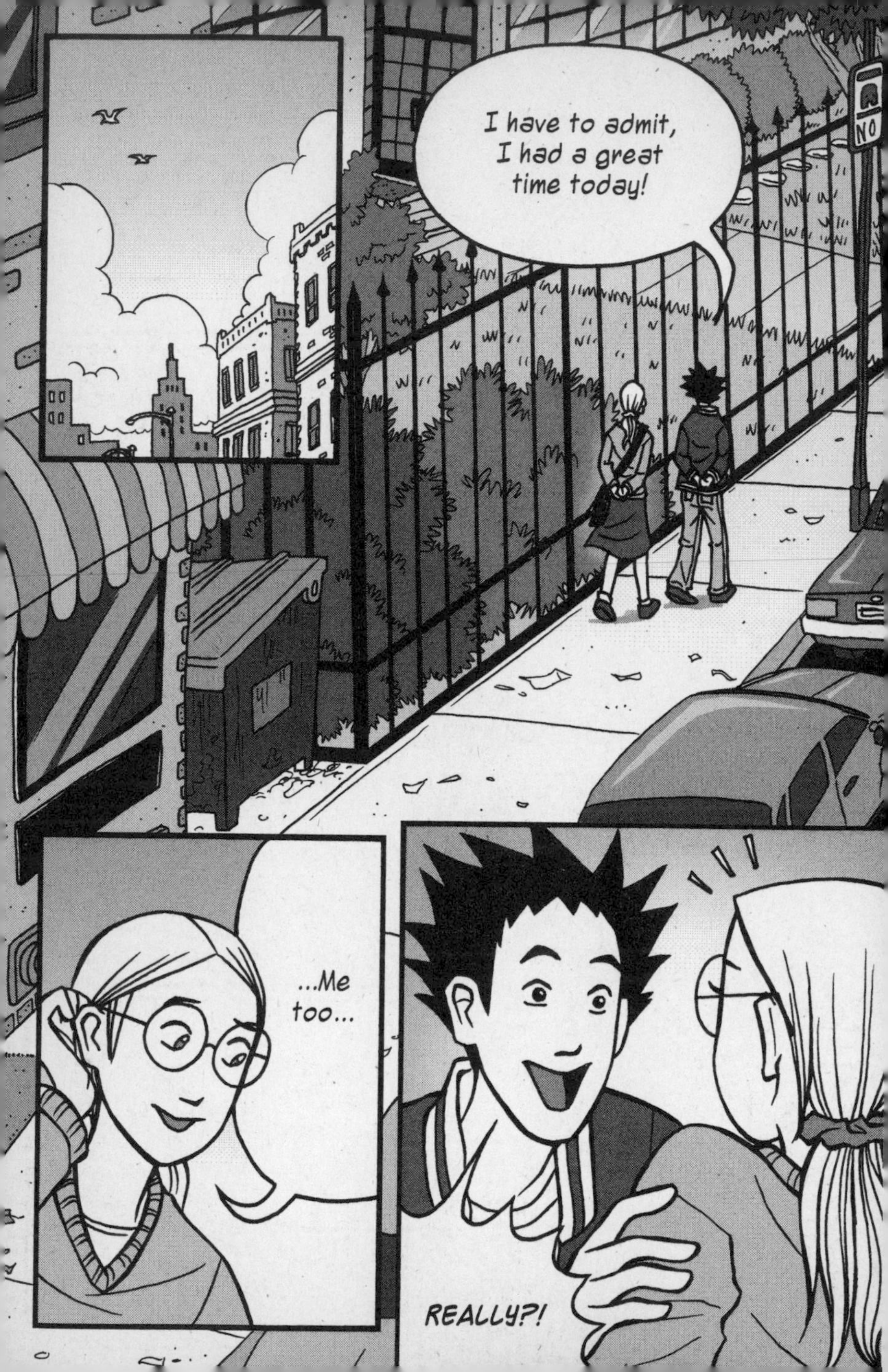
I have to admit, I had a great time today!
NO
...Me too...
REALLY?!

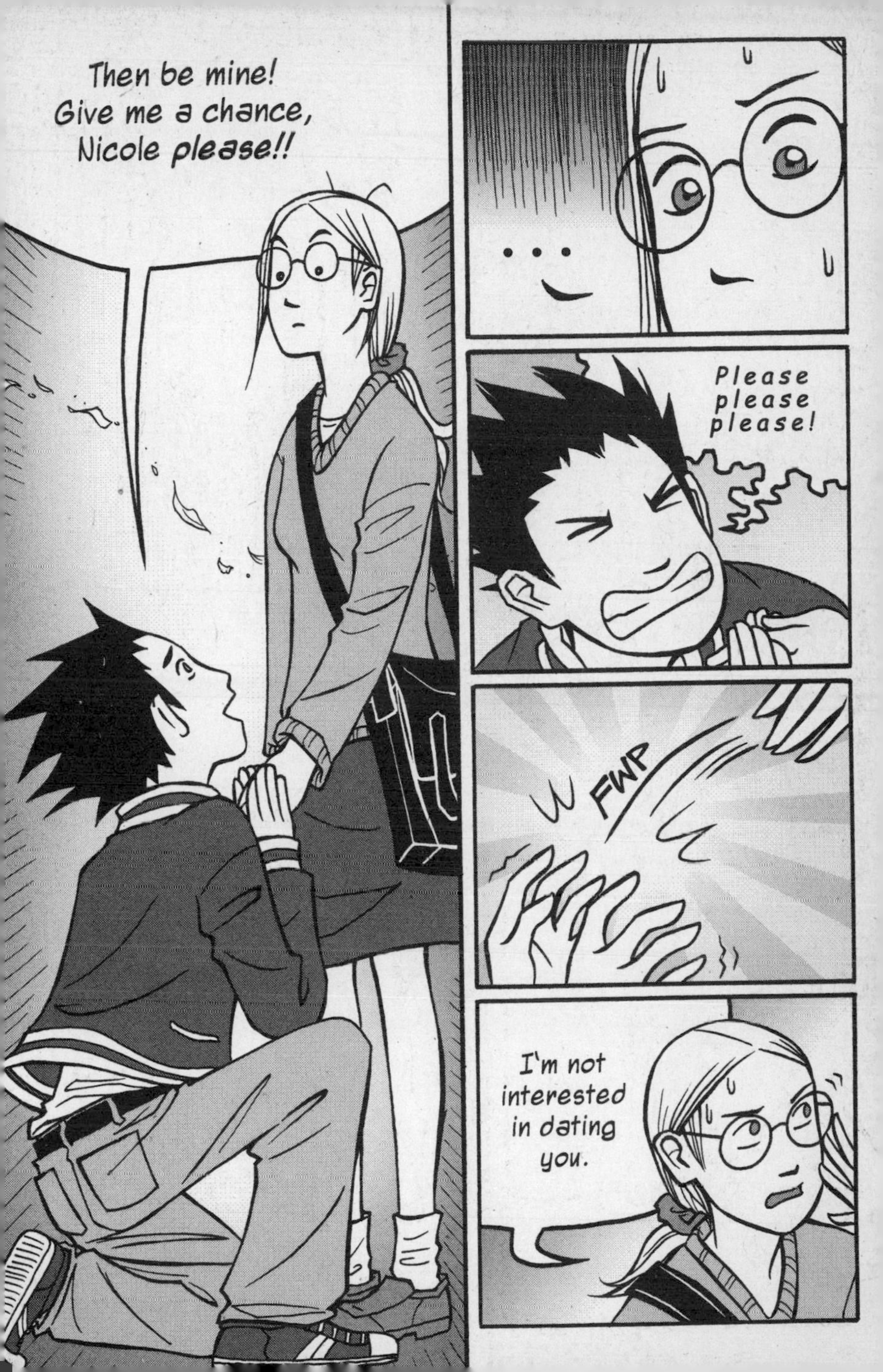
Then be mine! Give me a chance, Nicole please!!
...
Please please please!
FWP
I'm not interested in dating you.

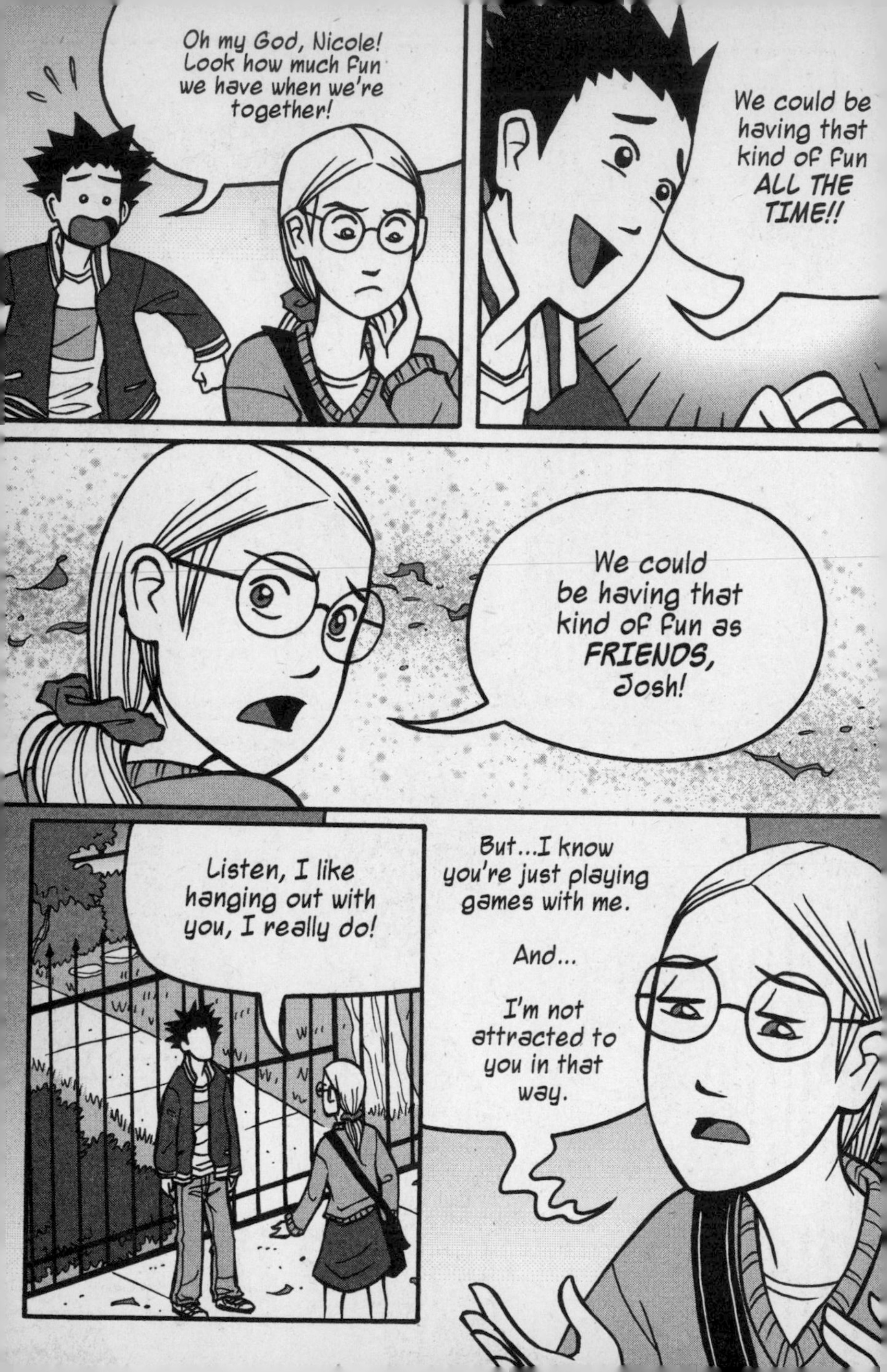
Oh my God, Nicole! Look how much fun we have when we're together!
We could be having that kind of fun ALL THE TIME!!
We could be having that kind of fun as FRIENDS, Josh!
Listen, I like hanging out with you, I really do!
...
But...I know you're just playing games with me.
And...
I'm not attracted to you in that way.

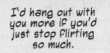

I'd hang out with you more if you'd just stop flirting so much.

What?! You can't ask me to do that! Flirting is in my nature!

It's like asking me not to have *awesome hair!!*

Well... I don't like it!

It's...It's insincere!

THNK

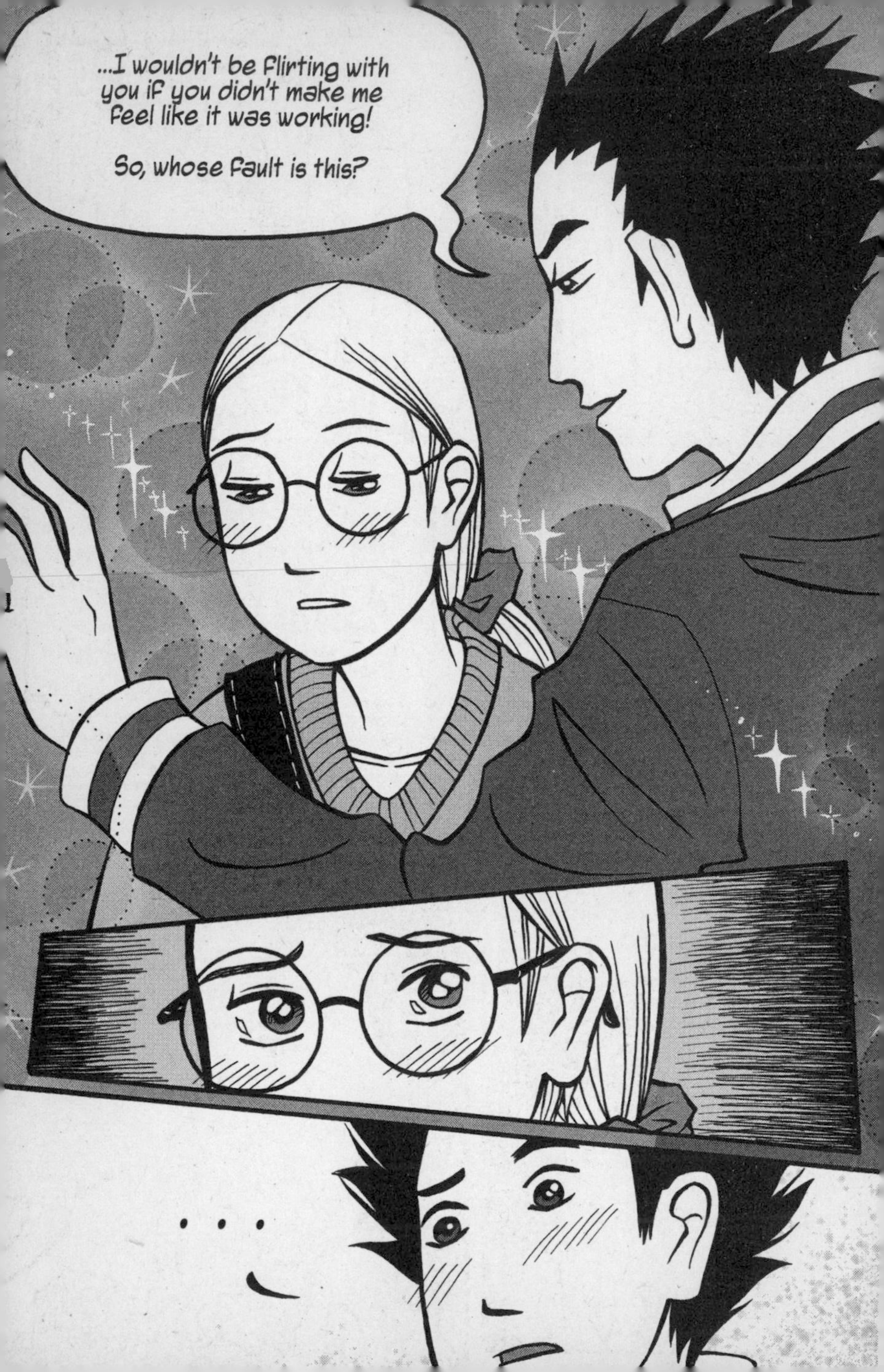
...I wouldn't be flirting with you if you didn't make me feel like it was working!
So, whose fault is this?
. . .

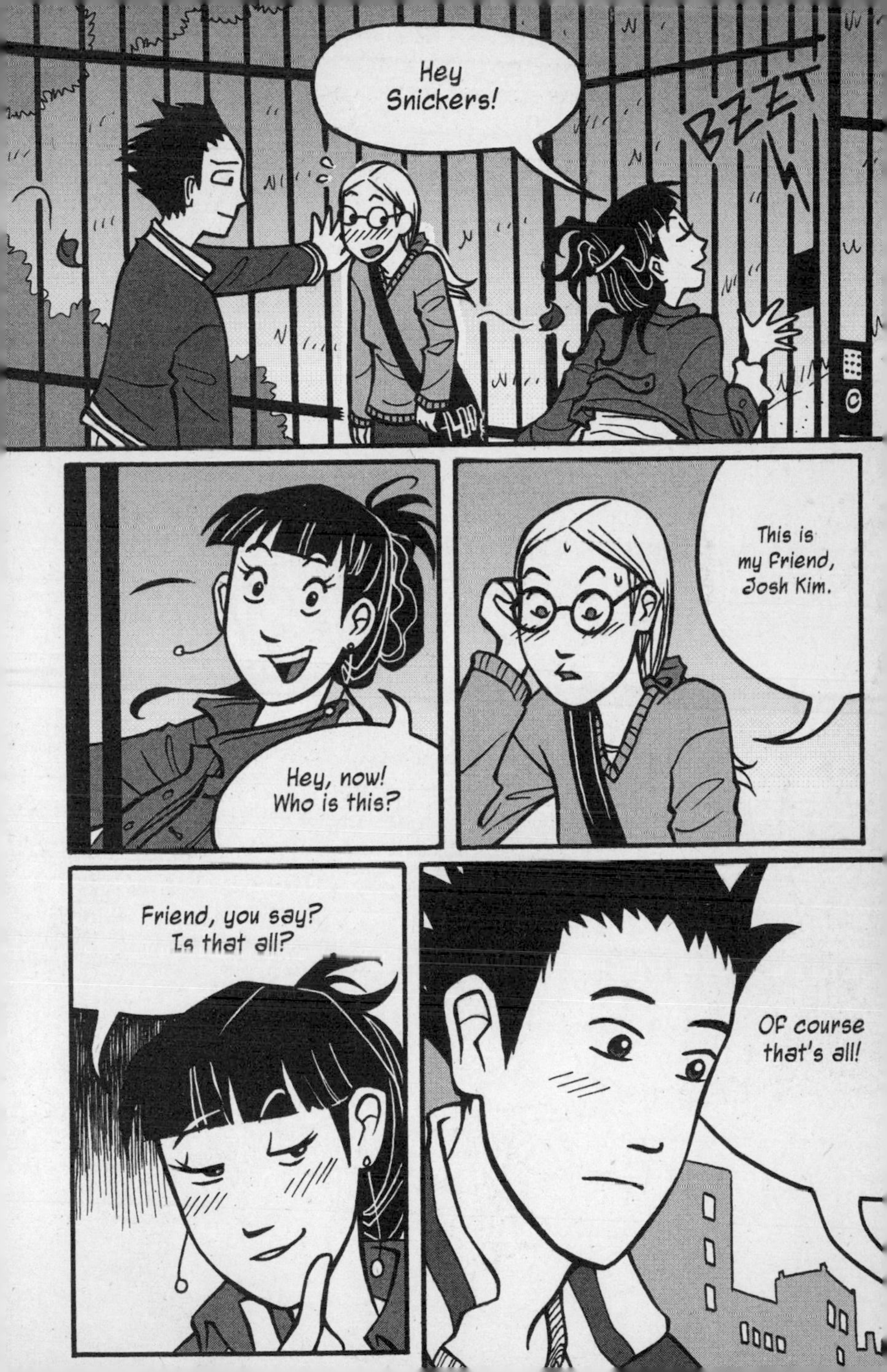
Hey Snickers!
BZZT
Hey, now! Who is this?
This is my friend, Josh Kim.
Friend, you say? Is that all?
Of course that's all!

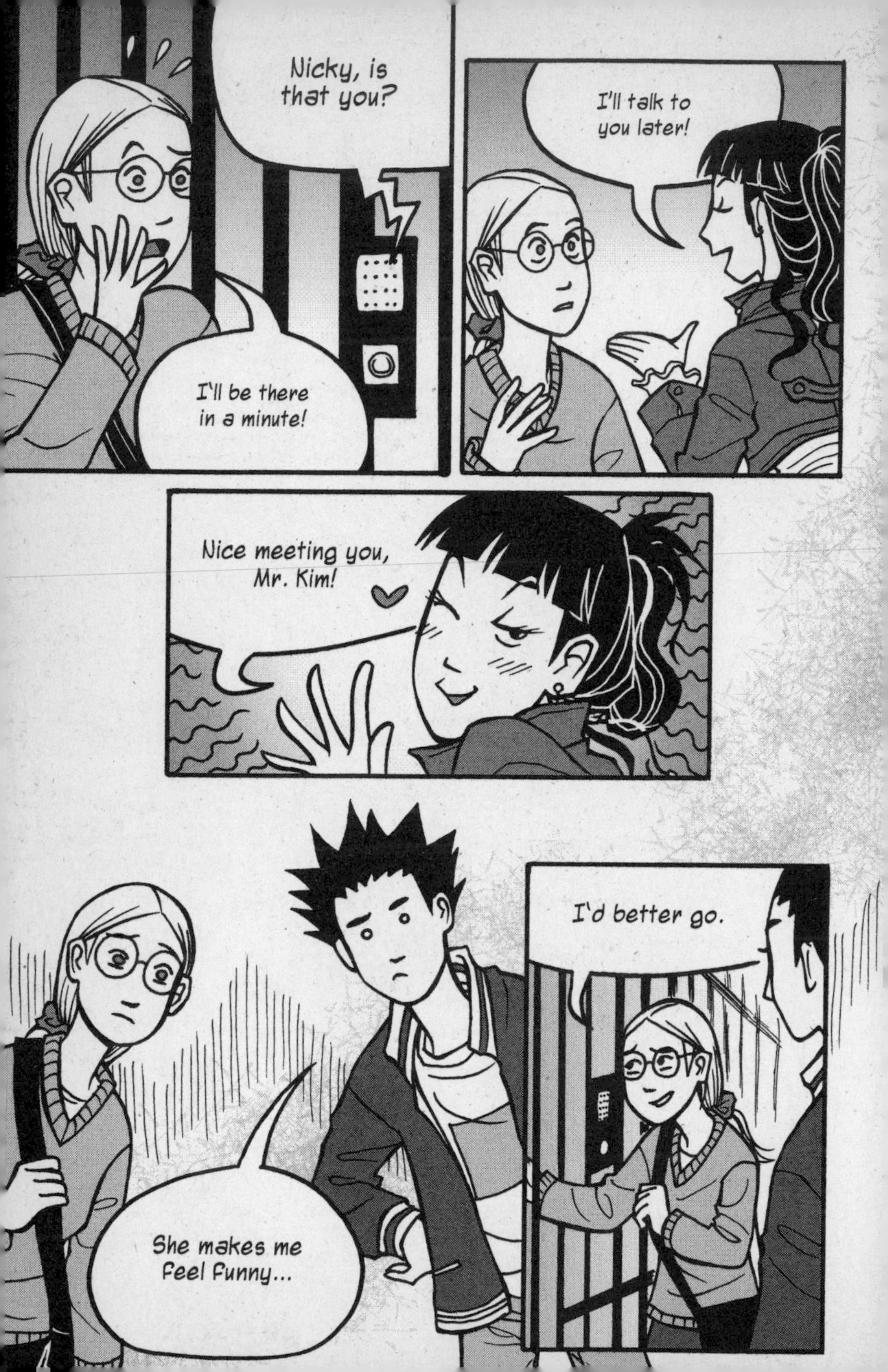
Nicky, is that you?
I'll be there in a minute!
I'll talk to you later!
Nice meeting you, Mr. Kim!
She makes me feel funny...
I'd better go.

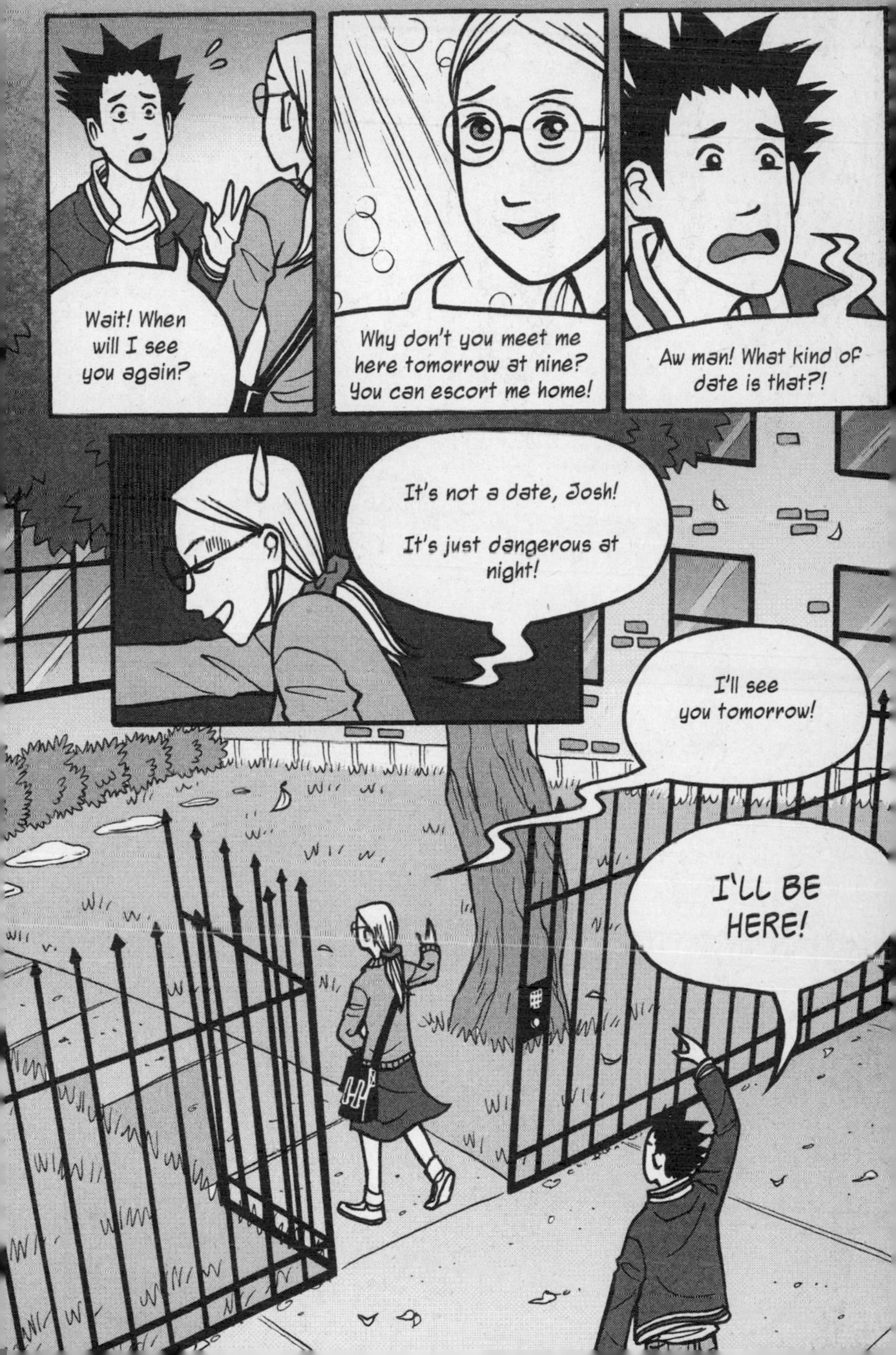
Wait! When will I see you again?
Why don't you meet me here tomorrow at nine? You can escort me home!
Aw man! What kind of date is that?!
It's not a date, Josh!
It's just dangerous at night!
I'll see you tomorrow!
I'LL BE HERE!

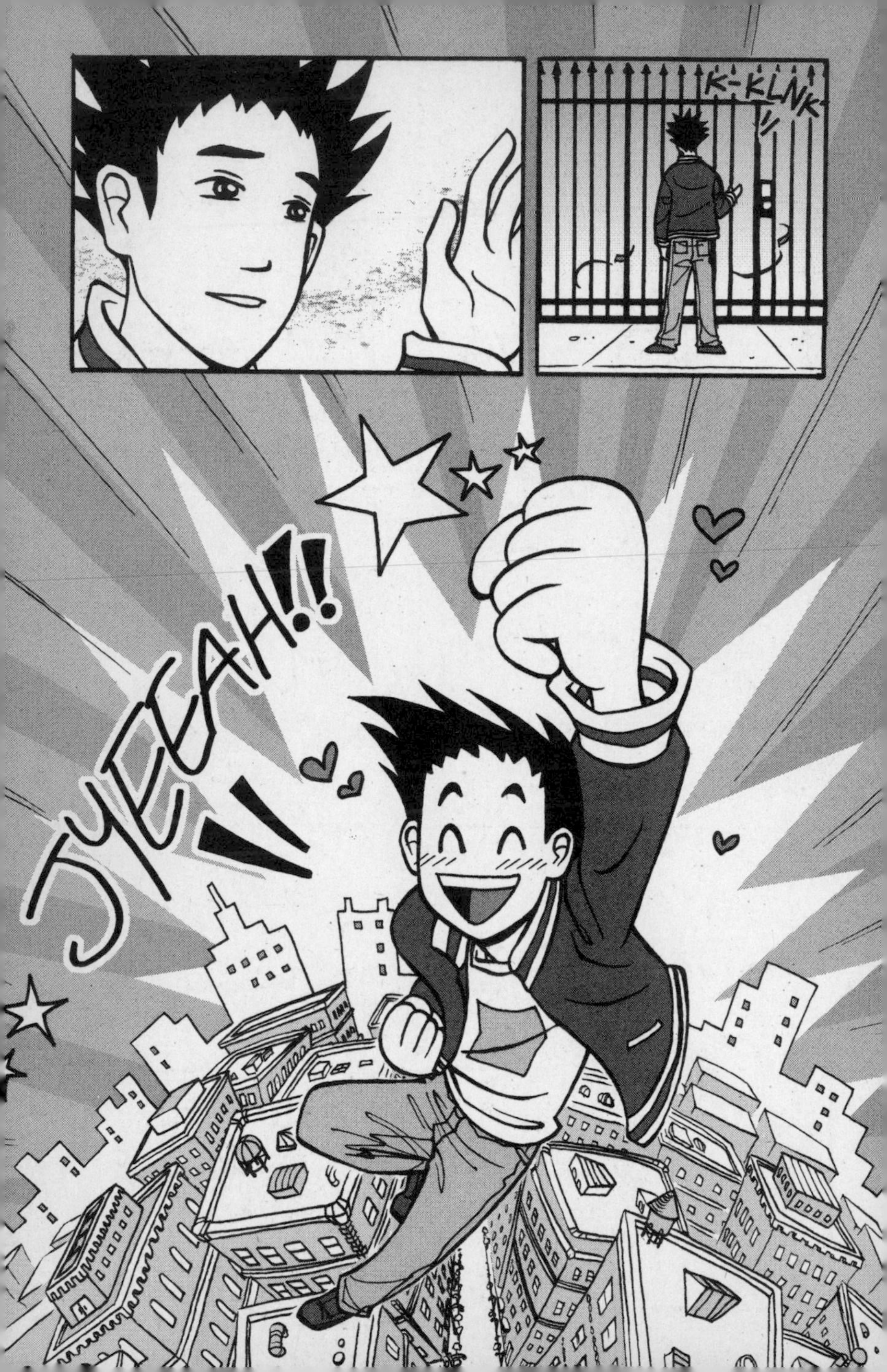
K-KLNK
JYEEAH!!

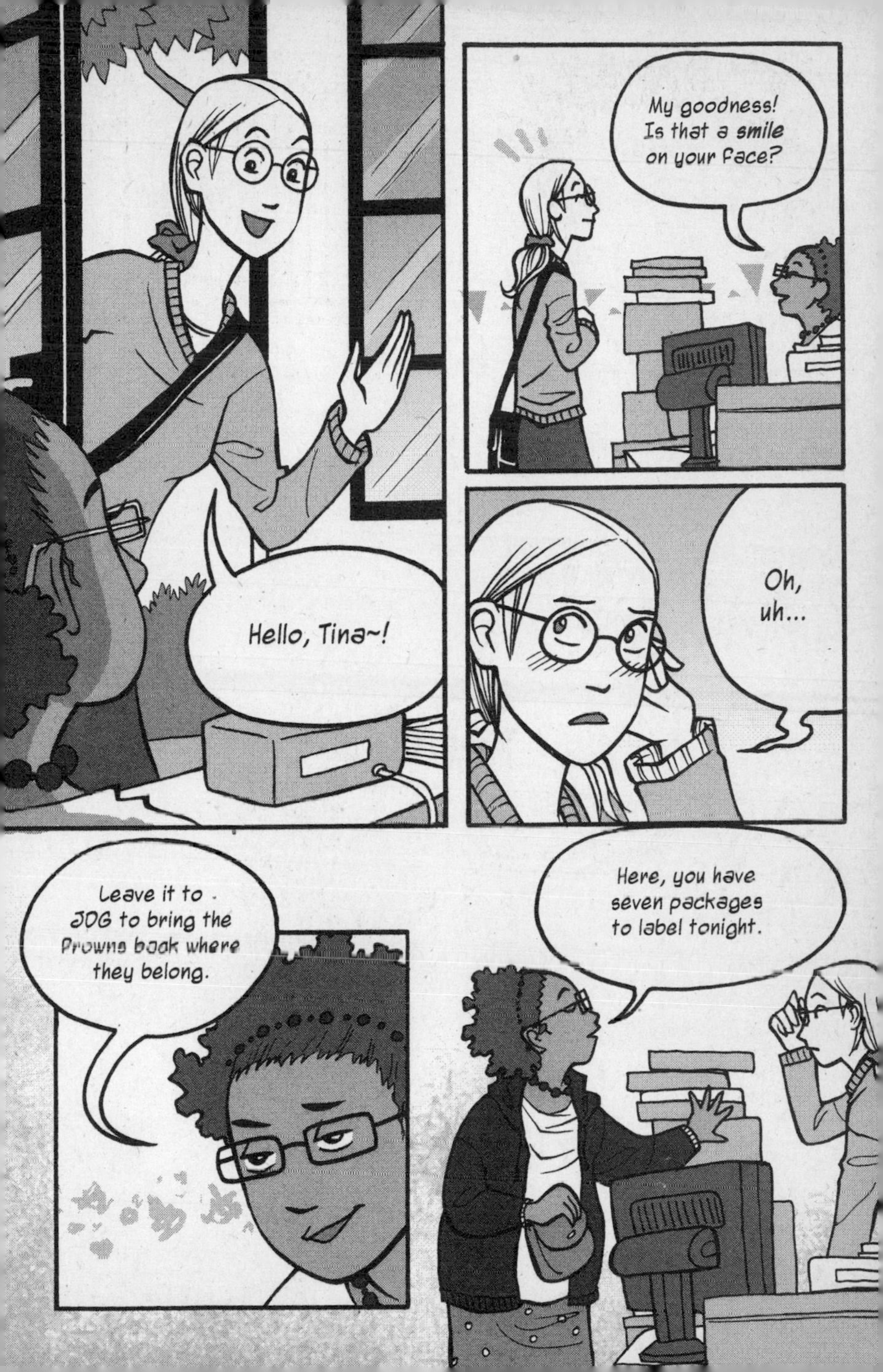
Hello, Tina~!
My goodness! Is that a *smile* on your face?
Oh, uh...
Leave it to JDG to bring the Prowns back where they belong.
Here, you have seven packages to label tonight.

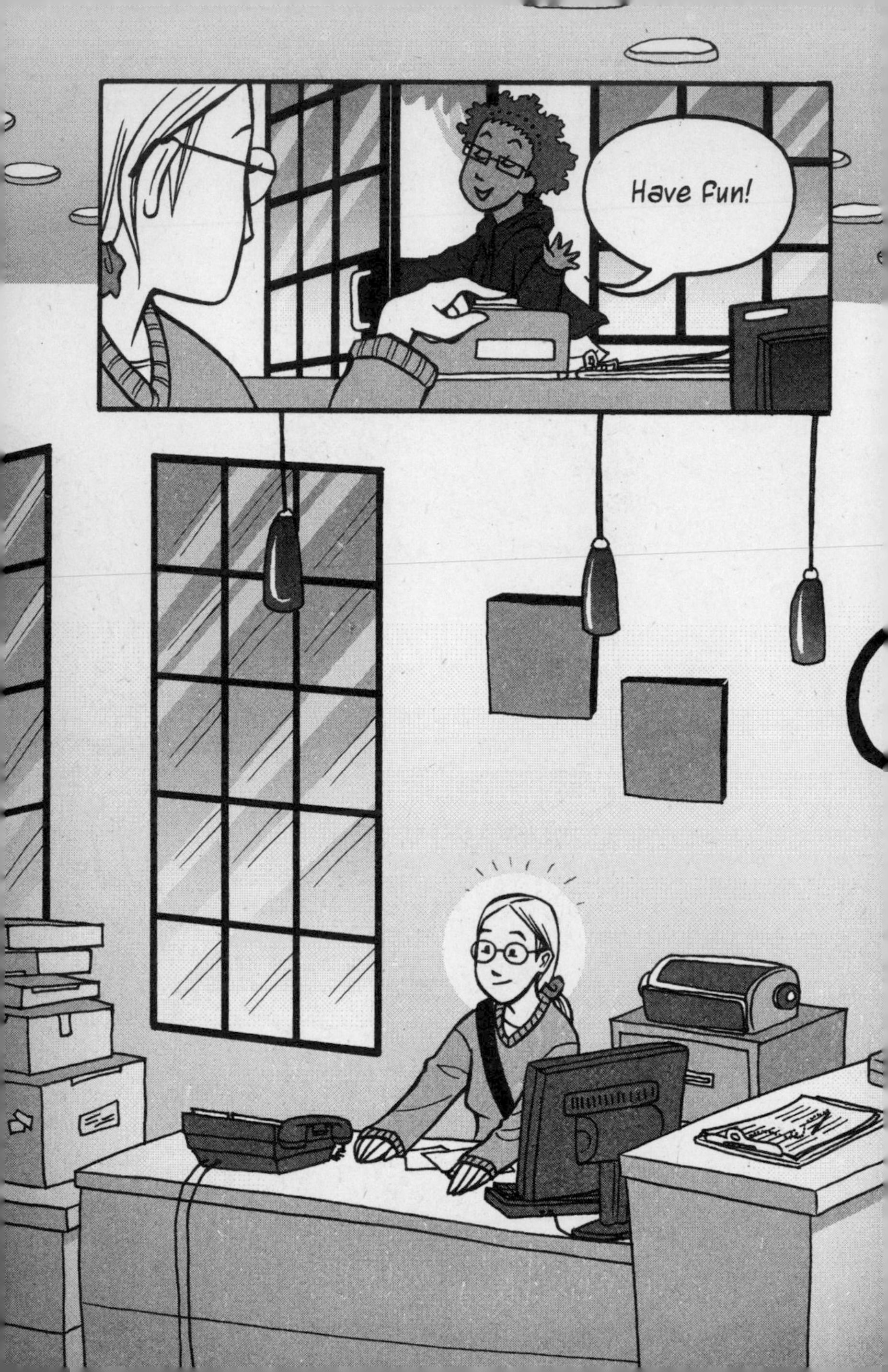
Have fun!

CHAPTER FIVE

Teaches A Lesson

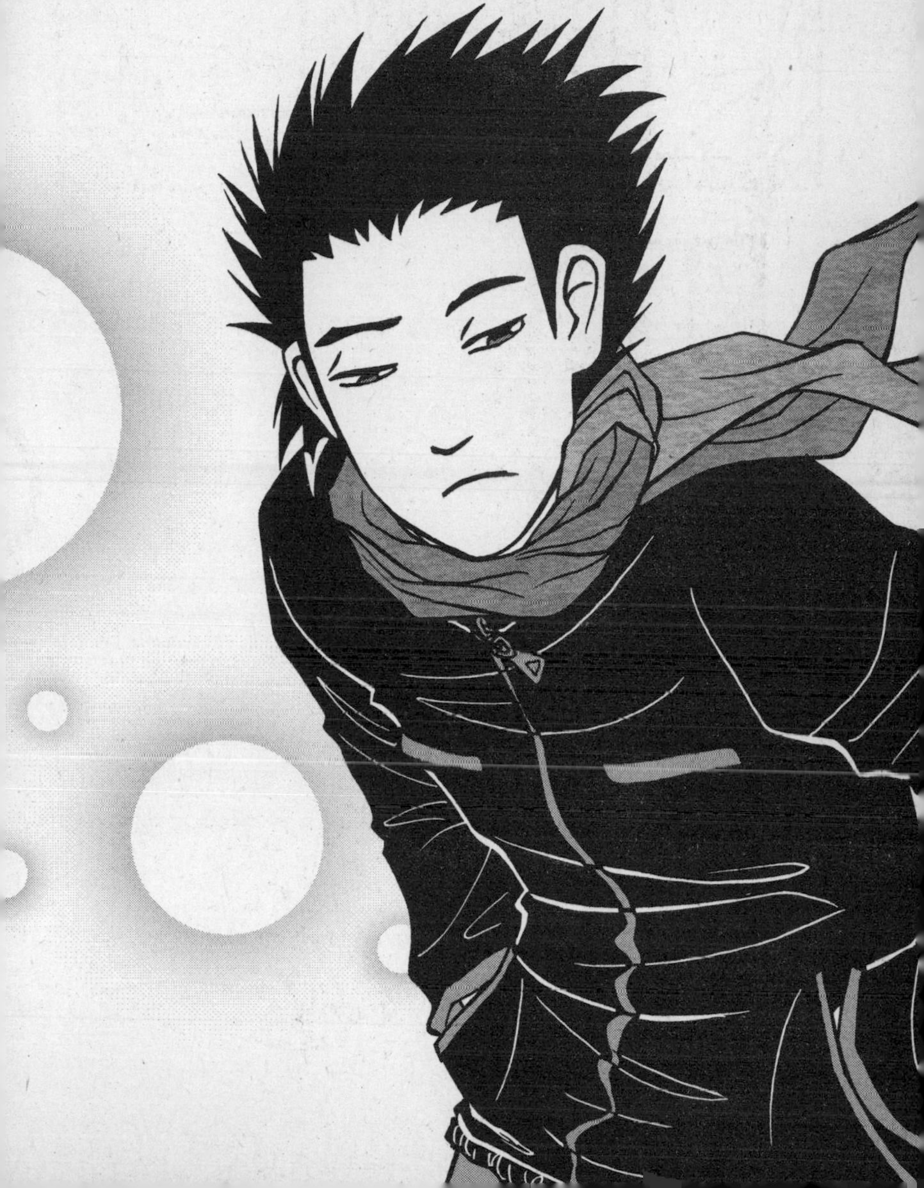

Being around
you made me
feel special...

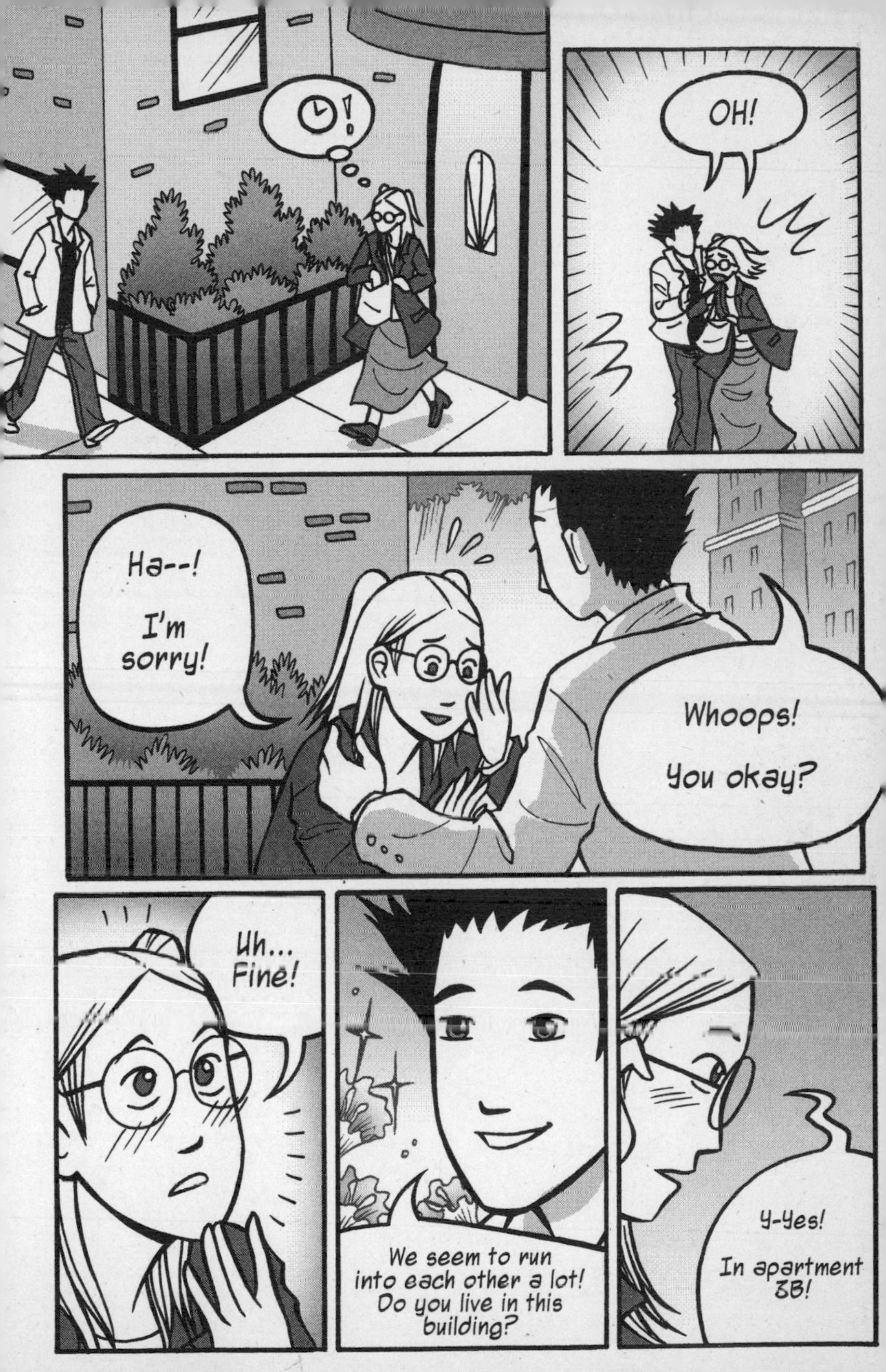
OH!
Ha--! I'm sorry!
Whoops! You okay?
Uh... Fine!
We seem to run into each other a lot! Do you live in this building?
Y-Yes! In apartment 3B!

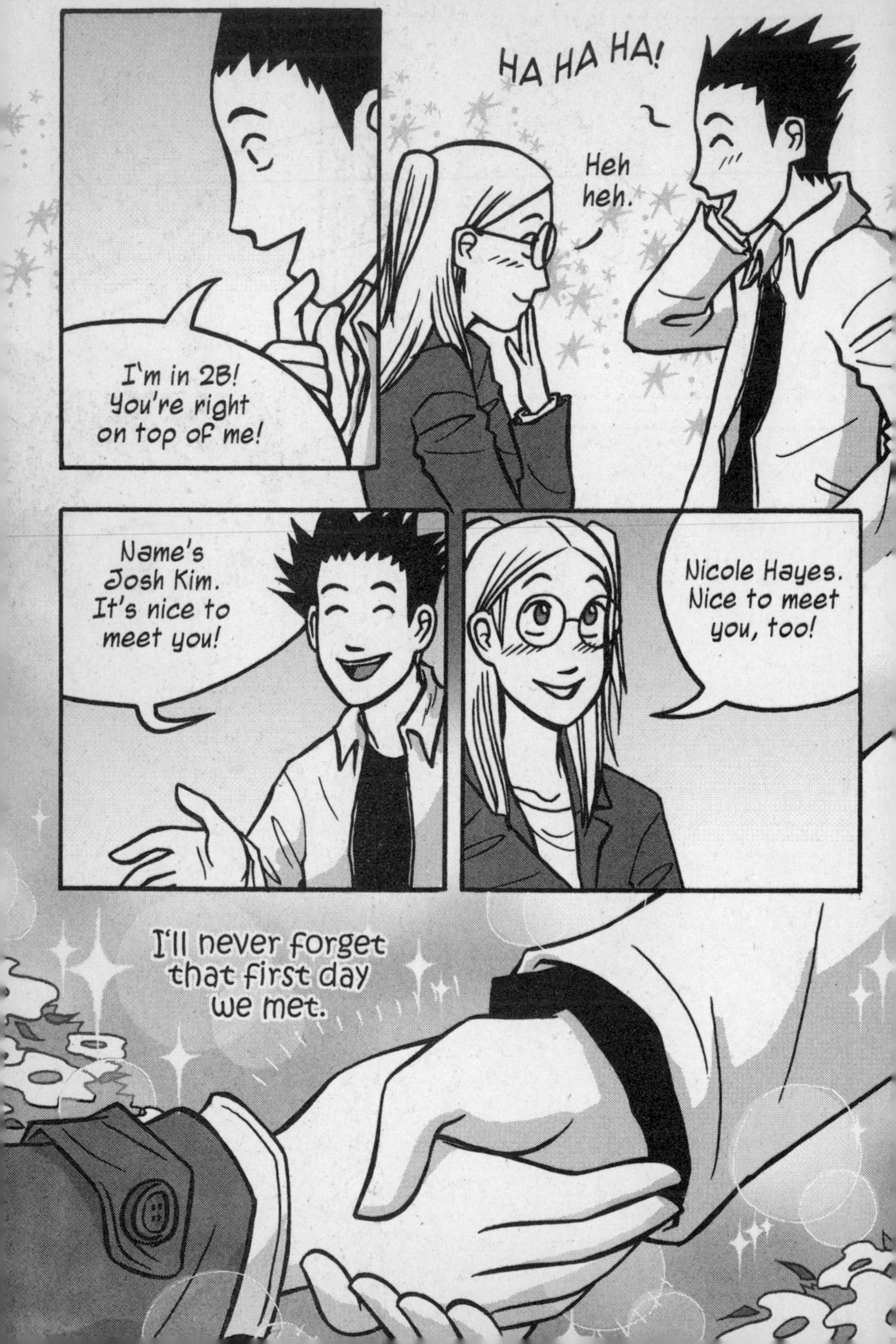

I'm in 2B! You're right on top of me!
HA HA HA!
Heh heh.
Name's Josh Kim. It's nice to meet you!
Nicole Hayes. Nice to meet you, too!
I'll never forget that first day we met.

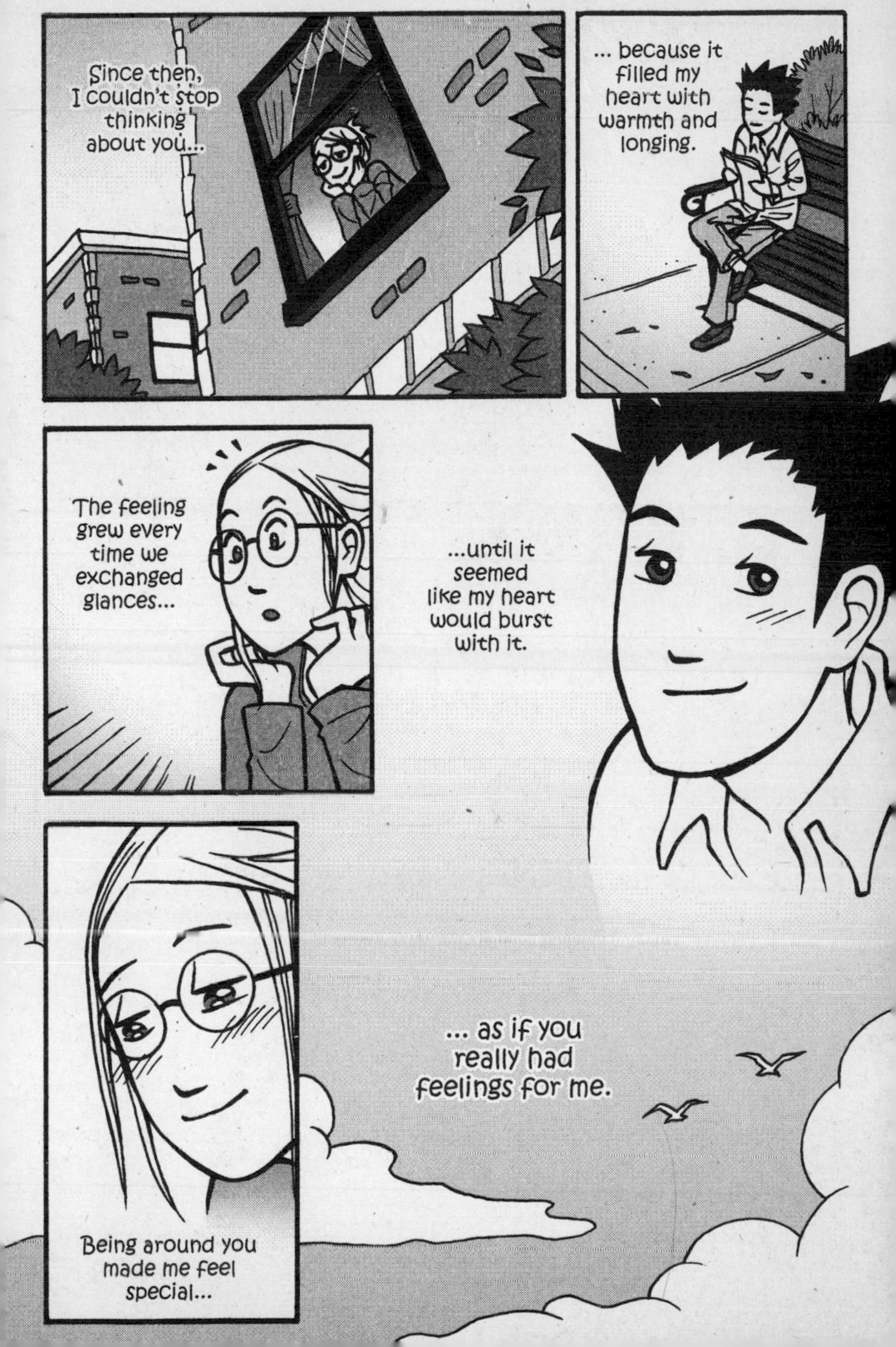
Since then, I couldn't stop thinking about you...
... because it filled my heart with warmth and longing.
The feeling grew every time we exchanged glances...
...until it seemed like my heart would burst with it.
Being around you made me feel special...
... as if you really had feelings for me.

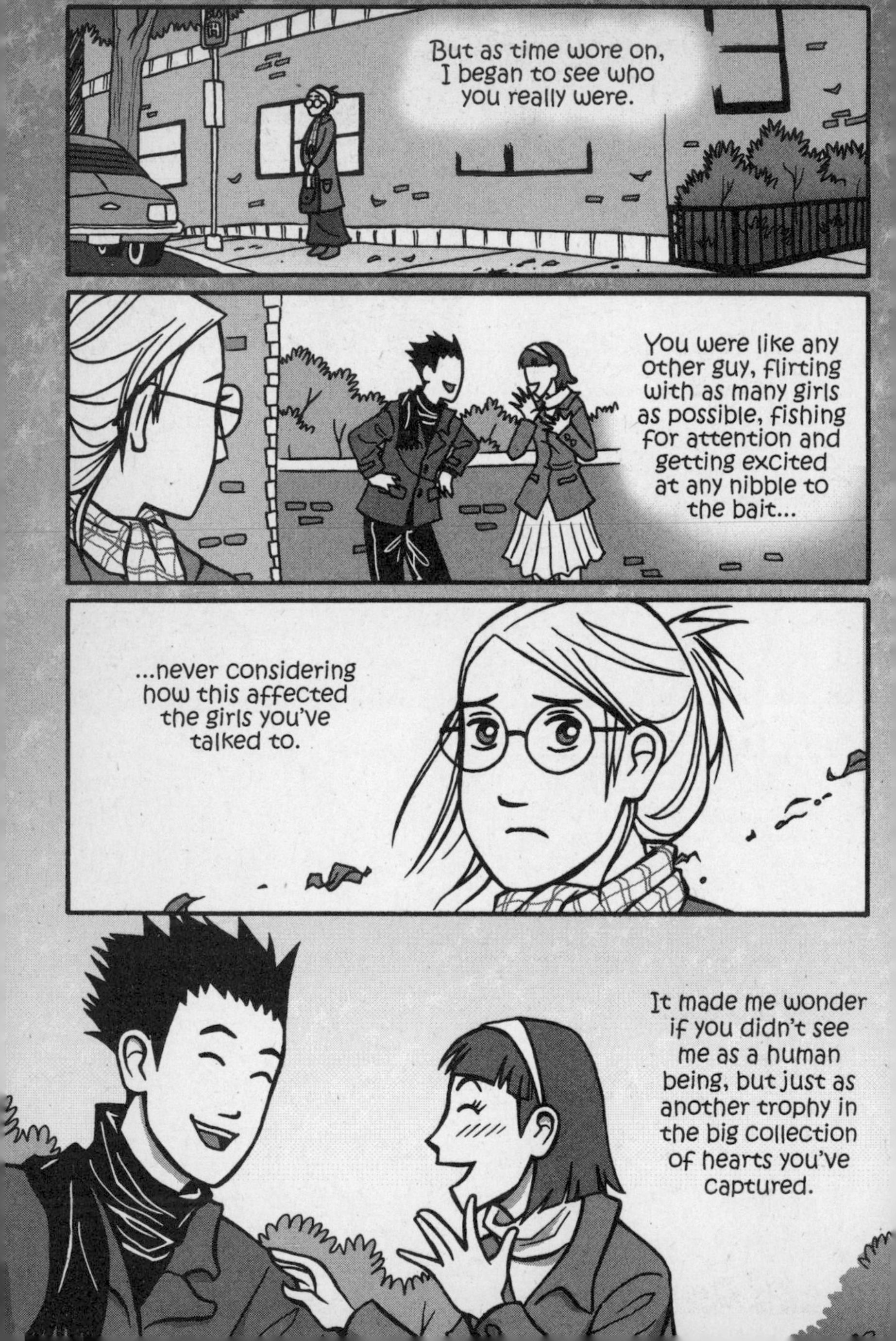
But as time wore on, I began to see who you really were.
You were like any other guy, flirting with as many girls as possible, fishing for attention and getting excited at any nibble to the bait...
...never considering how this affected the girls you've talked to.
It made me wonder if you didn't see me as a human being, but just as another trophy in the big collection of hearts you've captured.

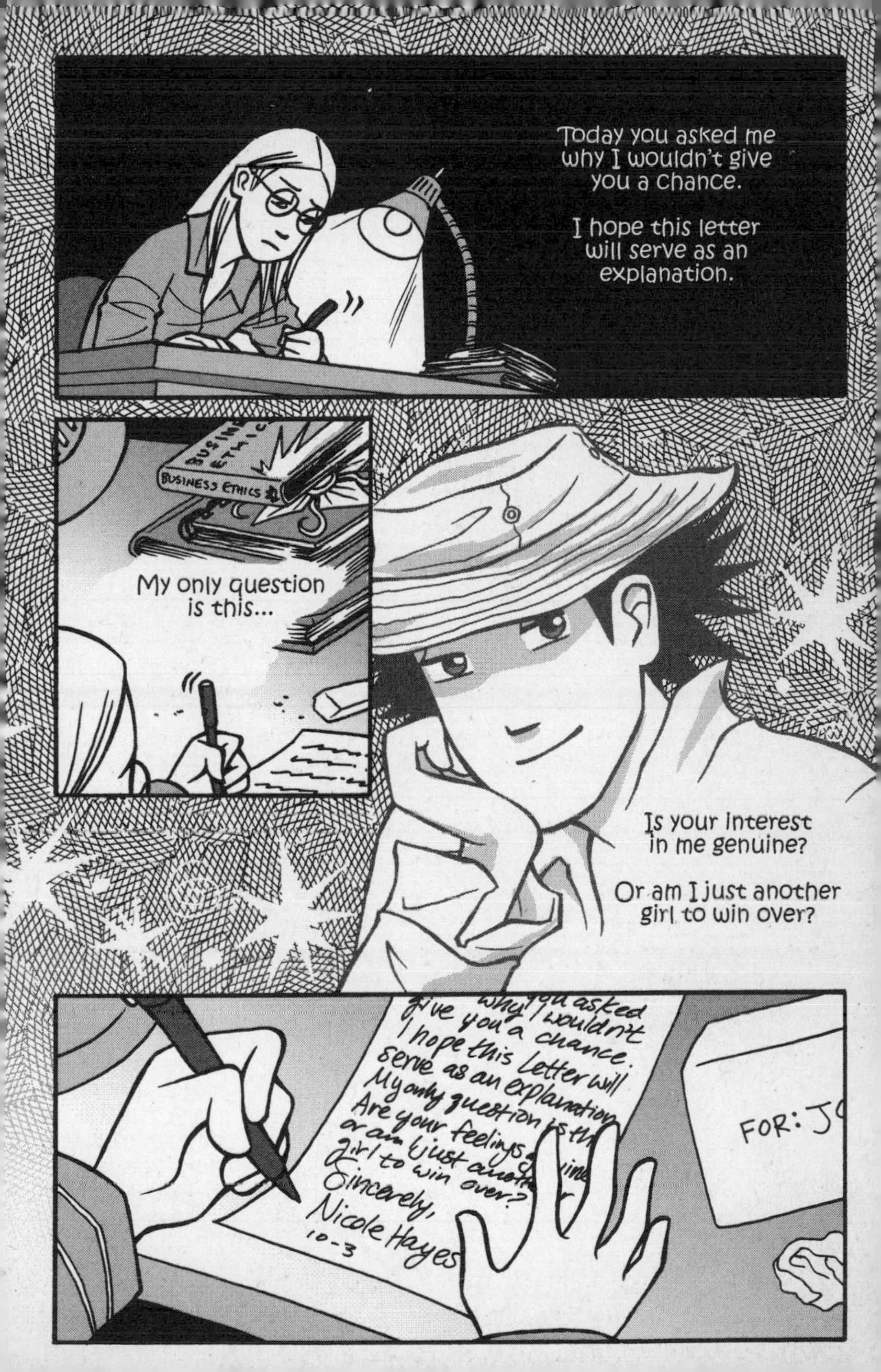
Today you asked me why I wouldn't give you a chance.
I hope this letter will serve as an explanation.
BUSINESS ETHICS
My only question is this...
Is your interest in me genuine?
Or am I just another girl to win over?
why you asked
I wouldn't
give you a chance.
I hope this letter will
serve as an explanation
My only question is th
Are your feelings
or am I just anoth
girl to win over?
Sincerely,
Nicole Hayes
10-3
FOR: J

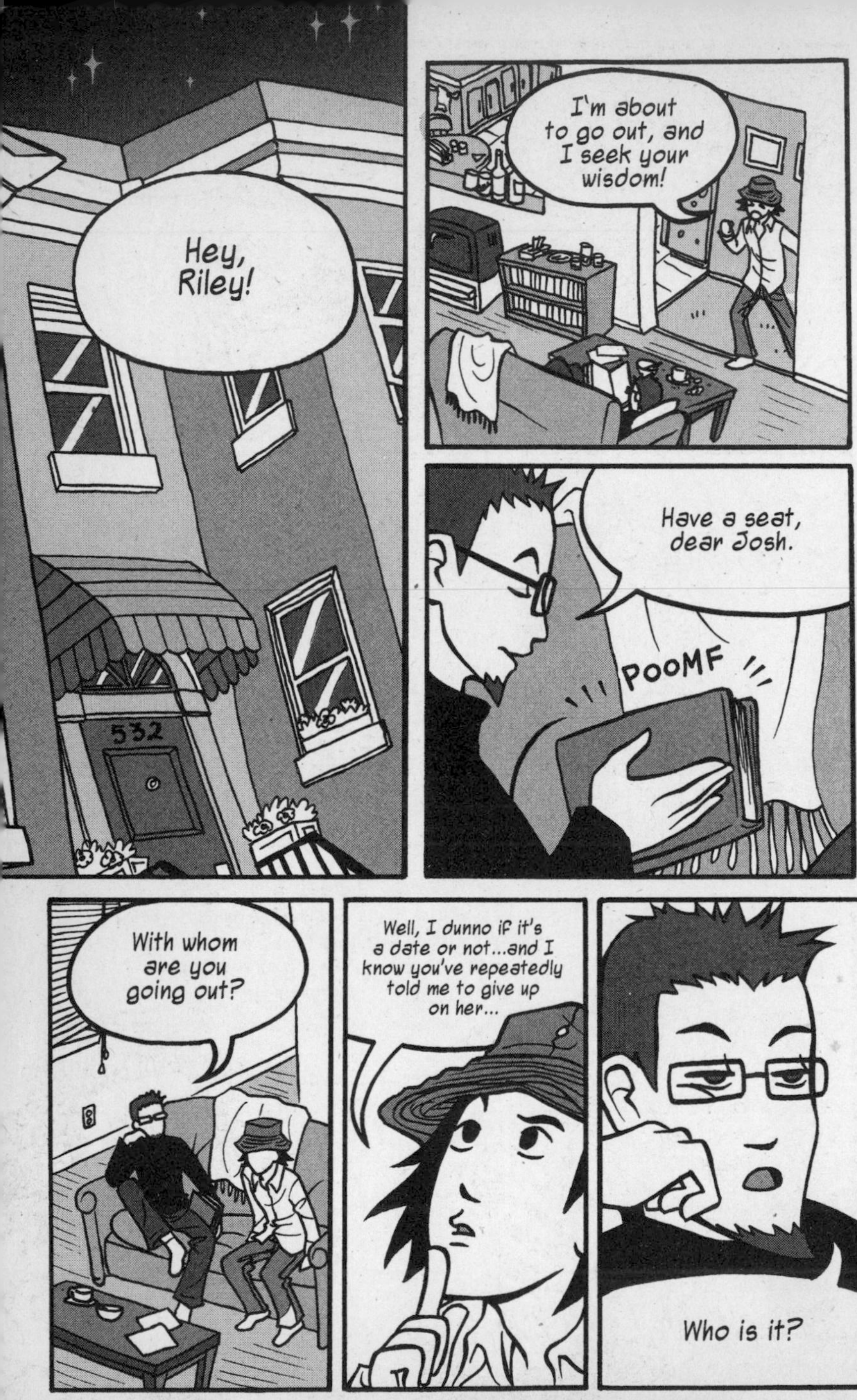
Hey, Riley!
532
I'm about to go out, and I seek your wisdom!
Have a seat, dear Josh.
POOMF
With whom are you going out?
Well, I dunno if it's a date or not...and I know you've repeatedly told me to give up on her...
Who is it?

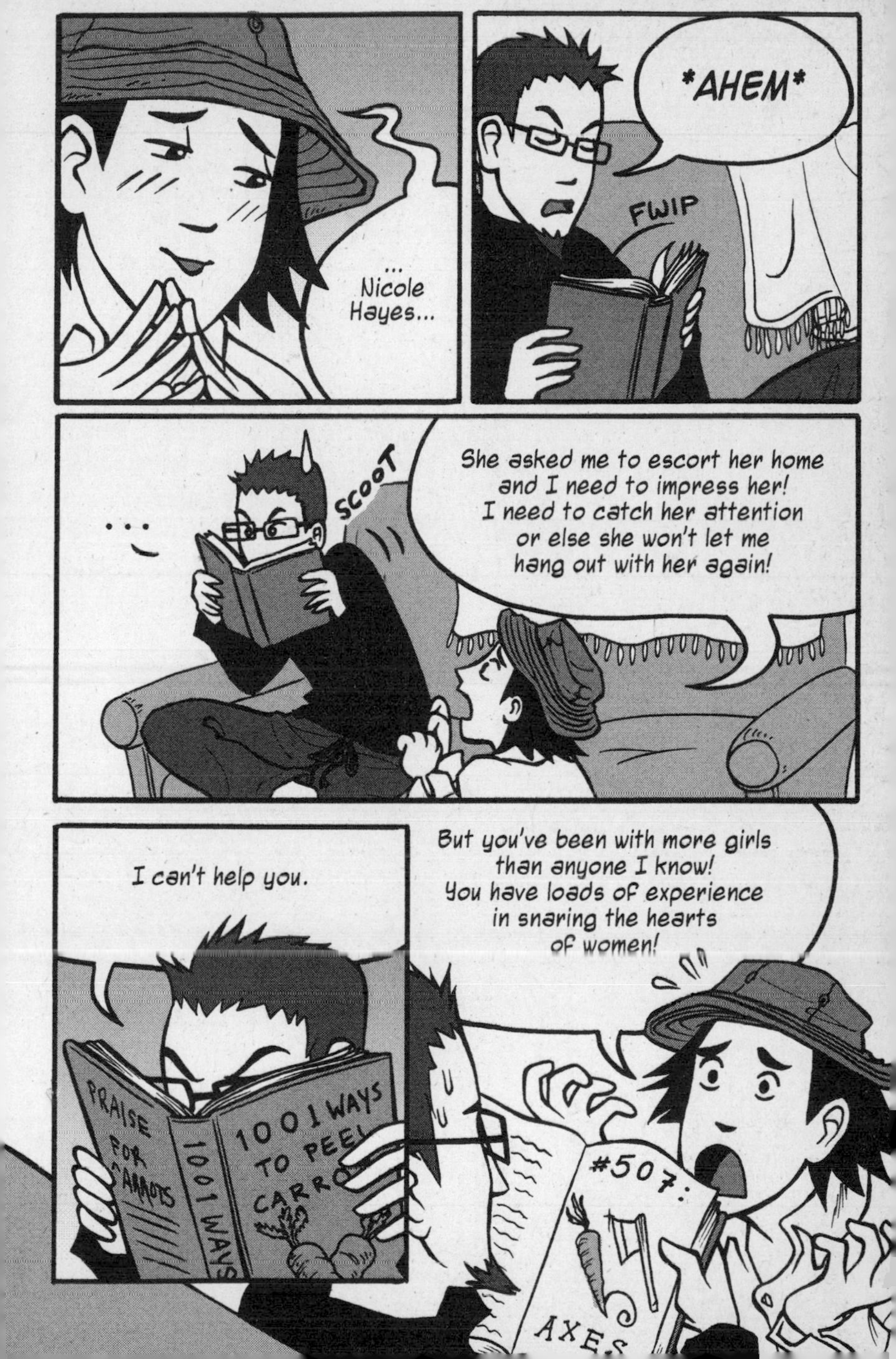

... Nicole Hayes...
AHEM
FWIP
SCOOT
...
She asked me to escort her home and I need to impress her! I need to catch her attention or else she won't let me hang out with her again!
I can't help you.
But you've been with more girls than anyone I know! You have loads of experience in snaring the hearts of women!
PRAISE FOR CARROTS
1001 WAYS
1001 WAYS TO PEEL CARRO
#507:
AXES

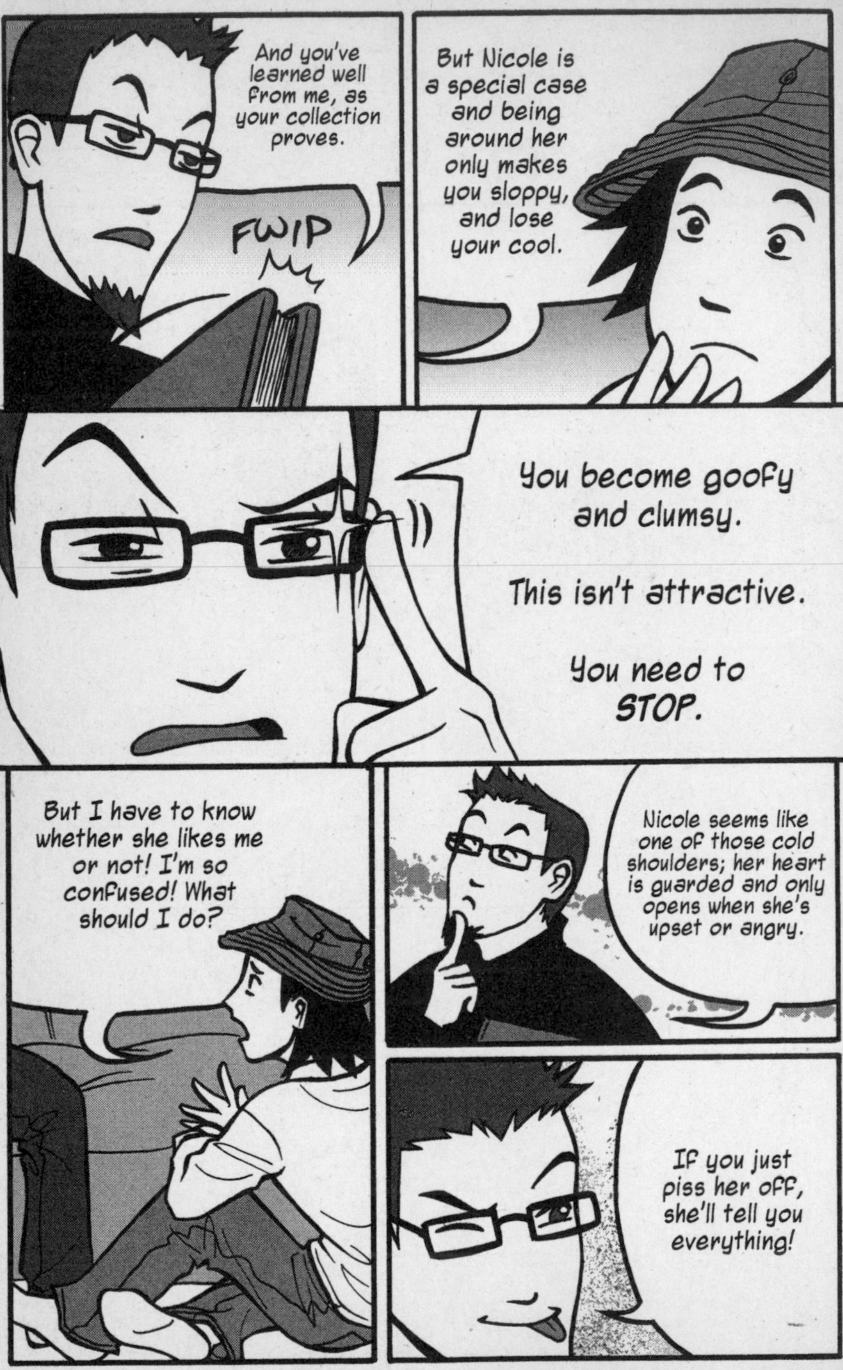
And you've learned well from me, as your collection proves.
FWIP
But Nicole is a special case and being around her only makes you sloppy, and lose your cool.
You become goofy and clumsy.
This isn't attractive.
You need to STOP.
But I have to know whether she likes me or not! I'm so confused! What should I do?
Nicole seems like one of those cold shoulders; her heart is guarded and only opens when she's upset or angry.
If you just piss her off, she'll tell you everything!

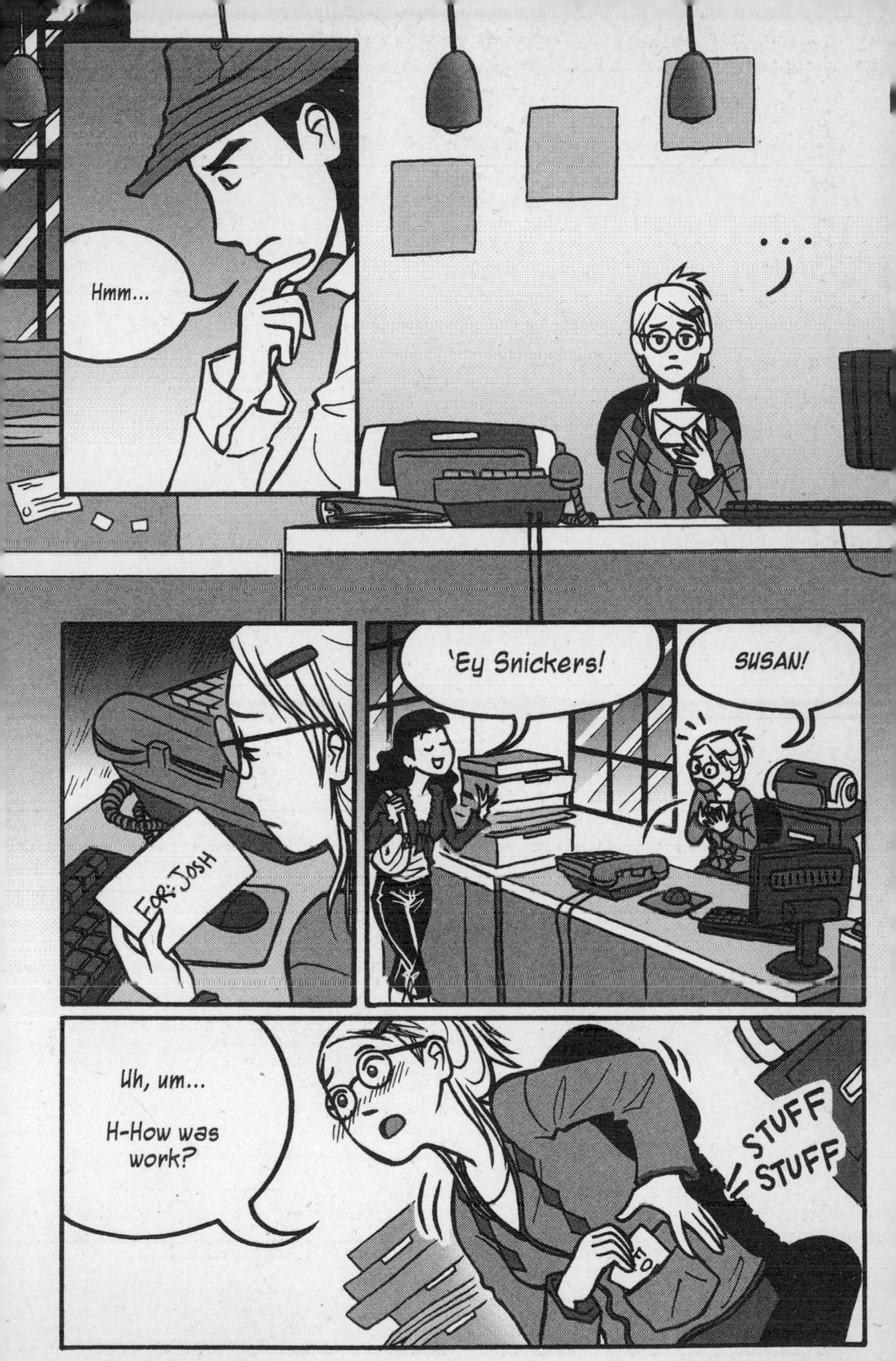
Hmm...
...
FOR: JOSH
'Ey Snickers!
SUSAN!
Uh, um...
H-How was work?
STUFF STUFF

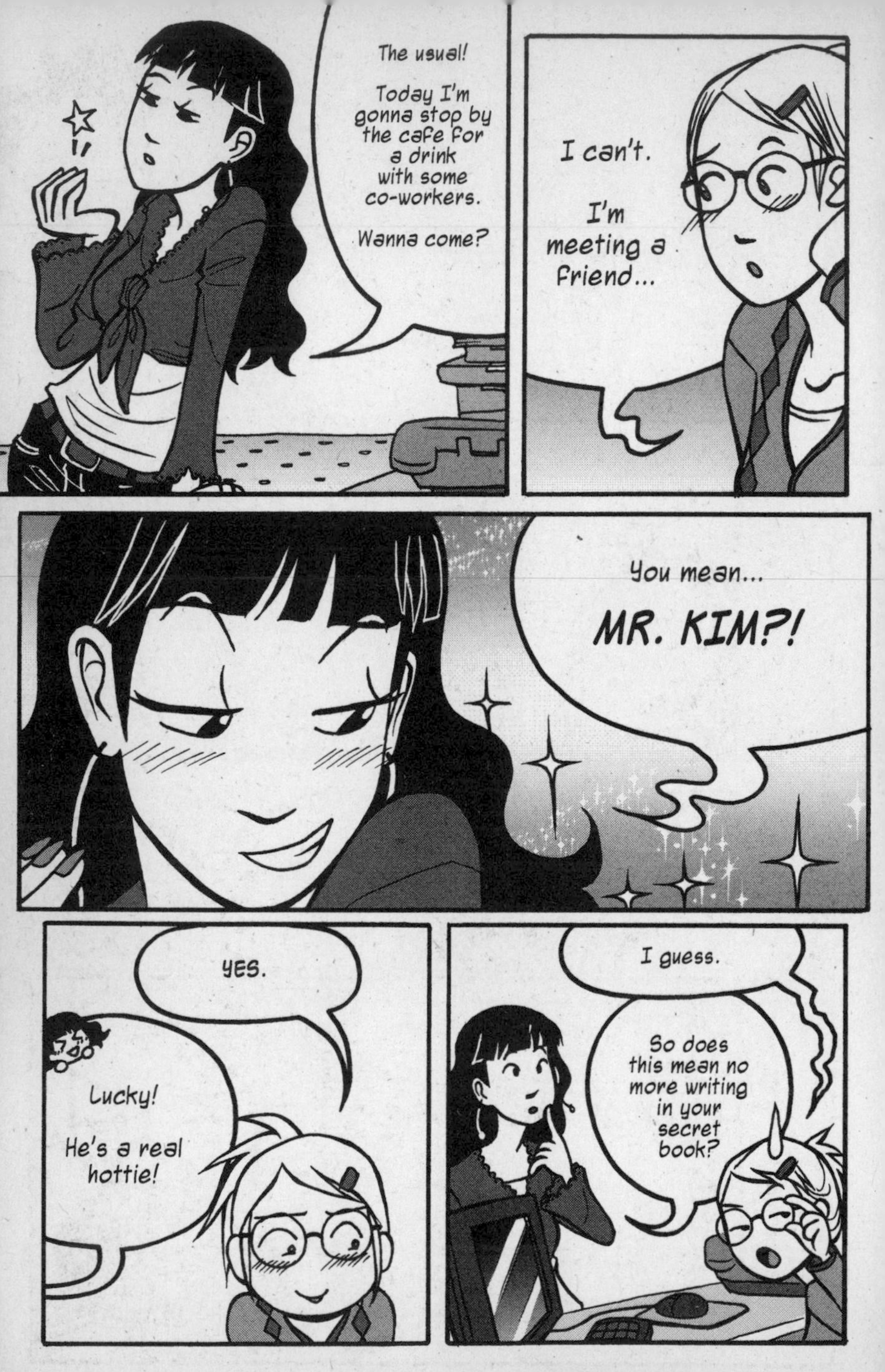
The usual!
Today I'm gonna stop by the cafe for a drink with some co-workers.
Wanna come?
I can't.
I'm meeting a friend...
You mean...
MR. KIM?!
YES.
Lucky!
He's a real hottie!
I guess.
So does this mean no more writing in your secret book?

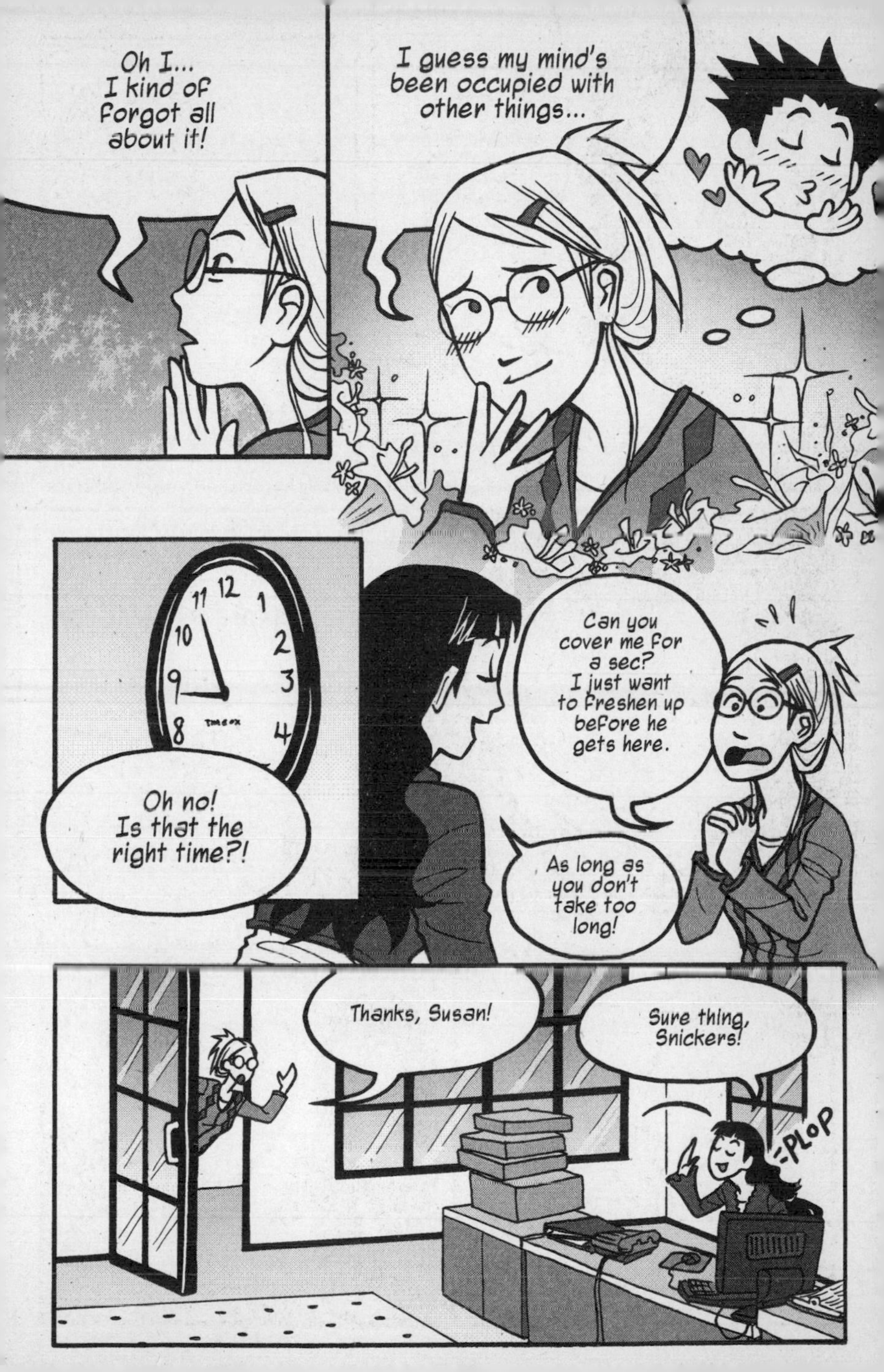
Oh I... I kind of forgot all about it!
I guess my mind's been occupied with other things...
Oh no! Is that the right time?!
Can you cover me for a sec? I just want to freshen up before he gets here.
As long as you don't take too long!
Thanks, Susan!
Sure thing, Snickers!
PLOP

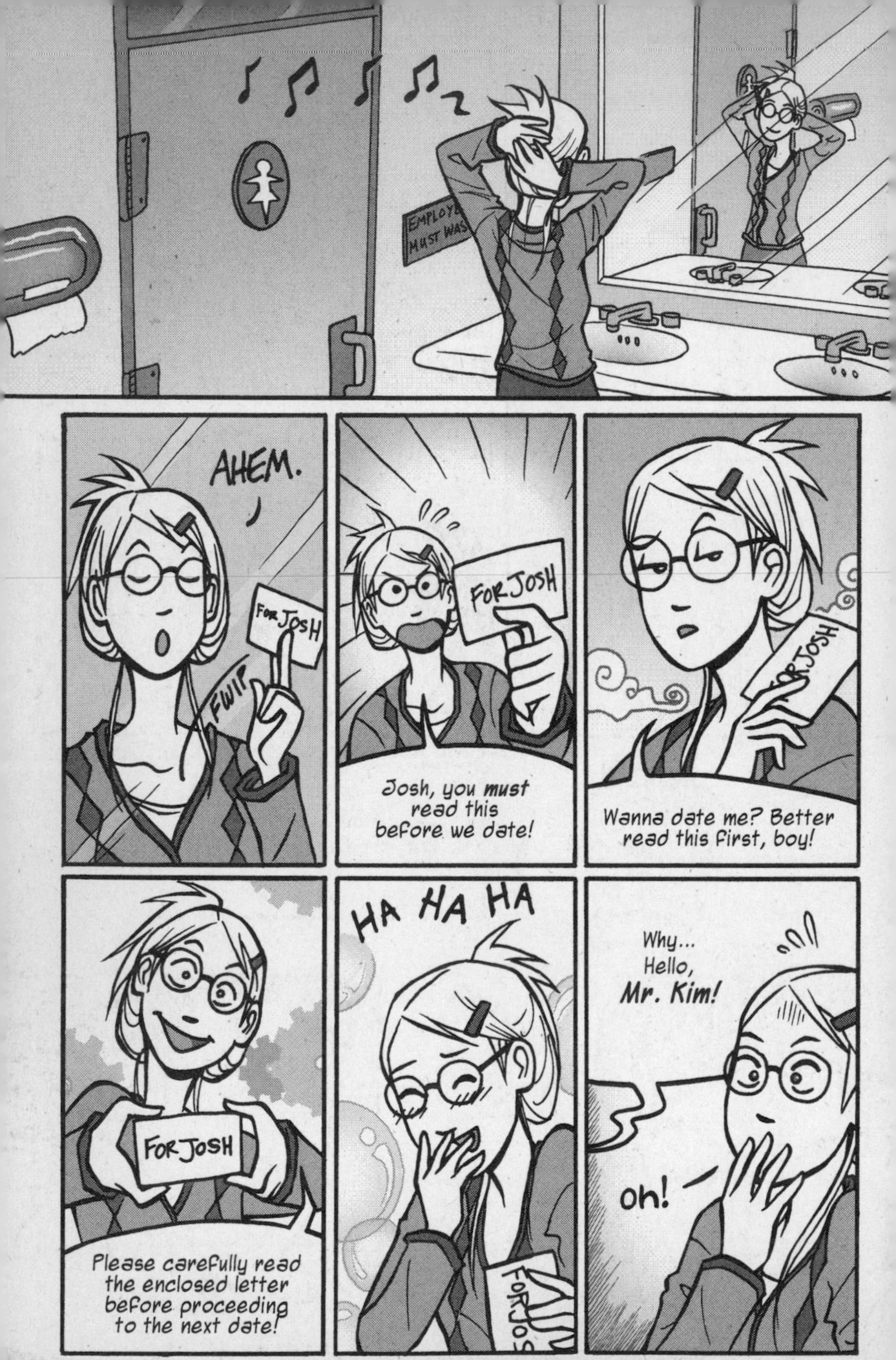
AHEM.
FOR JOSH
FWIP
FOR JOSH
Josh, you **must** read this before we date!
FOR JOSH
Wanna date me? Better read this first, boy!
FOR JOSH
Please carefully read the enclosed letter before proceeding to the next date!
HA HA HA
Why... Hello, **Mr. Kim!**
Oh!

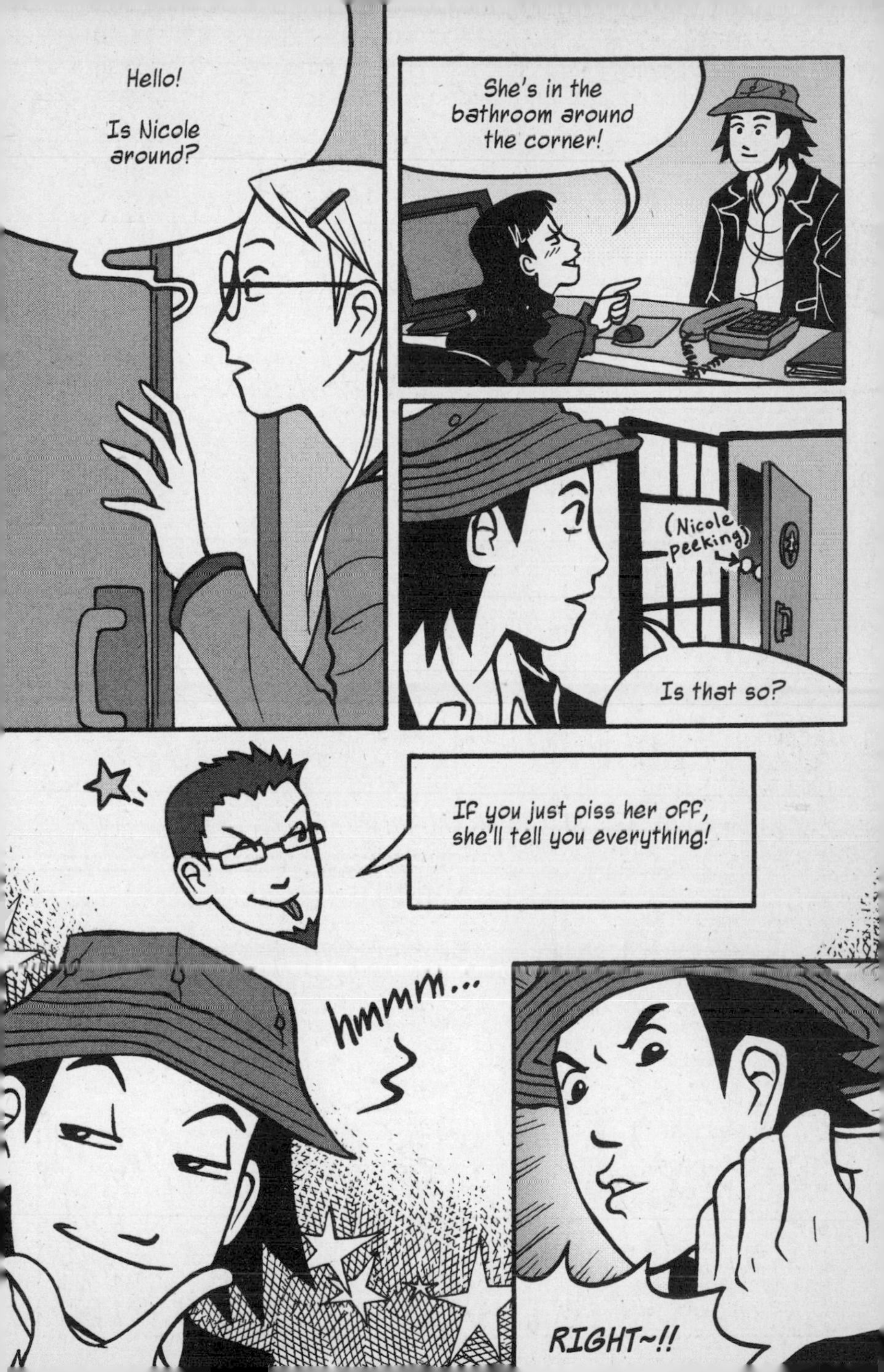
Hello!
Is Nicole around?
She's in the bathroom around the corner!
(Nicole peeking)
Is that so?
If you just piss her off, she'll tell you everything!
hmmm...
RIGHT~!!

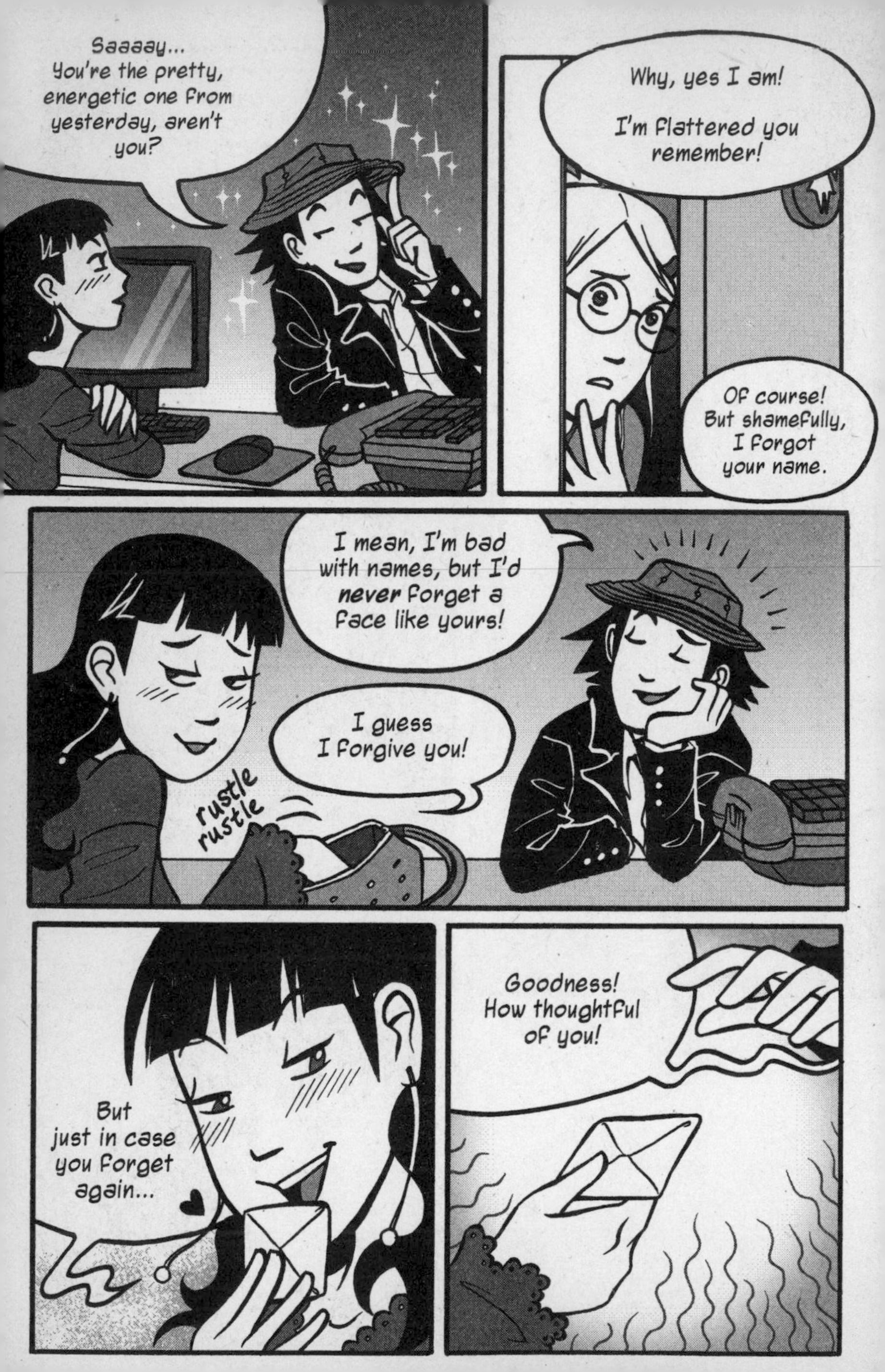
Saaaay... You're the pretty, energetic one from yesterday, aren't you?
Why, yes I am!
I'm flattered you remember!
Of course! But shamefully, I forgot your name.
I mean, I'm bad with names, but I'd **never** forget a face like yours!
I guess I forgive you!
rustle rustle
But just in case you forget again...
Goodness! How thoughtful of you!

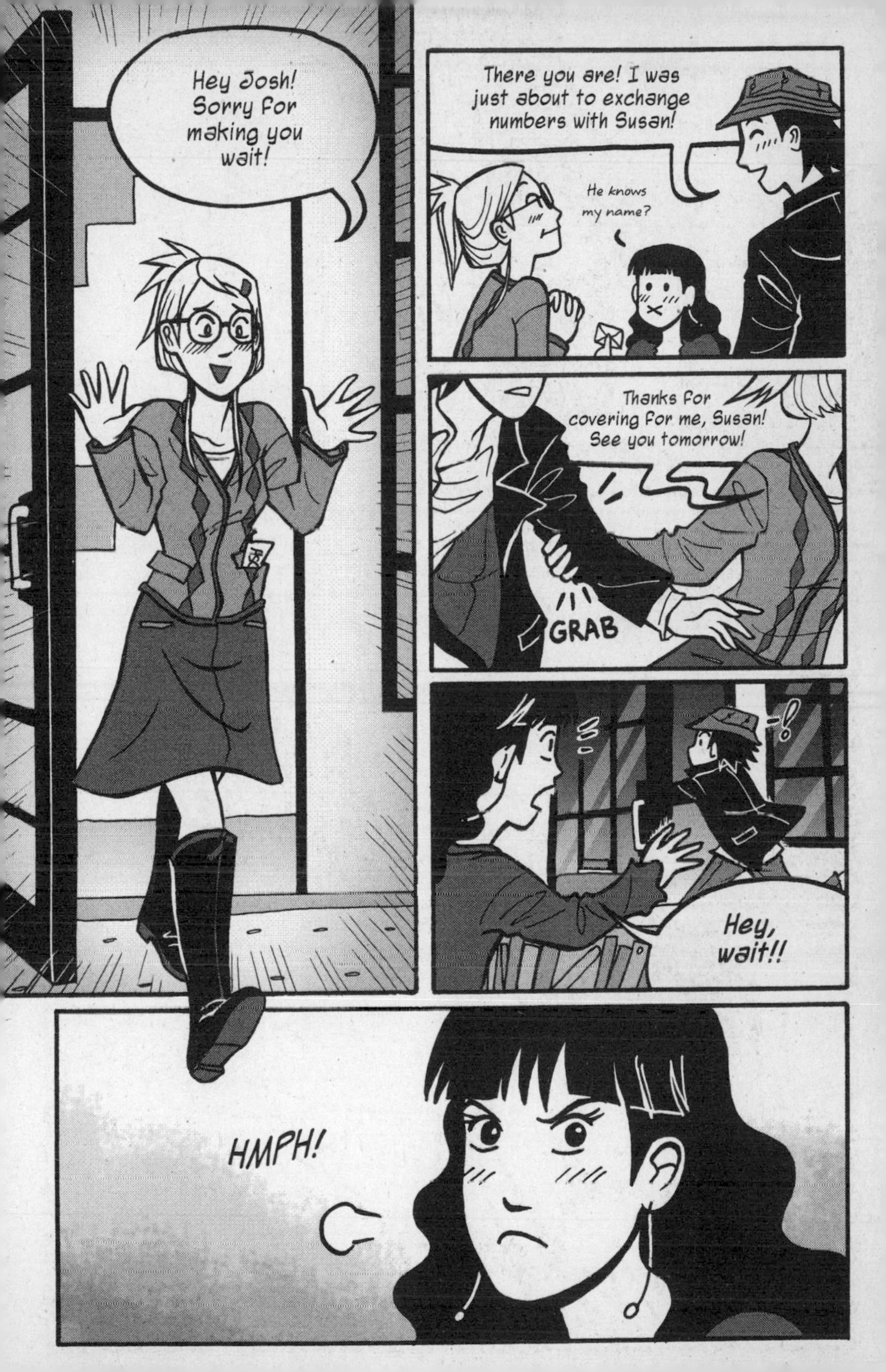
Hey Josh! Sorry for making you wait!
There you are! I was just about to exchange numbers with Susan!
He knows my name?
Thanks for covering for me, Susan! See you tomorrow!
GRAB
Hey, wait!!
HMPH!

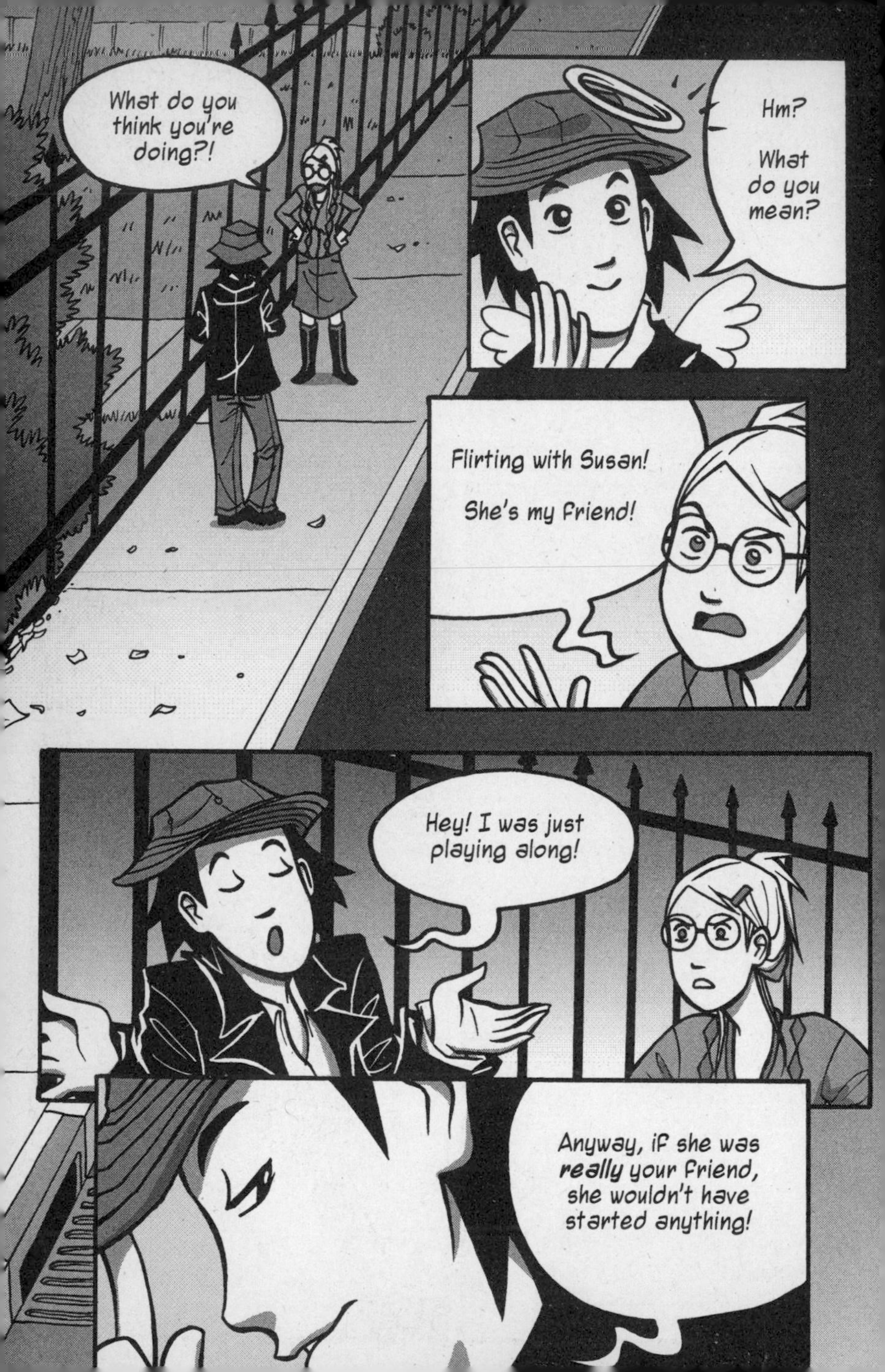

What do you think you're doing?!
Hm? What do you mean?
Flirting with Susan! She's my friend!
Hey! I was just playing along!
Anyway, if she was *really* your friend, she wouldn't have started anything!

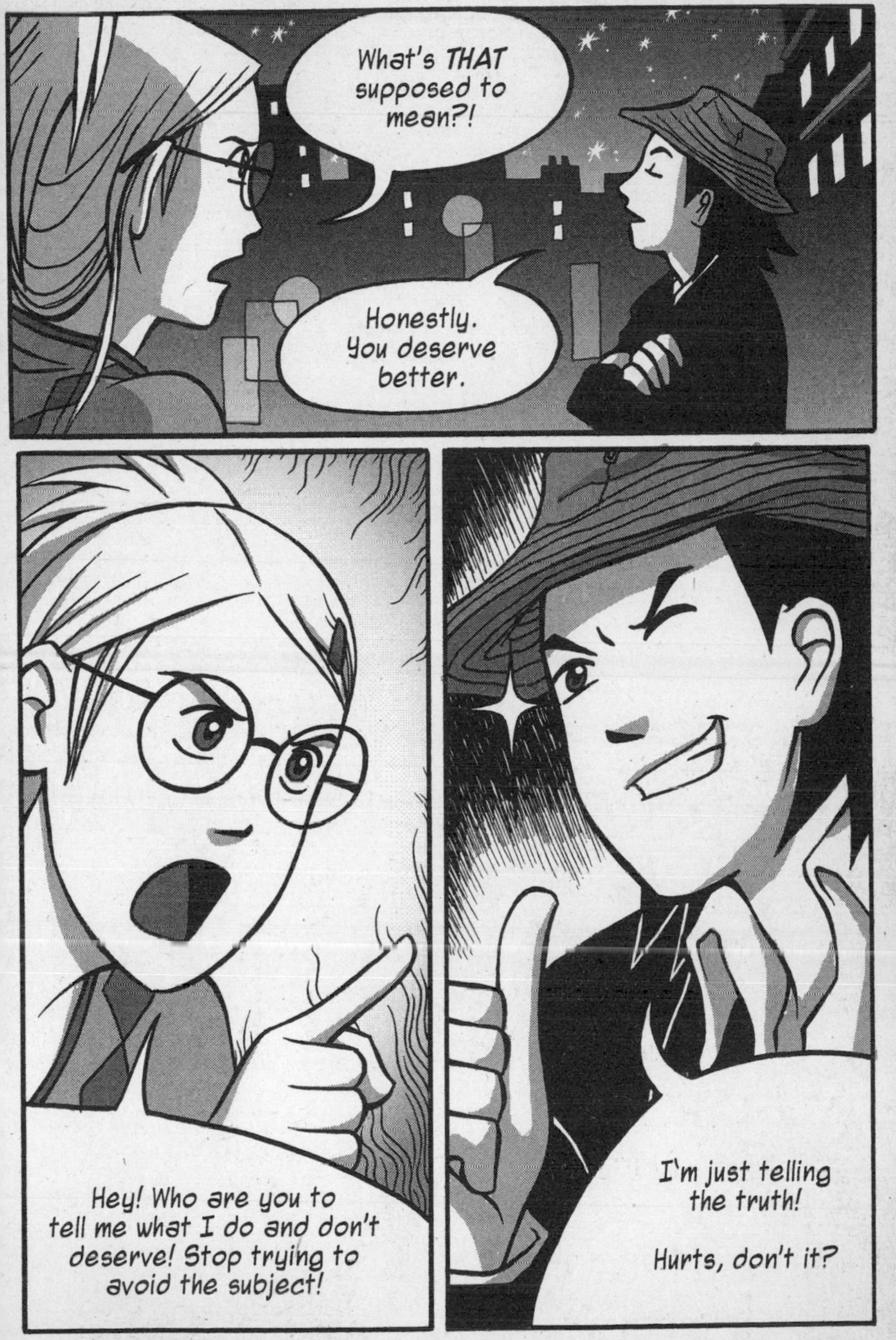
What's THAT supposed to mean?!
Honestly. You deserve better.
Hey! Who are you to tell me what I do and don't deserve! Stop trying to avoid the subject!
I'm just telling the truth!
Hurts, don't it?

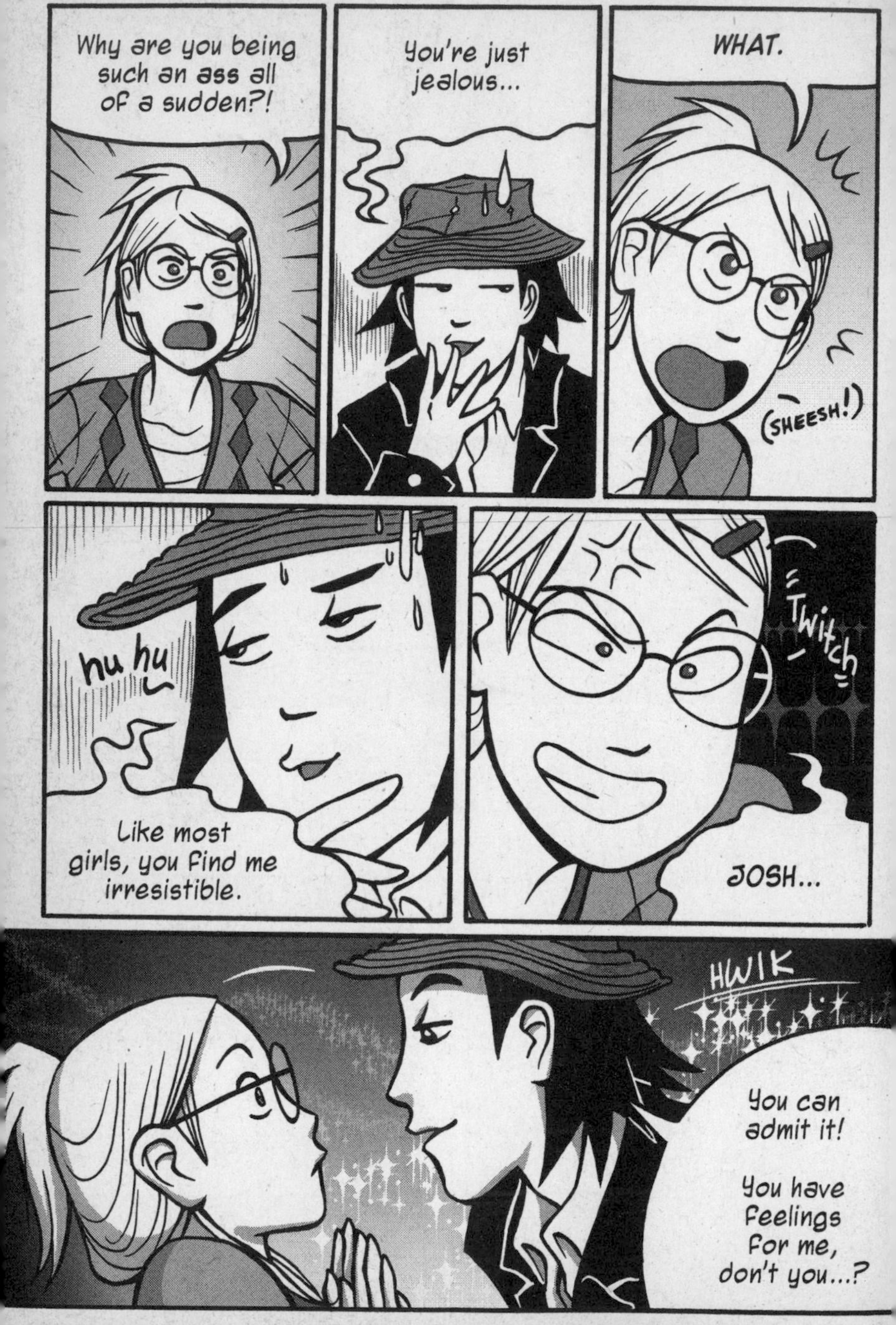

Why are you being such an ass all of a sudden?!
You're just jealous...
WHAT.
(SHEESH!)
hu hu
Like most girls, you find me irresistible.
TWITCH
JOSH...
HWIK
You can admit it!
You have feelings for me, don't you...?

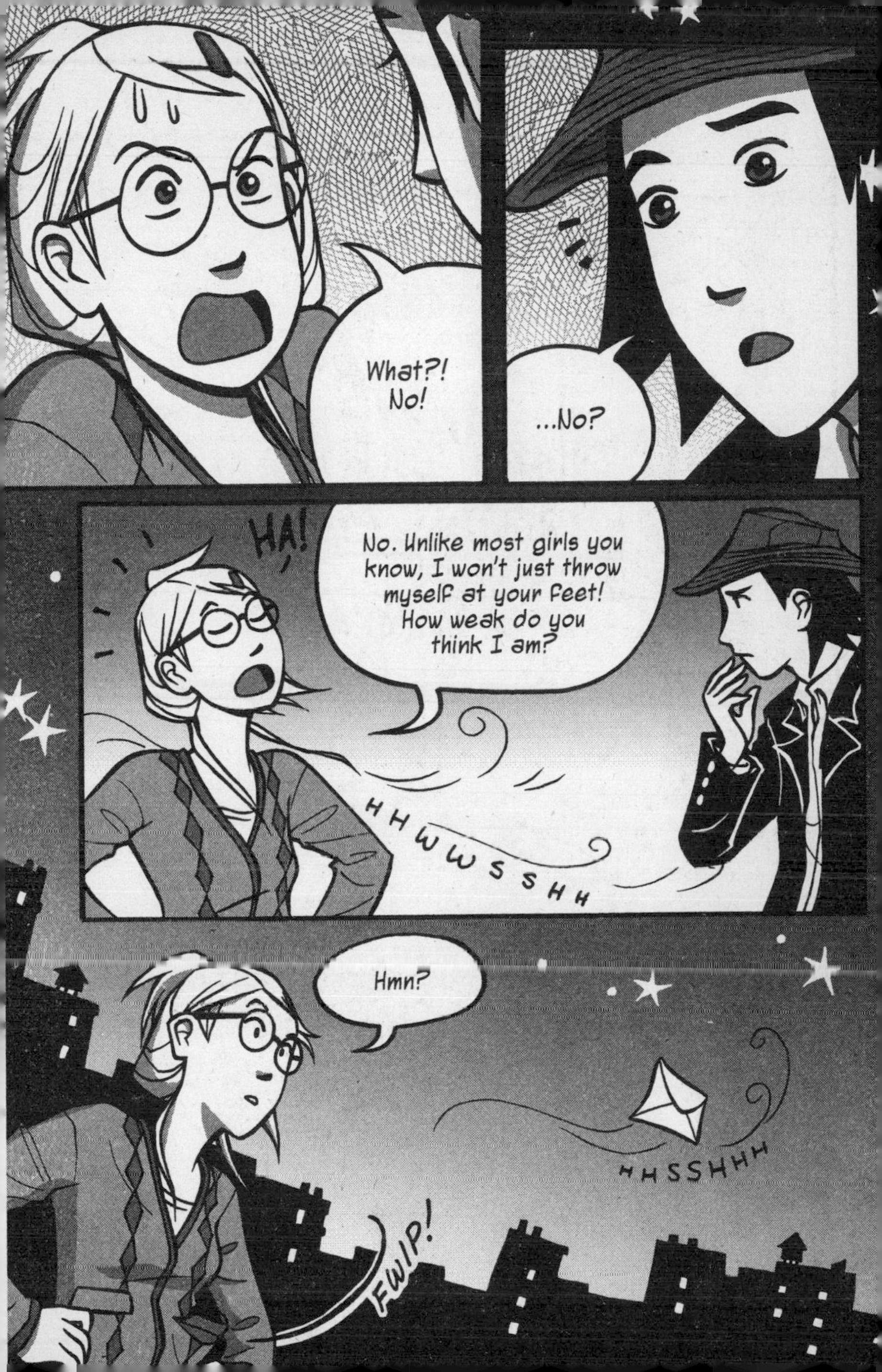
What?! No!
...No?
HA!
No. Unlike most girls you know, I won't just throw myself at your feet! How weak do you think I am?
HHWWSSHH
Hmn?
HHSSHHH
FWIP!

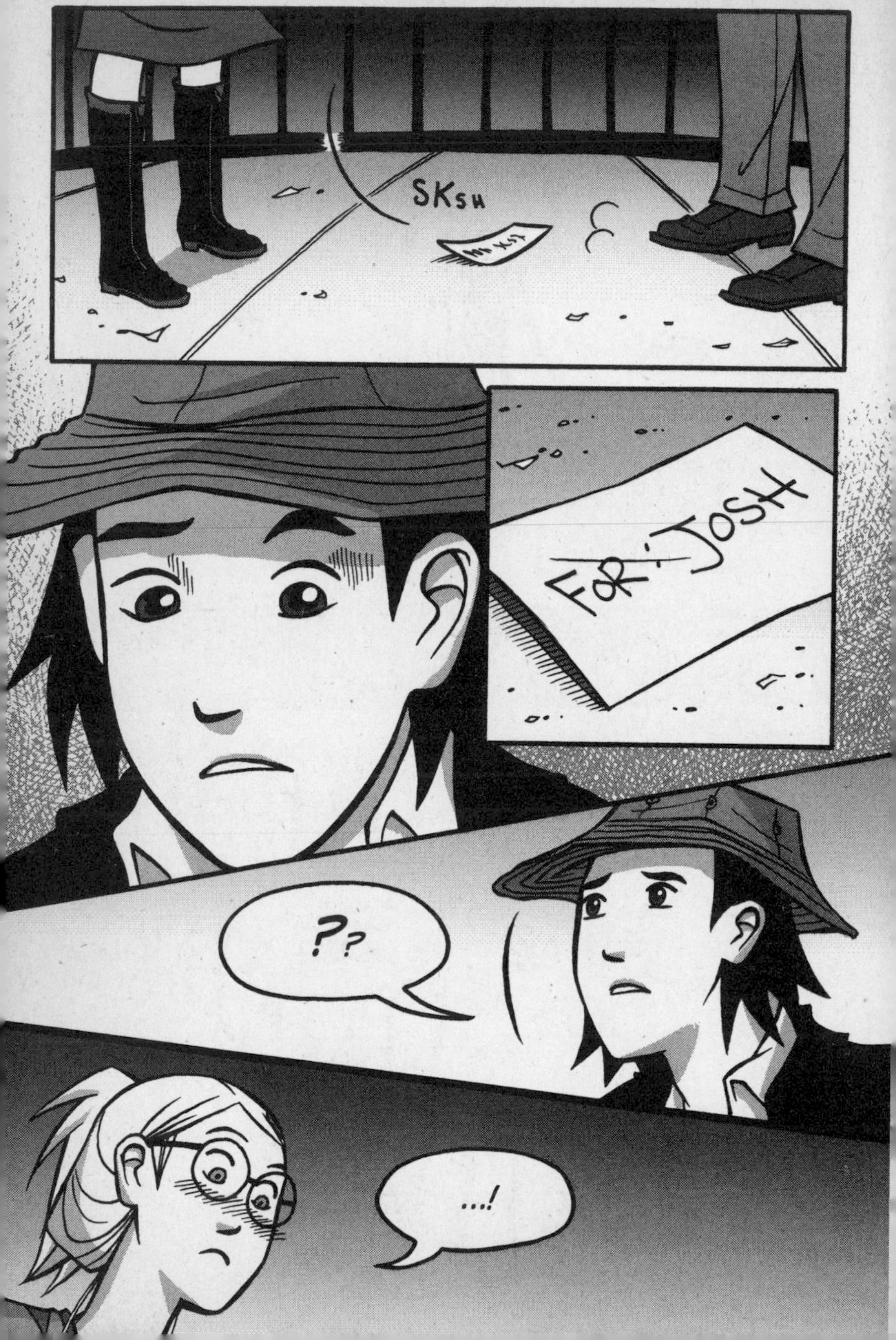
SKSH
FOR: JOSH
??
...!

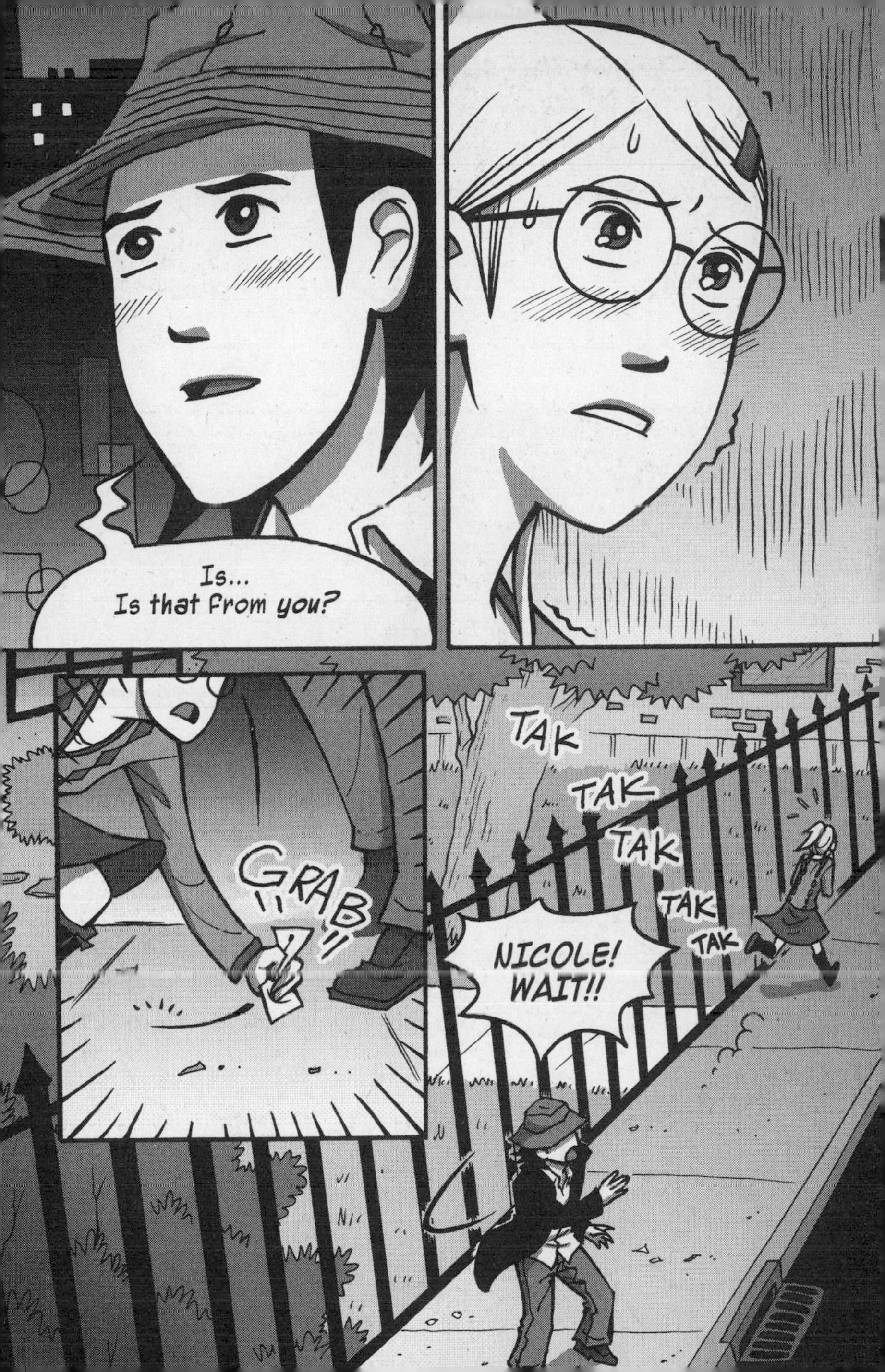
Is...
Is that from you?
GRAB!!
TAK
TAK
TAK
TAK
TAK
NICOLE! WAIT!!

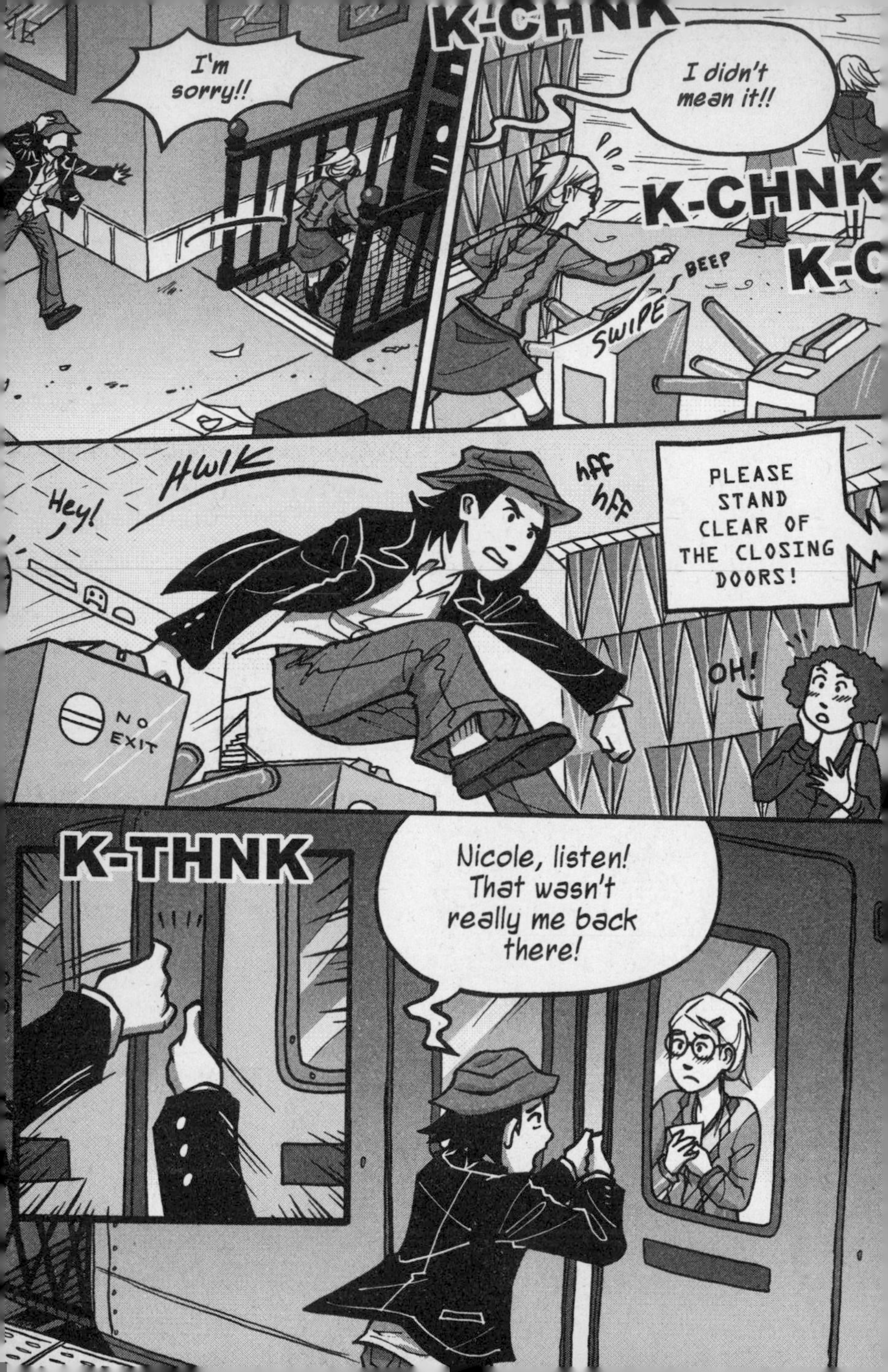
I'm sorry!!
K-CHNK
I didn't mean it!!
K-CHNK
K-C
BEEP
SWIPE
HWIK
Hey!
hff hff
PLEASE STAND CLEAR OF THE CLOSING DOORS!
NO EXIT
OH!
K-THNK
Nicole, listen! That wasn't really me back there!

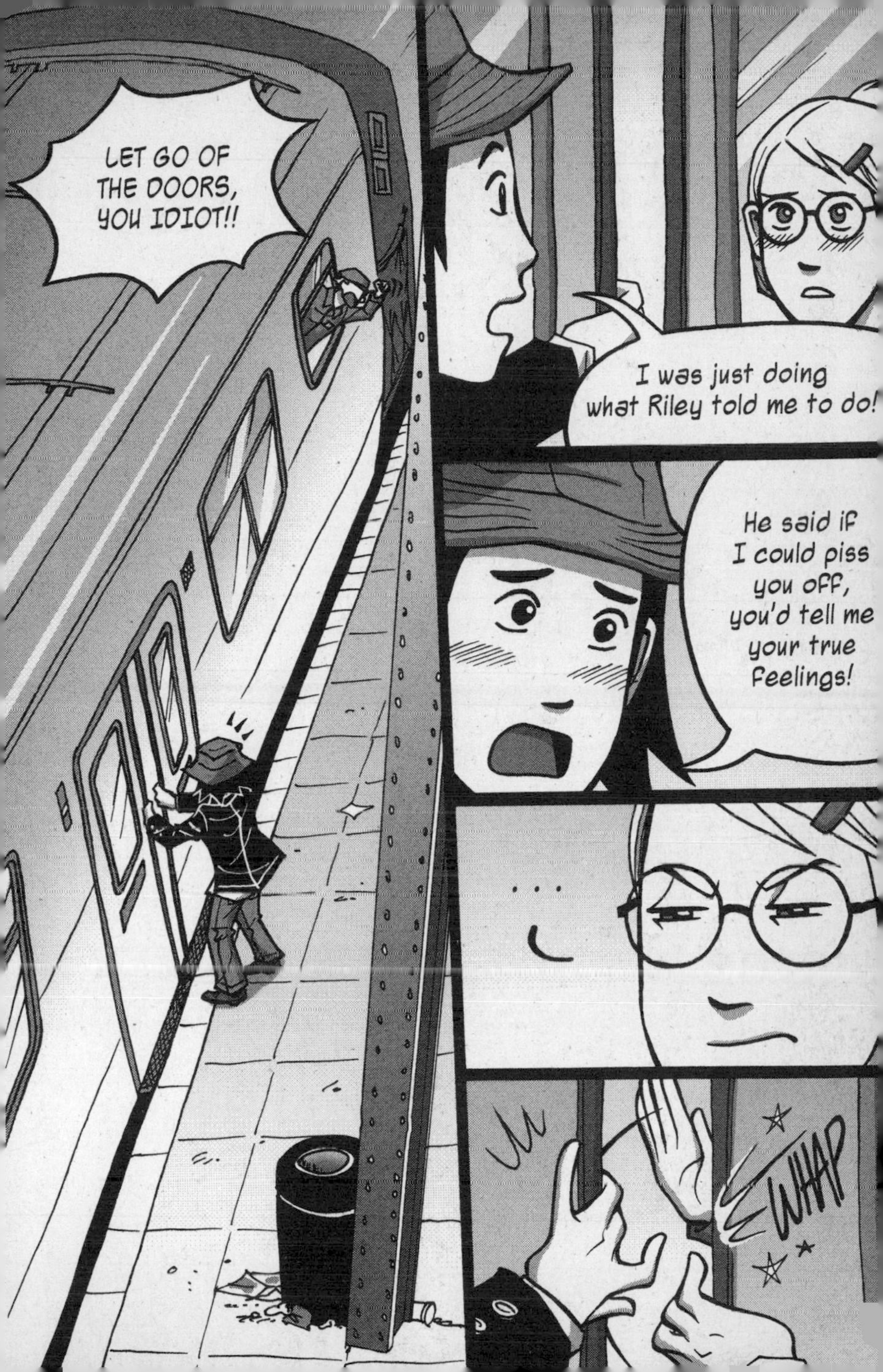

LET GO OF THE DOORS, YOU IDIOT!!
I was just doing what Riley told me to do!
He said if I could piss you off, you'd tell me your true feelings!
...
WHAP

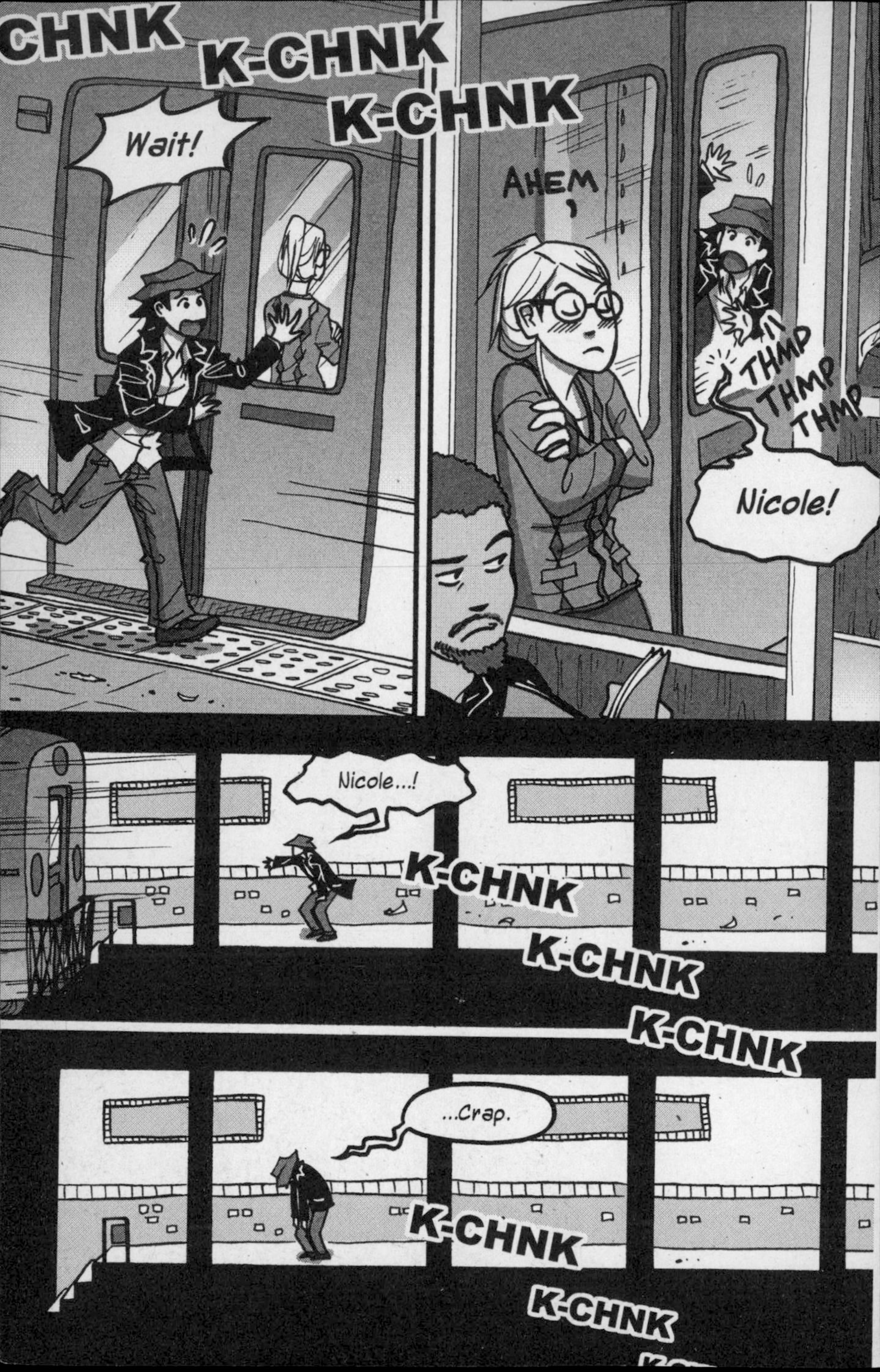
CHNK
K-CHNK
K-CHNK
Wait!
AHEM
THMP
THMP
THMP
Nicole!
Nicole...!
K-CHNK
K-CHNK
K-CHNK
...Crap.
K-CHNK
K-CHNK

CHAPTER SIX

Ends With A Vision

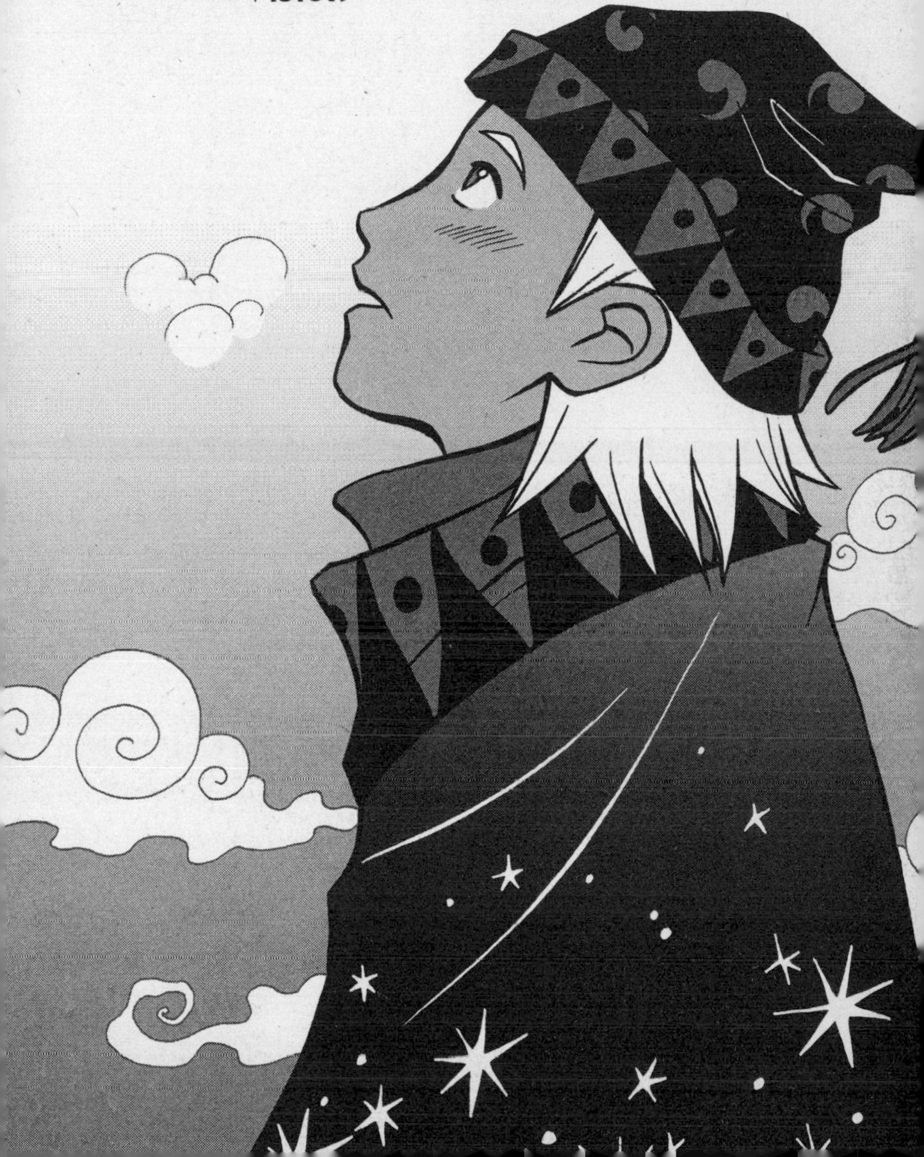

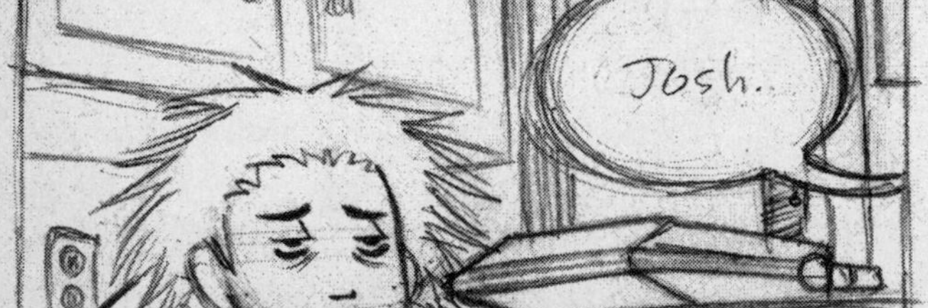
Josh..

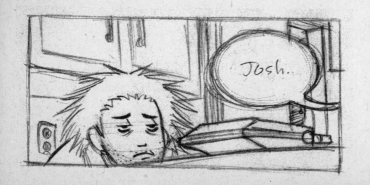

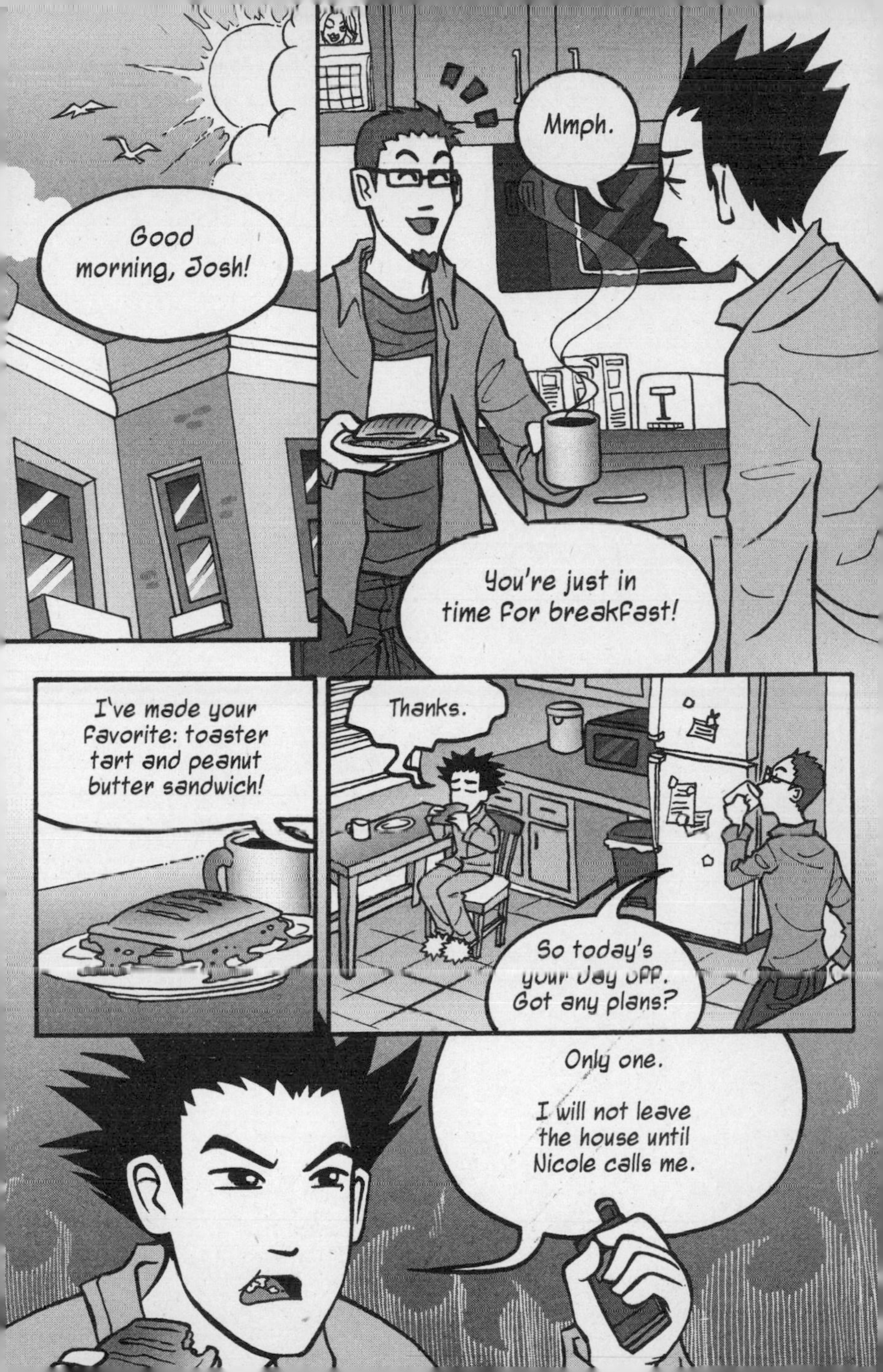
Good morning, Josh!
Mmph.
You're just in time for breakfast!
I've made your favorite: toaster tart and peanut butter sandwich!
Thanks.
So today's your day off. Got any plans?
Only one.
I will not leave the house until Nicole calls me.

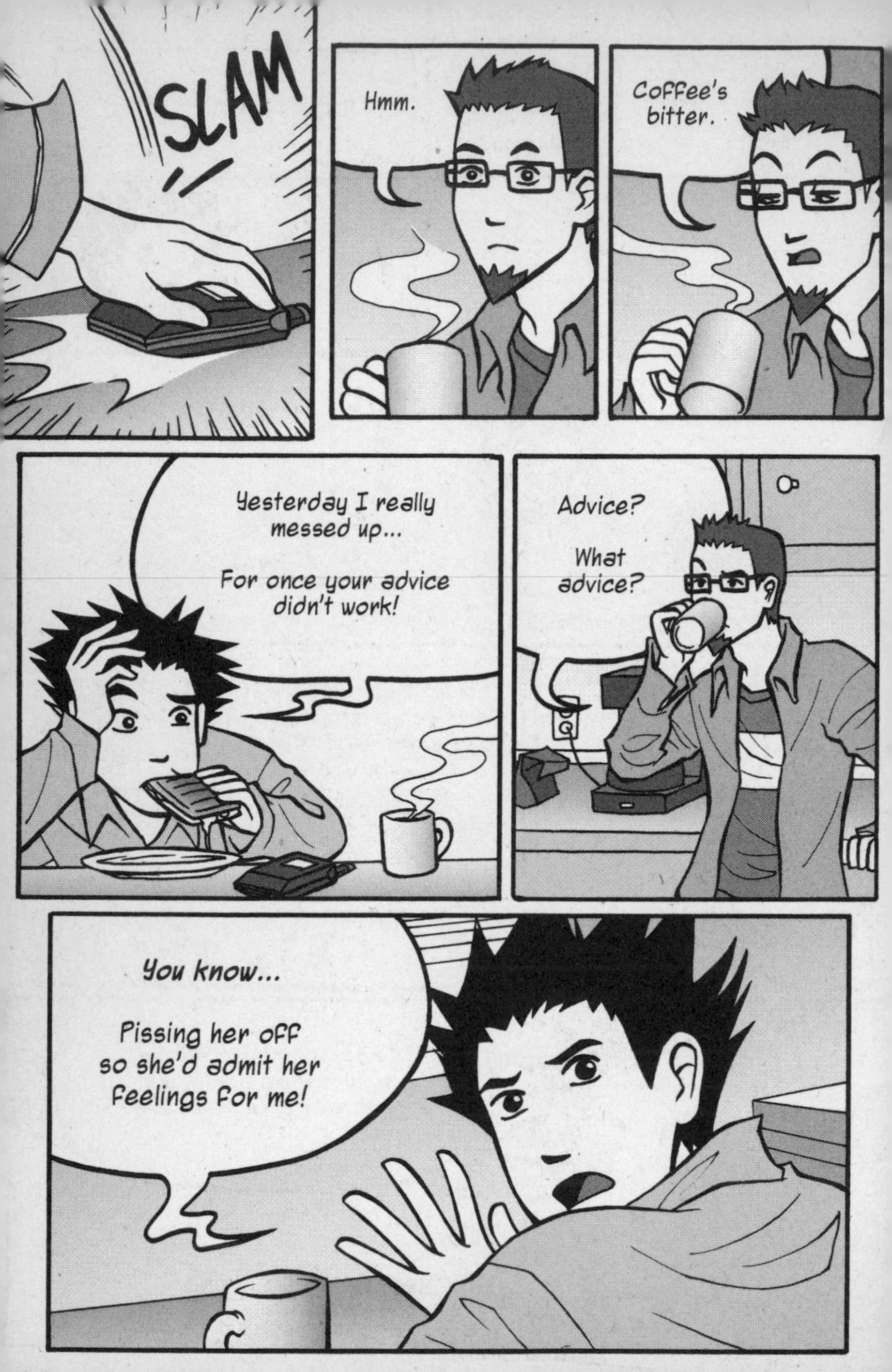
SLAM
Hmm.
Coffee's bitter.
Yesterday I really messed up...
For once your advice didn't work!
Advice?
What advice?
You know...
Pissing her off so she'd admit her feelings for me!

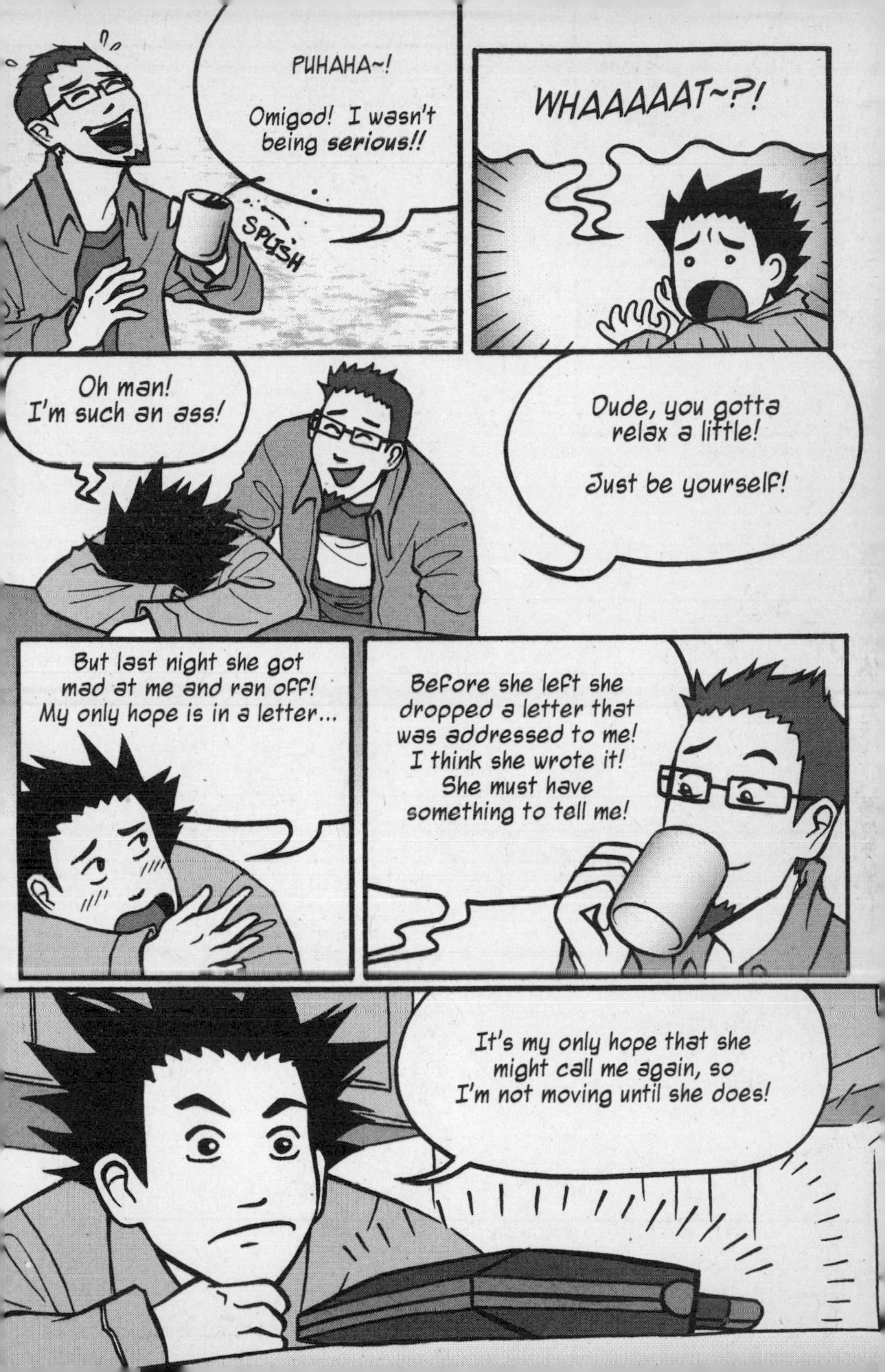
PUHAHA~!
Omigod! I wasn't being serious!!
SPLISH
WHAAAAAT~?!
Oh man! I'm such an ass!
Dude, you gotta relax a little!
Just be yourself!
But last night she got mad at me and ran off! My only hope is in a letter...
Before she left she dropped a letter that was addressed to me! I think she wrote it! She must have something to tell me!
It's my only hope that she might call me again, so I'm not moving until she does!

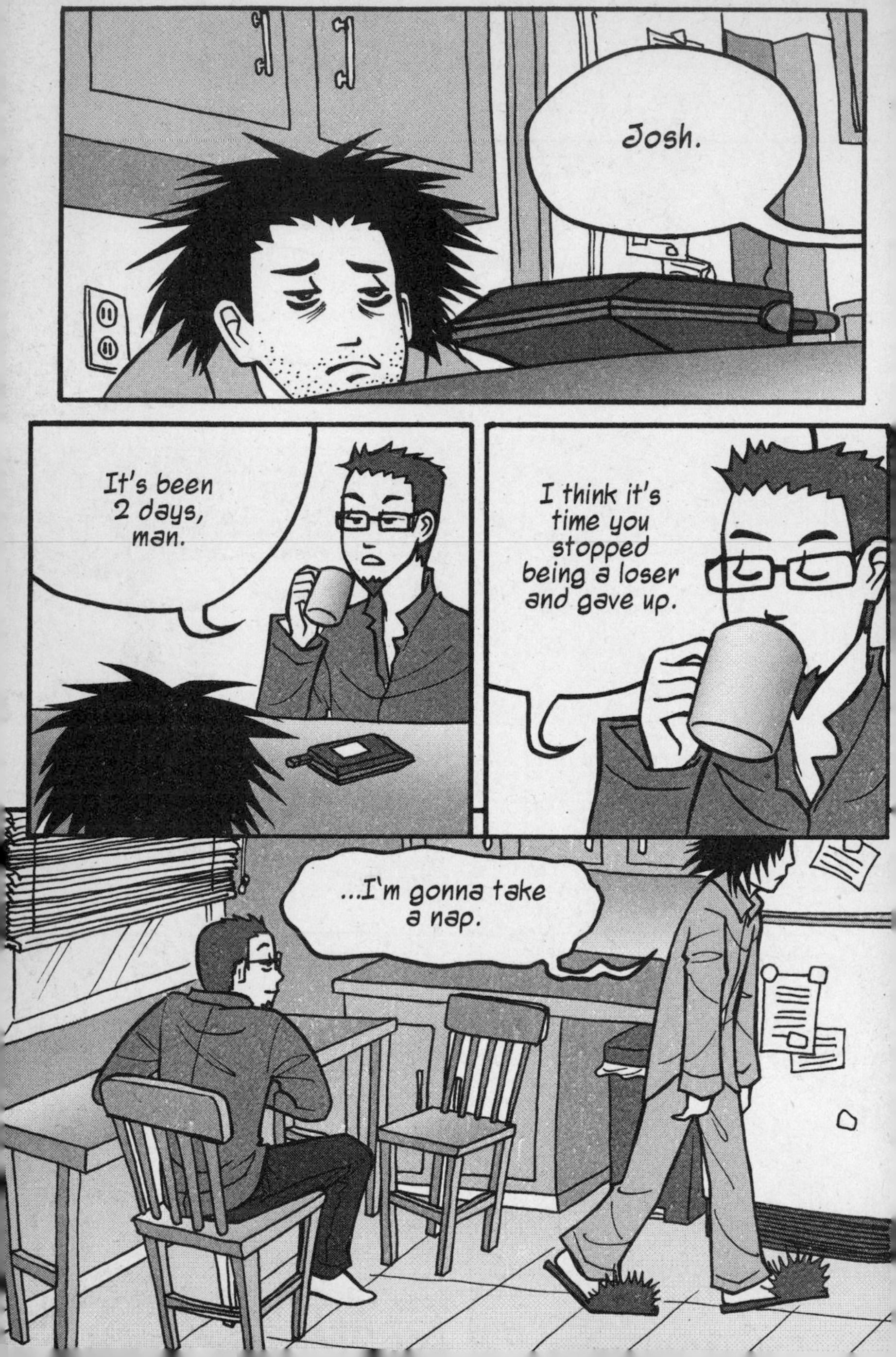
Josh.
It's been 2 days, man.
I think it's time you stopped being a loser and gave up.
...I'm gonna take a nap.

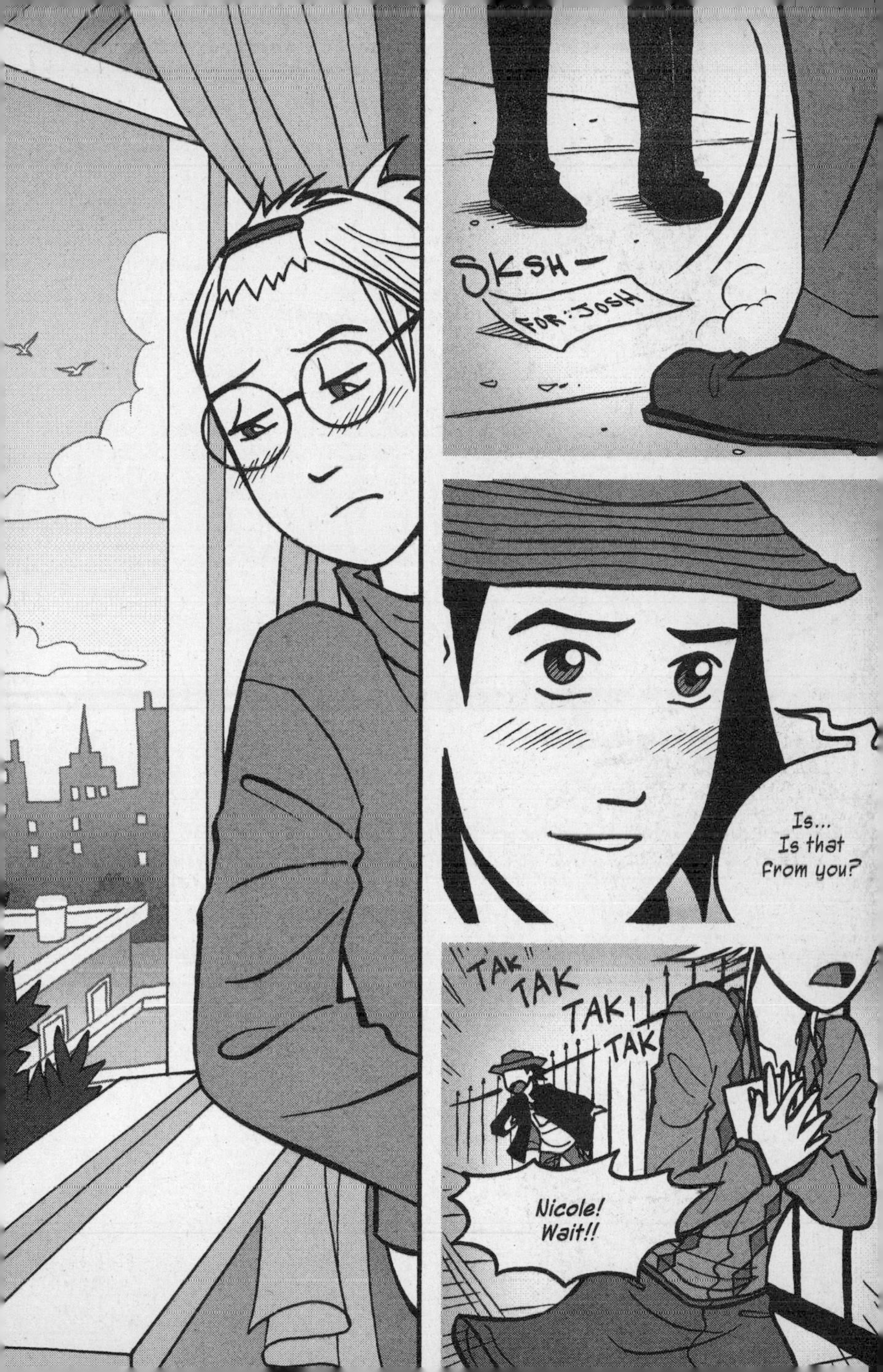
SKSH—
FOR: JOSH
Is...
Is that
from you?
TAK TAK TAK TAK
Nicole!
Wait!!

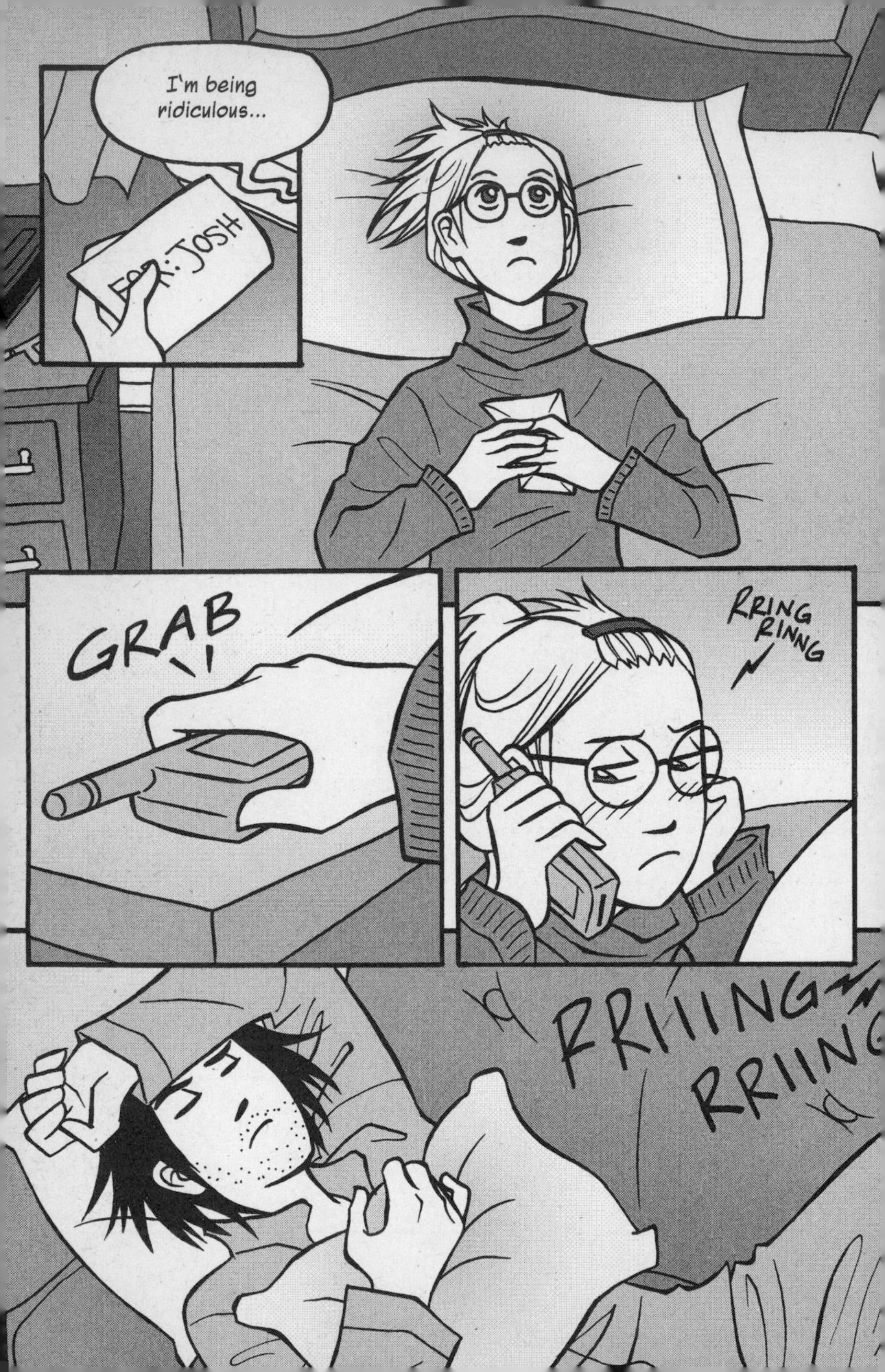
I'm being ridiculous...
FOR: JOSH
GRAB
RRING RINNG
RRIIING
RRIING

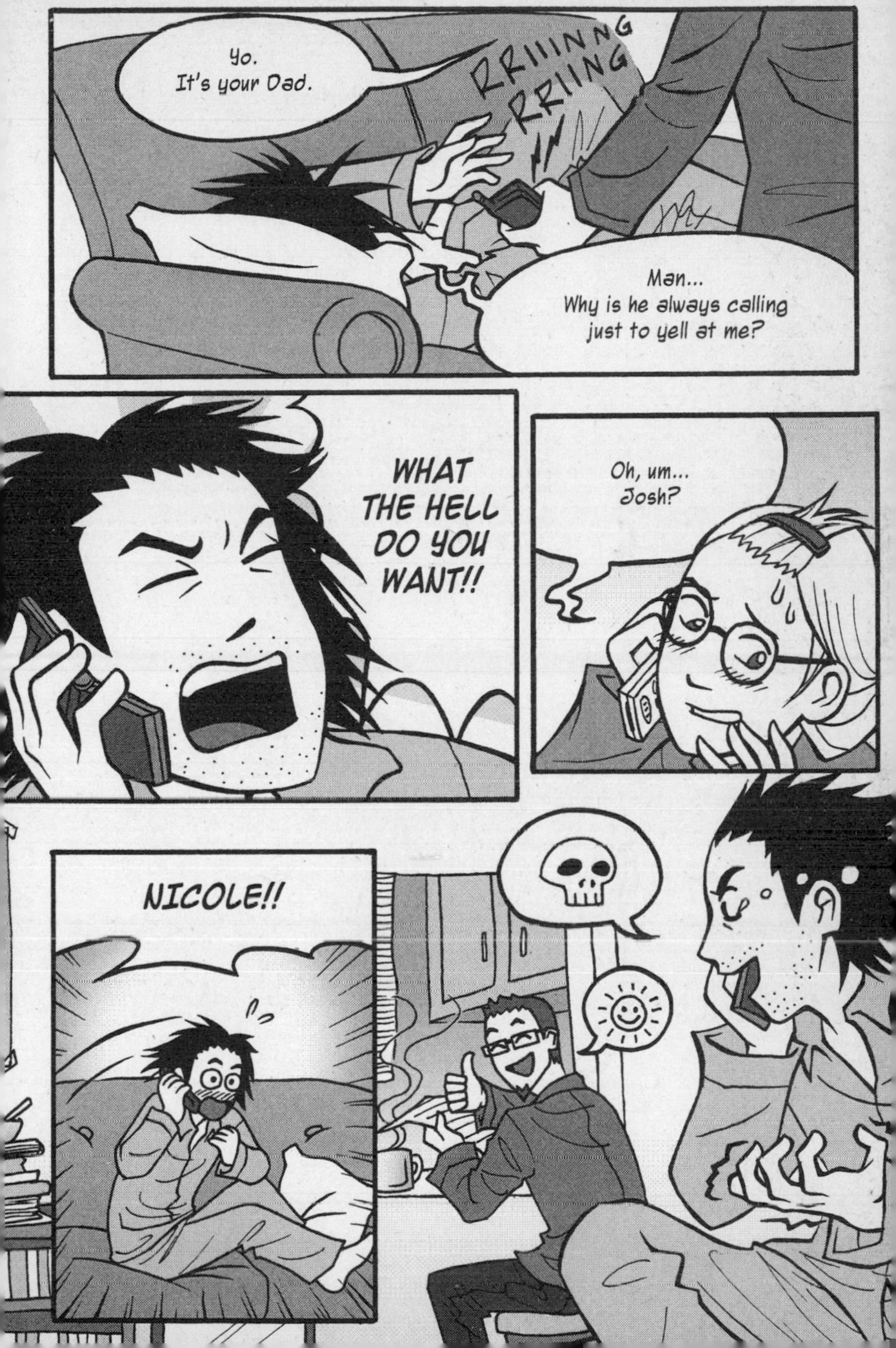
Yo.
It's your Dad.
RRIIINNG
RRIING
Man...
Why is he always calling
just to yell at me?
WHAT THE HELL DO YOU WANT!!
Oh, um...
Josh?
NICOLE!!

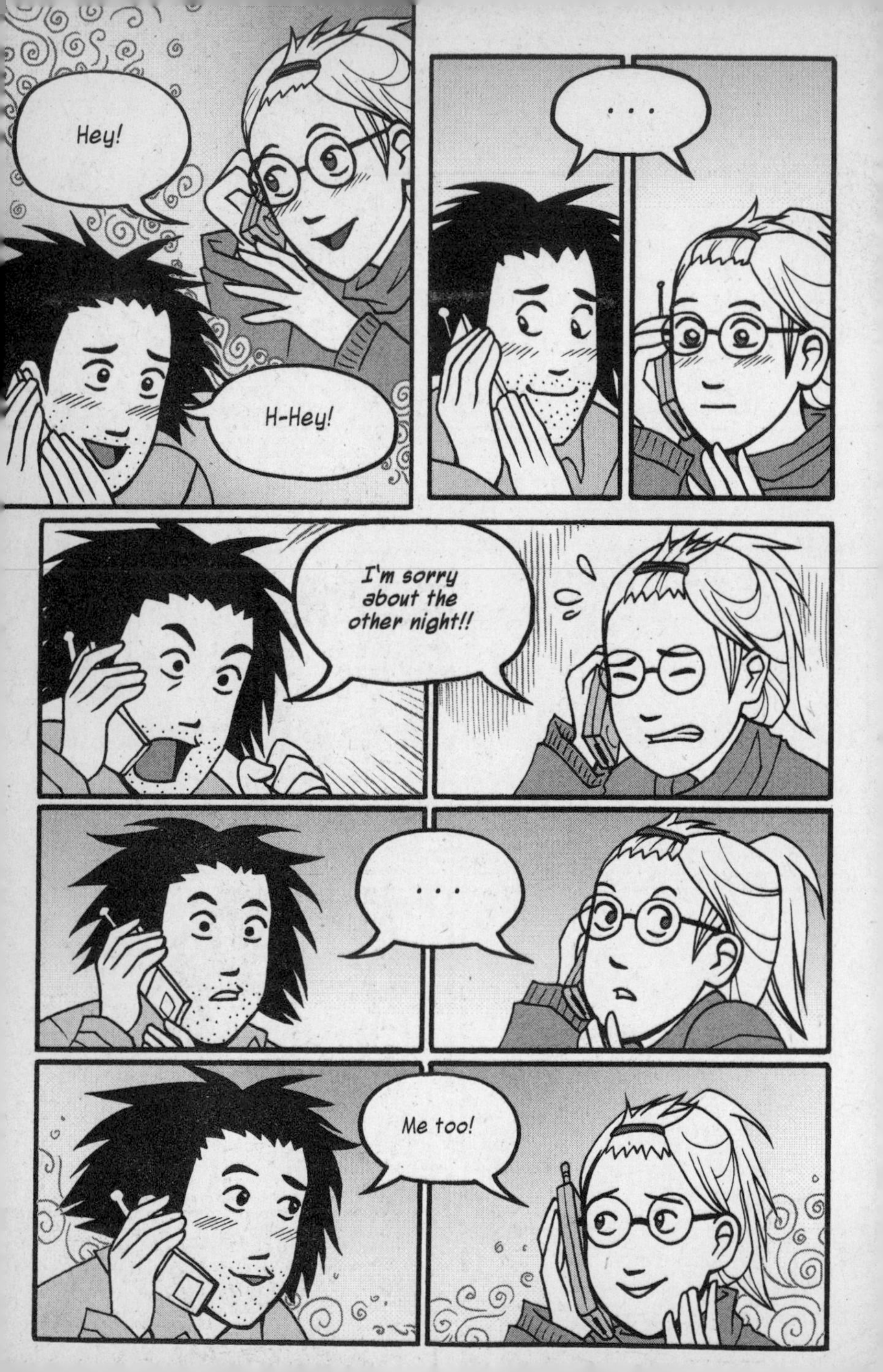
Hey!
H-Hey!
. . .
I'm sorry about the other night!!
. . .
Me too!

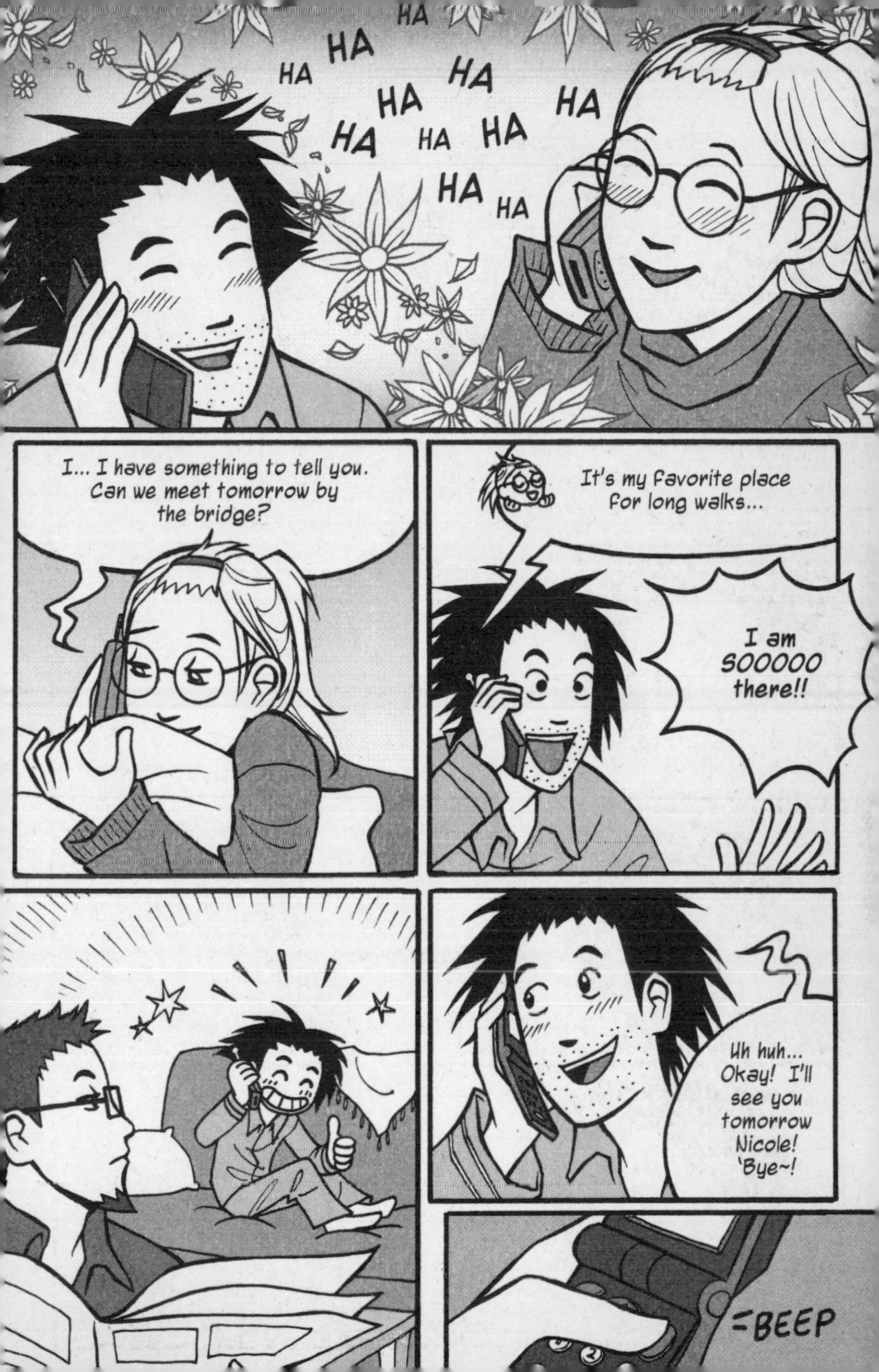
HA
HA
HA
HA
HA
HA
HA
HA
HA
HA
HA
I... I have something to tell you. Can we meet tomorrow by the bridge?
It's my favorite place for long walks...
I am SOOOOO there!!
Uh huh... Okay! I'll see you tomorrow Nicole! 'Bye~!
BEEP

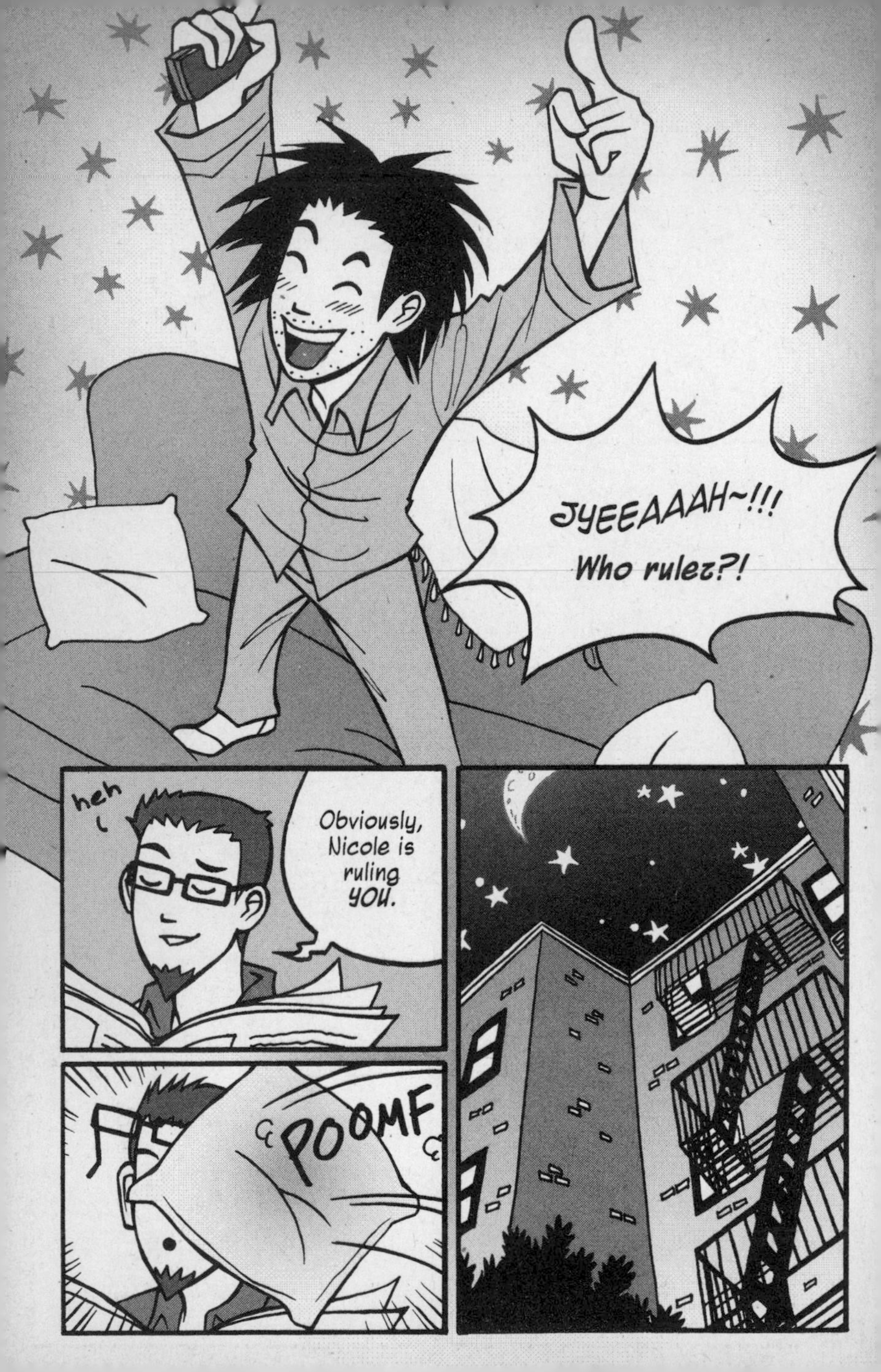
JYEEAAAH~!!!
Who rulez?!
heh
Obviously, Nicole is ruling YOU.
POOMF

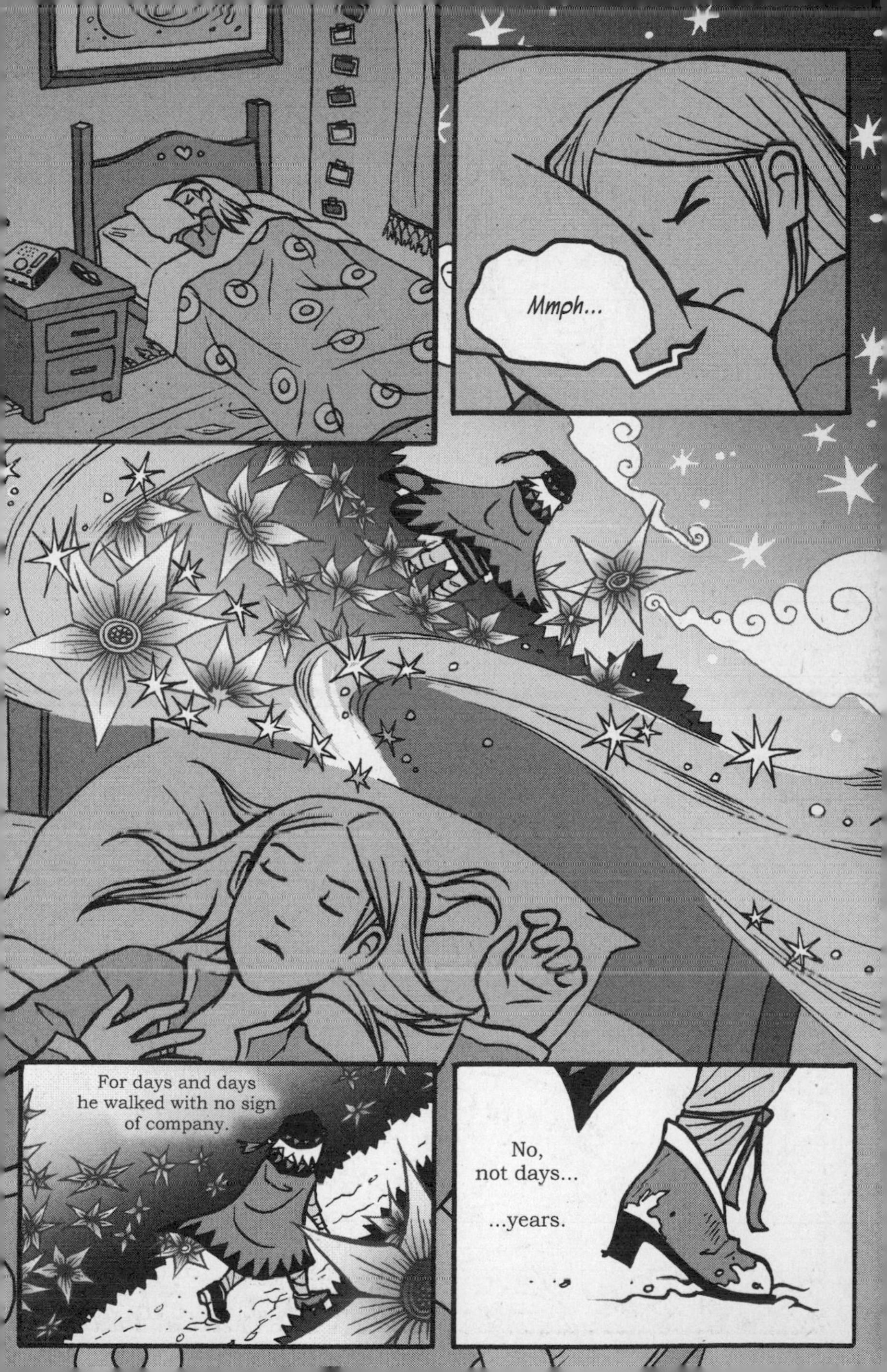
Mmph...
For days and days he walked with no sign of company.
No, not days...
...years.

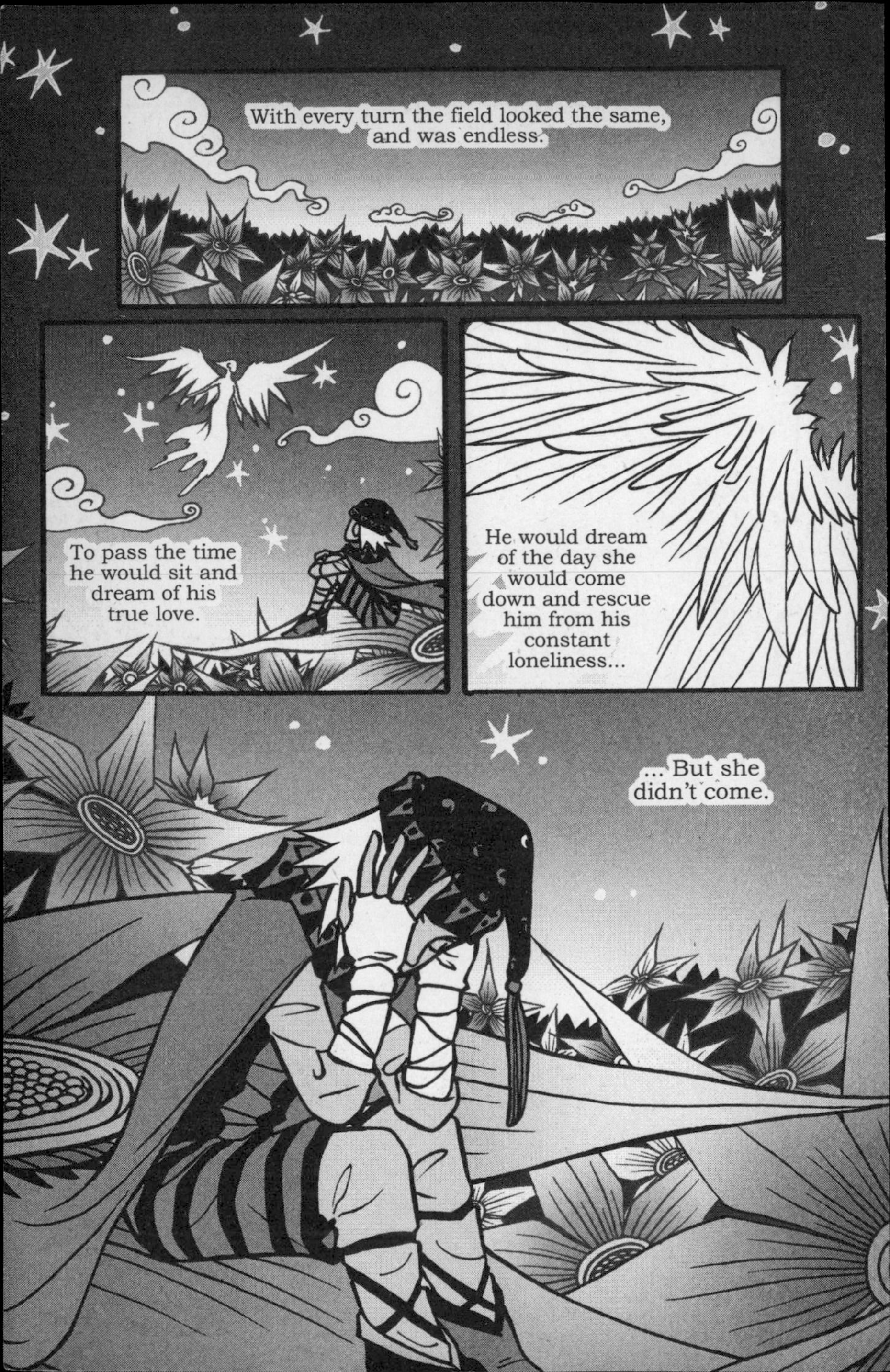
With every turn the field looked the same, and was endless.
To pass the time he would sit and dream of his true love.
He would dream of the day she would come down and rescue him from his constant loneliness...
... But she didn't come.

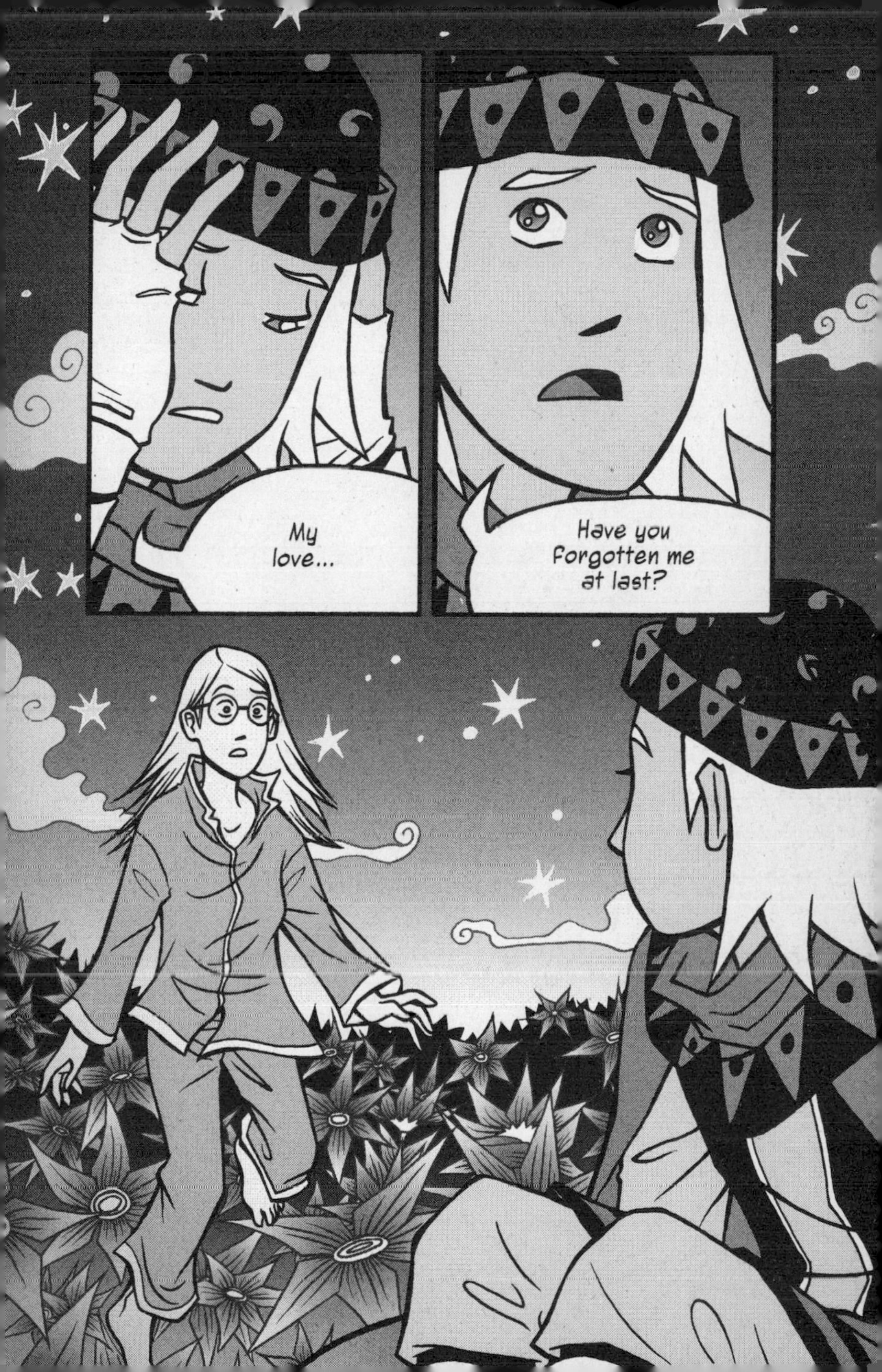
My love...
Have you forgotten me at last?

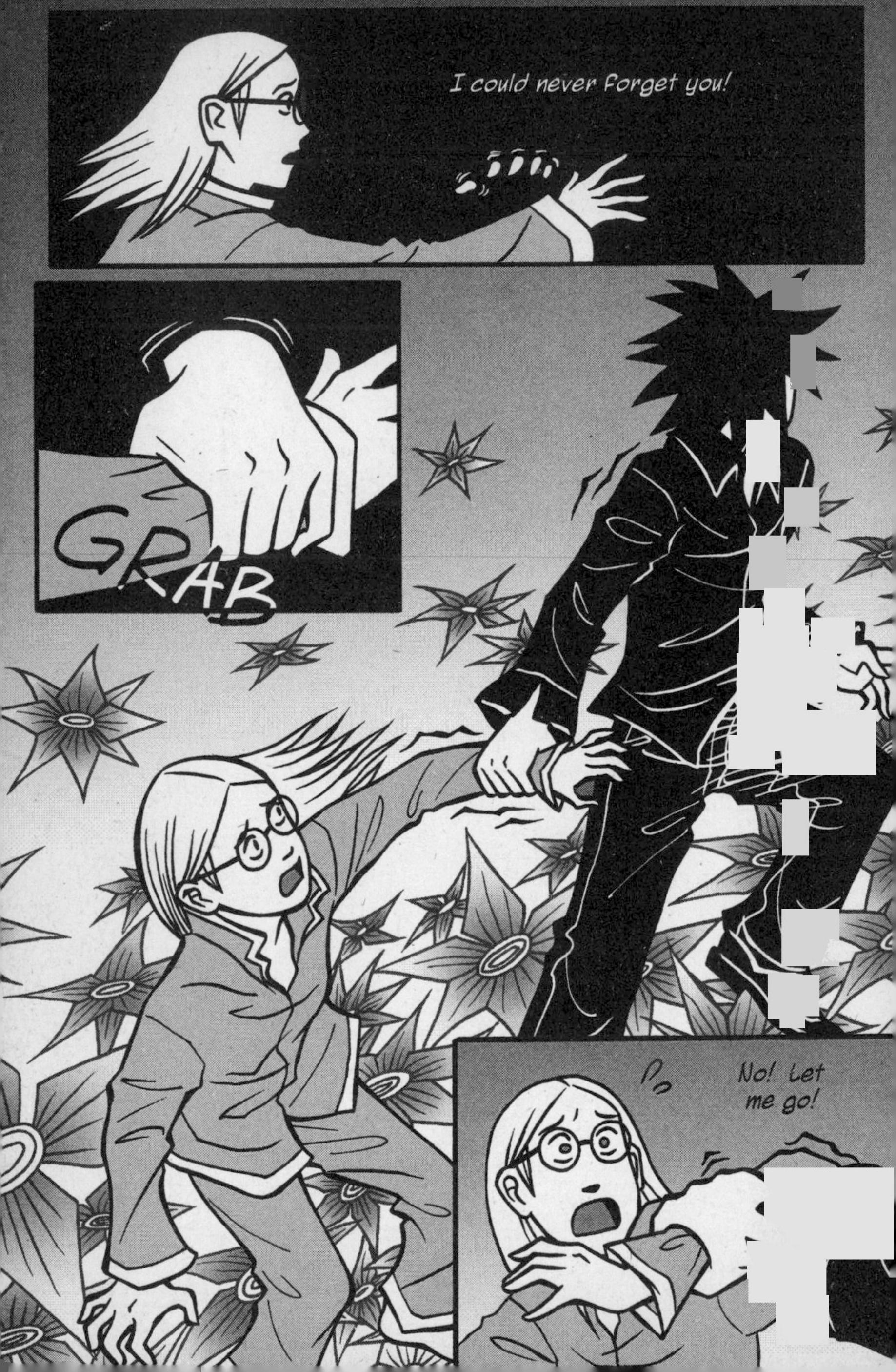
I could never forget you!
GRAB
No! Let me go!

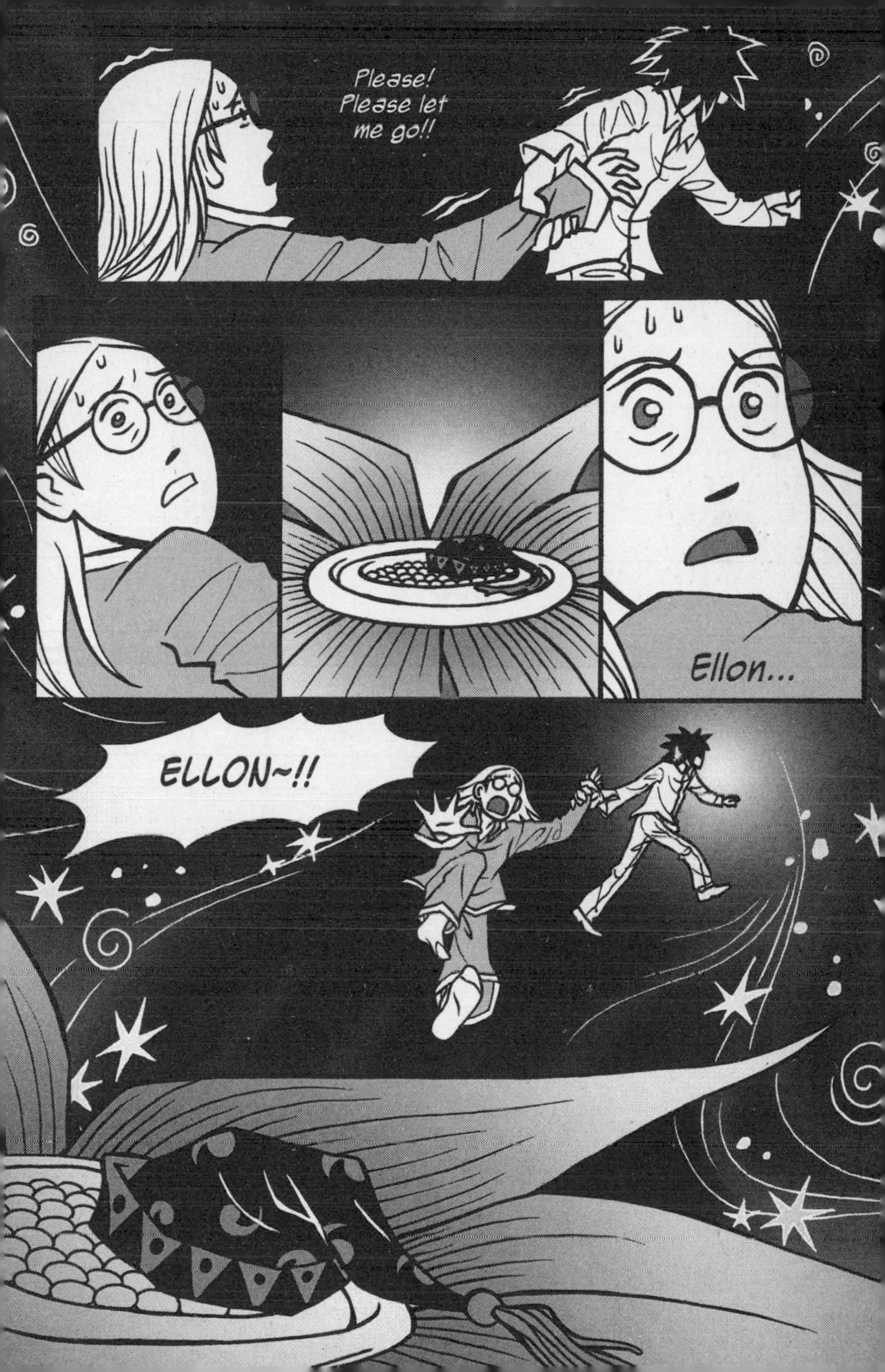
Please! Please let me go!!
Ellon...
ELLON~!!

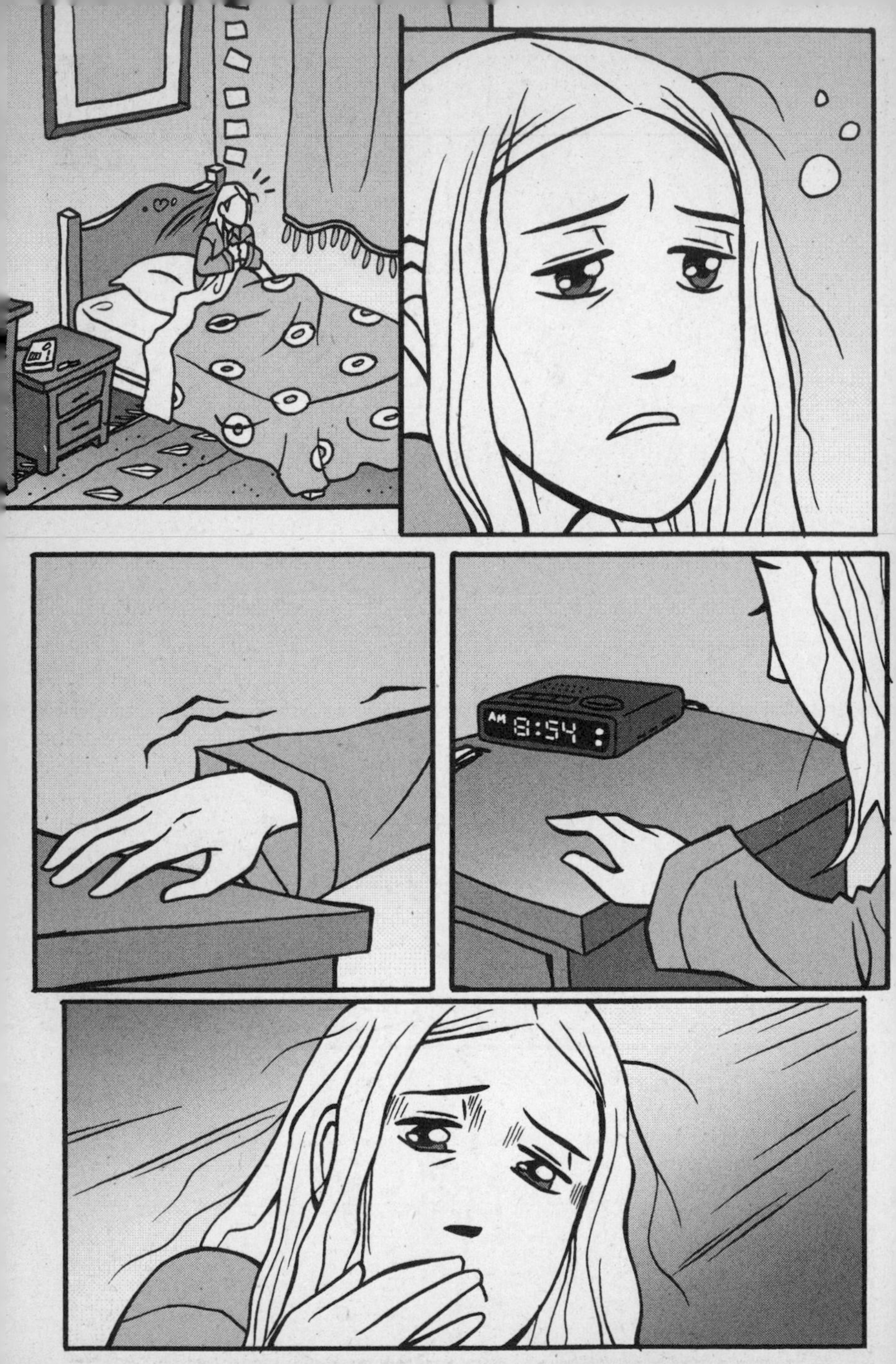
AM
8:54

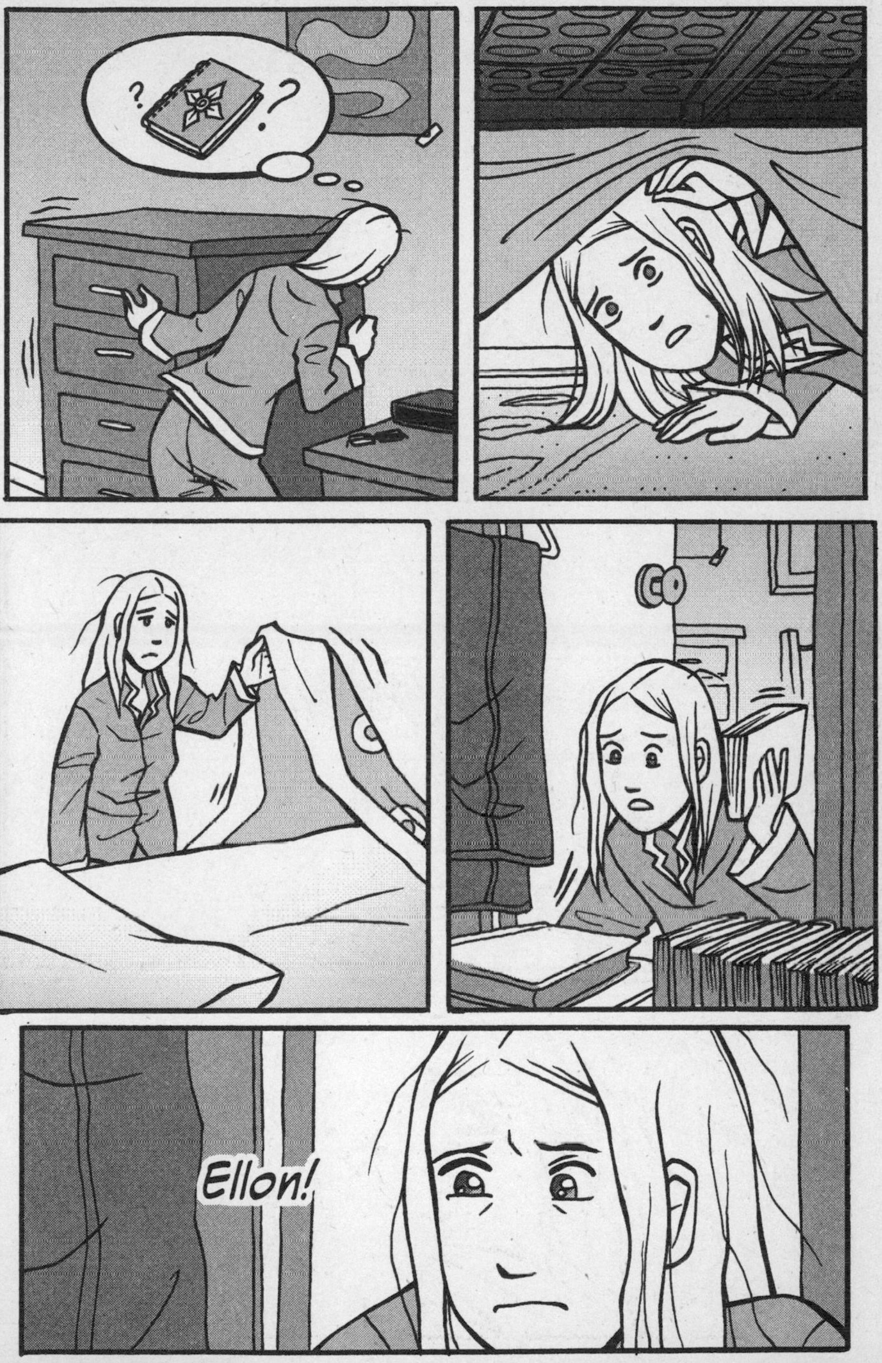
? ?
Ellon!

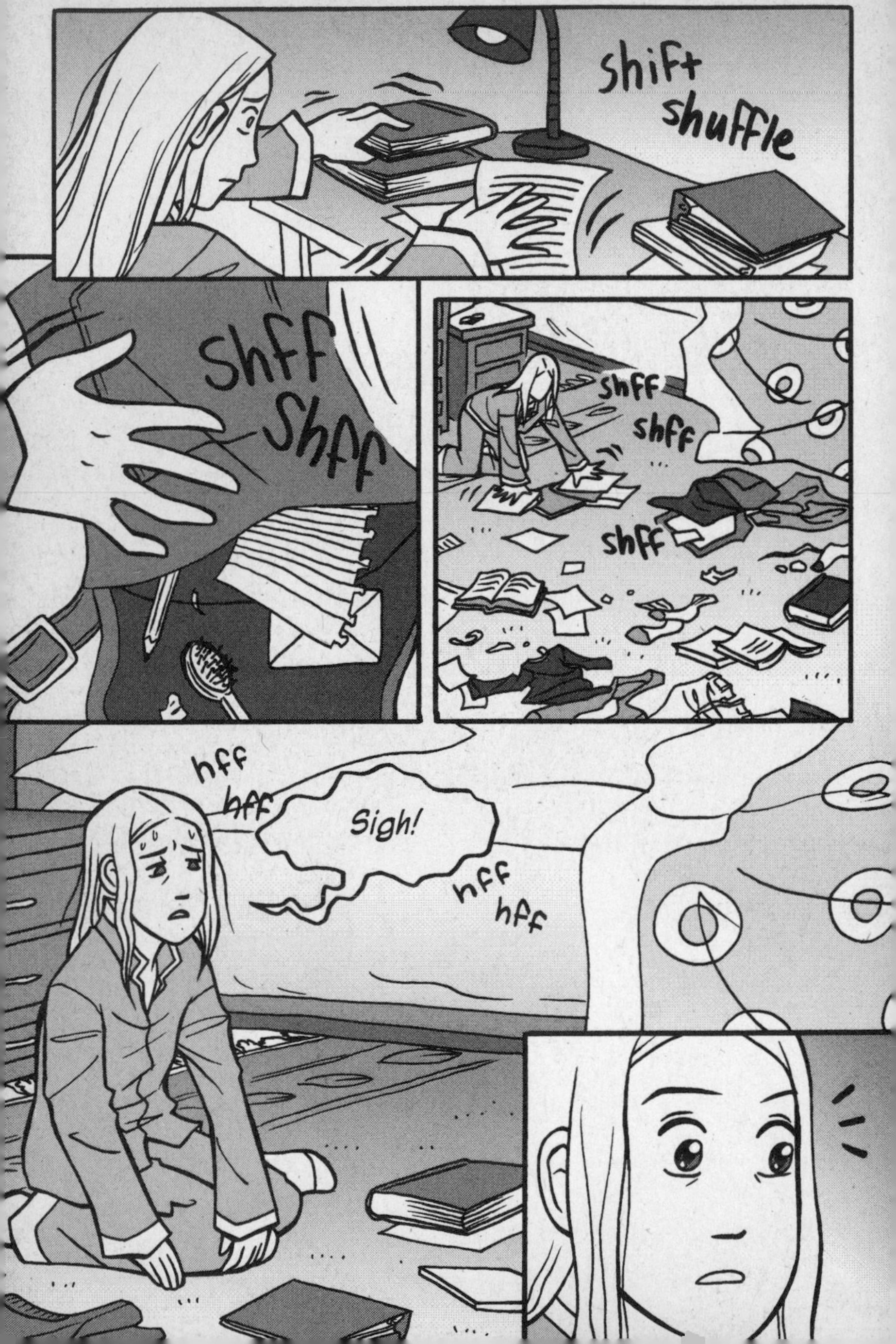
shift
shuffle
Shff
Shff
shff
shff
shff
hff
hff
Sigh!
hff
hff

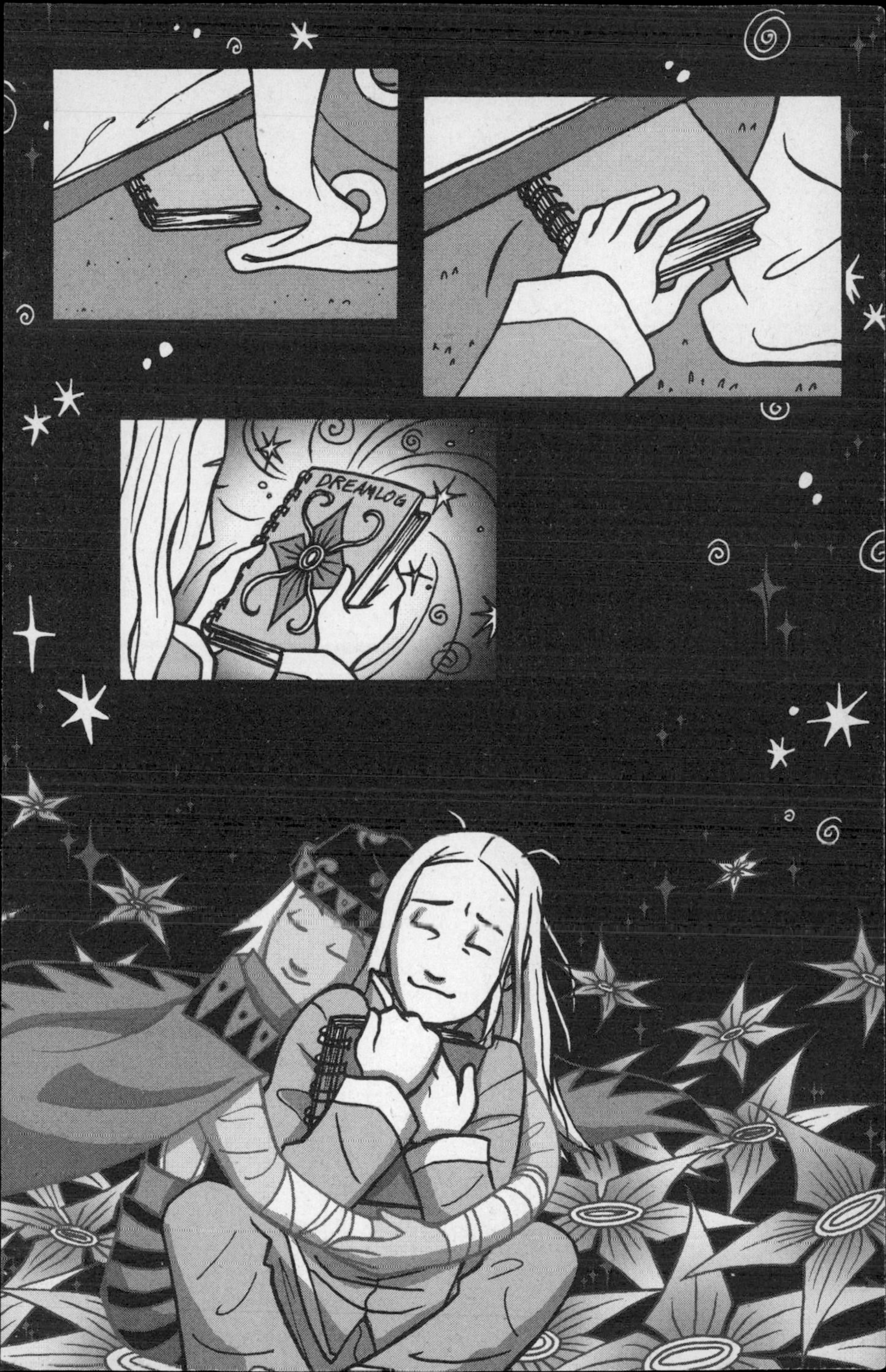
DREAMLOG

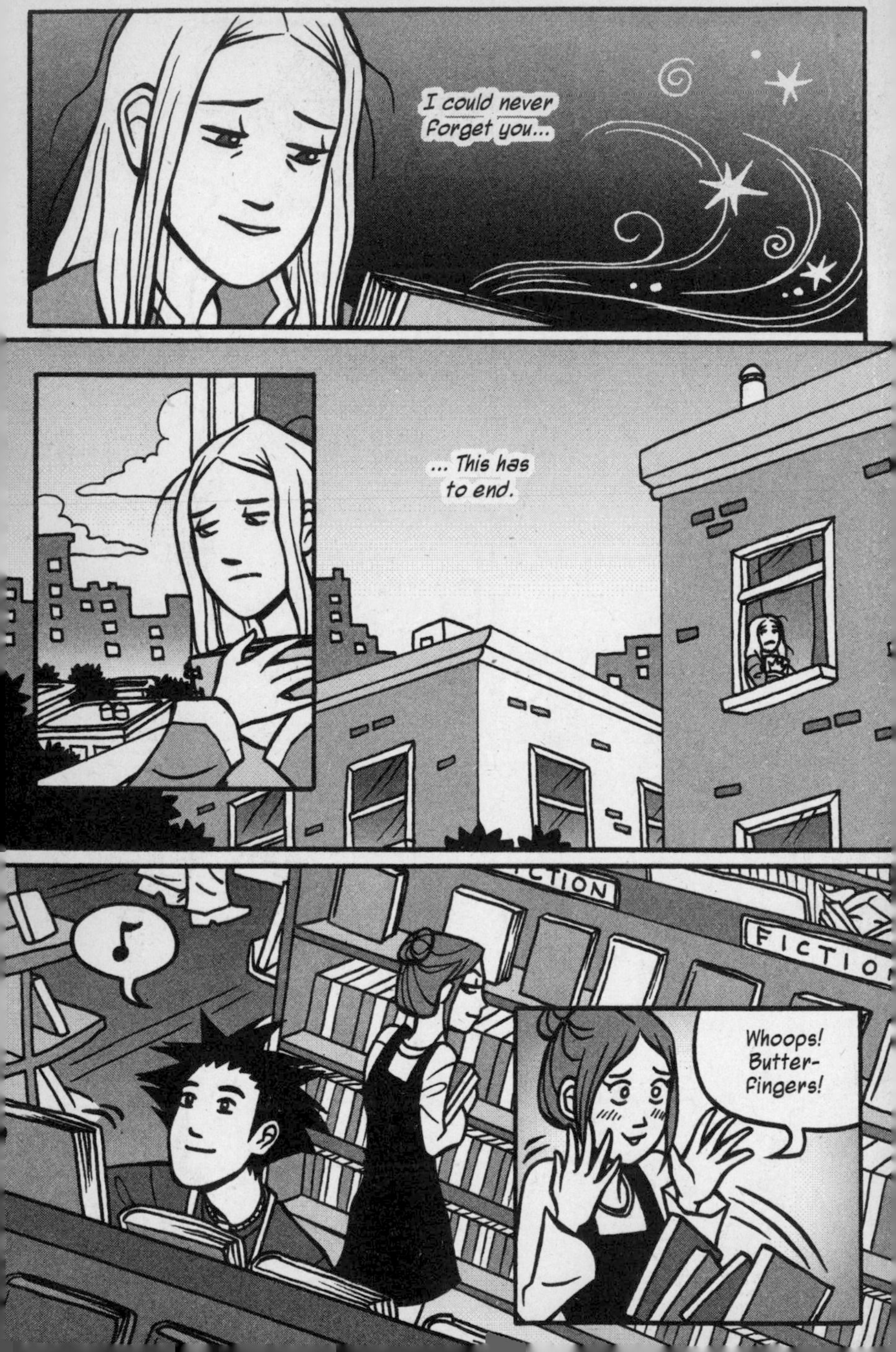
I could never forget you...
... This has to end.
FICTION
FICTION
Whoops! Butter-fingers!

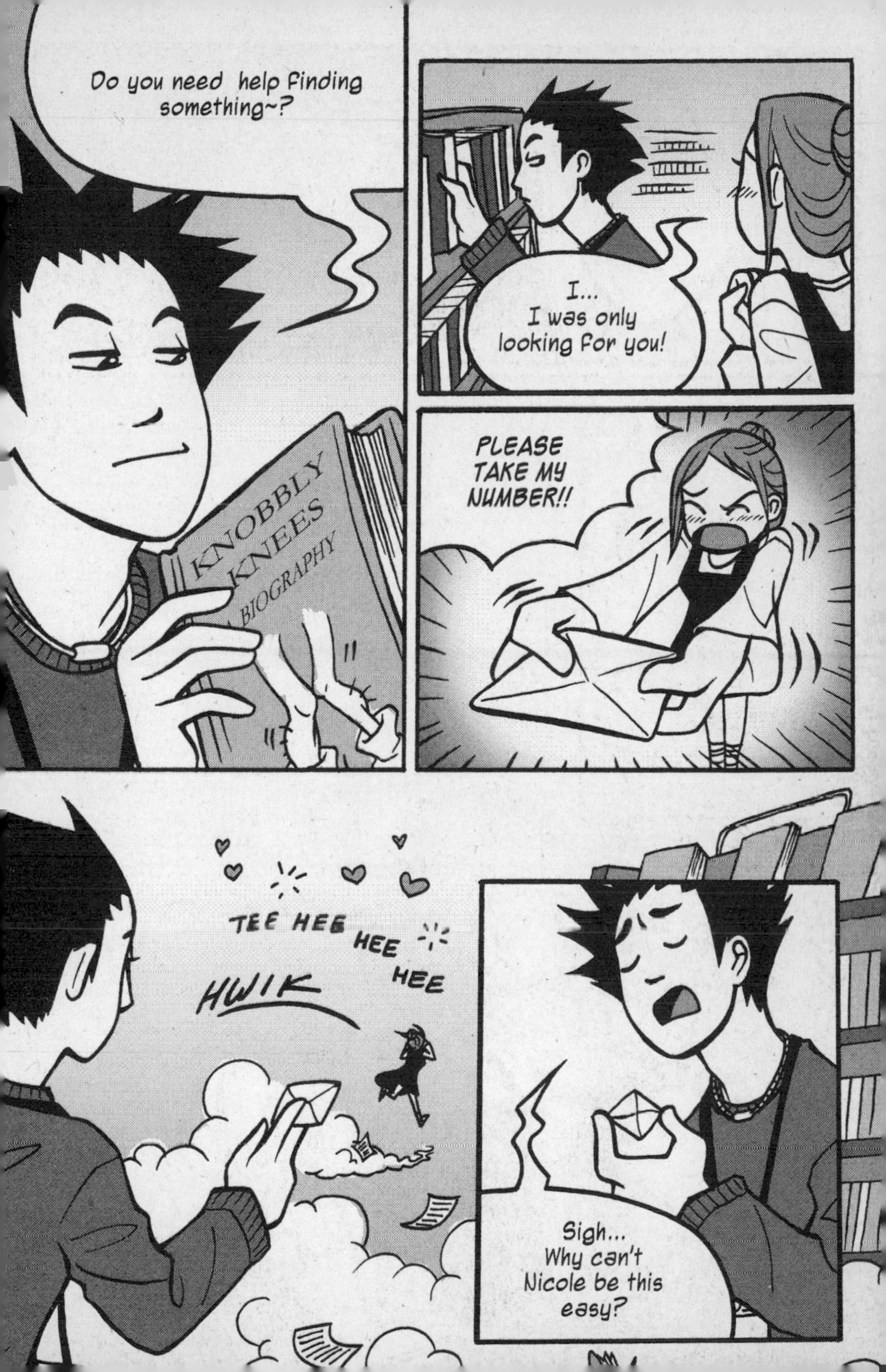

Do you need help finding something~?
KNOBBLY KNEES BIOGRAPHY
I... I was only looking for you!
PLEASE TAKE MY NUMBER!!
TEE HEE HEE HEE
HWIK
Sigh... Why can't Nicole be this easy?

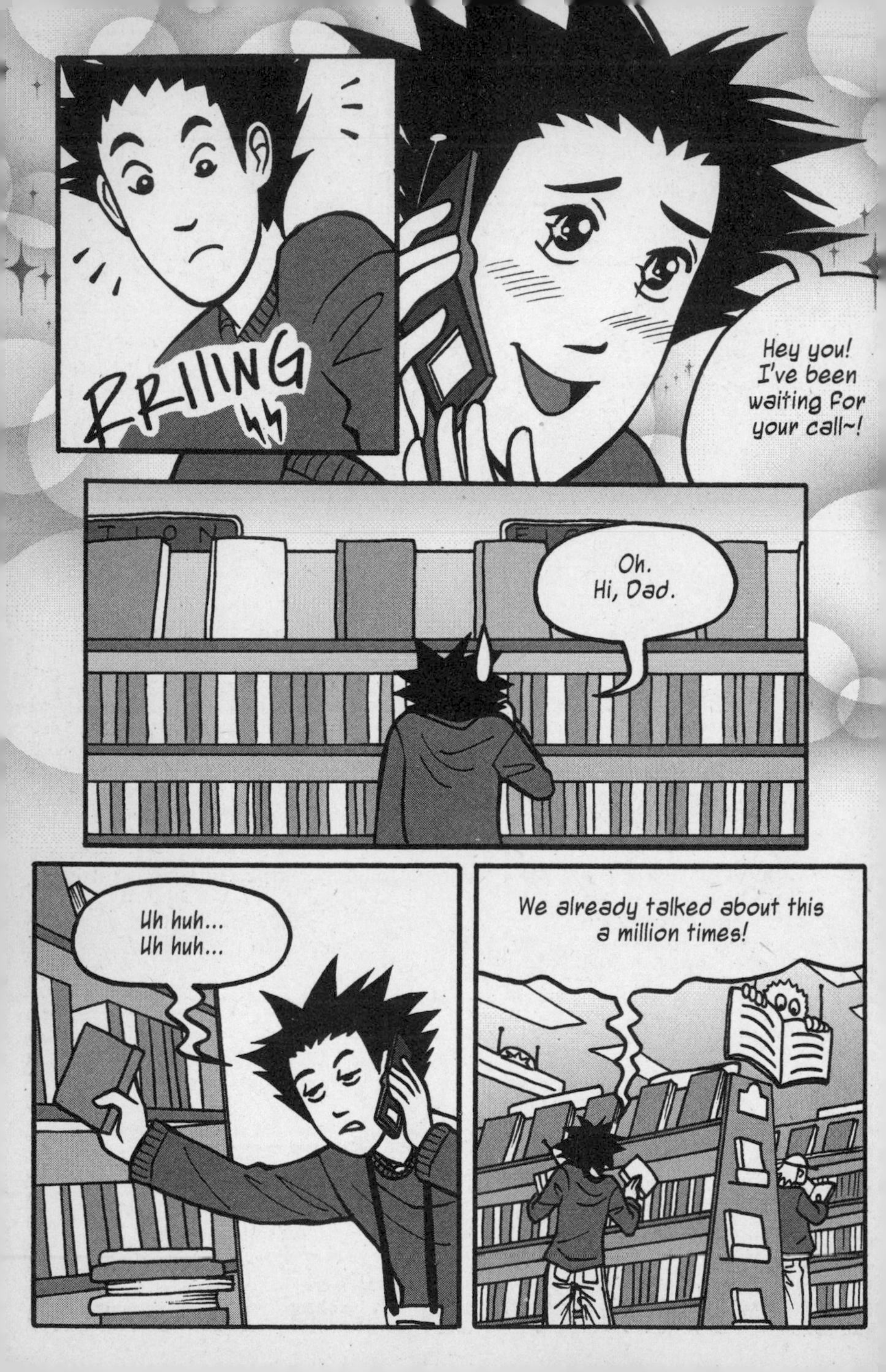
RRIIING
Hey you! I've been waiting for your call~!
Oh. Hi, Dad.
Uh huh... Uh huh...
We already talked about this a million times!

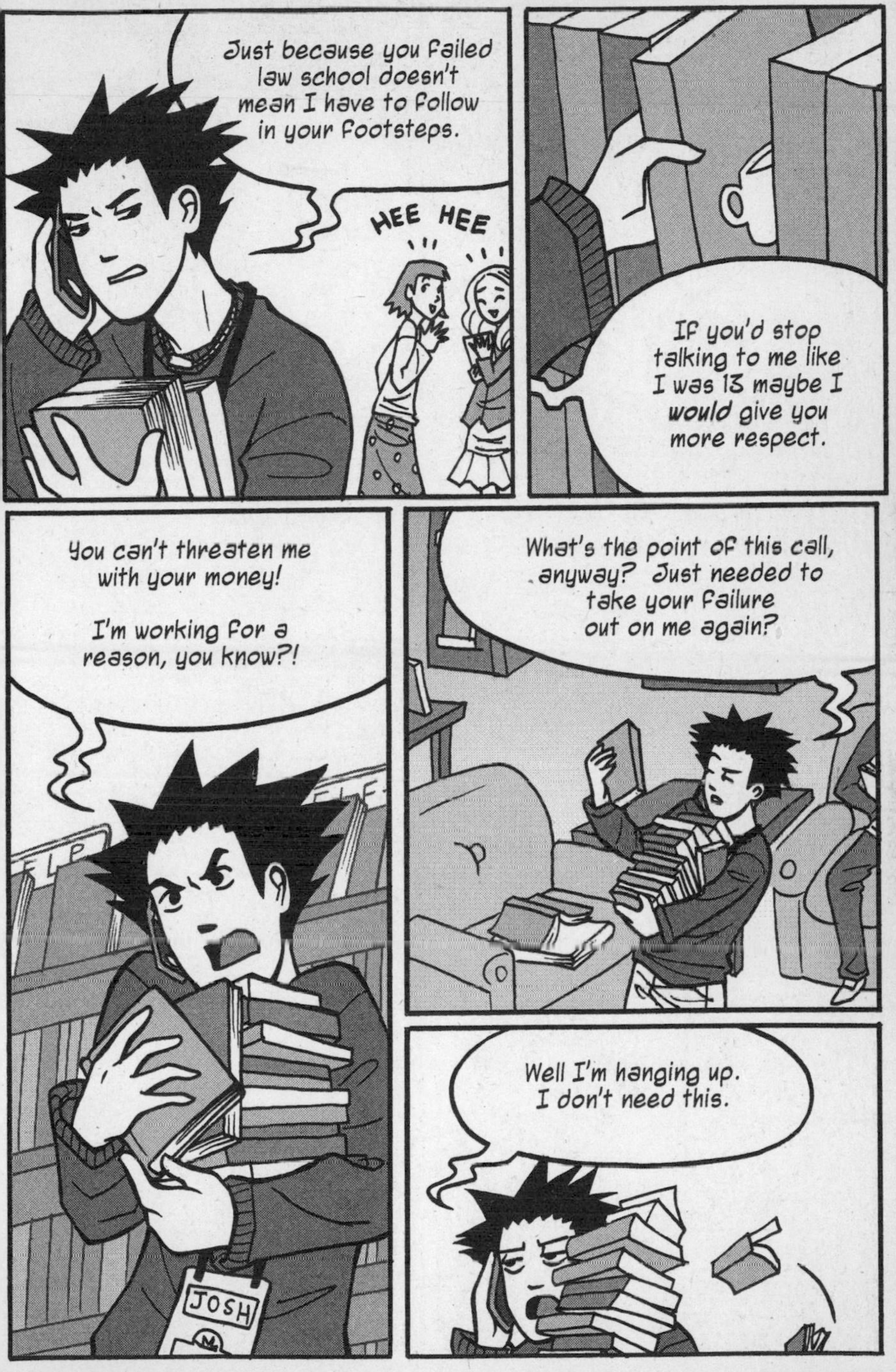
Just because you failed law school doesn't mean I have to follow in your footsteps.
HEE HEE
If you'd stop talking to me like I was 13 maybe I *would* give you more respect.
You can't threaten me with your money!
I'm working for a reason, you know?!
JOSH
What's the point of this call, anyway? Just needed to take your failure out on me again?
Well I'm hanging up. I don't need this.

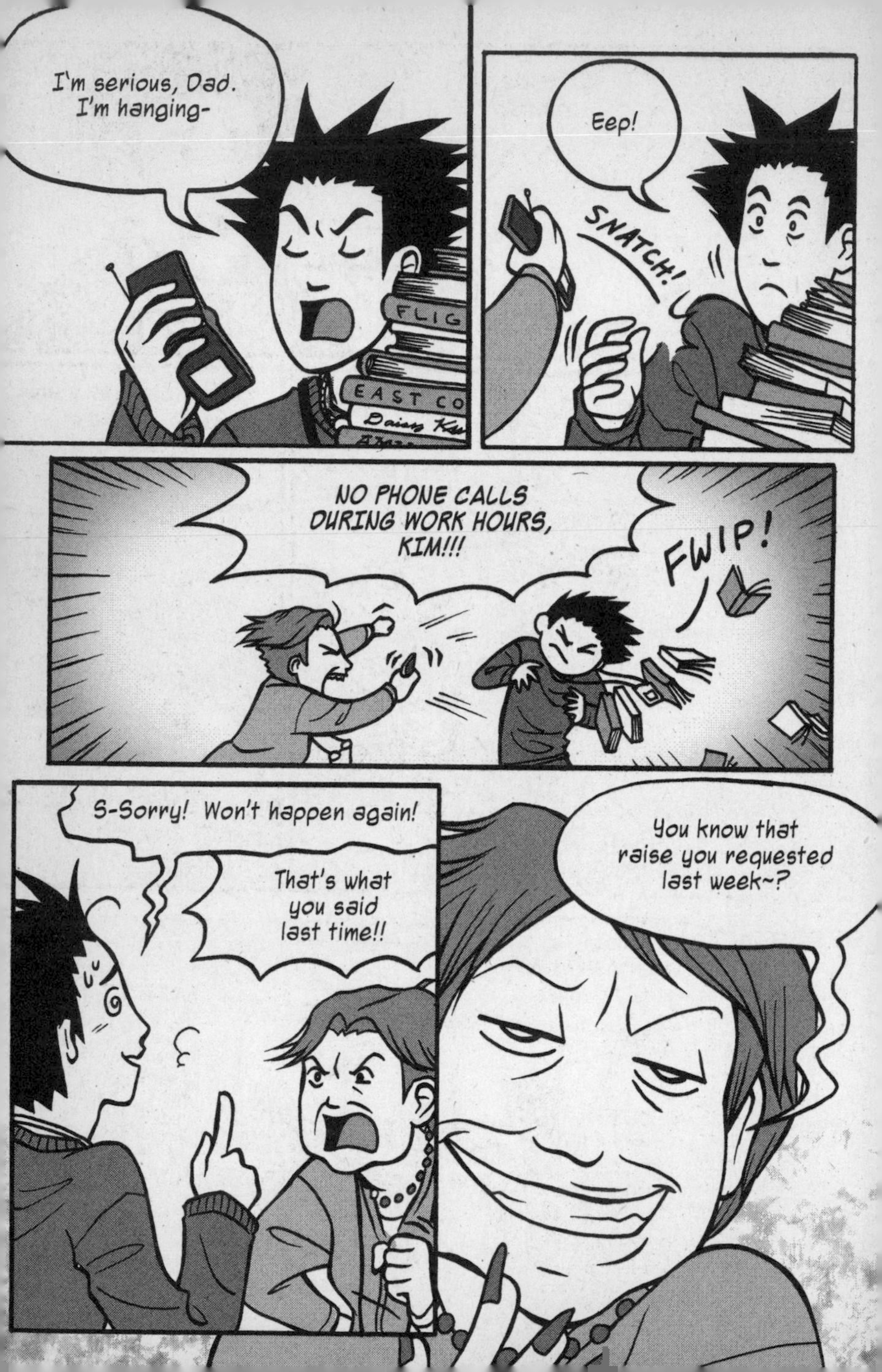
I'm serious, Dad. I'm hanging-
Eep!
SNATCH!
NO PHONE CALLS DURING WORK HOURS, KIM!!!
FWIP!
S-Sorry! Won't happen again!
That's what you said last time!!
You know that raise you requested last week~?

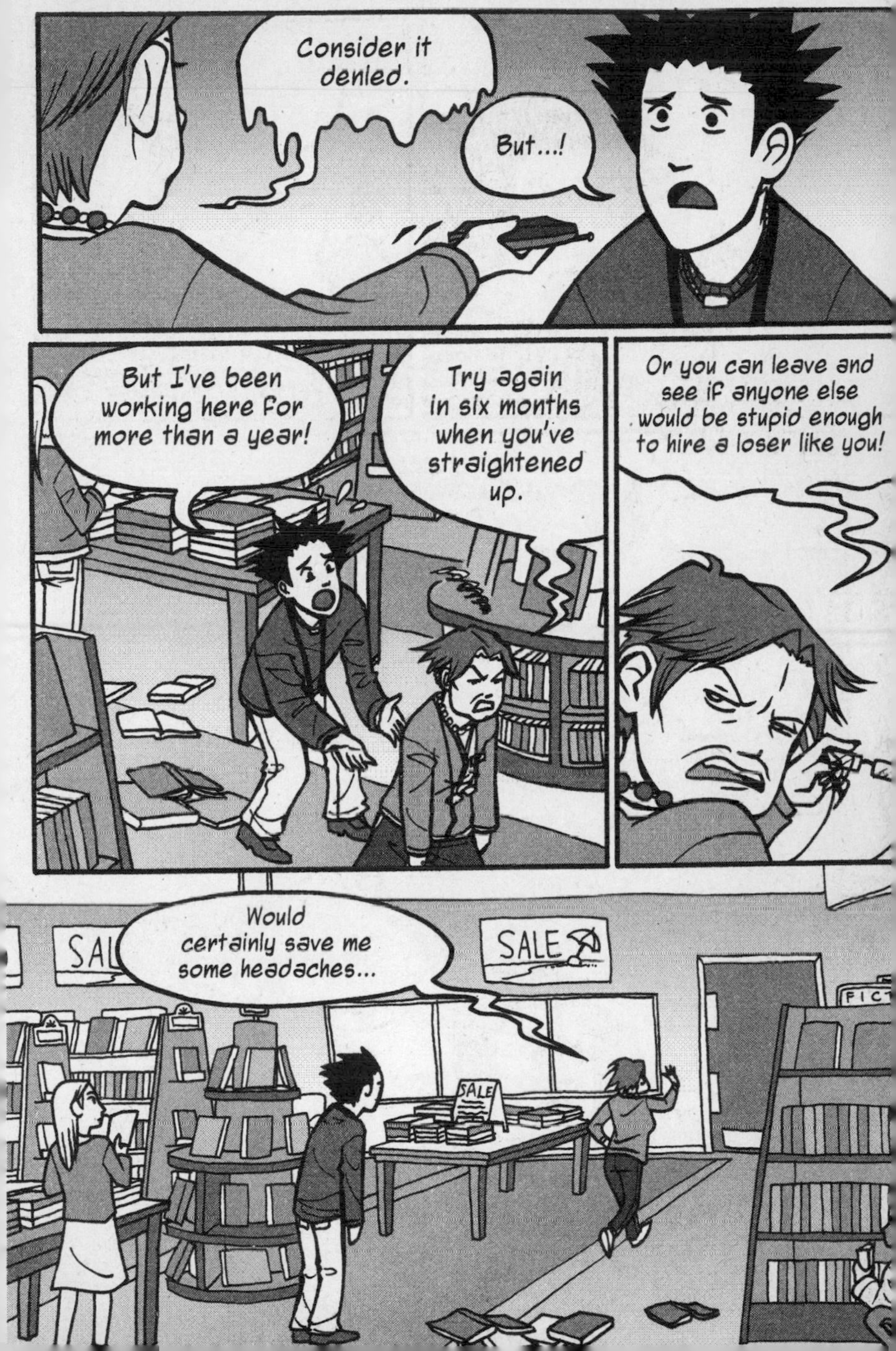

Consider it denied.
But...!
But I've been working here for more than a year!
Try again in six months when you've straightened up.
Or you can leave and see if anyone else would be stupid enough to hire a loser like you!
Would certainly save me some headaches...
SALE
SALE

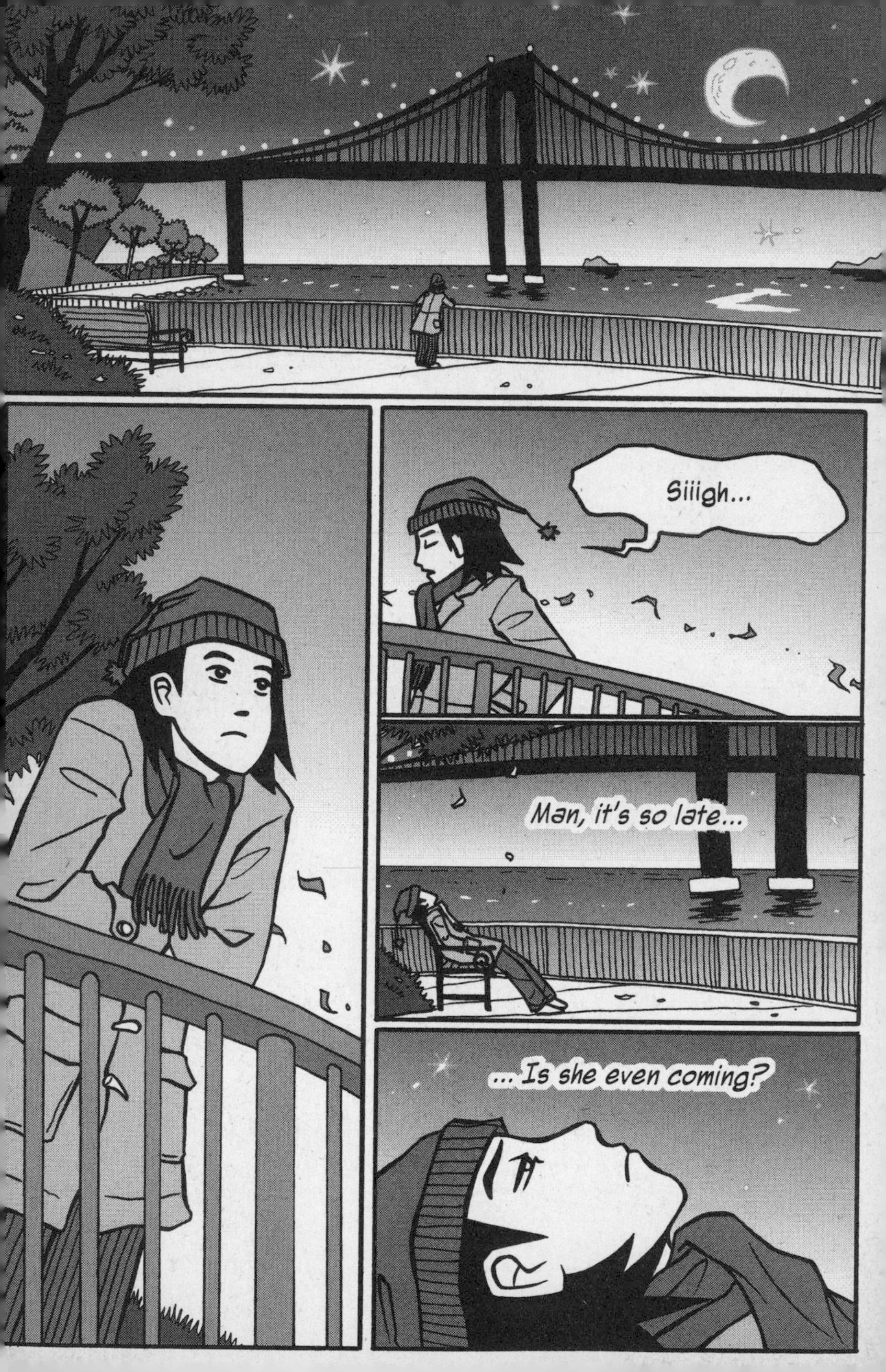
Siiigh...
Man, it's so late...
... Is she even coming?

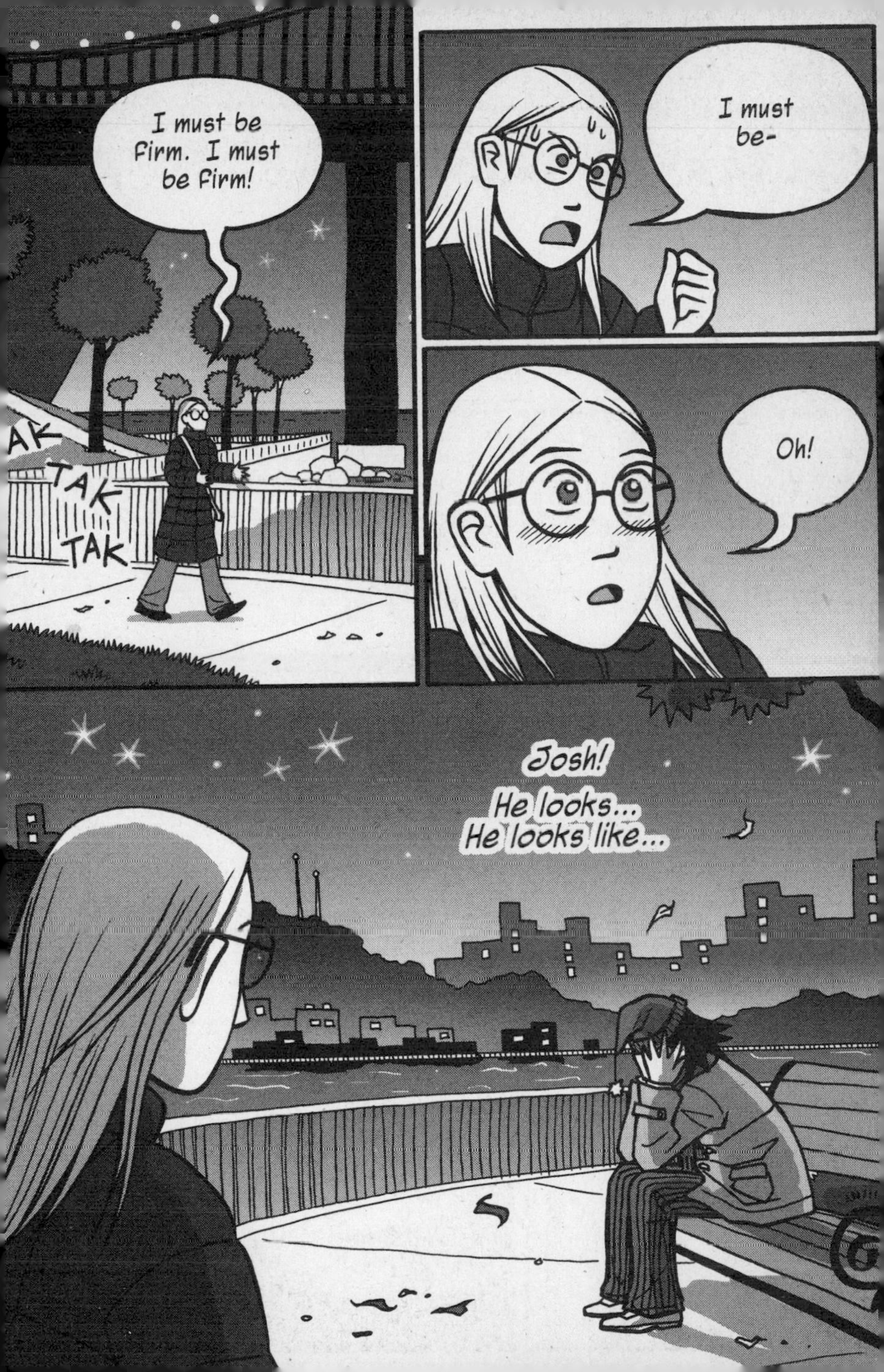
I must be firm. I must be firm!
TAK
TAK
TAK
I must be-
Oh!
Josh!
He looks...
He looks like...

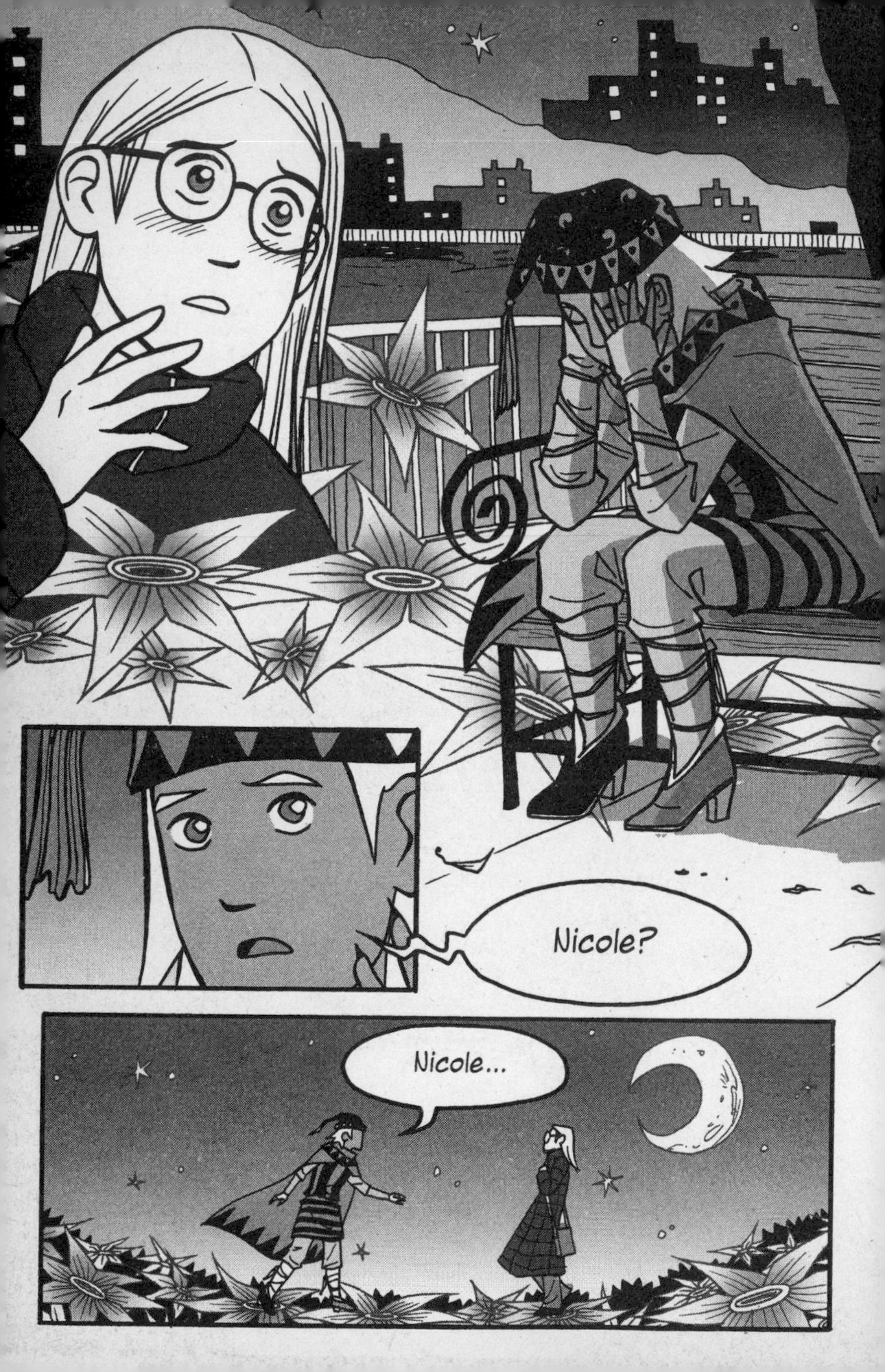
Nicole?
Nicole...

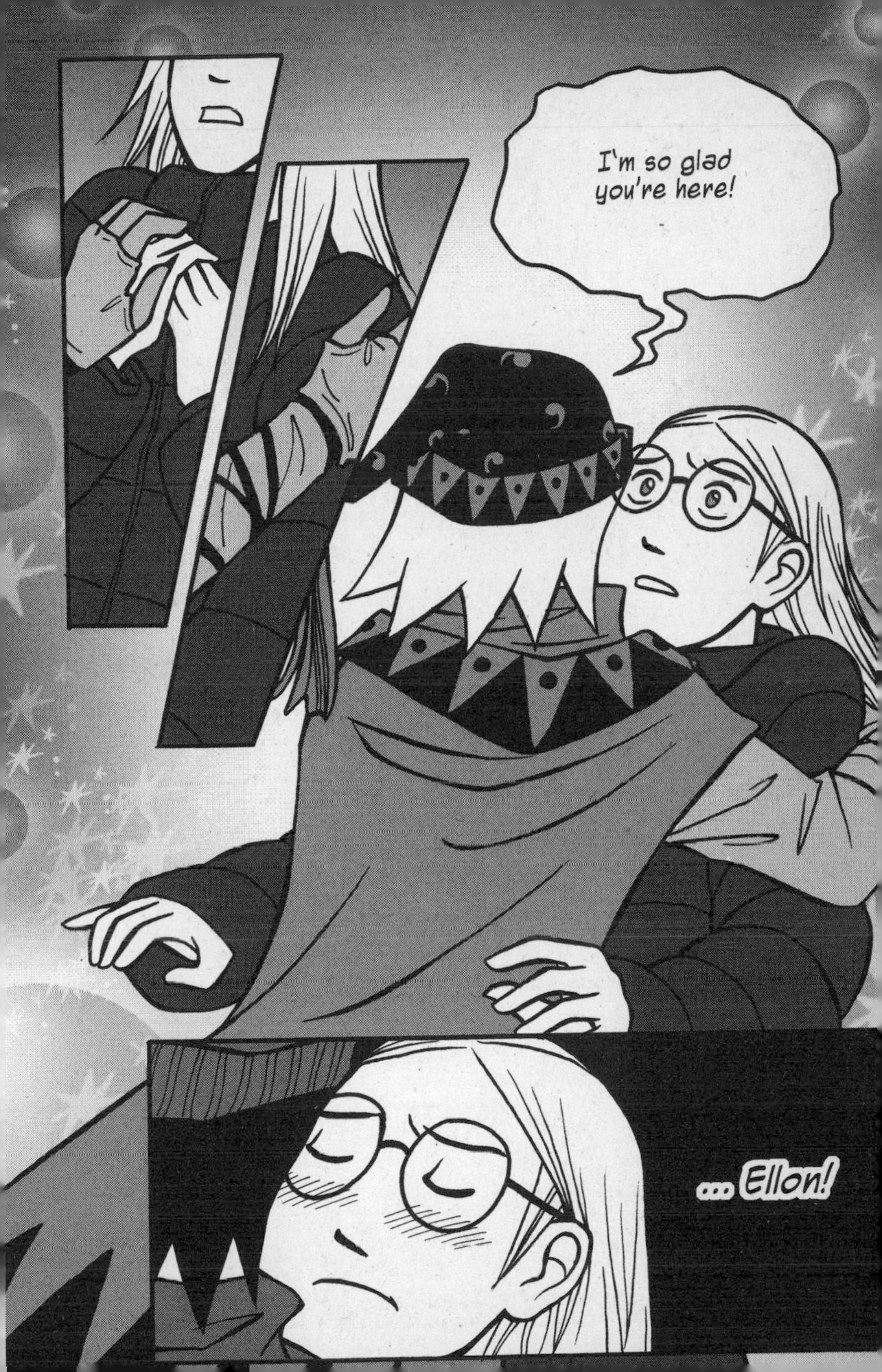
I'm so glad you're here!
...Ellon!

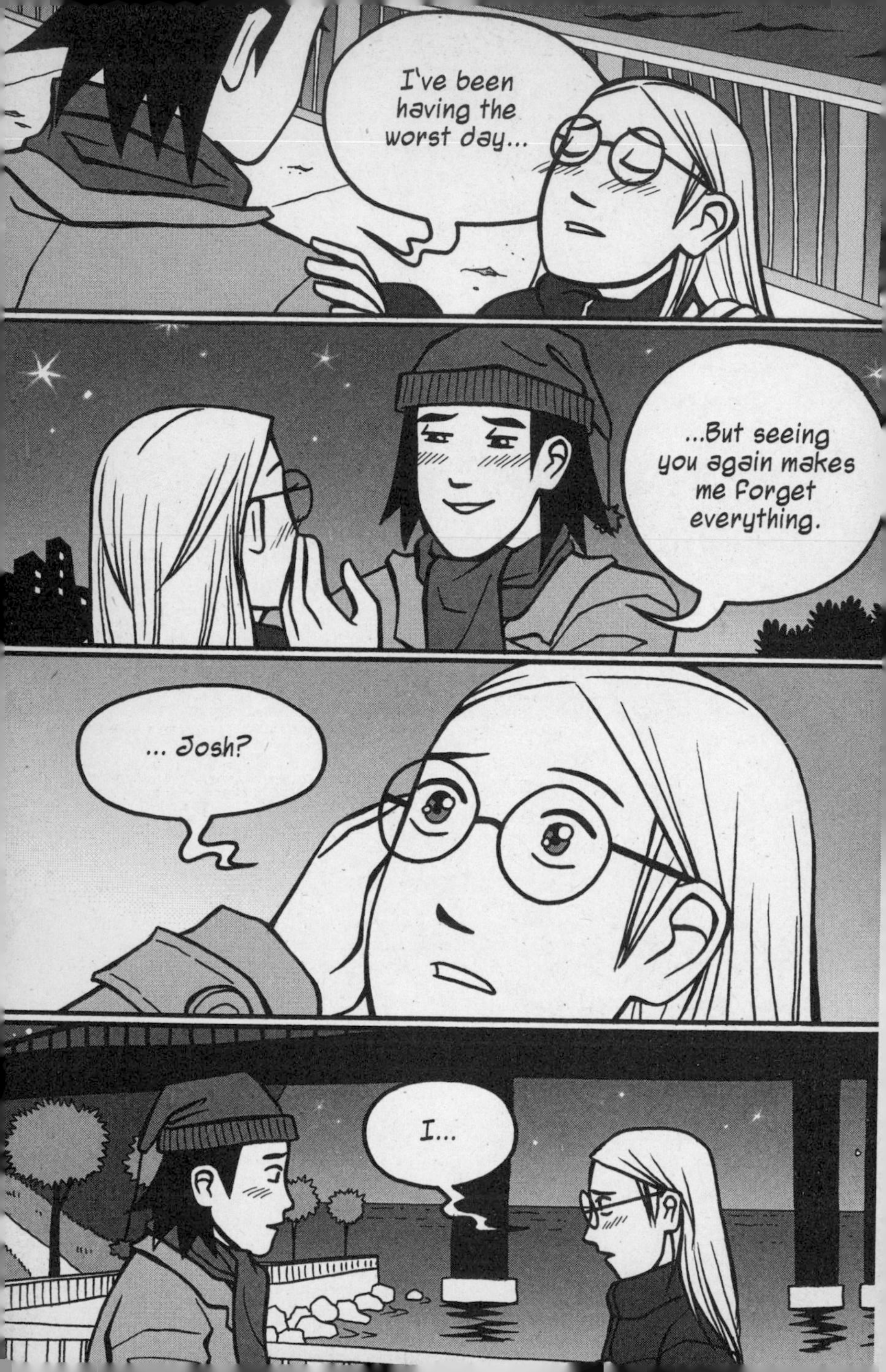
I've been having the worst day...
...But seeing you again makes me forget everything.
... Josh?
I...

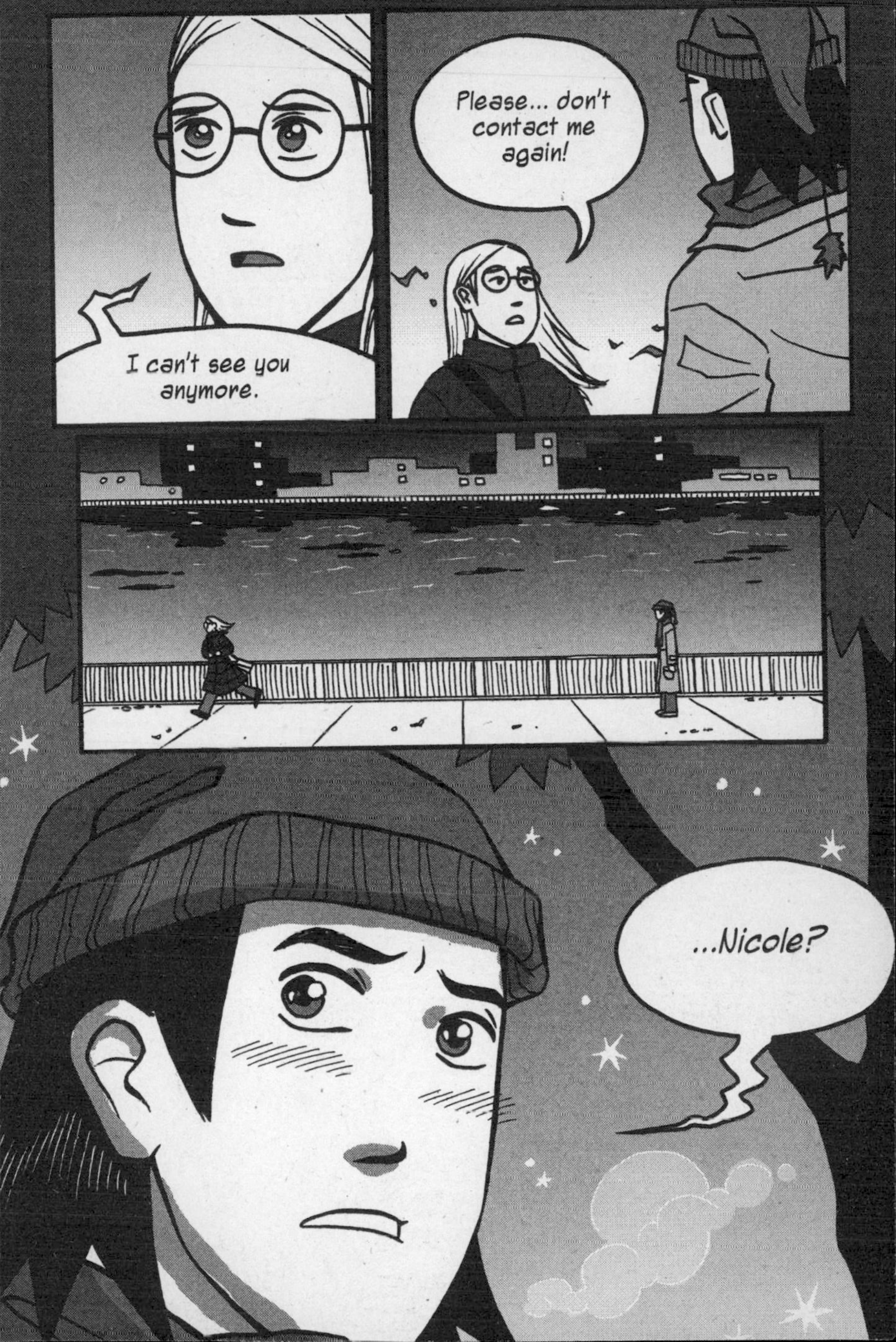
I can't see you anymore.
Please... don't contact me again!
...Nicole?

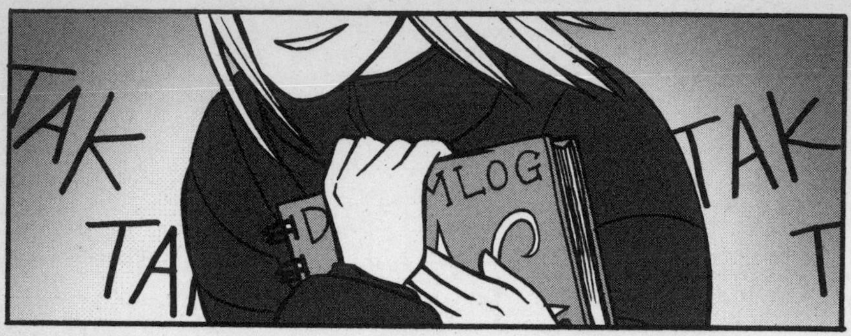
TAK
TAK

It's for the best!

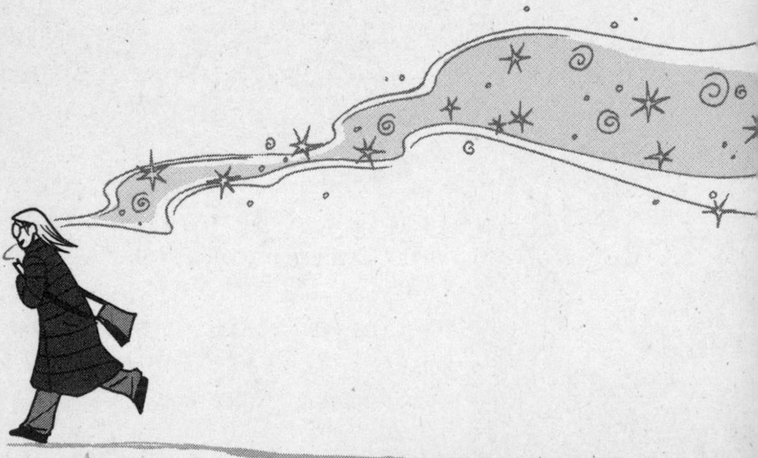

END OF BOOK 1

In the final volume of...

SORCERERS &

SECRETARIES

When Josh finally discovers Nicole's Dreamlog, he dedicates himself to helping her enter a writing contest for a fantasy magazine. But is this help she really wants?

Meanwhile, Josh seems to be inadvertently stealing away Susan's heart, and Riley finds a love of his own. Will Susan get in the way of Nicole and Josh's budding relationship?

Can Nicole ever overcome her fears? Will Josh ever do anything with his life besides work at a bookstore?

The answers to all of these questions--and more--will be yours in the final volume of *Sorcerers & Secretaries!*

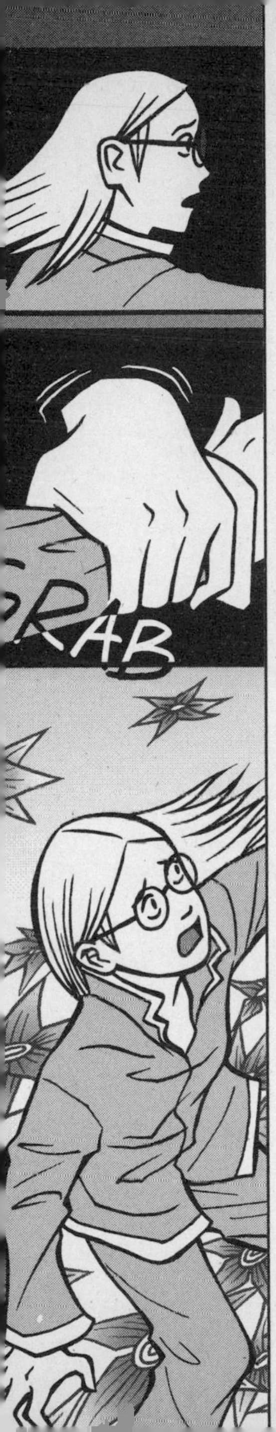
RAB

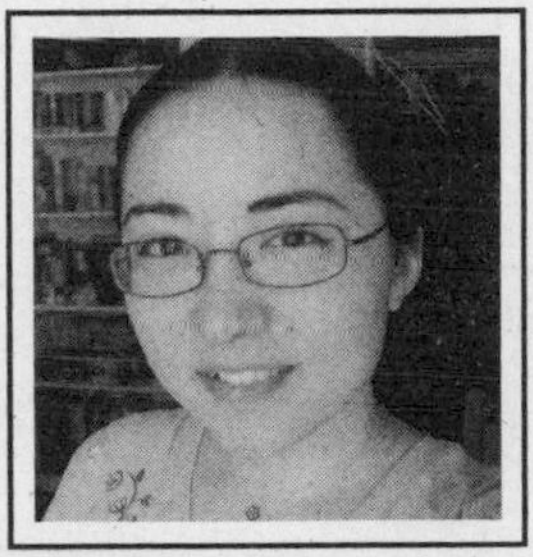

Amy Kim Ganter

Aside from her comics, Amy has worked as a freelance illustrator and animator, and holds a degree in Cartooning from The School of Visual Arts. In her spare time she contributes to the acclaimed *Flight* anthology, and also runs her website, Felaxx.com, where her romantic fantasy comic *Reman Mythology* was serialized. She currently resides in Alhambra, CA with her fiancé Kazu, who is also a graphic novelist.

TOKYOPOP SHOP

WWW.TOKYOPOP.COM/SHOP

Ayumu struggles with her studies, and the all-important high school entrance exams are approaching. Fortunately, she has help from her best bud Shii-chan, who is at the top of the class. But when the test results come back, the friends are surprised: Ayumu surpasses Shii-chan's scores and gets into the school of her choice—without Shii-chan! Losing her friend is so painful for Ayumu that she starts cutting herself to ease her sorrow. Finally, Ayumu seeks comfort in a new friend, Manami. But will Manami prove to be the friend that Ayumu truly needs? Or will Ayumu continue down a dark path?

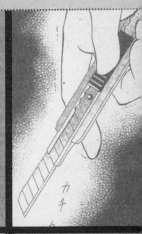

Volume 1

LIFE

Keiko Suenobu

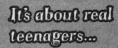

It's about real teenagers...

It's about real high school...

It's about real life.

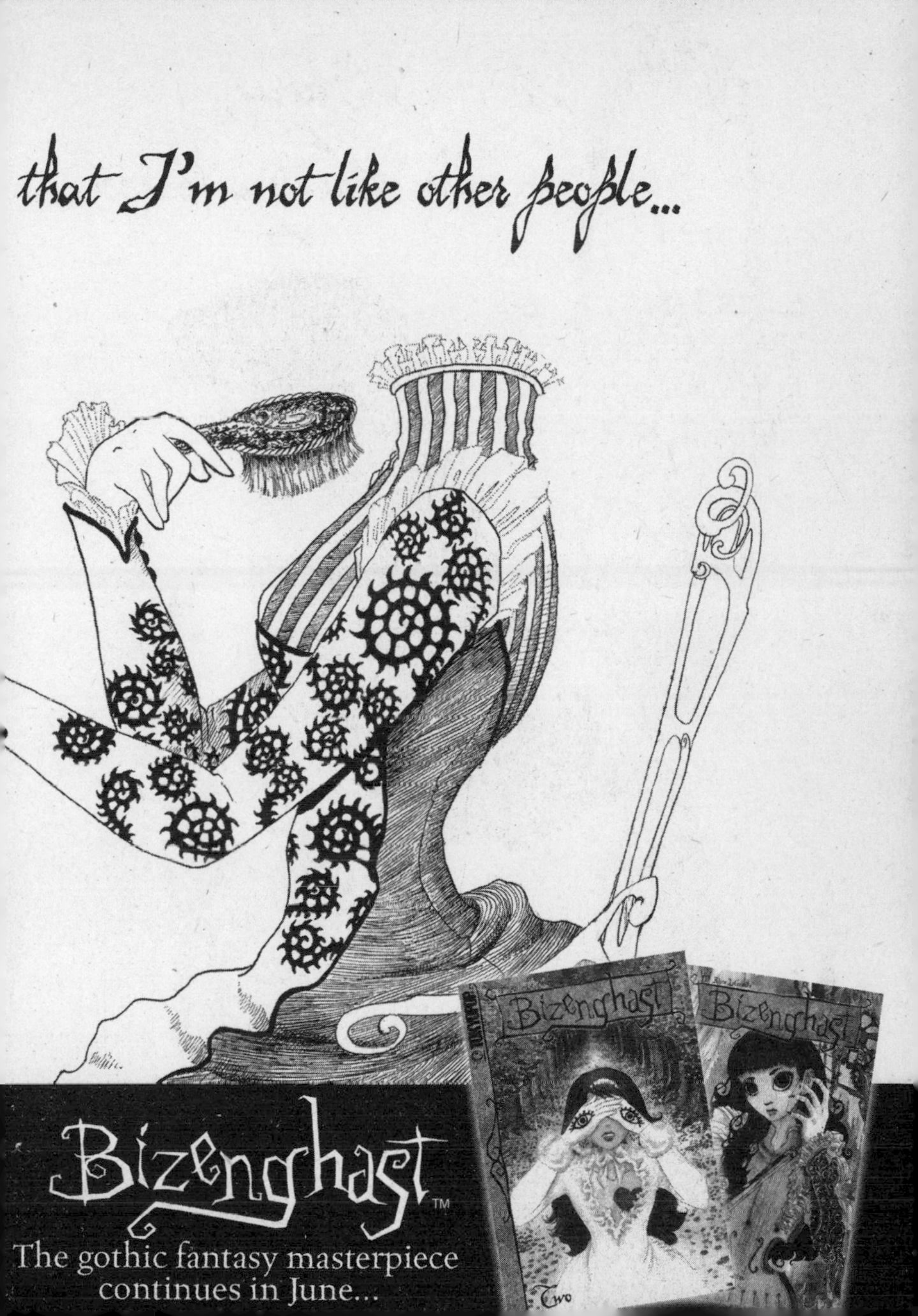
that I'm not like other people...
Bizenghast
Bizenghast
Two
Bizenghast™
The gothic fantasy masterpiece
continues in June...

TOKYOPOP PRESENTS

POP FICTION

For Believers...

Scrapped Princess:
A Tale of Destiny

By Ichiro Sakaki

A dark prophecy reveals that the queen will give birth to a daughter who will usher in the Apocalypse. But despite all attempts to destroy the baby, the myth of the "Scrapped Princess" lingers on...

THE INSPIRATION FOR THE HIT ANIME AND MANGA SERIES!

For Thinkers...

Kino no Tabi:
Book One of The Beautiful World

By Keiichi Sigsawa

Kino roams the world on the back of Hermes, her unusual motorcycle, in a journey filled with happiness and pain, decadence and violence, and magic and loss.

THE SENSATIONAL BESTSELLER IN JAPAN HAS FINALLY ARRIVED!

THIS FALL, TOKYOPOP CREATES A FRESH, NEW CHAPTER IN TEEN NOVELS...

For Adventurers...

Witches' Forest: The Adventures of Duan Surk

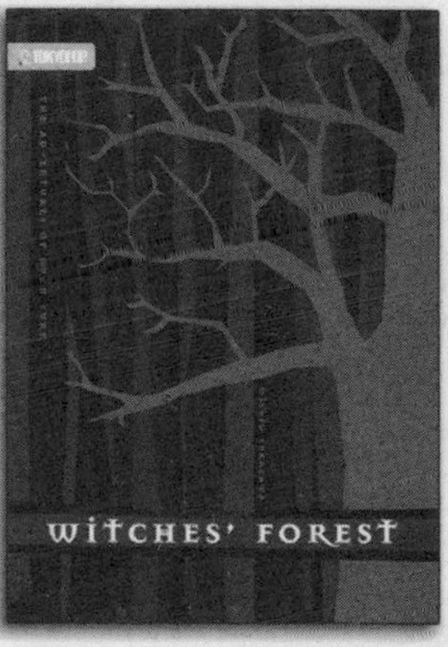
TOKYOPOP
WITCHES' FOREST

By Mishio Fukazawa

Duan Surk is a 16-year-old Level 2 fighter who embarks on the quest of a lifetime —battling mythical creatures and outwitting evil sorceresses, all in an impossible rescue mission in the spooky Witches' Forest!

BASED ON THE FAMOUS *FORTUNE QUEST* WORLD

For Dreamers...

Magic Moon

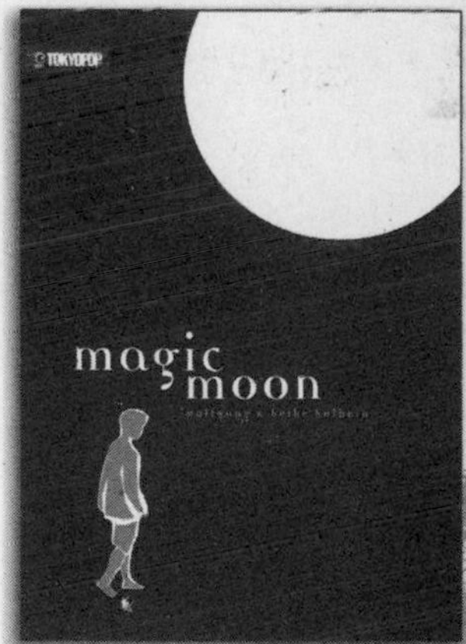
TOKYOPOP
magic moon

By Wolfgang and Heike Hohlbein

Kim enters the engimatic realm of Magic Moon, where he battles unthinkable monsters and fantastical creatures—in order to unravel the secret that keeps his sister locked in a coma.

THE WORLDWIDE BESTSELLING FANTASY *THRILL*OGY ARRIVES IN THE U.S.!

The breakout manga that put CLAMP on the map!

RG VEDA 聖伝

At the dawn of creation, the world was a beautiful and tranquil place. When a powerful warlord rebelled against the king, a violent, chaotic age began.... Three hundred years later, a group of noble warriors embarks on a quest to find the prophesied Six Stars before the land is torn apart!

© CLAMP